LEARNING OF AGGRESSION
IN CHILDREN

LEARNING OF AGGRESSION IN CHILDREN

Leonard D. Eron
University of Illinois, Chicago Circle

Leopold O. Walder
Behavior Service Consultants, Greenbelt, Maryland

Monroe M. Lefkowitz
New York State Department of Mental Hygiene

 LITTLE, BROWN and COMPANY *Boston*

For Caldwell B. Esselstyn
and his grand idea

PREFACE

When we embarked on this research program in 1955 we were only dimly aware of the compelling prominence of violence in our culture. Our concern then was primarily with mental disorder, how we could better understand emotional disturbance and promote conditions that would ameliorate and prevent it. We chose aggression as a variable for study because we felt it was a behavior that could be scientifically observed and manipulated better than vague constructs such as adjustment and mental health, which are difficult to define and to measure. This was in the days before Viet Nam, student protest, ghetto rebellion, assassination of public figures, and the formation of a National Commission on Violence. We were frankly more concerned at that time with testing theoretical notions about the learning of maladaptive behaviors than the implications our research findings might have for the understanding and control of violence. Now, fifteen years later, we present our findings in a different context. An aroused citizenry is concerned with this seemingly sudden, nationwide outcropping of aggression and violence against person and property. Although we are still interested in the theoretical relevance of our findings, we hope our results have some social relevance as well and that they will indeed point toward meaningful measures that can be taken to prevent and control aggressive behavior.

We have gone into the problems encountered in conducting field research on personality variables in no little detail. The solutions we devised for these problems should be of interest to serious researchers in personality and child development. We have included some consideration of the problems and their solutions in the text proper; for the most part, however, they are extensively treated in the appendices. For a complete understanding of the measures we used, why they were selected, and how they were derived, the reader should refer to the appropriate appendix.

In a research program of this size there are always many persons and organizations that are instrumental in implementing and facilitating the operation and who merit special mention and thanks. Our first debt of gratitude is to Dr. Caldwell B. Esselstyn, to whom this book is dedicated. As founder and executive director of the Rip Van Winkle Foundation, he envisioned a comprehensive, high quality medical care program that would be accessible to low- and middle-income persons in rural areas. He realized that in order to attract the best health care personnel to such a venture he would have to provide an academic atmosphere, one aspect of which would be an ongoing research program. It was to implement such a program that he invited me to join the Rip Van Winkle Medical Associates and provided support and encouragement in building a research organization. In addition to the Rip Van Winkle Foundation, which provided most of our financial support, we are also grateful to the National Institute of Mental Health of the Department of Health, Education and Welfare, which provided a substantial research grant for five years (Grant #M-1726). We are also indebted to the Columbia County, New York, TB and Health Association and the Hudson, New York, Lions Club, both of which made financial contributions to the research program. Members of the staff of the Rip Van Winkle Medical Associates who provided expert consultation and in general helped facilitate the research in many ways are: Dr. Frank Hladky, formerly Chief Psychiatrist of the Rip Van Winkle Medical Associates and now of the Tulsa Psychiatric Foundation; Mr. Robert Johnson, formerly Director of Health Education at the Rip Van Winkle Foundation and now Vice-President of the University of California; and Dr. Lewis Jarrett, psychiatrist, and Miss Mary Lawrence, social worker, both formerly at the Rip Van Winkle Clinic and now with the Community Mental Health Board in Columbia County. Drs. Robert Abelson and Irvin Child, both of Yale University, consulted with us on problems of theoretical relevance, instrumentation, design, and statistical analysis, especially in the early stages of the research. Their help is gratefully acknowledged.

Members of the research staff, in addition to the authors, who participated actively in the conceptualization and conduct of this research during the project were psychologists Dr. Thomas Banta, Dr. John Hurley, Mrs. Madeline Eron, Mrs. Florine Kopper, and the late Dr. Marjorie Collins; sociologists Dr. Jerome Laulicht and Dr. Romolo Toigo; and anthropologist Dr. Ethel Nurge. Expert secretarial assistance was provided during that period by Mrs. Ruth Gindin, Mrs. Marion Phillips, Mrs. Irene Quinn, and Mrs. Ann Yaeger, all of whom actually functioned as research assistants as well. We are indebted to Mrs. Catherine Johnson, Mrs. Jane Snow, and Mrs. Judy Klocek for typing the manuscript in its various stages.

The main body of data on which this report is based was gathered in 1960. Many, but by no means all, of the findings have been published in journal articles and have been reported at professional meetings. The opportunity to bring these all together and to integrate them with subsequent research done by my coauthors and me in varied settings was afforded me by a research leave from the University of Iowa and a Fulbright lectureship during the year 1967–1968. For both of these I am grateful. It was during this year, which I spent at the Vrije Universiteit, Amsterdam, Holland, that I was able to write a preliminary draft of this book. Thanks are due to Professor Dr. Jan deWit of the Paedologisch Instituut, who provided me with a comfortable office and research and secretarial assistance as well as with professional and intellectual stimulation. The draft I wrote in Holland was indeed preliminary. My coauthors have worked very closely with me in revising what I wrote and in adding considerable material. We have gone over the manuscript individually and in concert so many times that it is now difficult, if not impossible, to say who wrote what.

We are indebted to the following persons who read preliminary drafts of the manuscript and whose suggestions we incorporated into the final copy: Drs. Justin Aronfreed, Leonard Meyerson, James F. Williams, and mej. Drs. Suus van Hekken and Adrianna Stroo. We do not hold them responsible, however, for any misinterpretation of data or infelicity of expression. Students in seminars at the University of Iowa and the University of Maryland also made valuable suggestions. Thanks are due Miss Jane Aaron for her editorial assistance.

Our greatest debt is to the children and parents who served as subjects and who, of course, must remain anonymous and to the school personnel who facilitated the acquisition of the data and persevered with us through some community opposition. We would especially like to thank Miss Mary Dardess and Robert Costigan of the Chatham School District, Lester Benson of the Ockawamick School District, Robert Cullen of Claverack, Hughes Dearlove of the Roeliff-Janssen School District, Walter Howard of New Lebanon, the late Leveret Mansfield of the Ichabod Crane School District, Herschel Mortenson of Germantown, Jack Roosa of Greenport, and Robert Van Alstyne of Stottville.

L. D. E.

CONTENTS

LEARNING OF AGGRESSION
IN CHILDREN

INTRODUCTION

Chapter 1

The management of aggression is an important aspect of child training. Psychologists over the past thirty-five years have been devoting an increasing amount of research effort to problems in the development, expression, and control of this type of behavior in children. As in most beginning scientific endeavors, the early studies dealt with descriptions of such behavior and its frequency at different age levels (Dawe, 1934; Goodenough, 1931; Jersild and Markey, 1935). Later studies were concerned with the antecedents of aggression (Bandura and Walters, 1959; Sears, Pintler, and Sears, 1946; Sears, Maccoby, and Levin, 1957). More recently there have been attempts to predict and control this behavior (Bandura, Ross, and Ross, 1961; Hops and Walters, 1963; Lovaas, 1961).

Publication of the Yale University studies in frustration and aggression (Dollard, Doob, Miller, Mowrer, and Sears, 1939) marked the point at which descriptive endeavors began to yield to attempts to delineate cause and effect. The authors of this work formulated a theoretical proposition in terms that were susceptible to test. Subsequent experiment has modified the original formulation to some extent; this is discussed in Chapter 2. However, the contribution of the Yale group, demonstrating that theoretical constructs relevant to personality could be operationalized with fruitful results, has not been diminished. In attempting to substantiate their hypotheses the authors ingeniously used evidence from a variety of sources: laboratory researches (Bugelski and Miller, 1938), questionnaire investigations (Doob and Sears, 1939), observational studies (Sears, Hov-

1

land, and Miller, 1940), and analyses of data available from adventitious sources (Hovland and Sears, 1940). Subsequently there have been numerous studies investigating the antecedents of aggressive behavior under controlled laboratory conditions with animals (Azrin, Hutchinson, and McLaughlin, 1965; Miller, 1948; Seward, 1945), nursery school children (Chasdi and Lawrence, 1955; Sears, Whiting, Nowlis, and Sears, 1953), and college students (Buss, 1966a,b; Hokanson, 1961). However, only a few investigations have dealt specifically with parents' socialization practices as related to children's aggressive behavior.

The laboratory and field studies of Sears and his associates are notable among these investigations. These authors attempted to incorporate notions stemming from the frustration-aggression hypothesis as well as other behavior theoretical propositions into their investigative procedures. In their studies with nursery school children, the Sears groups related information obtained from parents about their child-rearing attitudes and practices to controlled observations in the nursery school situation (Sears et al., 1953; Sears et al., 1946; Levin and Sears, 1956). They also did survey studies in which they correlated parents' reports about the extent of aggression and other behaviors of their children and how they, the parents, responded to these behaviors (Sears et al., 1957).

In formulating our own research, it was obvious to us that anyone who would study aggression would have to examine carefully the formulations and procedures of Sears, the foremost researcher in socialization of aggression at that time. Thus the program of research in the antecedents of aggressive behavior of children which is reported in the current volume extended the work of Sears. Our approach was similarly grounded in behavior theoretical propositions. And our primary investigative procedures were also of the survey type. However, there are a number of differences between this study and the study of Sears et al. (1957) and most other survey studies of parental child-rearing practices. These differences will become apparent as the account of the present research is developed. They are briefly noted here.

1. The major dependent variable of our study is aggression as it is observed in the school situation. The Sears study, on the other hand, was not limited to the school context; and in addition to aggression, it was concerned with other child behaviors such as dependency, sex, and the development of conscience.

2. The subjects in the current study were in the third grade and thus approximately eight years old. The subjects in the Sears study were in kindergarten and thus approximately five years old.

3. Sampling procedures were different. Sears's subjects were 379 of the 640 children enrolled in the kindergartens in two suburbs of

a metropolitan area of New England. Included were only those children who were living with both parents. Excluded were twins, handicapped children, and those attending parochial kindergartens, as well as all cases in which either mother or father was foreign-born. The subjects in our study included all of the approximately 900 children in the third grade in a semirural county in New York.

4. Only mothers were interviewed in the Sears study. In our study both mothers and fathers were interviewed.

5. In the Sears study the criterion measure of aggression was a set of ratings made by the researchers on the basis of the mothers' reports. The criterion measure of aggression in the present study was obtained independently of the mothers' reports. This aggression measure was a rating made by the subjects' classmates. In contrast to the Sears and other studies, in the present research, criterion and predictor measures were obtained independently of each other.

6. The parent interview in the current study, although conducted individually in a face-to-face situation, used a standardized, objective, precoded format. The Sears interview was a structured but open-ended interview in which the mothers' reports were recorded. These audio tapes were then rated by members of the research staff on pertinent, predetermined variables.

Background of This Study

When the initial research team was formed, its charge was to determine the extent of mental health problems in a rural environment. The Rip Van Winkle Foundation, the organization which sponsored the research program, was interested primarily in medical practice in rural areas. It implemented this interest by, among other ways, sponsoring a group practice of medicine whose purpose was to bring high quality medical care to a semirural region, Columbia County, New York. Because of the public health orientation of this organization, the investigative procedures of the research team were expected to be primarily epidemiological in nature.

However, the difficulties of applying such investigative techniques to a behavioral area soon became apparent. The researchers were faced with two related problems: first, to establish an appropriate definition of mental health; and second, to obtain an adequate representative sample of the population in which to measure this condition. Thus it was decided to take just one behavior which most investigators would accept as an aspect of mental health. It would have to be a behavior which could be reliably observed and objectively measured (Eron, 1956). Aggression was considered to be such a variable.

We originally defined this behavior in a manner similar to Dollard

3

and his colleagues (1939): "an act whose goal response is injury to another object." In the course of the research this definition was changed ultimately to "an act which injures or irritates another person," since the final measure seemed to fit this more narrow definition (Walder, Abelson, Eron, Banta, and Laulicht, 1961, p. 539). Thus the criterion measure of aggression specifically taps extrapunitive aggression directed toward another person. See Chapter 3 for the operations by which this measure was derived.

To overcome sampling limitations, it was decided to study a 100 percent sample of a specific population — all children of one grade level throughout Columbia County. We selected the third grade in which the modal age of children was eight years. This was the earliest age at which we felt we could get children to cooperate with us and understand the group paper and pencil procedures we would be compelled to use in a large-scale survey study. Also by the time children are in the third grade they have established more or less stable patterns of behavior which are observable (Goodenough and Tyler, 1959). The third-grade population in Columbia County was distributed in approximately forty third-grade classrooms. The size of class ranged from a handful of students in a one room country school to groups of forty children in the city and in the consolidated school districts.

The basic research plan was to obtain data from three independent sources: mothers, fathers, and the children themselves. Throughout the five-year period during which measures were developed, pretested in various forms, and ultimately used in final form, approximately 2,600 children were tested in their classrooms and 1,800 parents were interviewed individually. The last group of third-grade subjects on whom the most refined measures were used included 875 children in 38 classrooms. We interviewed 713 mothers of these children (85 percent) and 570 fathers (71 percent). At least one parent was seen in 726 families and both parents were interviewed in 557 families.

The bulk of findings which are reported in this volume are based on 206 girls and 245 boys on whom we had complete data; i.e., the child was present at all three testing sessions conducted in the classroom one week apart and both his mother and his father contributed a scorable, personal interview.[1] When analyses are reported that are based on a fewer or greater number of subjects, this is noted. In addition a number of results on different populations are reported. Most of these results were obtained subsequent to the major study. These include laboratory researches as well as survey investigations

[1] Unfortunately the records of 10 children who met these criteria were lost in a computer editing routine. It is believed that this was an unsystematic selection.

4

with third graders and college students conducted in Iowa City and Cedar Rapids, Iowa; preschoolers and primary-grade children in College Park, Md.; eight-year-old school children in Amsterdam, Holland; and juvenile delinquents in Canaan, New York.[2] These results are discussed when they serve to amplify, corroborate, or help interpret the original findings.

As stated in a preceding paragraph and as developed in Chapter 2, the investigative procedures used in this study derived from certain theoretical notions about the development of aggressive behavior. Thus a paramount concern for the investigators was the translation of theoretical statements into operational terms. Once this had been done, pertinent variables could be measured and relations among them determined both in large-scale research using survey type methods and in laboratory studies in which variables are manipulated systematically. These procedures are discussed in subsequent chapters as each set of variables is described, the development of their measures detailed, and the findings presented.

It was felt that only in a survey with a large number of subjects would it be possible to identify the major sources of variance accurately. In laboratory experiments allocation of variance may be accomplished through random assignment of subjects to treatments. In a survey study, however, assignment of subjects to groups can be accomplished only after the data have been collected. It is impossible to make a priori judgments as to which subjects will fit into any given treatment group of an experimental design. For example, it is not possible to select in advance those subjects who exhibit a like amount of identification with parents so that the effect of reinforcement on aggressive behavior can be more effectively evaluated by keeping the extent of identification constant (see Chapter 6). To permit such controls, many subjects are required. In a field study where many variables are measured it is only by selection from a large reservior of subjects, on whom there is information on a number of variables, that effective controls can be instituted.

Setting of the Study

The survey of aggressive behavior of third-grade children and the socialization practices of their parents was conducted in Columbia County, a semirural area in the Hudson River Valley of New York State with a population of about 43,000. A brief description of this region and its inhabitants follows in order to give the reader an impression of the area in which the main body of the data reported in

2 Berkshire Farm for Boys.

this volume were collected. Beautifully situated in gently rolling hill country between the Catskill and Berkshire Mountain chains, the area is approximately 120 miles north of New York City. The principal industries are dairy and fruit farming and supporting activities. In addition, throughout the county there are a number of textile factories and other light manufacturing plants which employ a large portion of the labor force. Many persons whose primary occupation is farming are employed part time and seasonally in these mills. Hudson, which is the county seat and the only incorporated city in the county, has a population of approximately 12,000 persons. It is the site of two large cement plants as well as of several other factories which manufacture heavy, industrial equipment. Approximately 40 percent of the county population is located in Hudson and four incorporated villages, each of which has fewer than 2,500 persons. The remainder of the population lives on farms and in open country.

The area was originally settled by the Dutch and many descendants of the early settlers still live in the area. In addition, each major wave of immigration into the United States left its mark on the composition of the population; thus there are sizable proportions of Irish, Italian, Slavic, Jewish, and Negro inhabitants in the population. It is an area steeped in American history and its inhabitants tend to be conservative and proud of their heritage, whether natural or adopted. The organization sponsoring the research, the Rip Van Winkle Foundation, assumed a name which is indigenous to the location. Washington Irving for a time was tutor to the children of Martin Van Buren, who lived in Kinderhook, one of the incorporated villages in the county. Kinderhook is reputed to be the locale of the *Legend of Sleepy Hollow*.[3] The Van Tassels are still residents of the area and every generation has at least one Katrina. One of the large centralized school districts is named Ichabod Crane and there are countless taverns called "The Headless Horseman." Old Rip probably rolled his bowling balls through the hills and valleys of the Catskill Mountains as Washington Irving gazed westward across the Hudson River from his garret room in the Van Buren mansion. In addition to its unique traditions, Columbia County is considered representative of many counties in the United States in terms of social and economic characteristics, density of population, urban-rural characteristics, and ecological distribution, as well as the system of school administration (Toigo, 1962).

The extent of cooperation of the members of this community in

[3] It is interesting that the Americanism "OK" is reputed to have been derived from the abbreviation of Van Buren's political party, "The Old Kinderhooks," with which the eighth president of the United States initialed the documents of which he approved (Urdang, 1968).

6

the conduct of the research was both surprising and gratifying. From the beginning every school board approved and supported the research, including the one Roman Catholic parochial school. Support throughout the tenure of the study in the form of financial grants came from the Columbia County TB and Health Association and the Hudson Lions Club. In large part, such participation was due to the prestige of the organization sponsoring the research as well as to the concerted efforts by the members of the research team to be active, visible members of the community. We devoted much time and effort to public meetings and discussions of the purpose and nature of the research program.

During the first three or four years of the research we had contacts with 1,800 children, 500 parents, and at least 100 school teachers and administrators without noticing any measure of dissatisfaction with what we were doing. During this time we talked to countless PTA's, service clubs, church organizations, etc., and we were always well received. However, toward the end of our data-collection period, starting with an anti–mental health campaign by the Americanism Chairman of the Hudson Post of the American Legion, we began to get some indication of misunderstanding about our program. A local newspaper printed this man's accusations which had been taken from publications of the American Flag Committee, The American Mercury, Economic Council, and similar organizations. These allegations linked mental health with communism, world citizenship, etc. However, a resolution condemning the "mental health movement" and calling for an investigation of it, introduced by the Hudson Post at a meeting of the County Legion organization, was defeated at that level.

Unfortunately, this campaign was at its height at the time our final countrywide study was underway, and although it had no real effect on the cooperation of parents in Hudson itself, in one of the centralized school districts, a group of three or four families, under the direction of a local lawyer, voiced objection to our program. Public meetings were held and there was much publicity in the newspapers. The contention was that the school board had acted illegally in granting the Rip Van Winkle Foundation permission to test the children without specific authorization from the parents. In the meantime, many false rumors circulated about the kind of questions being asked of children and parents and the deleterious effect this would have on them.[4] Three families requested that their children's tests be destroyed and we complied with the request. After suspen-

[4] Coincidentally, a cancer survey was being conducted in the county and questions about sexual behavior and related topics were included. Probably our study was confused with this one.

7

sion of the program for a month in this school district, during an investigation by a subcommittee of the school board, the members of the board unanimously endorsed the program, the program was reinstated, and the opposition dissipated. At about the same time, the local newspaper that originally had supplied most of the bad publicity ran a series of articles on the meaning and importance of social science research in general and this project in particular. A letter written to one of the complainants by a representative of the National Institute of Mental Health (NIMH), was widely quoted. Members of the research staff appeared on an area TV station and spoke on the local radio station. The researchers themselves were concerned about the ethics of measuring behaviors frequently considered undesirable. We assured our subjects of confidentiality and were successful in preserving confidentiality throughout the course of the study.

We do not believe that the public expression of dissatisfaction by these few individuals, coming as it did toward the end of the data-collection period, had any significant effect on the data obtained. All classroom data had been collected by this time; and no differences in extent and quality of cooperation on the part of the respondents were noted before and after the voicing of these objections. The TB and Health Association subsequently made their annual contribution to the research program, thus giving us tangible evidence of their support, and indeed elected the first author president of the organization. The sequence of events, interpretations of their possible causes, and the resolution of the entire affair have been documented elsewhere (Eron and Walder, 1961).

Theoretical and Methodological Orientation

The assumption underlying the design of this survey was that there are antecedent-consequent relations between the attitudes and behaviors of parents on one hand and the kinds of aggressive behavior which children display in school on the other. It was believed that the different learning environments that parents provide in their attempts to socialize their children's behavior accounted for much of the variation in the aggressive behaviors which were to be studied. Parents use rewards and punishments in differing degree, hoping to influence the behavior of their children. Also, instigations to aggressive behavior exist to varying extents in the home environments of different children. Furthermore, most parents try to instill standards of behavior in their children and, at the same time, knowingly or unknowingly, also provide role models for their children to copy. Both the child's acceptance or rejection of parental standards and

8

his copying of a role model might be considered components of identification with parents. The punishment patterns of parents and the nature and extent of the instigations they provide (or, at least, do not prevent), the standards of behavior they attempt to instill in their children, and the kinds of models they furnish may vary with sociocultural factors. We thus were interested in four kinds of parent variables as predictors to aggressive behavior of children in school: reinforcers, instigators, identification, and socio-cultural factors. These conceptualizations are examined further in Chapter 2, and their interpretation is examined in later chapters. Our interest in these variables does not mean we are unmindful of other legitimate conceptualizations about the antecedents of aggression in children. Psychoanalytic and other instinctual theories (e.g., Ardrey, 1966; Lorenz, 1966; Tinbergen, 1951) have gained much currency. In addition, the recent research on neurological disorders (Loomis, 1965), chromosomal aberrations (Telfer, Baker, Clark, and Richardson, 1968), and gonadal hormones (Bronson and Desjardins, 1968) command attention. However, it was our intent to see whether we could account for aggressive behavior in children using a strictly behavioral orientation within a research design which focused on parental child-rearing practices and attitudes.

There are many equally defensible ways to set about studying children's aggression and its antecedents. Either extended field observations of groups of children interacting with each other or intensive case studies of small samples of deviant or normal children could yield a great deal of information about the dynamics of aggressive behavior. Laboratory studies with random samples of children or animals in which independent variables presumed to be antecedents are rigorously defined and systematically manipulated could also be fruitful. The latter approach was employed to some extent in the research reported here; however, as previously stated, the major focus was epidemiological.

This epidemiological emphasis required that the behavior of both children and parents be assessed with survey techniques. It was necessary for the children to be seen in groups in the classroom and for the parents to be interviewed with objective, closed-end inventories. A peer-rating procedure was developed in which every child present in the class on the day of testing rated every other child in the classroom on a series of specific behaviors. The derivation of this procedure is described in detail in Chapter 3. Ultimately scores on this peer-rating technique were related to aggressive performance in an automated laboratory situation. A marked positive relation obtained between scores on the peer-rating technique and overt behavior in a controlled situation. This supported the methodological assumption that we were dealing with valid behavior samples when we examined the ratings of each child made by his peers. Indeed, by asking the proper questions of the appropriate informants it was possible to obtain useful information. The assumption underlying this research strategy was that there is a response class, aggression, that can include a variety of behaviors exhibited in numerous situations all of which result in injury or irritation to another person. There should be consistency within the individual whether data are collected by sociometric procedure or in the laboratory. This point of view makes no distinction between accidental and instrumental aggression or between socially acceptable and anti-social aggression. For a discussion of these problems see Kahn and Kirk (1968).

Also described in some detail in Chapter 3 is the derivation of the large scale instrument used to assess parental practices and attitudes, the Rip Van Winkle Child-Rearing Questionnaire (see Appendix II.B). The major focus in this interview was on parent-child interactions. We were concerned with what parents do with and to their children that might be reflected in their children's aggressive behavior in school. One problem was to capture the essence of these interactions in brief interviews with the parents without doing violence either to their sensibilities or to the nature and quality of the events as they occur in real life. An equally important problem was to insure the veracity of the information we obtained from parents or, at least, to assess which information was useful and how much of a correction had to be made for the informant's lack of knowledge or candor. As we have said elsewhere, "when we interview the parent, we are dependent on an untrained observer who may also be a biased reporter" (Eron, Laulicht, Walder, Farber, and Spiegel, 1961, p. 306). Radke-Yarrow later examined this problem in detail (1963).

The Need for an Objective, Precoded Interview

Most studies of child-rearing practices in the past used open-ended interview procedures with parents. The amount of structure depended only on the specificity of the questions being asked (Bandura and Walters, 1959; Sears et al., 1957). The parents were permitted to talk at will, developing points as they went along and, with unstandardized prompting from the interviewer, ultimately focusing on the relevant topic. The interviews were usually tape-recorded so that everything the respondent said was preserved. Often typescripts were made of the tape. The interviewers then returned to their home base. They delivered the interviews to the researchers who, in the quiet and privacy of their own laboratories, reviewed the tapes and/or typescripts and made ratings of the relevant variables. The ratings were usually made on the basis of the tone and content of the respondent's communication according to a priori categories that the researchers had devised themselves or borrowed from related studies.

Although such interview procedures may have been fruitful, it was impossible for us to employ them because, as mentioned previously, we were committed to a large-scale survey. Thus this type of interview would have been impractical because it is expensive, requires a large corps of highly skilled and trained interviewers, which we did not have available to us, and is inordinately time-consuming. More important, however, this type of interviewing was judged not to be an appropriate method in a controlled research endeavor. Such interviews are difficult to replicate because both the original and follow-up questions are rarely asked in exactly the same way. While much of the record is irrelevant, there are often many gaps in the information and it is not known whether this is due to improper questioning or lack of knowledge on the part of the informant. When there are improper questions, no objective means are available for identifying and improving them. The researcher is dependent on an impressionistic evaluation of the effectiveness of the technique. In one recently published study (Stolz, 1967) in which thirty-nine sets of parents were interviewed separately, there were 8,862 double-spaced typewritten pages of transcript! However, there was only an average of 2.5 bits of coded information for each page — a great amount of effort for little yield.

Furthermore, it is difficult to guard against a halo effect in assigning ratings when the whole or a large portion of the interview is being rated at one time. But most important, there is a sacrifice in reliability since the information has to be filtered through at least three middlemen — the interviewer, the typist, and finally the rater. The interjudge reliability estimates of rating personality and behavioral variables on the basis of tape-recorded interviews and subsequent typescripts have been embarrassingly low in some major studies.

We decided that a completely objective, precoded interview was not only essential because of the magnitude of the task, but also desirable because of the unreliability of the open-ended, tape-recorded interview. Moreover, a focused, objective interview makes possible a more systematic study of the area. We chose to use parents as the primary informants about the antecedents of aggression. We made no interpretive leaps between what parents told us and what was ultimately punched on IBM cards. The interpretation came only after the analyses were done. If the interviewer was in doubt, the respondent, not the interviewer, chose the response category. Since there were interviews with both mother and father, we had a check on the reliability of the information. Also there were a number of controls built into the interview for the purpose of checking on the respondent's candor, knowledge, distortion, and inconsistency. Since all interviews contained standard questions and prompts, a poorly worded or ambiguous question could be identified and either improved or eliminated. This approach made possible the standardization of the interview and facilitated training of interviewers and applicability of questions. Objections to this type of interview include its possible artificial, stilted, and restrictive nature; but our experience demonstrates that closed-end questions are feasible and provide valuable data. Also parents cooperate easily with such a procedure. The interview can be conducted in one to one-and-a-half hours by interviewers with various backgrounds.

Significance of the Research

As noted above, when the present research was first conceived in 1955, aggression was viewed as merely one aspect of a larger mental health problem. Although the potentiality for violence was no doubt present at that time, the actual level of violent and aggressive behavior was not nearly as pronounced as it is today. It seems that with the war in Viet Nam, the continuing futility and frustration of urban life for the poor, along with student protest and rebellion seemingly generated by these conditions, a contagion of violence pervades the American scene and threatens to overwhelm us.

It has now become fashionable to study the phenomenon of aggression and ask the questions that we struggled with some fifteen years ago. Indeed, a National Commission on the Causes and Prevention of Violence was established by former President Johnson, who named such a prestigious figure as Dr. Milton S. Eisenhower as its chairman. Many theories, notions, and fancies about the origin of and cause for present-day violence are abroad. Most of these fall, as is noted in Chapter 2, into one of two categories: man is by nature aggressive; or, man learns to become aggressive. When the question of how to control aggression is considered, each of these positions leads to a different approach. The former might require an implementation of "law and order," and the latter unlearning or education in a generic sense. In the current research we were guided by the conviction that aggressive behavior is learned and our findings encouraged us to believe that it can indeed be unlearned. However, irrespective of the position one chooses, it requires only perfunctory analysis to demonstrate that aggression has been an integral component of nearly every major endeavor, institution, and function of the United States as well as of most other "civilized" countries. For example, it is almost banal to say that the founding of this country comprised a series of violent acts from the Boston Tea Party through the battles of the American Revolution to the Declaration of Independence. Indeed, aggressive acts were inflicted upon the first settlers of this country while still on European shores and they in turn inflicted aggression upon the aborigines of these shores.

Brown (1969) has traced the historical patterns of violence in America from the time of the wars between whites and Indians beginning in Tidewater, Virginia, in 1607, through today's urban riots and police violence. Brown argues that the implacable hostility between whites and Indians could readily have been avoided. Only a small Indian population existed in the continental United States and there was more than enough room for the white settler to expand. Racial prejudice and the desire for self-aggrandizement on the part of New England whites shattered the peaceful model of white-Indian relationships established by such Puritan statesmen as John Eliot and Roger Williams. Thus ensued almost 300 years of aggression between whites and Indians from 1600 to the latter part of the nineteenth century. Scalping and torture were an accepted part of Indian warmaking, and very soon the whites became adept at these barbaric practices. Broken promises and treaties, the slaughter of defenseless women and children, and the theft and destruction of property became a means to conquest for the white American. The effect on the American national character of this early savagery has probably not been a healthy one and may have established an immutable model for violence.

Coexisting with the Indian wars were pre-Revolutionary and Revolutionary violence. One example is the violence generated in American port cities by the conflict between patriots, such as the Sons of Liberty, and British troops, culminating in 1770 in the Boston Massacre. Another is the intimidation of Tories by Whigs, out of which developed the custom of tarring and feathering. In addition to the formal clash of the British and Continental armies, guerrilla warfare between Whigs and Tories pervaded the American hinterland. Lynch-mob violence against individual Tories who would not relinquish their support of the British government was initiated in 1767 by Colonel Charles Lynch and named for that person. At first lynch law meant the use of corporal punishment, either by hickory withes or whips, but later it meant indiscriminate hanging and killing of anyone the mob decided deserved such a fate. Lynch law violence has served as a model of instant justice from pre–Revolutionary War times to the present day. The brutal murders of civil rights workers, such as James Chaney, Michael Schwerner, and Andrew Goodman, are recent examples of lynch law.

Still another form of aggression expressed itself as the family feud. This form of violence occurred primarily in the Appalachian part of the United States but also in Texas and the Southwest. These family blood feuds began shortly after the Civil War and continued to the beginning of World War I. Brown (1969) suggests that the animosities generated by the Civil War served as a trigger for these feuds. The Appalachian area was polarized between Confederate and Union sympathizers. Marauding guerrilla bands slew each other without mercy. These hatreds did not abate after the Civil War, and indeed were exacerbated by the liberal use of moonshine in that area. Some of these families feuded for many years: the Hatfield-McCoy feud lasted from 1873 to 1888 in the Appalachians; and in Texas the great Sutton-Taylor feud lasted from 1869 to 1899. Thus the family feud served as a model of aggression for the children of these areas during their growth and development.

For at least a decade before the Civil War, aggressive acts between citizens of the North and South mounted. For example, the Fugitive Slave Law in the South produced the action of vigilance committees there and abolitionism in the North. Fights between slave holders and those against slavery literally devastated the territory of Kansas. In addition to the massive bloodletting of formal battles, irregular warfare and guerrilla strife were also taking a savage toll of life and property. Moreover, groups and countergroups — vigilantes and safety committees of all sorts — arose.

Historians are beginning to believe that no other event in American history generated more hatred and violence, the end of which is not yet foreseen, than the Civil War. Of course, any war is a form of institutionalized aggression. The sanctions against killing and against the destruction of property, inculcated during the entire period of child-rearing, are temporarily lifted. Young men are instructed to act aggressively and indeed are rewarded for such behavior. The enemy is caricatured as less than human and worthy of only hate and destruction. Indeed, not killing and destroying during war may bring serious negative consequences to any individual who finds himself under battlefield conditions. It may be impossible ever to assess the effects of these institutionalized periods of violence — the major wars in which the United States has been engaged. An indication, however, derives from recent research, which will be examined in subsequent chapters, showing the direct effects of an aggressive model on an observer. It is staggering merely to list the lawless groups which seem to have had their origins in our various national and international conflicts. Some examples are: the vigilante groups of North and South, the various components of the Ku Klux Klan, the lynch mobs, the White Caps, the Bald Knobbers, the Night Riders, and family feudists. Outlaw groups, such as the James Brothers, the Younger Boys, and the band of William Quantrell, dotted the western American landscape. More recently we have the Minutemen, the Whitehats of Cicero, Illinois, the Black Panthers, the Weathermen, the Crazies, and the reactive forces of police groups at the city, state, and federal levels. The vigilante movement is in itself a chapter on violence in American history extending from 1760 to the beginning of World War I. The violence of agrarian uprisings marks rural America from the latter part of the seventeenth century to the recent milk-dumping tactics of the National Farmers Association. Such events as Shays's Rebellion, the Whiskey Rebellion, and Fries's Rebellion comprise every schoolboy's history lessons.

The history of organized criminal violence in the United States is traceable to the early eighteenth century. Horse theft, cattle rustling, and counterfeiting antedate the Civil War. Train robbery, bank robbery, and blue- and white-collar organized crime of all kinds compose the voluminous criminal statistics of the twentieth century. Certain aggressors and kinds of aggressive behavior have, in a way, been apotheosized by Americans. Jesse and Frank James, the Younger Boys, Billie the Kid, Pretty Boy Floyd, John Dillinger, Clyde Barrow, and Bonnie Parker tend to be seen as social bandits. The gangland crime of the prohibition period and the 1930's features Al Capone and his gang in Chicago; Lepke Buchalter and Murder, Inc., in Brooklyn; and Legs Diamond, Arnold Rothstein, and the intricate and well organized system of violence practiced by the Mafia. This list hardly scratches the surface of criminal violence. Operating concurrently with the violence of criminal activity is the violence of racial, ethnic, and religious prejudice.

Free-lance violence, culminating in the murder of individuals, abounds. In the span of 100 years four presidents have succumbed to assassins' bullets. Recent multiple murders, such as those committed by Richard F. Speck of eight student nurses in Chicago and those by Charles Whitman from the top of the University of Texas Tower, killing thirteen people and wounding thirty-one, although current, are by no means unique.

Labor violence antedates the American Revolution, and the advent of the Industrial Revolution in the United States in the nineteenth century produced a crescendo of violence. To this day, strikes, lockouts, dynamitings, goon squads, hijacking, sabotage, brutal beatings, and assassinations are commonplace in labor strife. Both labor and management seem about equally culpable with violence on one side inciting violence on the other. More recently the politics of protest and confrontation has escalated the level of violence throughout the United States. Examples are the recent urban riots in Chicago, Los Angeles, Washington, Newark, Detroit, and other cities. Not to be ignored is police violence, as documented by the Walker report (1968), in Chicago at the 1968 Democratic Convention. The willingness of civilian soldiers to fire live ammunition at point-blank range into a crowd of student protesters at Kent State University is another instance of how primed we are to use violent tactics. These examples seem to be part of a fabric of violence which is becoming increasingly pervasive throughout the United States.

The preceding is a thumbnail sketch of merely some of the highlights of violence occurring in this country prior to and since its inception. Stokely Carmichael's aphorism that violence is as American as cherry pie vividly elucidates the rationale for the resort to violence by individuals and groups excluded from the mainstream of American life. If Americans are to break their recourse to aggression in order to gain their ends, it is imperative that the phenomenon come under scientific study. The present research on aggression, although limited in scope, will, we hope, reveal information on the antecedents of aggression and on techniques for its mitigation. If we can determine how children learn to be aggressive, perhaps we can then set ourselves to the task of determining how this type of behavior can be unlearned and how we can arrange conditions so that alternative, pro-social behaviors are strengthened.

Summary

This chapter has set the background of our study in terms of the considerations leading us to a particular methodology for studying aggressive behavior in children and its antecedent learning conditions. We were committed to large-scale survey procedures for assessing the behavior of both the children and their parents. The appraisals of children and parents were carried out independently of each other. The subjects, 875 children, the total population of children in the third grade in a semirural county of New York, were group-tested in the classroom. The parents were independently interviewed in a face-to-face situation, usually in their own homes. New procedures were devised to assess variables which had been selected for their theoretical relevance to the learning of aggression. The theoretical orientation itself is explained in Chapter 2. The derivation of the measurement procedures is described in detail in Chapter 3. The procedures included measures of reinforcement, instigation, identification, and sociocultural variables, and findings grouped under these headings are detailed in Chapters 4 through 7, respectively. A synthesis of the findings, presenting an integrated picture of how children learn to be aggressive, appears in Chapter 8. Chapter 9 then examines the implications of these findings for child-rearing.

THEORETICAL ORIENTATION TO LEARNING OF AGGRESSION IN CHILDREN

Chapter 2

When we embarked on this research it was our firm conviction that aggressive behavior was influenced to a large extent by learning. We were aware of another body of theory and evidence exemplified by the concept of instinct as developed in psychoanalysis. Both of these orientations contributed something to the determination of the objectives and operations of our data-gathering. Although the variables we chose were largely experiential (e.g., rewards and punishments) we did not neglect the unlearned antecedents (e.g., frustration). Subsequent work (Aronfreed, 1969; Azrin and Holz, 1966; Bandura, 1968; Gewirtz and Stingle, 1968; Walters and Parke, 1967) provides more recent discussion of the two theoretical approaches. These later developments will be introduced where appropriate, primarily in the discussion of the interpretation of our findings. The current task, however, is to set forth the theoretical framework from which the study developed. It should be remembered that this development was in a time period before the most recent formulations noted above.

Psychoanalytic Theory

Two related but distinct theoretical notions about the causation and character of aggressive behavior have dominated twentieth-century psychology. Freud, in his second theory of the instincts (1922), postulates the presence of two drives or instincts present in all individuals: *Eros,* the instinct of life; and *Thanatos,* the death instinct. Aggression is considered to be the expression of the death instinct. Every person, according to this theory, is genetically endowed with a given quantum of energy that is directed toward destructiveness and must inevitably be expressed in one form or another. If it is blocked or inhibited in its direct, external manifestation, it then seeks to express itself indirectly. If all external expression is blocked or prevented, then the aggression is turned back on the individual himself (Menninger, 1938).

In this view of the causation of aggression, the biological nature of destructive impulses is emphasized. Although experiential factors are not completely ignored in this theory, they are certainly underplayed. Melanie Klein, currently one of the exponents of this point of view, states: "Innate aggressiveness is bound to be increased by unfavorable external circumstances and, conversely, is mitigated by the love and understanding that the young child receives, and these factors continue to operate throughout development. But although the importance of external circumstances is by now increasingly recognized, the importance of internal factors is still underrated. Destructive impulses, varying from individual to individual, are an integral part of mental life, even in favorable circumstances" (1963, pp. 3 ff.). This psychoanalytic view and other biological points of view will be discussed later in the interpretation of our findings (see especially Chapter 5).

Learning Theory

An alternative point of view, while not denying the possible biological underpinnings of aggression, stresses the importance of experience (i.e., learning) in the causation and mode of expression of aggression. This is exemplified by the Yale studies in aggression (Dollard et al., 1939). Exponents of this point of view hold that aggression is not an inherent, genetically given quantum of energy that seeks expression in some form or other. Rather, aggression is the by-product of frustration.[1] Initially it is the invariable response to frustration, and since frustration of basic drives is both inevitable and universal, aggressive responses at the start of life are also universal.

Important in determining the nature and extent of future aggressive behavior are the learning conditions attendant upon the initial responses to frustration and the subsequent reinforcement

[1] This point of view is consonant with Freud's earlier thinking, e.g., his statement that "if the object is a source of unpleasurable feelings, . . . this can essentially lead to . . . an aggressive inclination against the object, . . . an instigation to destroy it" (1915, p. 137).

19

history of those responses. Thus reinforcing factors are accorded an important role in the development of instrumental aggression.

Instigation

Most modern behavior theorists more or less accept the formulation which includes instigation and reinforcement, although experience and experiment have elaborated this formulation to some extent. In an article written soon after publication of the original frustration and aggression monograph by Dollard et al., one of the authors points out that they did not mean that frustration could have no other consequences than aggression or that instigation to aggression need eventuate always in overt aggression (Miller, 1941). Thus, Miller says, "Frustration produces instigations to a number of different types of responses, one of which is an instigation to some form of aggression" (*ibid.*, p. 338). The strength of instigation to aggression is said by the authors of the monograph to vary with the strength of instigation to the frustrated response, the degree of interference with the frustrated response, and the number of frustrated response sequences. More recently, arbitrariness of frustration (Pastore, 1952) and expectancy (Berkowitz, 1962) have also been noted as limiting variables. Perhaps the work of Azrin, Ulrich, and their colleagues on pain-elicted aggression represents the high intensity end of the frustration continuum (Azrin, Hake, and Hutchinson, 1965; Ulrich, Hutchinson, and Azrin, 1965).

The specific form the aggression takes is determined by the amount of instigation, the inhibiting effects of punishment, the characteristics of the target, including the possibility of displacement to another object, and the opportunity for catharsis which might serve to reduce the tension. Although aggression is a very likely response to frustration it is not the only one. Other responses to frustration which have been studied but do not concern us here are regression, withdrawal, and constructive striving.

It has been demonstrated that frustration often does increase the probability of aggressive response. Following Premack (1959), the opportunity to commit an aggressive act would then become reinforcing, that is, the probability of occurrence of the aggressive response would increase. Premack states that the opportunity under deprivation conditions to engage in a high probability response reinforces any immediately preceding behavior of lesser strength. His example of a reinforcing activity is eating under deprivation conditions. The work of Azrin, Hutchinson, and McLaughlin with pain aggression in animals (1965) substantiates this prediction about the reinforcing value of aggression following instigation.

Reinforcement and Punishment

While some behavior theorists have questioned the inevitability of aggression as the sole response to frustration, others more recently have questioned frustration as the necessary antecedent condition to aggression. Reinforcement and modeling have been presented as alternatives.

The reinforcement position is exemplified by Buss (1961) who argues that frustration is actually not a very potent antecedent to aggression. Aggression, he says, occurs primarily if it has instrumental value, i.e., if the individual gets what he wants by an aggressive act, eliminates an annoyance, or fends off an attack. Berkowitz, one of the current proponents of the frustration-aggression hypothesis (1962), counters that the deprivation of some object or goal which the individual attempts to obtain by aggressive behavior is in itself a frustration, as are annoyers and attacks by others.[2]

It is clear that frustration is an important instigator to aggression and that aggression is very likely an unconditioned response to frustration. Whether or not the presence of an aggressive response always presupposes some frustration and frustration always leads to some form of aggression is of secondary importance. However, as indicated above, when an aggressive response occurs as the reaction to frustration, its future development depends on the reward or punishment subsequent to the aggression.

The likelihood that an individual will perform an aggressive act is actually a function of both his aggressive and his nonaggressive tendencies. Anxiety about expressing aggression is an important contributor to nonaggressive tendencies and acts as an inhibiting force, while the aggressive tendency is a facilitating force. The resultant behavior depends on which force is stronger at any given moment. Training in aggression is an important determinant of the relative strength of these two tendencies. It is hypothesized that the child who is rewarded for aggressive behavior in a given situation will tend to respond aggressively in similar situations; and the child who is punished for such behavior will develop anxiety about its expression and will tend not to react with aggression in similar situations (Mowrer, 1939). Miller has stated that the "strength of inhibition of any act of aggression varies positively with the amount of punishment anticipated to be a consequence of that act" (1941, p. 337).

[2] Thus the aggressive act, by reducing the frustration, reinforces itself. This hypothesis can be used as one explanation of the paradoxical findings that, in many cases, parental punishment leads to expression of aggression rather than to its inhibition.

Furthermore, it is important to know the extent to which the child is rewarded for performing nonaggressive behaviors in order to assess more completely the interaction of rewards and punishments in producing aggression. When responses other than aggression lead to reward, these responses compete with the aggressive response, and whether or not a response in a particular situation will be aggressive depends on the relative reinforcement histories of the two responses. If the nonaggressive response has been rewarded systematically and the aggressive response punished systematically, the aggressive response tendency should be weakened.

There is empirical support for these formulations. The effect of reward for aggression on subsequent aggressive behavior has been demonstrated in a number of laboratory studies with children. Davitz (1952) gave one group training in aggression by rewarding them with praise and encouragement for any aggressive behavior they exhibited while playing a series of games, the goal of which was to injure some object. Another group was encouraged and rewarded for constructive play activities such as drawing murals and completing jigsaw puzzles. In a pretest the two groups of Ss ranked equally in both aggressiveness and constructiveness. However, after an interpolated frustration, the agressively trained children behaved more aggressively than the constructive group.

Subsequent to the collection of data in the current study, a number of laboratory researches have demonstrated that it is possible to shape aggressive responses using a variety of reinforcers (Lovaas, Baer, and Bijou, 1963; Walters and Brown, 1963). Walters and Brown, for example, trained boys to strike a Bobo doll. Two of the groups were reinforced with marbles, one on a continuous reinforcement schedule and one on a fixed ratio schedule. A third group received no reinforcement. After training, half of each group was frustrated. In the test period, each child was paired with another child who had not been trained to hit the doll, and the two competed in physical contact games and aggressive responses were recorded. It was found that there was no difference in aggression between the frustrated and nonfrustrated subjects but that the subjects trained on the fixed ratio schedule exhibited significantly more aggression than the other groups. Patterson, Littman, and Bricker comment on these studies:

> Such investigations simply show that in a laboratory setting aggressive behaviors can be brought under the control of reinforcing stimuli, such as adults' social approval or being given marbles. It is unlikely, however, that the culture is programmed to dispense these classes of reinforcers for assertive behaviors or that the reinforcers are on the same kind of regular schedules

used in laboratory studies, such as continuous or fixed ratio. An adequate understanding of the child's acquisition of aggressive behavior requires identification of the actual consequences and schedules provided by the social culture for his . . . aggressive behaviors [1967, p. 5].

The effect of punishment as an inhibitor of aggression has also been demonstrated in the laboratory with animals (Kahn, 1951; Scott and Marston, 1953; Seward, 1946). In addition, one laboratory investigation with nursery school children demonstrated that children who were punished for aggressiveness during initial play sessions exhibited significantly less aggression during later sessions than did children who received no punishment (Chasdi and Lawrence, 1955). Perhaps it is useful, before a few more studies are cited, to present Azrin and Holz's definition of punishment: "Punishment is a reduction of the future probability of a specific response as a result of the immediate delivery of a stimulus for that response. The stimulus is designated as a *punishing* stimulus; the entire process is designated as *punishment*" (1966, p. 381). Notice that the crux of the matter is not the "punishing" *appearance* of this stimulus but rather the decrease in the subsequent probability of the response. It is often observed that parents complain that they punish bad behaviors but that it either has no effect or it seems to increase the undesirable behaviors. Furthermore, the availability of an unpunished, possibly rewarding alternative behavior is important. Azrin and Holz state that "the alternative response situation leads to a greater suppression by a given intensity of punishment than does a single response situation, whether the aversive stimulus is a period of time-out, an annoying noise, electrode shock, or whether the subjects are human or pigeon" (*ibid.*, p. 406). In Chapter 4, as results of the current study are examined, data are presented that support the position that suppression of aggression by punishment will be more effective when a rewarded, alternative nonaggression is available.

Survey studies have not been as uniform in their results. Lesser (1952) found some indication that punishment for aggression as reported by parents was associated with the inhibition of aggression, whereas reward for aggression was associated with increased aggression. The latter relation was more marked than the former. Other large-scale survey studies of child-rearing practices and aggression, however, have not found this predicted relation between increased punishment and lowered aggression (Bandura and Walters, 1959; Glueck and Glueck, 1950; Sears et al., 1957). In fact Sears and his colleagues conclude that punishment is "ineffectual over the long term as a technique for eliminating the kind of behavior toward

23

which it is directed" (*ibid.*, p. 484). The Azrin and Holz definition quoted above would suggest that the behaviors which parents and/or interview-raters label as punishment may actually function as facilitators.

Aside from possible methodological problems in survey studies (Radke-Yarrow, 1963) which are discussed in Chapter 3, one of the possible reasons for the contradictory results of field studies of aggressive behavior is the lack of precise control of other contributing conditions. For example, the interaction of rewards and punishments with frustration complicates predictions of future aggressive behavior. What has been called punishment has two conceptually distinct aspects when it follows an aggressive act. First, it can serve to heighten anxiety about aggression and therefore reduce the probability of aggression in similar situations. In this way, it functions as a punishment as defined by Azrin and Holz. Second, however, punishment can facilitate aggressive behavior in at least two ways: it can serve as a frustration which increases aggressive need at least temporarily; and it can serve as an aggressive parental behavior to be copied by the child. Punishment as an aggressive act to be imitated is examined later in this chapter and in Chapter 6. The role of punishment as a facilitator of aggression in some families and as an inhibitor in others is examined in Chapters 4 and 6.

Although it is not clear how the first two opposing tendencies stemming from punishment combine to determine aggressive behavior, it is hypothesized that if punishment for aggression subsequent to frustration is severe enough, then aggressive behavior should decrease. Also, if the frustration is *not* removed or the child does not associate the removal of the frustration with his aggressive act, aggressive behavior following such frustration is less likely.

Similarly, reward following an aggressive act should increase the tendency to act aggressively in similar situations; but at the same time it should at least temporarily reduce frustration and, therefore, the momentary instigation to aggressive behavior. It is hypothesized that if the aggression subsequent to frustration is rewarded (e.g., by the removal of the frustration) and the child somehow associates the removal of the frustration with the aggressive act (Sears et al., 1953), then aggressive behavior following such frustration is more likely. Contributing to the total frustration level of the individual child and thus increasing the instigation to aggression are a number of factors: rejection, disharmony in the home, severe toilet training, general restrictive or permissive attitudes of parents toward children and child-rearing, lack of home nurturance, dependency conflict, and so forth. These should be investigated in a study delineating antecedents of aggression. A number of years ago, Goodenough (1931) showed that interference at home with goal-seeking behavior of preschool children was the most frequent source of anger in these children. Merrill (1946), who observed mother and child interacting, found a positive relation between aggressive behavior of the child and controlling, restrictive behavior of the mother. Lesser (1952), whose subjects were in the fifth grade and thus two years older than our subjects, found a direct relation between peer-rated aggression and parental rejection. Chasdi and Lawrence (1955) found a direct, positive relation between the amount of frustration at home and the extent of aggression expressed in fantasy. These empirical studies strengthened our conviction that frustration at home was antecedent to child aggression. However, a direct, straight-line relation was not anticipated because it had also been demonstrated that other characteristics of the child, no doubt produced by previous responses of socializing agents to the child's aggression, also influenced this relation. For example, Block and Martin (1955) compared children who had been previously characterized as undercontrollers and overcontrollers according to their responses to a situation in which they were not permitted to play with some attractive toys they were exposed to. While the overcontrollers settled for the less attractive toys with which they continued to play constructively, the undercontrollers made many aggressive responses. Otis and McCandless (1955) similarly examined two groups of children, one characterized as having a strong need for "power" and the other a strong need for "love and affection." The former responded more aggressively to a potentially frustrating situation than the latter.

Identification

Another limiting condition affecting the relation between punishment and inhibition is the extent to which the child identifies with the punishing agent. Specifically, to what extent does the child incorporate the standards of the parent and to what extent does he copy the punishing behaviors which the parent as a model furnishes? Perhaps the closer the identification, the more likely are rewards and punishments to work in the way the parent desires. Identification is a construct borrowed from psychoanalysis that has been incorporated into behaviorally oriented studies and theories of child development. For a review of this concept and especially its relation to modeling and imitative behaviors, see Gewirtz and Stingle (1968). Levin and Sears (1956) found that by introducing the variable of identification into their design they were able to predict more efficiently from antecedent learning conditions to the criterion. They observed children in two doll-play sessions and found that the frequency of aggressive behavior was positively related to the degree of identification with the like-sexed parent, provided that particular parent usually administered the punishment.

The modeling theorists have stressed the importance of observational learning in the acquisition of aggressive behavior. A situation that is postulated to have a strong influence on the learning of aggressive responses is one in which an observer performs an aggressive response after seeing another person perform similar behavior. This can be the exact imitation of either an old or a new response in the observer's response repertoire or a nonidentical behavior in the same general class as that observed (Gewirtz and Stingle, 1968). Although modeling should occur according to this formulation whether or not the observer has been previously instigated to aggress (Bandura and Huston, 1961; Kuhn, Madsen, and Becker, 1967), experiments in modeling usually include instigation as a necessary condition for eliciting the behavior (Berkowitz, 1965). Also, modeling is more effective when the observer sees the model being reinforced (Bandura, Ross, and Ross, 1963a; Rosenbaum and Tucker, 1962; Walters, 1966); although in at least one study, the modeling phenomenon was obtained without any opportunity for observing the model being reinforced for his aggressive behavior (Bandura, Ross, and Ross, 1963b). Gewirtz and Stingle (1968) propose a most reasonable analysis for imitating a model's reinforced behavior. Their analysis rejects the notion of vicarious reinforcement and suggests instead that situations in which behavior is appropriate for a model are also situations in which that behavior is appropriate for the imitator. Thus the imitator can reasonably expect to be reinforced for those behaviors that he has observed being reinforced in the model. Williams (1970), following the lead of Gewirtz and Stingle, demonstrated that what has been called vicarious reinforcement is a very arbitrary, manipulable relationship between the reinforcement and nonreinforcement of the model and the probability of the imitative response occurring.

It has also been demonstrated that the power status and other stimulus qualities of the model are important conditions of the effectiveness of modeling (Epstein, 1966; Hicks, 1965; Lefkowitz, Blake, and Mouton, 1955). At any rate, the modeling effect seems to be enhanced when certain kinds of instigation, reinforcement, and characteristics of the model are taken into account. A field study attempting to furnish a comprehensive account of the antecedents of aggressive behavior should therefore include measures of each of these variables: instigation, reinforcement, and modeling.

Observational learning (copying a model) is considered to be relevant to the notion of identification. As indicated above, the latter concept was developed by Freud to help account for the con-

26

tinuity of conscience between generations and for the appearance in children of the values, desires, and manners of their parents as well as those of their own sex (Freud, 1923).

Actually Freud distinguished two processes: anaclitic identification, in which the child takes on the attributes of the loved parent who has been a source of comfort and nurturance; and identification with the aggressor, in which the child defends against anxiety by taking over the attributes of a punitive parent (A. Freud, 1937). According to Sears, Rau, and Alpert (1965), the relevance of modeling to identification is that the child, "by performing acts which, in the mother's behavior repertoire, have become secondary rewards or reinforcers for the child, now has a mechanism by which he can reward himself. By imitating his mother, he can provide a substitute for her when she begins withdrawing affectionate interaction and nurturance from him" (p. 4). The other process of identification which Anna Freud described more fully, identification with the aggressor, perhaps could also be stated in reinforcement and/or behavioral terms. It may be argued that the dichotomy between the two kinds of identification is spurious because they can both be encompassed by a role model theory. Either kind of situation fosters imitation since each can provide extrinsic reinforcement for the imitator. Further, within the psychoanalytic model the development of conscience, i.e., the internalization of standards, is the result of either anaclitic identification or identification with the aggressor. This consequence of identification, internalization of standards, may be more difficult to state in terms of rewards, punishments, and secondary reinforcement. However, in this study guilt behavior manifested after the child has performed a prohibited act has been used as evidence for the presence of internalization. The child behaves not only as a child in breaking the rule but also as a parent in punishing for that behavior. These speculations deserve further empirical research. In the meantime they represent the theoretical orientation from which this research stemmed. Assuming that a majority of parents would like to discourage aggression in their children, a simple relation is predicted between identification and aggression: identification should serve to inhibit undesirable behavior and encourage desirable behavior.

Sociocultural Variables

We have considered three major related sources of aggression: instigation, reinforcement, and identification. The distribution of these variables may differ from one sociocultural group to another. A tentatively important variable here is social class which is usually measured by the occupation and education of the status parent (Warner, Meeker, and Eells, 1960). Also important are ethnicity (Barabee and von Mering, 1953), mobility orientation (Farber and Jenne', 1963), and attitudes which are conditioned by social class (Christie, Havel, and Seidenberg, 1958). These sociocultural characteristics determine a style of life which in turn influences the interaction between parent and child. The sociocultural groupings had been relevant in other studies (Allinsmith, 1954; Davis, 1948; Maccoby and Gibbs, 1954; McKee and Leader, 1955; Miller and Swanson, 1958), and thus we expected them to be important in our study. Another obvious but fundamental variable was sex of parent and child. The literature indicates unexceptionally that boys are more aggressive than girls and have different learning experiences. They relate differentially to fathers and mothers and vice versa. This variable is so pervasive (Anastasi, 1958) that it will not be treated extensively in any one chapter, but will appear as a control variable in almost every analysis. We will be looking at fathers and mothers and boys and girls separately, usually in four combinations: father/ boy; mother/boy; father/girl; and mother/girl. Gender is also important as a cue associated with the potential target of aggression (Buss, 1966b). In our own culture, if not in others, children learn early in life that girls are not appropriate objects of physical aggression.

Summary

This chapter has attempted to state our theoretical position at the time this study was initially planned some fifteen years ago and the main body of data collected five years later. This is awkward to do now since our theoretical notions have advanced on the basis of both our own findings and the writings of others. However, it has been our purpose here to describe our thinking at the time so the reader might understand from what source our hypotheses about important variables derived and consequently why we attempted to develop the measures we did. Occasionally in this chapter we have indeed referred to works published after 1960, but this is only when those authors produced pertinent findings or stated more cogently or elegantly what we had in mind.

On the basis of behavior-theoretical and psychoanalytic propositions, we assumed that the important antecedents to aggressive behavior were instigation, reinforcement, and identification. We had reason to believe that various sociocultural factors influenced the expression and formation of these antecedents so they became a fourth class of variable that we attempted to investigate. Subsequent chapters examine each of these four sets of variables to determine how they are related to the appearance of aggressive behavior in school. On the basis of the relations we find and the inferences we draw from these relations, we then return to a theoretical analysis of how children learn to be aggressive.

METHODOLOGICAL CONSIDERATIONS

Chapter 3

As outlined in previous chapters, our theoretical position concerning antecedents of aggressive behavior derived primarily from manipulative, laboratory experiments with animals. However, it was necessary to operationalize these concepts with large-scale assessment procedures in order to obtain the data required for the study of children. Measures of both the criterion (child aggression) and predictors (primarily parent behaviors) would have to be built with theoretical relevance as well as psychometric soundness. The following data-gathering procedures were devised: (1) a peer-rating measure of aggression to be used with the children; and (2) an objective, precoded interview schedule to be used with mothers and fathers. Furthermore, for validative purposes we had recourse to the following methods: (3) use of existing clinic and school records; (4) analysis of newspaper accounts of antisocial behavior of parents; and (5) observation of behaviors of preselected children in a laboratory situation.

Derivation of the Criterion Measure of Aggression

The construction of large-scale techniques for assessing the aggressive behavior of children in the primary grades was not an easy task. There were a number of requirements for such a measure. First, it had to fit our definition of aggression, "an act whose goal response is injury to another object," derived from the definition used by

Dollard et al. (1939), which obviously referred to hostile, extrapunitive aggression and excluded accidental aggression. Furthermore, the technique had to be suitable for assessing the behavior of large numbers of children in the classroom. It also had to demonstrate sound measurement characteristics: (1) yield a stable score, summarizing a three- or four-month sample of behavior in the classroom; and (2) exhibit high interjudge agreement. It was also desirable to obtain separate subscores as to type of aggression (whether physical, verbal, acquisitive, or indirect), object of aggression (whether against adult, peer, or nonhuman objects), and provocation level (whether justified or not). Finally, the measure of aggression had to relate to overt behavior and enter into meaningful relations with other variables. It was believed that these requirements could be met by a modified sociometric procedure in which each child in the class rated every other child on a series of specific items of aggressive behavior. Such a procedure would summarize a large number of observations of each child's behavior by many individuals who had had an extended opportunity to interact with him.

The peer-rating procedure, which would at least measure reputation for aggression, would also include items relevant to the child's (1) popularity among his classmates, (2) interpersonal activity level, and (3) aggression anxiety (the child's judged reluctance to be aggressive because of severe punishment for such behavior in the past). The first of these had to be included since there are likely to be differences in the quality of aggressive behavior of children who are popular among their peers and those who are rejected by them (Lesser, 1959). An estimate of interpersonal activity level was necessary as a correction for aggression scores. There are children who interact with others only occasionally but always aggressively and others who, because they interact so frequently with others, are bound to have high aggression scores. The assessment of anxiety about expressing aggression was to be included in order to represent the low end of the aggression scale. Children who were rated high on aggression anxiety, it was felt, would be ones who obtained few or no nominations on the aggression items. A study by Peterson (1971), to be described in Chapter 4, indeed indicates that low aggressive boys inhibit aggressive responding in situations where they are very apt to be punished for such behavior. However, when there is no chance of punishment they respond as aggressively as high aggressive boys.

The procedure which was devised to obtain peer-ratings involved giving each child a booklet made up of a number of identical pages each of which contained a page number and the names of all the children in the class. The names were arranged in two lists, one with the boys' names and other with the girls' names. The positions of the names in the two lists were randomized. The children were instructed to mark the names of everyone who fitted each question as it was read aloud to them by the examiner. One page was used for each question, and the pages were color-coded so that the examiner and his assistant, by glancing around the room, could rapidly determine that all children were marking names on the correct page. The children were permitted to mark as many names in each list as they thought fitted the question; however, they were required to cross out at least one entry in each list. This was possible since "No Boy" and "No Girl" appeared as names on each list. In this way we knew that an unmarked list was the result of carelessness and did not signify that no one fit that description. There was no restriction on the number of names that could be crossed out since the number of nominations made by any subject could be of interest in itself as a psychological response.

The aggression score that each child received was based on the number of judges who chose him as fitting a particular behavioral description. Thus, if ten of the twenty-seven members of a class crossed out Johnny Jones's name as someone who said mean things, Johnny's raw score was 10 for that item. If he were selected a total of forty-five times for the other nine items, his score on the whole set of items would be 55. These raw scores were converted into percentages in order to make scores of subjects who were in different classrooms more comparable.

The ten aggression items appearing in Table 3.1 comprised the criterion measure of aggression used in the final countywide survey. All results reported here, except where noted, refer to this measure of aggression. These were the items retained after a long series of preliminary studies in which approximately 1,800 third-grade children served as subjects. An account of these studies is detailed in the monograph by Walder, Abelson, Eron, Banta, and Laulicht (1961). The development of the measure is briefly summarized in Appendix I.A. Although this procedure is integral to the study as a whole, for purposes of continuity of presentation, an account of its development is placed in the Appendix. However, since the problems we faced in devising a paper and pencil measure of aggression as well as the solutions we achieved are central to the area of personality measurement and propaedeutic to this research, we recommend that the Appendix be examined carefully.

The final peer-rating procedure also included two aggression anxiety items, two popularity items, three success in aggression items, and three activity level items (see Table 3.1). Originally, there were four each of the popularity and aggression anxiety items, activity

TABLE 3.1
Peer-Rating Items

Category	Number	Question
Identification	1	Who are you?
Warm-up	2	Who are the children who always sit around you?
Popularity (MPOP)	3	Who would you like to sit next to in class?
Aggression (MAGG)	4	Who does not obey the teacher?
Aggression	5	Who often says, "Give me that"? (asked with emphasis)
Success in aggression (MSAG)	6	Who are the children who fight well?
Aggression	7	Who gives dirty looks or sticks out their tongue at other children?
Activity (MACT)	8	Who is too busy to talk to other children?
Activity	9	Who is very quiet?
Aggression	10	Who makes up stories and lies to get other children into trouble?
Aggression	11	Who does things that bother others?
Aggression	12	Who starts a fight over nothing?
Aggression	13	Who pushes or shoves children?
Aggression	14	Who is always getting into trouble?
Success in aggression	15	Who gets what they want by fighting?
Aggression	16	Who says mean things?
Activity	17	Who is always in and out of things?
Aggression	18	Who takes other children's things without asking?
Aggression anxiety (MANX)	19	Who says, "Excuse me," even when they have not done anything bad?
Success in aggression	20	Who pesters until they get what they want?
Aggression anxiety	21	Who will never fight even when picked on?
Popularity	22	Who are the children you would like to have for your best friends?

level was rated by the teacher, and there was one rejection item and no items specifically measuring success in aggression. The rejection item was eliminated in the final version because in all of the preliminary factor analyses it loaded so highly on the first general aggression factor that it would have been redundant to include it. This was important since we were trying to shorten the peer-rating procedure. For similar reasons only the two popularity items and the two aggression anxiety items which had the highest loadings on their respective factors were retained.

Since peer-ratings of aggression constitute the major dependent variable of the research reported in this volume, it is desirable to examine whether the statistical properties found with the earlier versions of the peer-rating index (which are described in Appendix I) were also present in the data obtained with the final form. Three tables of intercorrelations summarize these data. Table 3.2 reports the intercorrelations of five different composite scores: aggression, success in aggression, aggression anxiety, popularity, and activity level. Table 3.3 contains the intercorrelations of the ten aggression items which together constitute the aggression composite score. Table 3.4 represents the relation of each of the ten aggression items to each of the five composite scores. The top row of Table 3.4, showing the correlation of each of the aggression items to the aggression composite score, is actually an array of the item-total correlations of the aggression scale.

TABLE 3.2
Intercorrelation of Composite Scores

	MAGG	MSAG	MANX	MPOP	MACT
AGG	1.000	.841	-.335	-.286	.039
SAG		1.000	-.242	-.058	.126
ANX			1.000	.611	.647
POP				1.000	.554
ACT					1.000

N = 725 (all children present on the day the peer-rating procedure was administered).

TABLE 3.3
Intercorrelation of the Ten Aggression Items

	04[a]	05	07	10	11	12	13	14	16	18
04	1.000	.726	.734	.778	.780	.707	.726	.870	.727	.694
05		1.000	.783	.775	.776	.758	.744	.747	.767	.757
07			1.000	.816	.773	.774	.776	.781	.823	.746
10				1.000	.820	.841	.838	.846	.858	.813
11					1.000	.758	.806	.840	.797	.756
12						1.000	.821	.806	.850	.791
13							1.000	.822	.827	.748
14								1.000	.832	.753
16									1.000	.786

N = 725
[a] Number of the specific items as they appear in Table 3.1.

The relation between aggression and activity level, now rated by the children themselves, was of the same zero order as when rated by the teacher. The relations between aggression and popularity and between aggression and aggression anxiety were unchanged. And there was still a substantial correlation between aggression anxiety

TABLE 3.4
Intercorrelation of the Ten Aggression Items and Five Composite Scores

	04	05	07	10	11	12	13	14	16	18
MAGG	.868	.863	.886	.931	.906	.898	.905	.932	.917	.866
MSAG	.673	.717	.682	.763	.742	.819	.816	.789	.804	.718
MANX	-.296	-.322	-.312	-.260	-.321	-.287	-.309	-.316	-.280	-.264
MPOP	-.221	-.272	-.295	-.271	-.253	-.259	-.256	-.235	-.256	-.259
MACT	.042	.008	.040	.072	-.004	.054	.038	.031	.071	.044

$N = 725$

and popularity. The exceptionally high correlation between the ten-item aggression composite score and the three-item success in aggression score indicated they were probably both measuring the same thing. Indeed, each of the ten items in the aggression composite correlated highly with success in aggression, although not as highly as with the aggression composite score itself. This finding very likely means that children who are not rewarded by their peers for aggression do not aggress against them or at least do not act aggressively in their presence. Thus their behavior would not have been noticed and reported here. This is discussed further in Chapter 4 when we deal with reinforcers. The same order of relation obtained when the peer-rating measures were used with large groups of third-grade children in Cedar Rapids, Iowa (Semler, Eron, Meyerson, and Williams, 1967), and also with ninety-seven eight-year-old school children in Amsterdam, Holland (Stroo, 1970). The latter findings are examined in Chapter 7 which deals with sociocultural variables.

The interitem correlations in Table 3.3 range from .69 to .87; the item-total correlations in Table 3.4 range from .86 to .93. Thus the scale's homogeneity is not in doubt for this age group. It was possible in Table 3.4 to arrange the five composites in order of size of relation to the aggression items. It can be seen that in each column (i.e., for each item) the absolute values decrease with no inversions. Such regularity within the peer-rating data is, of course, not the whole picture. We were interested in seeing how the peer-rating data related to data from other sources. The remaining chapters of this book are devoted primarily to detailing these relations. The implications of the interrelations between the aggression items, the aggression composite score, and the other composite peer-rating scores are examined later in this chapter. Notice that caution is indicated lest the relations be overinterpreted. Much of the relation may be a function of method variance and, at least in the case of success in aggression (SAG), similarity of the item content. However, a real relation is very likely, as is explained below and in subsequent chapters.

One technical consideration in the administration of the peer-rating procedure that had to be resolved was what effect, if any, the test-administrator himself had on the nominating behavior of the subjects. Experiments in role-modeling would indicate that the sex, status, verbal behavior, and other characteristics of the experimenter might have an important influence (Bandura, Ross, and Ross, 1961; Berkowitz, 1965). Thus, since three different examiners administered the procedure to the subjects in thirty-eight different classrooms, one of the first assessments that had to be made was the extent of systematic differences among the classrooms in aggression score according to examiner. An analysis of variance was performed. The influence of four independent variables on the aggression score was assessed. The four variables were: (1) examiner; (2) sex of child as object of choice; (3) sex of child as chooser of other children; and (4) classroom, treated as a random replication factor. This analysis yielded non-significant Fs for all effects of examiner with respect to aggression scores (Toigo, Walder, Eron, and Lefkowitz, 1962). The lack of examiner effect was attributed to the standardization of administration of the peer-rating procedure. Also all the examiners were males of approximately the same age. More recently, Marcus (1966) did a study using both male and female test administrators with the peer-rating procedure and found no significant effects on peer-rating score attributable to sex of examiner. The finding of no difference due to sex of examiner broadens the general utility of the peer-rating index. A major requirement in the development of our procedures was that they should be standardized in order to insure replicability. The finding of no examiner effect with the peer-rating index therefore marks a methodological achievement. We then looked forward to examining the Rip Van Winkle child-rearing questionnaire with parents for the same characteristics (see p. 54).

A related procedural matter which had to be dealt with was the effect of classroom membership in general upon the relations obtained. We had used all our subjects in one single pool and to this end we corrected each child's sociometric score for class size by assigning percentage scores on the basis of the number of choices obtained by any S divided by the total number of choices made in his class. Conceivably there could be other factors about a class, such as clique structure, teacher's personality, etc., which might affect the level of aggression and/or the relations obtained among our classroom and parent interview measures. The correlational approach was used to test in a general way the notion of class as a

TABLE 3.5

Five Peer-Rating Mean Scores on 118 Absent and 796 Present Third Graders

	MAGG	MANX	MPOP	MSAG	MACT	$\overline{X}$	n^a
Absent	11.88	15.92	19.64	11.69	14.80	14.78	118
Present	13.00	17.68	23.35	14.72	15.66	16.88	796
$\overline{X}$	12.85	17.45	22.87	14.33	15.55	16.61	914

[a]The ns include fourth graders who were present in double classes with third graders. Their scores were not used in any substantive analysis.

moderator variable. Five peer-rating scores, ninety-seven parent interview scores, and the subjects' IQ and game-preference scores were intercorrelated in one analysis. The intercorrelations included the total correlations among scores for the entire group ($N = 451$ complete data cases), and we also obtained within-classroom correlations on the same subjects. These were calculated in terms of the deviation of each score from the classroom mean for that score. If there had been a consistent reduction in correlation when proceeding from total correlation to within-classroom correlation, it would have meant classroom membership had to be taken into account. However, this was not so; for most analyses we were justified in using all the subjects as one pool.[1]

A final procedural matter with which we had to deal was the effect of presence or absence of a particular child on the day the peer-ratings were done. Table 3.5 shows the effect of absence on the peer-rating score of aggression as well as on the other peer-rating scores examined below (see pp. 46–47). The ratings of those present were consistently higher than those absent ($p < .025$), indicating that presence-absence is a relevant dimension of the peer-rating procedure itself. It may be hypothesized that peer-ratings by third graders are at least partially based upon direct observation of the children who are nominated. This increases our confidence in the relevance of the peer-ratings to the behavioral referents of the items. However, it also argues against using the scores of those who were absent during the peer-rating procedure. Therefore, the bulk of the analyses reported in this volume are based only on the scores of those children who were present on the day the peer-rating procedures were completed.

[1] See Appendix I, Table I.5, for all correlations between aggression score and any variable that were significant for either total correlation or within-classroom correlation. For other relevant material, see the discussion of classroom atmosphere in Chapter 7.

Validity of the Peer-Rating Aggression Score

The account of the derivation of the peer-rating measure of aggression, detailed in Appendix I and on the preceding pages, furnishes ample evidence of the reliability of this instrument. This is seen in both interjudge agreement and test-retest reliability (Appendix I, pp. 175–183) as well as in the lack of susceptibility to error due to artifacts of procedure. Some examples of these artifacts are examiner differences, classroom membership, placement of name on list, ability to understand and follow instructions, and activity level. Validity was also demonstrated in a number of ways during the conduct of the research. Initially, there was the internal evidence of validity, noted in Appendix I in the derivation of the instrument. The results of factor analysis, consistent across samples, was one instance. The fact that boys always received higher scores than girls was another, since a consistent observation of most investigators is that boys are more aggressive than girls. The similar shape of the distribution of scores from class to class, with scores piled up at the low end as is expected in antisocial behavior (Allport, 1934), was a further preliminary indication of validity.

The face validity of the items as seen in agreement among expert judges and in the ability of the children to discriminate both good and bad aggression from good and bad nonaggression, were also encouraging (Appendix I, Table I.4). The high interrater reliability is in itself evidence of validity because the raters must have been basing their judgments on observation of the same specific behaviors in order to get such substantial agreement. Similarly, agreement of peers' judgments with teachers' judgments is an indicator of validity. In addition to "instant" validity data deriving from the measurement characteristics of the instrument and accompanying its construction, there were instances of other types of validity which accrued as research with the peer-rating score progressed. The search for validity eventuated in close correspondence between the peer-rating measure and overt behavior in a controlled laboratory situation. This is discussed below and in subsequent chapters.

Construct Validity

Construct validity in terms of the consistently meaningful relations into which the aggression score entered was gradually developed. The relations that were found to parent interview data and other sources constitute the major portion of this book. They include the consistent relation of the peer-rating score to: (1) punishment by the parents, especially the mother; (2) instigation to aggression in the home, as reported by either parent, but especially the father; (3) identification with parents, defined both as internalization of standards and modeling of behavior; and (4) various aspects of social class membership.

There was other evidence of construct validity. For five years, a file was maintained by the research staff of all reports of antisocial activity on the part of residents of Columbia County that appeared in the two newspapers in the county, one daily and one weekly. A search of this file revealed thirteen boys and fifteen girls in our study population whose mothers and/or fathers were involved in some kind of antisocial behavior reported in the newspaper (ranging from vagrancy to rape and from disorderly conduct to assault with a deadly weapon). Of the thirteen boys, twelve had aggression scores above the median for the entire group of boys (mean score of this group is 32.00, mean for all boys is 14.19) and only one below the median. Of the fifteen girls, twelve had scores above the median (mean score of this group is 22.92, mean for all girls is 9.23) and three below. This could not have been a function of social class since the occupational classification (according to the United States Census Index) of the fathers ran the entire range. Moreover, there was no concentration of occupations of any particular class among these twenty-eight boys and girls. Although these findings are based on a very small number of cases out of the total population, the instance of being mentioned in the newspaper for antisocial behavior is a rare event and the fact that it discriminated any of our subjects is impressive (Meehl and Rosen, 1955). These data, showing that markedly aggressive parents have aggressive children, have an obvious relation to the concept of role model.

A number of questions were inserted into the child-rearing interview with parents to make it sound plausible to the respondent and to gain his cooperation. In a common-sense way, the relation to aggressive behavior of many questions that we asked must have seemed remote to the parents. Therefore, randomly interspersed throughout the interview were items having to do with such matters as attendance at PTA meetings, TV habits of the children, comic books, and Spock's manual on child-rearing (1957). These items were subsumed under one classification, facetiously called "Ladies Home Journal." The computer, unaware of our jokes, analyzed these responses along with the others. It was found that the number of hours children watched TV per week and the violence rating of their three favorite TV programs were both highly related to aggression as rated by peers (Eron, 1963).[2] There was a significant positive relation between the violence ratings of children's favorite programs and aggressive behavior in school, although the relation between total number of hours watched and aggressive behavior was significantly negative. These findings, relating TV viewing habits and aggressive behavior in real life, corroborate the results obtained in the carefully controlled, and thus necessarily artificial, laboratory experiments of Bandura and his associates (1961, 1963a,b).

More recently the peer-rating measure has been administered in an urban community in another part of the country, Cedar Rapids, Iowa (Semler et al., 1967). These data were gathered in order to study the relation between aggression score and readily available data in school records, e.g., number of times tardy, IQ, and achievement test scores.[3] For 567 pupils in twenty-five third-grade classrooms there was an increasing monotonic relation between number of times tardy during the school year and aggression score obtained in that year. This was significant beyond the .001 level of confidence. See Table 3.6 for means and standard deviations. Tardiness in school might easily be interpreted as an act of aggression against the teacher, if not against the other pupils. This result was exactly replicated in the following year with 863 pupils in forty-three third-grade classrooms (Semler and Eron, 1967). It should be noted that divergent studies yielded consistent findings, indicating that the peer-rating measure was indeed robust.

In the light of earlier findings of the lack of relation between a nonverbal measure of IQ and aggression score,[4] the results with these same two samples (third-grade school children in two successive years) are interesting and provide evidence for the discriminant validity of the peer-rating measure. In the first, there was a significant but low negative correlation between Otis Quick Scoring IQ and aggression score ($r = -.22$) and a moderate negative correlation between aggression and achievement test score ($r = -.39$). IQ and achievement test score correlated highly positively ($r = .67$). Thus there was the possibility that the relation between aggression and achievement was spuriously high since both are reliably related to

[2] The number of hours and the favorite programs were reported by the parents. The violence in the programs was rated independently by two assistants with high reliability.

[3] This study also replicated the internal consistency data reported on previous pages. This suggests the measure was operating in the same way in this new community as in the original community.

[4] Actually, in the final study reported here there was a correlation of $-.31$ with IQ based on a verbal test, the California Test of Mental Maturity (Sullivan, Clark, and Tiegs, 1957).

TABLE 3.6
Means and Standard Deviations of Aggression Scores
by Number of Times Tardy per Year

	Number of times tardy per year				
	0	*1*	*2*	*3*	*4+*
N	397	90	32	13	35
X̄	14.98	19.72	21.83	23.02	26.16
σ	15.87	20.27	21.45	14.72	17.99

IQ. The relative importance of achievement and intelligence in this network of relations was estimated, using partial correlation procedures. The net relation of aggression to achievement was reduced very little, from —.39 to —.34, when IQ was held constant, indicating that the finding that the aggressive child does not achieve as well as the nonaggressive child is independent of measured intelligence. However, when achievement test performance was held constant, the correlation between intelligence test score and aggression dropped to .06 from —.22. These results were also replicated in the following year with a new group of third graders (Semler and Eron, 1967). Thus the lack of relation between measured intelligence and peer-rated aggression, established in the original studies in the derivation of the peer-rating measure, was corroborated. The negative relation between aggression and achievement in fifth-grade boys has also been demonstrated by other researchers using different measures of aggression (Morrison, 1967; Barsky, 1966).

Empirical Validity

At the time the peer-rating data were attained, there were a number of sources of information available from which estimates could be made relevant to overt aggressive behavior. For example, some of the schools in the Columbia County sample had child guidance clinic services supplied by the Rip Van Winkle Clinic, and it was possible to check out those children on whom we had scores who had also been seen in the clinic. Those who were known to have problems in aggression consistently had scores above the median for their respective classrooms (Eron, 1960). Again, as with our newspaper study, only a small and extreme portion of the total population is included; but it is impressive that any of our subjects at all were discriminated by this criterion, and it demonstrates that the aggression measure is sensitive to the same child behaviors as are reflected in a clinical referral.

Another source of concurrent validity data was the ratings made by persons other than peers. There was a modest, positive relation between ratings of children's aggression made independently by the parents and the peers. This relation was more pronounced when the mothers and fathers agreed on their ratings than when they disagreed. (See p. 51 in this chapter for a comparison of mothers' and fathers' interviews and Chapter 4 for results.) The correlation between fathers' and mothers' ratings of their children's aggression was .31. Fathers' ratings correlated .22 with the peer-rating, and mothers' correlated .16. The relation of peer-rating to teachers' rating was somewhat higher (ranging from .41 to .63). The higher relation between teachers' and peers' ratings than between parents' and peers' ratings probably results from the greater similarity among the situations in which the children are observed by teachers and peers than among the situations in which children are observed by parents and peers. In the same way, mothers and fathers also observe their children in somewhat different situations (see Chapter 4 for examination of similarity between ratings of mother and father). The relation of peer-rating to self-rating was .33. (Self-ratings were obtained only with early versions of the peer-rating procedure.) Although this correlation is significantly better than zero, self-ratings are certainly not interchangeable with peer-ratings. In fact, self-ratings do not correlate as well as teacher-ratings with peer-ratings. The low relation indicates that self-ratings cannot be accepted as a valid criterion of aggression. This finding is consistent with the findings of Leibowitz (1968), who used the Buss-Durkee self-rating inventory and found it did not relate well to overt behavior as measured on an aggression machine. Buss (1967) also reports that there is no relation between self-ratings and aggression machine scores. It would seem that the self-incriminating nature of self-ratings is too difficult to overcome. In this regard it is interesting to note that the aggression self-rating did relate fairly well to other self-rating scales, viz., Sarason Anxiety and Test Anxiety Scales (Eron, 1960).

Despite all the evidence of internal consistency, construct validity, and concurrent validity, we still had no real evidence that the peer-rating measure related unequivocally to overt behavior that could be observed under controlled conditions, the ultimate achievement in empirical validity. To demonstrate such validity, it was desirable to devise an automated laboratory situation in which the behavior that was exhibited could be reliably observed and would closely fit the semantic definition of aggression implicit in the peer-rating questions on which the child had been previously rated. The behavior would also have to be of the type that other investigators in the area agreed was aggressive.

In order to get observational reliability, it was decided to use an automated situation suggested by the "aggression machine" of Buss (1961). However, instead of electric shock, we used noxious sound (Williams, Meyerson, Eron, and Semler, 1967).[5] The child was led to believe that by pushing buttons on a panel he was delivering sounds of increasing noxious intensity to the earphones of one of his classmates. The choice of button (intensity of sound) made by S as well as the latency, duration, and frequency were all recorded automatically by pen recorders which were connected to the buttons and made ink tracings of the data. Automatic timers controlled the whole procedure. (See photograph of apparatus, below.)

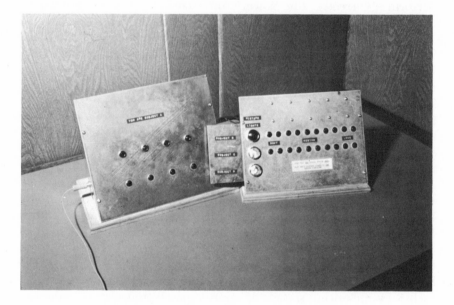

The nature of this situation is such that it closely resembles the semantic definition of the peer-rating measure of aggression — "an act which injures or irritates another person." Furthermore, this machine situation seems to be consonant with the definitions of aggression used by many previous investigators. Dollard et al. (1939), in their quite specific definition, stressed both intent and the necessity of performing the act toward another person before the act could be termed aggressive. Buss (1961) deemphasized intent in his defini-

[5] Thanks are due Professor Milton Rosenbaum for his initial suggestions with regard to this procedure.

tion but specified that the response must be made in an interpersonal situation. In the least specific definition, Bandura and Walters (1959) maintained that the act had only to be potentially pain producing — i.e., an act which could injure if it were aimed at a vulnerable object. Thus, since the nature of this button-pushing task does imply intent and is carried out in an interpersonal situation, it certainly comes within the scope of all these definitions.

Ss were run three at a time. They were brought into the experimental room and told they were to play a cooperative game in which each S in his own booth had to turn off one of a series of four amber lights by pressing the appropriate button under the lights. This was purposely made a very simple task so that all Ss would be sure to perform it correctly. The Ss were told that in order to win the game all three teammates had to complete three trials in a row correctly. After every trial each S was informed by a light signal (called the mistake light) which of his teammates made an error, and he could inform that teammate of his error by pressing one of the ten buttons next to his mistake light. The buttons were ordered in intensity of sound that they delivered, with sounds increasing in unpleasantness from right to left.[6] In the original experiment with the aggression machine, Ss were selected on the basis of their peer-rating aggression score — sixty boys and sixty girls, half of whom had been rated as high aggressive and half as low aggressive. They were brought to the experimental room three at a time and fitted with earphones. Sexes were tested separately and there was systematic grouping of high and low aggressive children — either all three high aggressive, all three low aggressive, two highs and one low, or two lows and one high.

The children were told that each button caused a different sound to be heard by their teammate and the farther right the button, the louder the sound. Buttons one, five, and ten were demonstrated to each S by presenting sounds of approximately 100 Hzs. delivered at 96 db., 105 db., and 111 db. SPL, respectively, for a duration of one second.

Eighteen trials were administered, on the first fifteen of which each S was led to believe that he was solving the problem correctly but his teammates were not (on his own panel his mistake light never lit up, but the lights for his teammates did). The last three trials were rigged as success trials for all teammates. Thus, in each of the first fifteen trials, S was required to depress one of ten buttons graded in intensity of the sound he could deliver to the earphones of his teammates. Actually, the apparatus was switched off after the

[6] In a more recent experiment (Peterson, 1971), third-grade Ss were actually asked to rate the sounds for unpleasantness, and indeed the results were very consistent with the a priori judged irritability of the sounds.

44

demonstration and no one received any sound; after the experiment each S was told the apparatus had broken down so no one had received any sound at all.

The aggression score, automatically recorded by a moving pen, was the numeral of the button pushed (intensity of aggression), length of time the button was depressed (duration), the time elapsing between onset of the mistake light and the button-pushing response (latency), and the number of times the button was pushed (frequency). It was found that high peer-rated aggressive Ss of both sexes pressed the button at significantly greater intensities, for longer durations, with shorter latencies, and more frequently than low aggressive Ss. These results thus provided the validation with an overt measure of aggression that we sought for the peer-rating procedure.

There were some other interesting findings. Boys always obtained significantly higher intensity scores than girls, but there was no difference for latency, duration, or frequency. It seems that girls are stimulated to aggression as quickly and as frequently as boys and maintain the aggressive response for as long as boys; they just do not hit as hard as boys. In nonlaboratory studies this difference could be attributed to less developed musculature. The present result, however, indicates that the lower intensity of girls' aggressive responding is a function of learning rather than constitution, since the required muscular effort for button-pushing is minimal. A study by Peterson (1971) demonstrated that low peer-rated aggressive boys will respond more aggressively toward other low aggressive boys than toward high aggressive boys. Furthermore, when they are assured there is no possibility of retaliation, they respond even more aggressively than high aggressive boys. On the other hand, high aggressive boys respond more aggressively toward other high aggressive boys and especially so when they are certain they will be retaliated against. It seems that while threat of punishment inhibits the aggression of low aggressive boys, it facilitates the occurrence of aggression in high aggressive boys. This is considered in greater detail in Chapter 4 when the findings on punishment are examined.

Other Classroom Measures

In addition to the criterion measures of aggression and aggression anxiety, other measures were also obtained in the classroom. These are briefly examined here for purposes of convenience, although they might be classified more correctly as predictors, conditions of learning, or control variables than as criterion measures. The classroom data were gathered by three senior staff members (the authors of the current volume). It was possible to obtain all the data in any one class in three 45-minute sessions conducted on three successive half days.

Activity Level

Since total aggressiveness of the child may be a function of total amount of interaction with his peers, a measure that would provide control for the total amount of interaction with peers was essential. Originally this measure was provided by the teachers. They were asked to designate approximately 10 percent of their class who were the most withdrawn and 10 percent who were the most interactive with others. This permitted a three-fold classification of amount of interpersonal interaction. Our first large-scale study revealed no relation between this classification and aggression score (r ranged from $+.22$ to $-.33$ in six classrooms, with median r of 0). This was surprising since previous observational studies (e.g., Dawe, 1934) had shown that the total number of aggressive acts in a given period is a function of the total number of acts. It was felt that one reason for the lack of confirmation of this finding could have been that the questions were directed at the wrong informant, the teacher. Therefore, it was decided to have the children rate each other on this variable during the sociometric procedure (see Table 3.1). This change in procedure, however, did not affect the previous findings. There remained no significant relation between activity level score and aggression score. However, in Holland we found a significant negative correlation ($r = -.38$) between aggression score and activity level.

Popularity

This was measured by two sociometric items (see Table 3.1). Originally there were four items in addition to one rejection item (see Table I.1 in Appendix I) to measure popularity. This is detailed in the account of the derivation of the aggression measure earlier in this chapter. In all our studies relating these two measures, a moderate negative correlation (circa $-.30$) always obtained (see previous discussion and Appendix I.A). The same order of relation was found by Lesser (1959) between peer-rated popularity and overall aggression scores in his study of lower-class boys in the fifth and sixth grades in an urban school system. However, when he divided his aggression score into its components, he found a tendency toward positive correlations of this magnitude between popularity and provoked physical aggression only (e.g., "Who will fight back if you hit him first?"). Our final aggression measure did not contain any such items. However, as explained in footnote 2 of Appendix I (p. 183), provoked aggression is highly related to our aggression measure and thus the differential relation found by Lesser would not hold for our total sample.

Success in Aggression

One of the surprising findings in our first study relating aggression in school to parental behaviors was the consistently positive relation between punishment for aggression at home and the appearance of that behavior in school. One explanation for this was that the parents are not the only socializing agents for aggressive behavior. Perhaps peers are at least equally important sources of reward and punishment for aggression. The child who tends to get beaten up in fights will not be as likely to get into fights as the child who always wins and succeeds in getting what he wants by fighting. The instrumental value of aggression has been emphasized by Buss (1961). Therefore, in later studies, items in which the children rated each other on how successful their aggressive behavior was were incorporated into the sociometric procedure (see Table 3.1). The relation between these two peer-rating scores (aggression and success in aggression) is examined further in Chapter 4, since success in aggression pertains to reinforcement.

Intelligence

In order to assess the effect of intellectual level on the learning and performance of aggressive behavior, the Davis-Eells Games (1953), a nonverbal test of general intelligence or problem-solving ability, was used originally in our studies. However, no significant relations at the .01 level of confidence were found between scores on this measure and scores on the aggression procedure. This result seemed unusual, and in the final study, a verbal measure of intelligence was used, the California Mental Maturity Scale, Short Form (Sullivan et al., 1957). There was a moderate negative relation ($r = -.31$) between this measure of intelligence and school aggression. However, studies in a different community five years later using the Otis Quick Scoring Test again demonstrated no relation between measured intelligence and peer-rated aggression score when achievement was held constant (see above, pp. 40–41).

Identification

A number of measures of identification were utilized, some obtained from parent interviews (See Chapter 6) and some obtained directly from the children themselves in the classroom (see Appendix I.B). The latter will be mentioned here.

1. Masculine-Feminine Identification. A measure of sex typed behavior was included in order to get an indication of preferred sex identification (Lefkowitz, 1962). This game, called "Would You Rather?" (Games and Activities Preference in our own nomenclature), included a paired list of activities, one of which seemed more appropriate for boys and one for girls (See Appendix I.B, p. 187, for pairs of items). The subject selected which one of the two he would rather do. A scoring scheme based on the responses of two hundred boys and girls to the twenty-one item pairs was devised. Items were classed as masculine (or feminine) if 60 percent or more of boys (or girls) preferred them. Thus it was possible to develop a masculinity scale and a femininity scale on the basis of respective endorsement of items ranging from 60 percent to 100 percent for each sex. By dividing this range of 40 percent into eight intervals, it was possible to assign weights from one to eight for each preference. Thus the responses of each subject were scored for masculinity or femininity according to norms based on these two hundred cases. Results with this and other measures of identification are treated in Chapter 6.

2. Figure-Drawing (Draw-a-Person). Originally used as a buffer, it was believed that figure-drawing might be useful as a measure of masculine-feminine identification. A random sample of 354 pairs of drawings selected from the first large-scale study showed that 85 percent of the subjects drew their own sex first. This reinforced the notion that sequence may be an indicator of preferred identification, at least in this age range. See Appendix I.B for instructions for administering figure-drawing so that the sex of the first figure drawn was correctly noted.

3. Expressive Behavior Profile (Profile Identication). This procedure for measuring identification is a variation of the Semantic Differential Technique (Osgood, Suci, and Tannenbaum, 1957). Each child rated himself on a series of eighteen bipolar self-descriptive adjectives having to do with perceived expressive behavior (see Appendix I.B). To deal with one of the problems of response set, adjectives were chosen which had no obvious value loading on either end of the continuum. In the parent interview, each parent also was asked to rate himself or herself on the same series of adjectives. A comparison of the child and parent measures thus gave us an indication of actual similarity in perceived self-expressive behavior between parent and child. The rationale underlying the use of the expressive behavior profile was that a child copies and internalizes not only the moral precepts of significant figures in his environment but also the manifest motor behavior of these persons. Essentially, this instrument attempted to assay the extent to which the child captures and incorporates the stance and style of the physique of the socializing agents. Thus, copying of patterned styles of physical movement was postulated to be one component of identification. The D

score described by Cronbach and Gleser (1953) was used to assess the dissimilarity between profiles of the subject and his mother and father. Similarly, a D score was calculated to assess dissimilarity between S's evaluation of himself and the modal self-evaluation by his own sex peers.

4. Occupational Aspiration. Another index of identification was obtained by comparing the child's occupational aspiration with the parent's response to what he would like the child to do when he grows up (see Appendix I.B). Conforming to parental desires in the area of occupation would seem to be one component of the larger complex of role model. In this test the child is presented with a list of occupations which is a modification of the *1950 Census of Population, Classified Index of Occupations and Industries,* from which he picks the one he would most like to be. The parent's choices are also classified according to this scheme.

Discarded Measures

A number of other measures were tried and abandoned in the course of the investigation and before the final survey. These have been summarized in Appendix II.A, Table II.7, along with measures from the parent interview.

Derivation of the Rip Van Winkle Child-Rearing Questionnaire

The data emanating from the parents' interviews are of vital importance to the study because most of the independent variables were derived from these data. In the process of devising this interview (see Appendix II.A), which went through two major revisions, we talked with more than five hundred mothers and fathers. The final result was a 286-item, completely objective, precoded interview, made up of forty-two scales constituting primarily the predictor variables which were generally of four kinds: instigators, reinforcers, identification, and sociocultural variables. A number of the scales also constituted control variables.

All of the scales went through the usual stages of initially loose conceptualizing, theorizing, item-writing, pretesting, homogeneous item selection, and finally empirical tryout before the final version of the parent interview was ready. As with the building of the criterion measure of aggression, the first step was the adoption of a clear-cut definition for each variable. An operational definition was required which would make the concepts distinctive. This permitted meaningful tests of their individual and combined relation to overt aggression in school. Each definition had to be distinctive in meaning and point directly to questions. No definition was accepted for a variable until items could be written which were judged by a number of experts to fit that definition. This was not an easy task. We had assumed that such terms as "rejection," "permissiveness," and "nurturance" had common accepted meanings among experts so that item-writing should be a straightforward procedure. However, our examination of a number of interview schedules employed in previous researches indicated that different investigators used the very same items to tap different variables (Sears et al., 1957; Sears et al., 1953; Glueck and Glueck, 1950; Loevinger and Sweet, 1956; Schaeffer and Bell, 1958). It became apparent that although the names associated with these concepts were routinely used in many interviews, there was no agreement among the interview constructors as to the behavioral referents for any one concept, and thus the same name was used to refer to different concepts. We found it necessary to go back to the literature and also to interview clinicians exhaustively as to what behaviors they had to observe in their clients in order to use such diagnostic words as "rejection," "dependency," and "permissiveness." For example, what specific evidence did the clinician need before making the judgment that a child was rejected? With some prodding we found that the experts could indeed point to specific cues in the behaviors and attitudes of parents which represented distinctive concepts and thus we were able to write relevant items. We accepted concepts from a variety of theoretical orientations, always insisting on distinctive, objective, behavioral definitions.

It was possible also to construct closed-end questions with predetermined alternative responses because of the considerable groundwork laid by the Sears group (Sears et al., 1953; Sears et al., 1957) with open-ended interviews in which the respondents' answers, previously sound-recorded, were rated independently from typescripts by a number of judges. Other items were taken from the Lesser interview (1952), a closed-end questionnaire; the Bandura and Walters interview (1959); the Kohn interview (1959b); and the Schaeffer and Bell (1958) and Loevinger and Sweet (1956) inventories.

One important issue was whether to use attitudinal or behavioral questions. The problem was one of item construction, establishment of rapport, and the nature of the variables being measured. Since we were interested in how the adult's behavior affects the child's behavior, we relied *primarily* upon behavioral items.

The first set of variables that we constructed, with definitions and sample items for each, appears in Appendix II.A, Table II.1 (pp. 193–195). A preliminary test of the relation between the classroom measures and the parent interview variables was carried out by interviewing the parents of sixty children selected on the basis of their school aggression score. These children were chosen from a pool of 152 students, the total population of six third-grade classes, from divergent socioeconomic areas.

From this total group of 152 third graders, ten boys with the highest aggression scores, ten boys with the lowest, ten boys about the median, and three similar groups of girls were selected to represent both sexes at three levels of aggression. Interviews were obtained with all mothers and fifty of the fifty-eight available fathers of this group of sixty preselected children.

The results of this study were utilized as a basis for making improvements in the interview. The specific steps in this interview-building procedure are described in Appendix II.A.

Agreement between Parents

In such a survey study as we devised, each parent serves as an observer of his child and as an observer of himself. On the one hand, one would hope that the two parents would tend to agree on those interview variables that are built to describe the child. An example of this is the home aggression measure: if we are to know from interviewing parents how aggressive a child is at home, the parents as judges must tend to agree in order that we can have confidence in their ratings. On the other hand, there are interview variables that were designed to describe the parent himself. For example, it is not necessary for the parents to agree on the variable of their punishment for the child's aggression. The question of confidence in the data does not mean that lack of perfect agreement between mother and father represents inadequate measurement. Actually, low agreement may be as informative about a family as high agreement.

Indeed, as illustrated in Appendix II.A, findings from an early interview study demonstrated that mothers and fathers do not always agree on the information about their children that they give to the interviewers. However, they not only disagree when they tell us about their children, but, even when there is agreement of scores on certain variables, those scores do not then relate to scores on other variables in the same way for both mother and father. This was demonstrated by Eron, Banta, Walder, and Laulicht (1961) in comparing data obtained from mothers and fathers. Results presented in that article showed that prediction to the criterion was improved when data from both mother and father were considered jointly. There is little question of the necessity for interviewing both mothers and fathers in child-rearing studies. The importance of the father as a socializing agent has long been neglected. We found it both possible and practical to interview fathers and looked upon their inclusion in the study as the addition of both a new dimension and a new method. In other words, aside from the father's influence on the socialization process itself, we also considered the potential use of the father as a *method* in child-rearing practices research. Agreement between mother and father can be an indication of the reliability of information we secure from either. In large-scale research, perhaps only those children should be included in the sampling whose mothers and fathers agree in evaluating their child's behavior. Although, by doing this, we may overlook important differences in parents and the effect of these differences on the children, it helps increase confidence in the accuracy of information obtained. Where mothers and fathers disagree, it is necessary to conduct separate analyses. The techniques of information-gathering may have to be revised, for indeed parents do have different perceptions of their children. This is perhaps based on the fact that a child relates in different ways to each parent. In this research, separate analyses for those parents with good agreement were done to see if prediction of the criterion was improved by such an increase in presumed accuracy of predictor data. (For example, see Chapter 4, pp. 62–64, for the relation between mother's and father's ratings of home aggression and how these ratings in turn related to school aggression.) Allowance also has to be made for the order of interviews, whether mother and father were interviewed at the same time, and, if not, which one came first and the amount of time elapsing between interviews. It was our experience that two parents evaluating the same child three months apart can give quite different pictures of the child's behavior and both be accurate for the time rated. Other controls for acuity of observation and knowledge of the child on the part of the respondent, who is, after all, one of our chief measuring instruments, were included in the revised interview as the result of our earlier experience. Two such controls were to ask the parents to predict the child's intelligence and his popularity with peers in school. We had independent estimates on both of these variables. It is likely that those parents who can predict these scores accurately know their children better than parents who cannot predict accurately, and we can thus have confidence in the information they impart. Another control variable was parental presence: judgments of a child's behavior made by the parent who is rarely at home perhaps should not be treated the same as judgments of the parent who has greater opportunities for observation. These are but a few indications of how our initial experiences in interviewing both mothers and fathers alerted us to ways in which, by using these two sources of information, we were able to improve the precision of our predictor measures.

The interview questions and the manual of directions which accompanied the questionnaire appear in Appendices II.B and II.C. The variables covered in the interview, the number of items per variable, and the question numbers in the interview associated with each variable are summarized in Table II.11 of Appendix II.A. As previously noted, these variables are considered either instigators, reinforcers, identification, or sociocultural factors. In addition, there are a number of control variables. The derivation of the measures for each variable as well as the relation of the measures to the criterion and among each other will be discussed in later chapters.

Overcoming Response Bias

Not enough attention has been paid to problems of response bias in field studies of parent-child relations (Radke-Yarrow, Campbell, and Burton, 1968). We were sensitive to response bias and the cumulative effect of the questions. However, experience with our interview indicated that parents were not disturbed by the kinds of questions we asked. There was much evidence to indicate that they were making a real effort to be candid. The questions were worded to allow parents to admit to socially unfavorable behaviors in nonobvious ways. For example, items were quite specific in content and thus had unfavorable connotations only when scored as a composite. Further controls were used in the analysis of the data as an additional aid in overcoming response bias.

We also adopted a Kinsey-like tactic in interviewing (Kinsey, Pomeroy, and Martin, 1948) by asking questions that assumed our respondents did everything. Instead of asking, "Do you ever . . . ," we asked, "When was the last time you. . . ." For example:

How often does NAME disobey you? Does it happen:
  5 At least once a day?
  4 At least once a week?
  3 At least once a month?
  2 Less than once a month?
  1 Never?

When is the last time NAME was rude to you? Was it:
  5 Today or yesterday?
  4 Just a few days ago?
  3 In the past week?
  2 In the past month?
  1 More than a month ago?
  0 Never?

In administering this type of question, the interviewer was required to read the most frequent or most recent alternative first.

53

If the respondent said "yes," the interviewer would exit to the next question. If the respondent said "no," the interviewer would offer the next alternative, continuing to do this until he received an affirmative response. In this way, it was made more difficult for the respondent to give the socially acceptable response. Such a format encouraged the use of more socially incriminating response alternatives in these items; the acquiescent response style and social desirability response set were presumably working in opposite directions.

Controlling for Interviewer Bias

Although there were a number of internal controls throughout the interview to maximize accuracy of reporting on the part of the parents, it was necessary to make an assessment of how much influence the interviewers themselves had on the information they obtained. A total of twenty-one interviewers collected the data, some interviewers contacting more parents than others. Although the interviewers were all carefully screened and trained, it was necessary to determine if any bias occurred as the result of the variation in number of interviews completed, interviewer personality, etc. This problem was handled in a rough way by grouping together all interviews obtained by any one interviewer. Four scales were then selected that might be most susceptible to such bias: rejection, recency of aggression, interviewer rating, and F Scale. Mean scores on these scales for all subjects interviewed by each examiner were then calculated. There was very little variation in mean score. The mean aggression score of the corresponding children, obtained independently of the interview, was also calculated. The range in mean score for aggression in school appeared, if anything, wider than for any of the interview variables (see Table 3.7). Thus it is very likely that the effect of interviewer bias was minimal, and it is justifiable to consider all interviewers to have contributed to one pool of subjects.

Final Selection of Items

Improvements in the interview, resulting in the final instrument used in the countywide study, were based primarily on the results of the preliminary investigation (Eron, Banta, Walder, and Laulicht, 1961) relating school aggression to parent interview variables (see Appendix II.A). Decisions as to the retention or revision of items and scales were made in light of item-total reliabilities and interrelations among measures. The former were used to ensure homogeneous scales; the latter to ensure relevant scales. Items were retained because they had substantial item-total correlations and favorable distribution characteristics or because they belonged to item sets bor-

54

TABLE 3.7
Mean Score on Four Variables from Interview Obtained by Each of Twenty-one Interviewers and Mean Aggression Score of Corresponding Children

	Mother interview variables				Noninterview variable		Father interview variables				Noninterview variable
IN	RJ	RA	IR	FS	AGG	IN	RJ	RA	IR	FS	AGG
00	14.25	24.13	19.38	28.63	19.63	00	12.93	19.60	25.07	27.27	6.33
01	11.75	26.50	21.00	27.75	25.00	01	12.44	17.56	25.33	26.00	12.67
02	13.75	21.38	23.38	27.13	5.25	02	12.73	21.36	25.27	23.45	15.36
03	12.80	21.00	20.40	24.40	4.40	03	13.30	24.40	25.30	27.00	15.20
04	12.73	18.82	24.27	25.55	5.00	04	14.00	23.75	20.25	26.00	11.25
05	14.05	19.84	22.16	28.00	13.53	05	12.00	16.25	25.63	25.88	6.25
06	14.13	22.38	22.88	27.13	20.00	06	15.67	12.00	25.00	31.33	6.67
07	13.88	21.88	19.08	28.62	11.69	07	12.54	17.23	25.38	26.00	11.08
08	13.70	23.20	23.60	29.90	15.30	08	13.80	15.00	22.40	27.20	3.60
09	12.38	17.25	20.81	27.75	10.00	09	13.82	19.73	23.36	23.18	12.55
10	13.42	15.61	22.95	29.29	12.29	10	12.68	11.41	23.45	27.27	8.27
11	13.31	20.45	24.41	28.86	10.86	11	13.11	17.49	23.89	27.27	10.24
12	13.69	22.53	21.17	29.22	11.67	12	13.53	17.53	21.59	27.76	6.94
14	13.10	18.10	22.74	27.38	8.46	14	12.26	14.26	23.53	28.16	11.79
15	12.75	15.50	18.13	28.63	8.00	15	12.75	17.81	22.00	25.50	7.44
16	13.21	15.61	18.32	28.07	9.96	16	12.00	16.00	22.60	27.60	10.60
17	12.79	20.64	21.59	29.22	11.36	17	12.92	17.96	18.98	28.23	10.77
18	14.57	17.43	23.61	29.71	8.38	18	13.36	16.57	22.57	26.85	8.14
19	14.23	22.62	23.25	27.22	11.88	19	12.75	16.64	24.47	27.11	12.00
20	13.39	23.52	20.61	28.61	14.45	20	12.86	21.09	21.88	28.58	13.78
21	13.34	20.45	25.38	29.67	15.79	21	12.49	16.29	26.14	28.35	13.62

IN = Interviewer
RJ = Rejection
RA = Recency of Aggression
IR = Interviewer-rating
FS = F Scale
AGG = School aggression measure

55

rowed from other studies to be used as reference variables. Examples of this latter case are the Reversed F Scale (Christie et al., 1958) and Walters and Zak's Personal Opinion Inventory (1959).

Table II.7 in Appendix II.A summarizes all variables and items which figured in the study at one time or another. Also included there are the ultimate status in the final interview of all items retained as well as reasons for deletion of those items dropped. A more extended account of the history of those scales which were retained appears in the appropriate chapters and appendices that follow. Tables II.8, II.9, and II.10 in Appendix II.A detail results with the control variables. One such variable (not included in the appendix tables) was interviewer-ratings, a six-item composite score dealing with the amount of difficulty the interviewer had in arranging and conducting the interview and how much the interviewer liked the respondent. This score had very little relation to scores on any of the variables since it was related beyond the .01 level of confidence to only four out of ninety-six variables [7] for father (highest r obtained was .15) and three for mother (highest r was .21). Interviewer-ratings for father did not correlate significantly with interviewer-ratings for mother. Obviously, how the interviewer felt about the respondent had little influence on the information obtained.

An acquiescent response style was measured by Christie's Reversed F Scale (1958), scored for acquiescence (see Table II.9 in Appendix II.A). Acquiescence did not have much influence except perhaps for self-ratings of aggression (Walters and Zak, 1959). In this instance acquiescence correlated .42 for fathers and .26 for mothers. Additionally, acquiescence correlated .33 with punishment for aggression for fathers and .27 for mothers. For the age at which nocturnal enuresis ceased, there was a correlation with mothers' acquiescence score of .51, although for fathers it was only .01. Mothers are obviously more involved in this area. Finally, for education of parent, acquiescence correlated —.30 for fathers and —.17 for mothers. The largest influence of acquiescent style on response for both mothers and fathers was with the self-ratings of aggression (Walters and Zak's Personal Opinion Inventory). This scale had been used without any attempt to modify its format or content as we had done with most others in line with our concern for response bias. It included items such as, "Horses that don't pull should be beaten and kicked," "I easily lose patience with people," and "I've been in trouble with the law," with which the respondent had to agree or disagree. The remaining ten items were equally as obvious and potentially self-

[7] These correlations come from a 105 × 105 matrix including eight classroom scores and ninety-seven scores derived from the parent interview.

incriminating. It is not surprising that people who admitted to foolish and/or reprehensible behaviors on one scale also admitted to them on another scale (e.g., on the F Scale, where one item reads, "Sex criminals deserve more than prison; they should be whipped in public or worse").

In general, the correlations obtained between acquiescence and father interview variables were higher than mother interview variables. This suggests that information supplied by mothers may be more pertinent to the content of the question than to the format of the response. This is not as true for fathers. In addition to data which will be examined later in this book, other studies support this observation (Lefkowitz and Cannon, 1966; Walder, Cohen, Breiter, Warman, Orme-Johnson, and Pavey, 1970).

Another control for overenthusiastic interpretation of relations was achieved by constructing a random scale to determine how many significant relations it entered with the other scales (see Harris, 1967, for statistical rationale and footnote 1 in Appendix II.A of this volume). This constituted a base line for random significant relations. The number of these relations that could be expected for any one variable was calculated by arbitrarily constructing a composite score of thirteen scale items randomly selected from the interview and randomly scored. This composite score was then related to scores on the 104 other variables (see Table II.10 for significant correlations). In the fathers' interviews this composite correlated with three variables at the .01 level of confidence or better — the correlations were .13, .14, and .29. In the mothers' interviews there were fourteen correlations with the random composite score significant at the .01 level of confidence ranging from .13 to .32 with a median of .14. Neither fathers' nor mothers' random composite score correlated higher than zero with any of the eight independently obtained classroom measures. It would seem that correlations between any two interview measures below .30 should be considered with some skepticism. This stringent requirement need not be instituted for consideration of correlations between interview and classroom data since method variance is not a consideration here. Following these rules, we may feel confident that the relations among variables in the interview and between interview measures and classroom measures reported and interpreted in this volume are not likely to be a function of chance alone.

Confidence in the parent interview is bolstered by results with a modified version used in Holland with seventy-two mothers of eight-year-old boys and girls (Stroo, 1970). A factor analysis, in which the five peer-rating scores were included with twenty-two scales from the interview and a dichotomous classification by sex of child, revealed five factors. These accounted for at least 40 percent of the variance of most of the scales, especially those which had to do with factual information such as occupation, education, and frequency and recency of aggression. Also accounted for, however, were more subtle scales such as rejection, confession, and respondent's aggression. Further consideration of the Dutch results is in Chapter 7 which deals with sociocultural factors.

Summary

The development of the data-gathering procedures employed in this research was described in this chapter. A paper and pencil measure of aggression for use with children in school was the first procedure discussed. Third-grade children were selected as the subjects because this was the earliest age at which we believed it was possible for children to cooperate in large-scale paper and pencil procedures. It was necessary that the subjects be able to read and to write and to discriminate among the behaviors exhibited by their peers. A peer-rating procedure, in which each child in a class rated every other child in that class on a series of specific behaviors, was selected as the best possible method because it yielded a large number of observations on each subject by observers who had had many opportunities to interact with him. The final measure of aggression was highly reliable in terms of interjudge agreement, temporal stability, and independence from procedural artifacts. A number of validities were demonstrated for the peer-rating measure: (1) content validity in terms of agreement by expert judges that the items did indeed tap aggression of various types, objects, and provocation levels; (2) construct validity in terms of the meaningful and theoretically predictable relations into which the measure entered; and (3) empirical validity in terms both of prediction of overt behavior, as measured in a controlled laboratory situation with automatic recording of aggressive responses, and of relation to other indicators of aggression.

Other classroom measures described in the chapter were aggression anxiety, popularity, activity level, success in aggression, IQ, and various measures of identification. These included masculine-feminine identification, ratings of expressive behaviors, occupational aspirations, and drawings of the human figure.

The derivation and description of a completely precoded, objective interview that was used with parents in an individual, face-to-face situation were also included in this chapter. The final interview contained 286 items comprising forty-one variables consisting of one to twenty-seven items each, with a median number of five items per variable. The variables were classified largely into four types: reinforcers of aggression, instigators to aggression, identification, and sociocultural variables. In addition, there were a number of control variables to take into account, including the respondent's candor, consistency, reliability, and knowledge of his child. In assembling this interview a number of test-construction procedures not usually associated with interview-building were utilized. These included: (1) judgment of content validity of items by a panel of experts; (2) selection of items on the basis of their difficulty and spread as well as relation to the criterion individually; and (3) establishment of homogeneous scales by inter-item and item-total correlations. Extensive pretests were done. Responses of mothers and fathers were compared with each other and related to the criterion singly and in combination. Factor analyses of mothers' and fathers' interviews done separately strengthened our belief that it was necessary to separately interview both parents since there were some areas of parent-child interaction in which mothers were better informants, some where fathers were better informants, and still others in which responses of both parents had to be combined. Because of the variety of controls instituted in these data-gathering procedures, we were reasonably satisfied that the information obtained and the relations demonstrated were valid representatives of the real-life behaviors of these subjects.

Now that the general methods of data-gathering have been presented, we can turn our attention to the specific measuring techniques and the results obtained with them. Each of the next four chapters considers a different set of variables: Chapter 4 is concerned with reinforcers; Chapter 5, instigators; Chapter 6, identification; and Chapter 7, sociocultural variables. As each set of variables (e.g., punishment in the chapter on reinforcers) is considered, its psychological function with respect to the learning of aggression is discussed. Occasionally, the relations of a set of variables suggest its relevance to a concept examined in one or more of the later chapters (e.g., instigation and identification). Thus the reinforcement aspects of this set are considered in Chapter 4; in Chapter 5 this set is reconsidered in terms of instigation; and in Chapter 6, in terms of identification. Other sets of variables (e.g., rejection) are handled in the first chapter that seems relevant (Chapter 5, instigation). Other interpretations are not plausible. Thus rejection is not considered later. In this way the hypotheses about the psychological functions of the sets of variables, the variables themselves, and the items comprising the variables, with reference to the learning of school aggression, are raised, tested, and discarded or retained. By Chapter 8 the various measures are classified according to function, interrelated, and summarized.

THE REINFORCEMENT AND
PUNISHMENT OF AGGRESSION

Chapter 4

One of the major hypotheses of this research was that aggression in children is a function of rewards and punishments for this behavior. Children who are rewarded for aggression will tend to be aggressive in situations similar to the ones in which they were rewarded. However, it would not be unreasonable to expect that, on the average, children who are more aggressive than others in one situation will tend to be more aggressive in another situation even though the absolute level of aggression might change. For example, Radke-Yarrow et al. (1968) reported that ratings by mothers of aggression at home correlated with ratings by teachers of aggressiveness in nursery school .39 for boys and .25 for girls.

Relation of Home Aggression
to School Aggression

It was felt that the extent of the child's aggressive behavior at home as judged by parents might be important in that this is the behavior which may have been evoked by instigation, strengthened and maintained by reinforcement, reduced by punishment, or increased or decreased to match a model. The quality of these judgments of home aggression was of concern from the outset of our research. In the early study described in Chapter 3 and Appendix II, the child's home aggression was rated by each parent on a frequency scale for the occurrence of each of thirteen aggressive behaviors. For example, we asked, "How often does NAME say mean things to another child?" The response alternatives were: "never," "rarely," "occasionally," "pretty often," "frequently," "daily"; these were defined in terms of specific frequency per unit of time. This measure had zero relation to school aggression. Furthermore, the correlation between mothers' and fathers' ratings was not significantly greater than zero. Finally, there was a very narrow spread of scores restricted primarily to the lower end of the frequency continuum. While these findings may have accurately described home and school aggression, it seemed proper to be concerned with the trustworthiness of the methods before accepting and interpreting the resulting scores. Actually, the results could have been due to a variety of factors imposed by the format of the interview in use at that time. For example, all the home aggression items appeared in one block toward the end of the interview, which, of course, encouraged a uniform response set. In addition, responses could easily have been influenced by responses to the punishment questions, which came earlier in the interview, about the very same aggression behaviors. Furthermore, despite our efforts, the response alternatives turned out to be ambiguous. Finally, the items were very obvious, and perhaps social desirability considerations did not permit the parents to admit to the occurrence of aggressive behaviors in their children. Because of these deficiencies, two new scales, described briefly in Chapter 3, were substituted for the home aggression measure: frequency and recency of aggression. These scales were designed to make it easier for parents to admit to presumably unfavorable characteristics of their children; and, since the items in the scale were scattered randomly throughout the interview, it was less easy for a respondent to adopt one type of response to all items.

These revised home aggression scales did indeed work much better than the previous one. There were now correlations significantly greater than zero between home and school aggression and between mothers' and fathers' ratings. However, the correlations themselves, even when significant, tended to be puny and of little practical interest, although they were of the same order as those reported by Radke-Yarrow et al. (1968). A technique more appropriate than product-moment correlation was finally used for evaluating the relations among the variables. This was a two-way analysis of variance with two interview scores as independent variables and school aggression as the dependent variable. In this two-way analysis, 3×3 tables were constructed by categorizing each S into one of three approximately equal groups — low, middle, and high — on each of the two variables. Nonpuny and often substantial trends were revealed by this type of unequal n analysis, which acts to partial out

TABLE 4.1

**Mean Peer-Rated Aggression Scores According to Mothers'
and Fathers' Ratings of Frequency of Home Aggression**

		Fathers' ratings			
		Low	Middle	High	Total
Mothers' ratings	Low	8.0 (63)[a]	9.5 (44)	11.9 (34)	9.8
	Middle	9.7 (37)	10.3 (50)	10.7 (63)	10.2
	High	13.4 (37)	15.3 (42)	16.9 (81)	15.2
	Total	10.4	11.7	13.1	

[a]The number in parentheses represents the number of subjects in the cell.

the effect of one classification variable from the other (Anderson and Bancroft, 1952; Eron, Walder, Toigo, and Lefkowitz, 1963).[1]

Although the correlations of aggression with mothers' and fathers' ratings of frequency of their children's aggression at home do not account for much of the variance, as alluded to above, the aggression means for the corresponding two-way analysis of variance presents a more convincing picture (see Table 4.1). Only the effect of fathers' ratings of home aggression on school aggression is significant ($p < .005$). The consistency of the trend of fathers' ratings at each level of mothers' ratings is substantial. Thus while mothers' ratings themselves do not relate to aggression, when the effect of mothers' ratings is controlled, it allows the relevance of fathers' ratings to become apparent. Although we expected a significantly positive relation between home and school aggression, our belief was that a "perfect" home aggression measure would not correlate highly with a "perfect" school aggression measure without the introduction of other controls.

Assuming that there is a "true" home aggression score for each child, one might expect parents who agree with each other about their child's home aggression to be, on the average, better reporters than those who disagree. Another consideration is that children who are consistent enough in their home aggression so that mothers and fathers agree in their ratings of this behavior are also likely to be consistent across situations (home to school). Therefore, an analysis relating home to school aggression controlled for the

[1] This procedure acts to equalize the ns in nine cells. Thus the marginal means are changed so that the main effect of fathers on school aggression is no longer influenced by the correlation of fathers' scores with mothers' scores. Although the unadjusted marginal means represent the numbers from which the puny correlations were calculated, the adjusted marginal means represent the relation between the variables that would be found in a manipulative experimental study. This was also done for punishment, instigation, identification, and social class. These findings will be discussed in the appropriate chapters.

amount of disagreement between parents on the home aggression measure. The home aggression measure, which was divided into appropriate thirds (low, middle, and high), is the average of the mothers' and fathers' ratings of frequency of aggression. The analysis is presented in Table 4.2 for boys and in Table 4.3 for girls. Included in this analysis are all children for whom we had two parent interviews and who were themselves present at the classroom session during which peer-ratings of aggression were obtained. As noted in Chapter 3, children who were present tended to get higher peer-rating scores than those who were absent.

Since the problem involved finding the largest sample of parents whose agreement on home aggression enhanced its relation to school aggression, the "difference" groupings presented here are cumulative. Thus the zero-difference group and the difference-of-1 group comprise the 0–1 difference group; the zero-difference and the difference-of-1 groups along with the difference-of-2 group comprise the 0–2

TABLE 4.2
Boys' Mean School Aggression as a Function of Frequency of Home Aggression with Difference between Fathers' and Mothers' Ratings Controlled

| | Difference in ratings | | | | | | |
| | Steps of difference | | | | | | |
Home aggression	0	0–1	0–2	0–3	0–4	0–5	All
Low	5.83	11.67	12.87	13.31	12.93	12.38	13.45
Middle	12.75	11.29	13.32	12.58	11.80	12.83	12.72
High	21.57	17.60	16.42	17.85	17.43	18.05	16.02
N	17	50	82	115	144	154	281

Note: Distributions cut into approximate thirds at score changes.

TABLE 4.3
Girls' Mean School Aggression as a Function of Frequency of Home Aggression with Difference between Fathers' and Mothers' Ratings Controlled

| | Difference in ratings | | | | | | |
| | Steps of difference | | | | | | |
Home aggression	0	0–1	0–2	0–3	0–4	0–5	All
Low	4.75	4.57	5.00	4.97	4.82	5.20	5.65
Middle	16.75	7.18	8.07	7.94	8.09	8.06	8.27
High	23.33	14.89	14.50	13.59	13.69	13.14	13.47
N	11	59	95	121	149	171	264

Note: Distributions cut into approximate thirds at score changes.

TABLE 4.4

Mean School Aggression Scores of Groups at Three Levels of the Home Aggression Composite Score for Girls and for Boys

		Girls	Boys
Home aggression	Low	4.30 (76)[a]	14.54 (69)
	Middle	8.06 (62)	13.12 (91)
	High	16.43 (68)	17.24 (85)

[a]The number in parentheses represents the number of subjects in the cell.

difference group; and so forth. It is clear that only the zero-difference group for boys and all the groups for girls show positive monotonic relations to school aggression. This finding increased our confidence in the frequency of home aggression measure for girls only. The reliability and perhaps the validity of the measure for boys whose parents disagree on frequency of home aggression by at least one step may well be affected adversely by a conflict in expectations: our society considers aggression an undesirable behavior in general but at the same time condones it as a necessary masculine behavior. Society and the parents have no such conflict about aggressive behavior in girls: aggression is not only generally undesirable, but it is also undesirable as a feminine behavior.

In order to predict school aggression from home aggression, it was necessary to find the most comprehensive measure of home aggression, taking into account both fathers' and mothers' responses to both types of questions. Appendix III.A contains a description of the building of this composite measure. Results with the final composite home aggression score appear in Table 4.4, where a positive, monotonic, significant relation between parent-rated aggression at home and peer-rated aggression in school is shown. This is significant, however, for girls only ($p < .005$). The conflict in expectations for boys, noted above, may help to explain this difference in findings between boys and girls.

Intensity of Reward and Punishment

Closest to the heart of our theoretical orientation was the relation between rewards and punishments for aggressive behavior and the appearance of that behavior in the school context. As noted in Chapter 1, survey and laboratory studies have produced contradictory findings when they have tried to relate child-rearing practices and conditions of learning to aggressive behavior of children. It was felt that a possible reason for the discrepancy was a deficiency in the application of theory in these studies. Although rewards and punishments (sanctions) for various behaviors had been categorized, rated, sorted, and studied for their relation to the later evocation of these behaviors, no effort had been made to determine the differences in intensity of various rewards and punishments. Thus, efficient prediction from antecedent to criterion was impossible. Laboratory studies in learning uniformly take the intensity of the rewards and punishments that are under study into consideration. This is because various theoretical formulations postulate that sanctions are related to behavior differentially according to their intensity (see Appel, 1963; Azrin, 1958, 1959, 1960; Azrin, Holz, and Hake, 1963; Breithower and Reynolds, 1962; Dinsmoor, 1952; Estes, 1944; Masserman, 1946; Nissen and Elder, 1935).

Most experimental studies with animals have treated intensity of sanctions in a straightforward way. They have usually dealt with unlearned primary rewards, and it is relatively easy, at least in animal studies, to vary systematically the amount of food intake, strength of electric shock, availability of sex object, and so forth. In survey studies of child-rearing practices and child behavior, however, where learned sanctions are mixed with primary sanctions, this experimental solution is not readily applicable. Such correlational studies (e.g., Sears et al., 1957) have either ignored intensity of sanctions or else invoked it post hoc, and no attempts have been made to operationalize this notion. Laboratory studies with children suggest that the relation between punishment and inhibition of response is complex. For example, Aronfreed and Leff (1963) report that when a child is required to make a simple discrimination between two toys which are considerably different in attractiveness, the punished response, i.e., choosing the forbidden toy, is readily suppressed by high intensity punishment. When the discrimination task for the child is more difficult, i.e., when choice is between two toys of comparable attractiveness, high intensity punishment is not effective in suppressing the punished response. The authors reason that the requirement of a complex discrimination in conjunction with high intensity punishment produces a high level of anxiety which interferes with adaptive learning. Furthermore, as noted in Chapter 2, the relation between punishment and inhibition of response is complicated by the fact that the punishing parent is both supplying a model of aggressive behavior to the child and also increasing his frustration level by administering the punishment.

Devising a Measure of Intensity of Reward and Punishment

We originally attempted to evaluate intensity of reward and punishment in the following manner. For thirteen aggressive behaviors which appeared in our interview schedule (and also in the peer-rating measure), the parent was asked an open-ended question, for example, "What do you usually do when NAME says mean things to another child?" We sought specific behavioral descriptions. When the respondent said, "I talk to him," the interviewer probed for what was said and how. Then a second question was asked: "What do you do if he does it again real soon?" or "If that doesn't work, what do you do then?" Such questions were designed to account for the fact that the same punishment may have different meanings or intensities for different children. Extensive preliminary explorations indicated that one major reason for a particular punishment varying in severity from family to family is that the promise or threat of another punishment of greater intensity might prevail in one family and not the other. The second question, then, was designed to elicit what is promised or threatened if the child does not respond to the first punishment. The parent does not necessarily have to warn the child that the second punishment may follow the first; all that is necessary for the postulated effect to occur is a somewhat systematic sequence of A followed by B, either now or in the past. The mechanism invoked here to account for the establishment of anxiety is classical conditioning with a second punishment or threat functioning as the unconditioned aversive stimulus. Thus some avoidance (nonaggressive) behavior develops which suppresses or interferes with the aggressive behavior.

In this preliminary study the individual responses to the questions (1,485 in all) were typed on cards and randomly assigned to nine decks. Each deck was sorted independently by three judges (nine judges in all participating) who knew neither the person administering the sanction nor the behavior that was being sanctioned. Eight categories were used: five intensities of punishment, two intensities of reward, and one category with neither reward nor punishment value for the child. Interjudge agreement was very high. There was perfect agreement in two-thirds of the ratings and more than one-step disagreement in only 1 percent of the ratings. Where there was lack of agreement, the median of the three ratings was assigned as the intensity value.

Two major analyses of these data were done. In the first analysis (Walder, 1961), punishment intensity for each of the thirteen items was evaluated by a two-way analysis of variance: high, medium, or low school aggression and sex of child, done separately for mothers and fathers. With every item for fathers, significantly more intense punishment was associated with high aggression, a finding especially true for boys. However, the same was not true for mothers, although the results were generally in the same direction. Similarly, a correlational analysis of total aggression score with total intensity of punishment score yielded an r of .31 for fathers and .03 for mothers (Eron,

Banta, Walder, and Laulicht, 1961). At that time these results were surprising since we had expected intensity of sanctions and aggression to relate generally according to Thorndike's Law of Effect so that children whose parents rewarded them for aggression would be more aggressive than children whose parents punished them for this behavior. This was the beginning of our recognition of how naive we were in expecting that the laws of the animal laboratory would apply to the data of the survey study. We had expected that parents would be able to recognize and label accurately even subtle interactions with their children and that they would be aware of time sequences between occurrences of their children's behavior and their own overt responses, but the parents probably needed help to appreciate the importance of timing. The interview-constructors erred in not assisting the parents to report better, and, in fact, they did not appreciate the importance of a particular behavior being followed by a particular sanction, as noted in the blind rating procedure described above. Also we did not ask the parents how they responded to and strengthened nonaggressive responses to frustration, which would build behaviors incompatible with aggression. In other words, we, as well as others, were just beginning to apply behavior theoretical concepts to events in the natural (nonlaboratory) environment and did not realize all the complexities. For example, Bandura's article on psychotherapy (1961) represents one of the first presentations of the application of learning principles to the understanding of human behavior in the natural environment.

It was believed at that time that perhaps the obtained results arose because the aggression score summarized a conglomerate list of behaviors. If punishment or reward for each item of behavior were related specifically to extent of that particular behavior, predictions from rewards and punishments might improve. Therefore, punishment [2] scores for each specific behavior were correlated with scores on that behavior in the school measure for the thirteen items that appeared both in the interview and in the school aggression measure. However, the results were not different from those obtained when either total punishment score or punishment for each behavior was correlated with total aggression score. The more punitive fathers on each item still had children with higher scores on that item in school. For fathers, all correlations were in the positive direction, and four of the thirteen single items were significant beyond the .01 level of confidence. For mothers, all correlations were in the positive direction, but none was significant at the .05 level.

These results were tentatively interpreted as showing that fathers'

[2] Since very few rewards for aggressive behavior were reported by parents, the scales originally designated as rewards and punishments or sanctions were redesignated simply as punishment.

punishment functioned either as an instigation or as a model of behavior to be copied by their children. However, the results might also have been caused by the specific methodology employed. We may have sampled only the middle range of punishment intensity. Perhaps only with the severest punishment does its inhibiting effect override the frustrating (instigating) effect (McKee, 1949). Becker and his colleagues (1962) found that, at least for girls, aggression in school as rated by teachers was related to punishment in a curvilinear fashion so that girls of both high and low punitive mothers showed less aggression in school than girls of moderately punitive mothers. The open-ended format of our questions did not encourage parents to admit to severe punishments. Thus it seemed essential to develop a closed-end version of the punishment for aggression measure since parents might be more likely to admit to more intense punishments when they are simply stated as alternatives. As a first step, a content analysis of each of the points on the intensity scale was accomplished by examining all rated sanctions for which there was perfect agreement on placement by all three judges. Thus each point on the scale was described by a series of representative sanctions, as shown in Table 4.5.

A cursory examination of these instances suggested that there was a strong relation between type of sanction and intensity rating. In order to investigate this hypothesis, all sanctions were sorted by three judges into types: verbal, deprivation of privilege, and physical. The amount of overlap between type and intensity ratings can be seen in the following percentages: Category 3 (mildest punishment), 91 percent verbal; Category 4, 71 percent verbal; Category 5, 2 percent verbal; Categories 6 and 7 (the harshest punishment), only 1 percent verbal. Thus, in assigning ratings, it was apparent that type and intensity of punishment were highly related. It was believed that perhaps it was impossible to construct completely independent measures of these two attributes of punishment in real-life situations.

Despite these problems, a number of other attempts were made to scale intensity of punishment. The children themselves, rather than experts, might be the best judges of how harsh various punishments were. However, despite many attempts with varied formats, we were unable to get the children to understand the kind of ratings we wanted. Therefore, we did the next best thing and obtained a sample of parents of eight-year-olds to make such judgments for us. We reviewed a wide variety of rated punishments that had been collected the year before and selected forty of them. We then had thirty different parents of third graders rate them on a nine-point scale from harshness to mildness, using the method of equal appearing intervals (Thurstone, 1929). Median scale values were calculated and all pun-

TABLE 4.5
Content Analysis of Sanction Items with Perfect Agreement
on Placement in Seven Intensity Categories

Category 7 (harshest punishment)

1. Spank very hard (>15 times on behind).
2. Isolate from friends a week or more.
3. Severely wash mouth out with soap.
4. Frighten dramatically.

Category 6

1. Isolate from friends more than one day.
2. Slap hard on face.
3. Spank hard (2-14 times).
4. Use strap or stick 1-3 times.

Category 5

1. Spank moderately on bottom or slap hard once on arm or bottom.
2. Deprive of movies one week (misses two movies).
3. Isolate from friends, etc., up to one day.
4. Force to sit on a chair up to half hour without anything to do.

Category 4

1. Scold severely with voice raised.
2. Force to apologize.
3. Force to sit in chair (can look at book) up to 15 minutes.
4. Deprive of friends, etc., momentarily.

Category 3 (mildest punishment)

1. Point out what's wrong with behavior but definitely show disapproval.
2. Privately, without display of anger, point out the child wouldn't like the same thing done to him.
3. Insist that child do task.
4. "Don't bother me now, I'm busy."

Category 2 (neutral)

1. Ignore it.
2. Don't butt in.
3. Let child work it out himself.
4. Overlook it.

Category 1 (reward)

1. Distract with something else.
2. Comfort child.
3. Give child a reward.
4. Pay attention to child.

ishments were ordered in terms of median rating of harshness. It was possible to distinguish clearly three categories of harshness. At each cutting point, ten punishments were deleted so that any punishment in a given category had little chance of having a true value in any other category. The items finally selected were those with the most agreement. (See Appendix III.B for materials and directions to parents.)

The punishment scale thus consisted of twenty-four items (see Table 4.6) having to do with likely responses of the parents to four kinds of aggressive behavior on the part of their children: two dealing with aggression toward the respondent, and two with aggression toward other children. Two specific punishments at each of the three levels of intensity were assigned to each of the four items. Each item received a weighted score if the respondent said he was likely to use that punishment: 1 for low punishment intensity, 2 for medium punishment intensity, and 3 for high punishment intensity. The types of punishment included physical punishment, love withdrawal, restraint, isolation, shame, threat, and corrective reasoning. Within each subset, the punishments were randomized and the subsets were randomly placed throughout the interview. The punishment score for each parent was the total of all his weighted *yes* responses. Separate subscores were developed for punishment for aggression against parents and punishment for aggression against children. Thus we were able to devise a precoded method of determining intensity values for parental punishment patterns that was independent of type. Both physical [3] and verbal punishments were included and a sufficient number of parents admitted to the use of harsh punishments to enable us to evaluate three widely spaced points on the intensity continuum. Thus, by furnishing high intensity punishments as given alternatives in this closed-end format, we were successful where before, with open-ended questions, we had failed.

Relation of Parental Punishment to School Aggression

Although our measurement operations changed, the results using this improved scale of punishment with the countywide sample corroborated the previous findings with the cruder scales. The data to

[3] Physical punishment was defined, for the purpose of this study, as the application by the socializing agent of an aversive stimulus necessitating the use of physical contact. On the other hand, nonphysical punishment was defined as the application of an aversive stimulus which might deprive the child of privileges, curtail his freedom of movement, or imply the threat of physical force, but in which no physical contact is used by the socializing agent.

TABLE 4.6
Items in Punishment Scale with Mean Intensity Ratings and Weighting

Items	Mean intensity rating	Weighting
If NAME were rude to you, would you:		
Tell him: "I will give you something you like if you act differently"?	1.4	1
Wash out his mouth with soap?	7.7	3
Remind NAME of what others will think of him?	4.6	2
Say: "Get on that chair and don't move until you apologize"?	5.7	2
Tell NAME that young men (ladies) don't do this sort of thing?	3.4	1
Spank NAME until he cries?	7.8	3
If you saw NAME grab things from another child, would you:		
Tell him that young men (ladies) don't do this sort of thing?	3.4	1
Say: "I would like to be proud of you"?	3.5	1
Make NAME apologize?	5.8	2
Tell NAME you don't love him?	7.7	3
Point out how some close friends of his behave better than NAME does?	4.9	2
Not let him play with his friends for two days?	7.7	3
If NAME got very mad at you, would you:		
Get very angry at him?	4.4	2
Slap him in the face?	7.9	3
Say: "That isn't a nice thing to do"?	3.5	1
Tell NAME you don't love him?	7.7	3
Tell NAME in a nice way how to act differently?	2.8	1
Send him to another room where he would be alone and without toys?	6.0	2
If you heard NAME say mean things to another child, would you:		
Tell him in a nice way to act differently?	2.8	1
Say: "Get on that chair and don't move until you apologize"?	5.7	2
Not let NAME play with his friends for two days?	7.7	3
Point out how some close friends of his behave better than NAME does?	4.9	2
Wash out his mouth with soap?	7.7	3
Say: "I would like to be proud of you"?	3.5	1

be reported here are based on scores of 245 boys and 206 girls and their fathers and mothers. These were all the children in the county-wide survey on whom we had complete data (see Chapter 1). Fre-

quency distributions of intensity of punishment scores were calculated separately for mothers and fathers, and each distribution was
divided into low, medium, and high groups. The cutoff scores divided the distribution into approximately equal thirds. Ninefold
contingency tables were then constructed conjoining mothers' and
fathers' intensity of punishment with these other variables. This type
of analysis was more fully explained in footnote 1 of this chapter (p.
62). The mean aggression scores of all children were entered in the
appropriate cells as in Table 4.7 (Anderson and Bancroft, 1952; Eron
et al., 1963). The consistency of results for mother-son, mother-
daughter, father-son, and father-daughter pairs is noteworthy. The
more the child is punished for aggression by his parents, the higher is
his peer-rated aggression score. The findings are significant beyond
the .01 level of confidence for all pairs except father-son, which, however, is in the same direction (Eron et al., 1963). These results corroborate the monotonous findings of survey studies of child-rearing
practices, but, as was pointed out in Chapter 2, they are not what
would be expected from some laboratory-derived theoretical statements about the socialization process. It has been postulated that
children who are punished for aggressive behavior will tend to develop anxiety about expressing aggression and will inhibit its expression when they are in situations similar to the one in which they
learned the anxiety (Child, 1954). Buss states that "the major inhibitor of aggression is punishment. . . . So long as punishment is administered after an aggressive response, the tendency to make the response is suppressed" (1961, p. 56). Although this has been confirmed
in carefully controlled laboratory experiments, it was neither our
finding nor has it been the general finding in survey studies.

TABLE 4.7
Mean Aggression Scores According to Severity
of Punishment for Aggression

| Punisher | Aggression scores | | |
	Low	Middle	High
		BOYS	
Mothers	13.32 (77)[a]	11.54 (82)	17.50 (86)
Fathers	12.20 (74)	13.78 (78)	16.12 (93)
		GIRLS	
Mothers	6.19 (68)	8.67 (70)	12.84 (68)
Fathers	6.22 (74)	9.52 (63)	12.19 (69)

[a]The number in parentheses represents the number of subjects in the cell.

However, the intensity dimension of punishment is considerably complex and is more readily understood through controlled manipulation in the laboratory than through questionnaires in field surveys. The physical punishment to which parents admit either may be severe enough to cause physical suffering by the child or, as Walters and Parke (1967) suggest, may actually inflict less pain and suffering than a child ordinarily encounters in play with other children. Although both behaviors involve physical contact, they probably do not lie on the same measurement continuum. Thus, survey studies that use graduated scales and linear correlations may make incorrect assumptions about the intensity gradient of physical punishment. This observation is particularly important for the present study since it was found that nonphysical punishment was unrelated to children's aggression scores (see pp. 75–78 in this chapter and also Chapter 6).

Because of ethical considerations, laboratory experiments to study the effects of the intensity of punishment on human subjects are infrequently performed. However, Aronfreed and Leff (1963) made a laboratory study in which varying intensities of noise were employed as aversive stimuli and the dependent variable was response inhibition. They found that when children were required to make relatively simple discriminations, transgression responses did not occur if intensity of punishment was high. When discrimination requirements were complex, however, children receiving high intensity punishment committed more transgressions than those receiving milder punishment. Parke and Walters (1967) examined the hypothesis that children who are administered relatively intense punishment are less likely to transgress than children administered milder forms of that punishment. Although equivocal, the results of their experiments tended to support the hypothesis.

Although our study corroborates findings of previous survey studies, it differs in procedure from earlier studies in that the criterion (child aggression) and predictor (parent behaviors) measures were obtained from different sources. Sears et al. (1957), for example, asked mothers both how aggressive their children were and what they did about it. It is not at all surprising that they obtained a positive relation. Actually, in his seven-year follow-up study, Sears used different informants to obtain the criterion measure and no longer obtained results in a positive direction (Sears, 1961).

Contrary to our earlier study with sixty subjects with extreme aggression scores (Eron, Banta, Walder, and Laulicht, 1961), the effect of mothers' punishment now seemed more pronounced than that of fathers' punishment. A two-way analysis of variance, relating both mothers' punishment and fathers' punishment in nine different combinations (i.e., stratifying mothers' by fathers' punishment and vice versa) to peer-rated aggression, showed a main effect only for mothers of boys; and there was no interaction between mothers' and fathers' punishment. The additive, rather than interactive, effect of a combination of mothers' and fathers' punishment is shown in Table 4.8. There is a steady increase in school aggression score from children of mothers and fathers who are both low punishers to children of mothers and fathers who are both high punishers. One exception is that boys of mothers who are moderate punishers tend to be less aggressive than boys of mothers who are minimal or severe punishers, regardless of fathers' punishment. However, the interaction and the difference between the low and moderate cells are not significant. These significant positive findings for mothers' punishment, when none obtained in the earlier study, may result from the more precise measurement of intensity of punishment and/or the larger number of subjects. The first study compared the highest, middle, and lowest groups (ten subjects in each group); the later study covered the whole range of intensity of school aggression with 245 boys and 206 girls. These results operate in the same way regardless of which parent is chiefly responsible for the child's discipline. It is interesting that fathers are rarely credited with being the chief disciplinarians (Eron et al., 1963). Becker, Peterson, Luria, Shoemaker, and Hellmer (1962) found discrepant results when they predicted from mothers' and fathers' punishment separately. However, when they summed punitiveness and hostility for both parents they too found an approxi-

TABLE 4.8
Mean Aggression Scores of Subjects According to Mothers' and Fathers' Punishment

| | | Mothers' punishment | | |
		Low	Middle	High
		BOYS		
	Low	12.30 (27)[a]	8.47 (30)	18.65 (17)
	Middle	12.92 (26)	12.33 (24)	15.82 (28)
	High	14.91 (24)	14.14 (28)	18.17 (41)
Fathers' punishment		GIRLS		
	Low	4.89 (36)	7.78 (23)	7.00 (15)
	Middle	8.15 (20)	9.56 (25)	11.00 (18)
	High	6.83 (12)	8.59 (22)	16.29 (35)

[a]The number in parentheses represents the number of subjects in the cell.

74

mately straight-line relation between punitiveness at home and aggression both in school and at home. The finding that mothers' punishment is more important than fathers' punishment is consistent with data, reported in Chapter 6, that show mother-child relationships involving identification to be almost always more relevant to school aggression than the corresponding father-child relationships. The mothers' impact on both boys and girls in the home is balanced by the fathers' influence, especially on boys, through their position in the community, i.e., through ethnicity, occupational and educational status, and mobility orientation (see Chapter 7).

Physical versus Psychological Punishment

In a continuing attempt to understand the consistent but frankly unexpected results with punishment, another analysis of the data was performed (Lefkowitz, Walder, and Eron, 1963). The goal was to clarify the ambiguous relation between punishment and aggressiveness in previous studies by distinguishing between physical and nonphysical punishment.

The distinction between physical and psychological punishment is important theoretically in terms of the relation of either form of punishment to identification and to the dependent variable of aggression. Modeling theory would predict, and indeed the research in this area demonstrates, that the physical, expressive behavior of adult models is readily imitated by children (Bandura and Walters, 1963), especially if external reinforcement of a child's behavior is contingent upon the child's behavior (Aronfreed, 1969). Specifically, the theory helps to explain the positive and statistically significant relation found in the present study between physical punishment by parents and aggression of their children in school. Allinsmith (1960) obtained very similar findings with a group of junior-high-school boys by using an incomplete-story technique in which the stem situation was always the frustration of the protagonist by an older authority figure. The story endings were classified according to how directly aggression was expressed. Boys whose mothers used physical punishment tended to express aggression directly, while boys whose mothers used psychological disciplinary techniques tended to express aggression indirectly or not at all.

A major difference obtains between physical and nonphysical punishment. The recipient of physical punishment sees the agent perform an aggressive act. Not isolated, this act occurs as a response contingency which makes salient to the recipient the use of force through physical contact. In effect, physical punishment becomes a

75

demonstration by a role model of how to act aggressively. The recipient of nonphysical punishment, however, is deprived, so to speak, of these sensory modes of experience. He neither sees the motor behavior of the punisher nor feels its effect. Nonphysical punishment is not demonstrated by the model in any direct way. This may account for the absence of any significant relation between nonphysical punishment and school aggression for the population under study.

Conceptually, therefore, various kinds of behavior, such as force applied through physical contact or deprivation of privileges, may nominally be classified as punishment. However, when evaluated in terms of their effects upon the dependent variable, only some of them function as punishments. Physical punishment, perhaps because of its modeling effect or because of its instigating effect, is one of the antecedents of aggressive behavior, whereas nonphysical punishment may not be such an antecedent.

The punishment data were analyzed on the basis of a dichotomy between physical and nonphysical punishment and on an intensity basis in which punishment was a scaled quantity ranging from zero to four physical punishments. This quantity pertained to the number of physical punishments the parent admitted using out of a possible total of four. For this analysis the sample of subjects consisted of 875 children, 555 of their fathers, and 699 of their mothers (all the available data). Table 4.9 shows the mean school aggression score of all the children classified by the number of physical punishments reported to be used by their mothers or fathers. Clearly evident in this table is the consistent increase in the children's mean school aggression scores as the number of physical punishment items chosen

TABLE 4.9
Mean Aggression Scores Classified According to Number
of Physical Punishment Items Admitted to by Parents

Physical punishment items	N	Aggression score	Boys	Girls
Mothers				
0	428	11.08	219	209
1	180	13.71	94	86
2	63	16.19	35	28
3 or 4	28	18.39	18	10
Fathers				
0	353	9.79	167	186
1	138	14.96	80	58
2	45	15.16	28	17
3 or 4	19	14.89	11	8

by mothers increases from zero out of four possibilities to three or four out of four possibilities. An analysis of variance for randomized groups was performed on these data that showed a significant difference in means beyond the .01 level of confidence. The increase in school aggression was not as consistent for fathers as for mothers: the largest aggression mean coincided with the next to the largest number of physical punishment items. However, an analysis of variance for randomized groups showed these means to be significantly different from each other, beyond the .01 level of confidence.

Each child was categorized into one of two groups on the basis of the total number of physical punishments admitted to by both of his parents: neither parent of children in the zero group admitted to using any physical punishments; and either or both parents of children in the other group admitted to using at least one physical punishment. The mean school aggression scores for the children in each of these two groups were compared. This relation of physical punishment by both parents to aggression in the classroom is shown in Table 4.10. This table indicates that in 233 or 43 percent of the families, neither mothers nor fathers chose any of the four physical punishments. The mean school aggression score of their children was 8.57. In 312 or 57 percent of the families, either fathers or mothers did choose one or more of the physical punishments. The mean school aggression score of their children was 14.07. These means are significantly different beyond the .01 level of confidence. The almost consistent increase in children's mean school aggression scores, paralleling the increase in physical punishment at home, suggests that physical punishment enhances rather than inhibits the expression of aggression. In spite of the fact that aggression anxiety may be assumed to be present because the children were punished for aggressive behavior (Mowrer, 1939), their aggression was not inhibited, at least as demonstrated in our analysis of the survey data. Further examination of the construct of aggression anxiety and other nonaggressive behavior alternatives begins on page 82 of this chapter.

TABLE 4.10
Children's Mean School Aggression Scores as Parents Use
or Do Not Use Physical Punishment

Physical punishment items	N	%	Aggression score
0	233	43	8.57
1+	312	57	14.07

To speculate, the overriding factor seems to be the use of physical punishment. The saliency of a role model performing an aggressive act may alter the inhibiting effect of aggression anxiety. Specifically, the experience of observing the socializing agent administer punishment through physical contact provides the young recipient of such punishment with learning conditions not present in the nonphysical punishment situation. The intensity of the punishment would probably have to be extremely severe (probably so socially unacceptable that few parents would admit to using it even to the most permissive of interviewers) for the inhibiting effect of aggression anxiety to overcome the facilitating effect of modeling.

Another attempt was made to clarify the relation between nonphysical punishment and aggression. Scores comprising the sum of all nonphysical punishment items endorsed were correlated with scores on aggression for 233 families analyzed in Table 4.10. No significant relation was demonstrated. Thus it appears that the relation between parents' punishment and children's aggressive behavior may be attributed to the physical component in the parents' punishment patterns.

Corroboration of this finding is seen in a study by Potter (1968) at a private school for male juvenile delinquents. This study attempted to determine the relation between fathers' punishment and boys' behavior. The boys were asked to rate their fathers on the kinds of discipline characteristically used: "talked to you"; "took away some privilege"; "slapped you with an open hand"; "beat you with a closed fist or some other object." Criterion measures were ratings by cottage staff on obstreperousness of boys (Katz and Lyerly, 1963) and mean number of conduct reports issued by their teachers. The results showed that as the boys' ratings of their fathers' disciplinary techniques increased in severity, the boys were viewed as being more obstreperous ($r = .27$, $p < .05$). The mean number of conduct reports issued for these boys was also related positively to severity of punishment ($r = .25$, $p < .05$). In addition, the ratings of a community service worker of fathers' obstreperousness was positively associated with the boys' ratings of fathers' discipline ($r = .28$, $p < .05$). These results are consistent with the hypothesis that punitive fathers serve as role models of aggressive behavior for their sons. Our results would indicate that either parent can serve as an aggressive role model (see Chapter 6).

An alternative explanation for the finding that increased punishment, especially physical punishment, is related to increased school aggression should be entertained. This is that physical punishment by the parent instigates school aggression. This and related interpretations will be discussed later in this chapter and Chapter 5.

Children's Judged Sensitivity to Punishment (JUP)

A method of measuring children's sensitivity to punishment was incorporated into the parent interview (see Appendix III.B). As described above (pp. 68–70), a small sample of parents rated forty punishments in terms of harshness for third graders. Those twenty items which had the largest dispersion (Q values) were selected to be rated by all parents on the same Thurstone (1929) type scale. By definition, these were the most ambiguous items with respect to harshness, and it was assumed that parents would indirectly reveal their tendency to use harsh or mild punishment by their average rating of these twenty punishments on the intensity continuum. For example, if a parent's intensity ratings were higher than average for the total sample, he would tend to be more lenient than a parent whose intensity ratings were lower than average. The relevant data appear in Table 4.11 which shows that fathers or mothers who judge a series of punishments as harsh tend to have girls who are rated less aggressive in school; but this is not so for boys. Identification, which the

TABLE 4.11
Mean School Aggression Scores as a Function of Parents' Judgment of Harshness of Punishment

Judged harshness of punishment	Girls	Boys
Judgment by mothers		
Harshest	7.19 (88)[a]	15.42 (86)
Less harsh	9.07 (91)	12.66 (96)
Least harsh	10.95 (85)	14.73 (99)
Total	9.05 (264)	14.23 (281)
Judgment by fathers		
Harshest	6.88 (107)	14.92 (71)
Less harsh	10.49 (75)	13.82 (111)
Least harsh	10.56 (82)	14.20 (99)
Total	9.05 (264)	14.23 (281)
Sum of judgments by fathers and mothers		
Harshest	7.18 (101)	14.71 (70)
Less harsh	8.91 (80)	12.74 (115)
Least harsh	11.48 (83)	15.67 (96)
Total	9.05 (264)	14.23 (281)

[a]The number in parentheses represents the number of subjects in the cell.

79

sex-linked aspects of these results suggest is a relevant concept, is examined in Chapter 6.

The tendency of parents to underestimate the harshness of the punishment experienced by their children might also be an indirect index to the frustration level of the home. Parents who believe that the punishments they administer to their children are not very severe are no doubt providing a less nurturant atmosphere than parents who believe that the same punishments are harsh. The relation of frustration at home to instigation is examined in Chapter 5.

Success in Aggression (SAG)

In an effort to relate aggressive behavior in children to the punishment patterns of parents, we may have neglected an important group of dispensers of rewards and punishments for aggression — other children. On the one hand, the child who never wins a fight or never gets what he wants by being aggressive will be very likely to evince less of this kind of instrumental behavior. On the other hand, the child whose aggression is successful will be likely to maintain and increase aggressive responses (Patterson, Littman, and Bricker, 1967). Therefore, items on success in aggression were included in the final peer-rating measure. As anticipated, there was a high positive relation between total aggression and success in aggression scores $(r = .84)$. This relation was corroborated in two successive studies done in another community (Semler, Eron, Meyerson, and Williams, 1967; Semler and Eron, 1967). However, whether the variance is accounted for by the intrinsic relation between success in aggression and the extent of aggression and how much is due to similarity of item content is uncertain. A better, albeit more expensive, procedure, which would have retained method independence, would have been to observe success in aggression as it occurred in the classroom.

Confidence in a real, rather than a method-bound, relation between success in aggression and aggression is bolstered by results obtained in the previously mentioned Amsterdam study (Stroo, 1970), in which success in aggression, although it related almost as strongly to aggression as it did in the United States, related in opposite ways to aggression anxiety and popularity. Our Dutch colleagues have interpreted these findings sensibly (see Chapter 7), which minimizes the possibility that method variance accounts for the relation between aggression and success in aggression.

At any rate, this high correlation does support the contention of Buss (1961, 1966a) that behaviors, including aggression, are strengthened or maintained by positive consequences. The results are further borne out in a study by Patterson et al. (1967), who for nine months observed children in a natural setting, i.e., nursery school, and counted the frequency of children's aggressive behaviors and the consequences supplied by their peers. They had predicted that when an aggressive behavior was followed by a positive reinforcement from the target of the aggression (e.g., when a desired toy was obtained from the target), "on the next occasion in which the same aggressor was involved he would select the same aggressive response and the same victim" (p. 38). They found significant support for this prediction. However, their most striking finding was with children who initially evinced few aggressive behaviors. These low aggressive children remained low aggressive except when they received positive reinforcement (e.g., obtained an object, got their way, etc.) in a situation requiring aggression for self-protection. Those passive children who were frequently attacked but who also engaged in a series of successful counterattacks showed a marked increase in occurrence of aggressive behaviors. Thus, our results, even though inflated by method variance, support the hypothesis that aggression increases when it has instrumental value. They are also consistent with a study by Leon (1967), in which children behaved more aggressively toward their mothers after being reinforced for hitting a Bobo doll in another room. The intervals in which aggression occurred changed from .70 to 2.07 out of 60 intervals, each 20 seconds long.

There have been very few studies of childhood aggression in which the mothers and children are observed in the laboratory under specified conditions. In Leon's experiment, mother-child interactions were observed before and after the children were reinforced for hitting a Bobo doll. In each of eight nursery school classes, the teacher and her assistant independently rank-ordered the children in terms of amount of aggressive behavior exhibited. (Interjudge agreement, Spearman ρ's, in the eight classes were .85, .91, .79, .89, .77, .76, .89, and .59; the mean ρ was .81 and the median ρ was .82). Fifteen boys ranked high in aggressive behavior for their class and fifteen boys ranked low were chosen for the study, representing high and low groups.

An observer dictated a description of the ongoing interactions of mothers and children as they occurred in the experiment. Another observer checked, for each twenty-second interval, whether or not the children had exhibited aggressive or restless behavior (percentage agreement ranged from 76.7 to 93.2 with a mean of 83.9), and if so, they then checked the mothers' responses to this (percentage agreement ranged from 91.7 to 100 with a mean of 97.3).

The mothers and children worked for twenty minutes on a questionnaire arranged so that responses had to be given by both in order to complete the task. Then the children were taken to another room where they were allowed to hit a toy clown until they received thirty trinket reinforcements on a fixed ratio schedule (FR-6). The mothers stayed in the first room and completed semantic differential and word association tasks. After the children earned their reinforcements, they were taken back to their mothers for another twenty-minute session in which both were again given a questionnaire to be filled out cooperatively. After the second twenty-minute period had elapsed, the mothers were given an opportunity to see their children hit the clown and were instructed to meet E in the hallway after their children had received three reinforcements. The observers continued to describe and rate the mother-child behaviors until the subjects left this room.

The results (see Table 4.12) indicated that the frequency of the children's aggressive behavior increased from the first to the second questionnaire session, but that their restless behavior did not. Wide individual differences were noted. Out of the thirty children, eleven had higher aggression scores in the second session than in the first; eighteen remained the same (usually no aggression either time); and only one child had a lower score in the second session than in the first. However, the children's aggressive behavior in the peer situation (nursery school) showed no relation to their aggressive or restless behavior with their mothers.

The mothers did not tend to respond differently according to which aggression group their children were in. The mothers tended to ignore their children's aggressive behavior, a response that increased in frequency in the second questionnaire session. A large proportion of the restless behavior was also ignored.

Aggression Anxiety

One way to understand a measure such as the peer-rating measure of school aggression is to determine those conditions which might bring about change in a subject's score. The survey study shows only which conditions are correlated with different levels of aggression; it does not manipulate these levels. Accordingly, an apparatus was developed which could measure and manipulate aggression and its antecedents, concomitants, and consequences in the laboratory. As reported in Chapter 3 (pp. 43–45), the peer-rating score is highly related to performance with this apparatus, the Iowa Aggression Machine (IAM). The score was based on the intensity of a noxious stimulus delivered by the S to a human target, as indexed by the number of a button in a graded series. Studies by

TABLE 4.12
Children's Aggression Scores for the Pre- and Post-Sessions[a]

| Group | Subject no. | Aggression scores | |
		Pre-session	Post-session
	1	0	3
	2	0	1
	3	1	2
	4	1	0
	5	0	0
	6	0	0
	7	0	0
Low	8	0	0
	9	0	0
	10	0	1
	11	0	0
	12	0	2
	13	0	0
	14	0	5
	15	0	0
	16	6	13
	17	0	0
	18	0	2
	19	0	0
	20	2	4
	21	0	0
	22	0	0
High	23	0	0
	24	3	5
	25	2	18
	26	6	6
	27	0	0
	28	0	0
	29	0	0
	30	0	0

[a]From Leon (1967).

Meyerson (1966), Edwards (1967), Daut (1969), and Peterson (1971) that utilize the aggression machine help us understand scores on the peer-rating measure of aggression.

Meyerson's study involved ninety third-grade boys, forty-five with high peer-rated school aggression scores (HA) and forty-five with low scores (LA). All ninety subjects were instructed on the use of the IAM and then were told to watch a 3½-minute silent film while the apparatus was "being prepared." Each of three treatment groups (each with fifteen HA and fifteen LA subjects) was shown one of three different movies designated as (1) machine aggression or similar aggression, (2) nonmachine aggression or non-similar aggression, and (3) nonaggression or neutral. The first two films both pictured aggressive behavior. The machine aggression film showed an adult male aggressing by using the IAM to present the most noxious sound (number 10 button) to a second adult male. The nonmachine aggression film showed the same two adults aggressing in a physical fight. The nonaggression film pictured nonaggressive behavior, showing the same adults at the IAM with the mistake light not going on, thus permitting no opportunity for aggression. Immediately following presentation of the movie, the apparatus was "ready" and all Ss performed on the IAM. (See Table 4.13 for mean scores.)

Analyses of variance were done on the mean intensity scores of the high and low peer-rated aggression boys in the three conditions—machine aggression (similar), nonmachine aggression (nonsimilar), and nonaggression (neutral). The analyses showed that the high aggression boys in all conditions aggressed at an equally high level (although not near the ceiling). However, the low aggression boys were differentially affected by the treatments (movies). The presentation to low aggression boys of the movie of an adult male model aggressing on the IAM (similar film) increased the low aggression boys' IAM aggression score to that of the high aggression boys. However, the presentation to low aggression boys of the nonmachine aggression movie of the two adult males physically fighting with each other did not increase their IAM aggression score. This latter finding suggests that the effect of the film was rather narrow; that is, only the specific aggressive behaviors shown were influenced by the content of the film. These results contradict Aronfreed's findings (1969) of the generality of aggression arousal through observation of an aggressive act. This is discussed further in Chapter 6.

TABLE 4.13
Mean IAM Intensity Scores[a] of High and Low Aggressive Boys After Different Film Conditions in Meyerson's Study (1966)

| | | Film condition | | |
		Machine aggression	Nonmachine aggression	Nonaggression
High aggressive	Mean	104.65	107.67	104.70
	σ	32.07	21.15	21.25
	N	15	15	15
Low aggressive	Mean	99.77	86.61	72.23
	σ	24.45	31.67	26.14
	N	15	15	15

[a]"Mean intensity score" refers to the sum of the numbers of the buttons pushed on all fifteen trials averaged over all Ss in that condition.

The influence of the aggression movies on the IAM aggression score of low peer-rated aggression boys and not high peer-rated aggression boys suggests that the difference between the two might be the function of aggression anxiety (or other nonaggression behaviors) in the low aggression boys. The Meyerson data suggest that the total difference is accounted for by the reduced anxiety (i.e., increased permissiveness of the situation) after the showing of the machine aggression movie. Observation of a model performing a specific aggressive behavior without subsequent punishment lowered inhibition, and the low peer-rated aggression Ss responded as high aggressive Ss.[4]

A study of Daut (1969) demonstrated that performing aggressively on the Iowa Aggression Machine [5] led to an increase in aggression anxiety in his Ss (female college students). Aggression anxiety was assessed from TAT stories told by the Ss immediately after they were forced by way of instructions to deliver noxious sounds of various intensities to the earphones of a peer. Half of Daut's Ss were instructed to push high buttons (buttons which they were told delivered noxious sounds), and half the Ss were instructed to push low buttons (buttons which they were told delivered mild sounds). The complete design ($2 \times 2 \times 2$ randomized between factor design) also called for variation in cue relevance and sequence of TAT cards, but these aspects need not concern us here. The measures of aggression anxiety were two ratio scores from Pittluck (1950) that took into account expressions both of unmodified physical aggression and of the defense against the expression of

[4] Aggression anxiety here refers to an hypothesized experience in the background of the LA subjects, i.e., that they once were HA people whose aggression was punished and thereby reduced. A study might be done that would show this to be so. From a pool of HA subjects, some are punished severely enough for aggression that aggression on the IAM goes down, and these are then LA subjects (with more aggression anxiety). The aggression score of other HA subjects who are not punished for aggression does not go down, and these subjects remain HA (with less aggression anxiety). The three movies from the Meyerson study are presented to some of each of these two groups (HA and LA). Obtaining the same results as Meyerson would support our interpretation of aggression anxiety (i.e., the previous punishment of aggression) as the relevant difference between HA and LA in the response to the films.

[5] The machine used with third graders was adapted for college-age subjects by Hedges (1967). In this adaptation, sawtooth noises of approximately 75, 95, and 115 db. were used. These noises were judged by audiology experts to be extremely noxious at high amplitudes, but not harmful. All the instructions were given to the subjects through earphones via tape recordings, and in experiments with college students the noxious sounds were actually delivered to the subjects' earphones as noxious stimulation in addition to the demonstration, when warranted by the particular experimental design.

aggression. For both measures of aggression anxiety, the Ss who were instructed to push high buttons had significantly higher scores than the Ss who were instructed to push low buttons. These results support the hypothesis that commission of an aggressive act increases aggression anxiety. Daut comments that of the Ss forced to push high buttons, several remarked that the sound must have really been annoying and two refused to push the high button, one pushing it briefly and then returning to low buttons. These observations corroborate the presence of aggression anxiety in subjects forced to act in an aggressive manner, i.e., to push high intensity buttons.

In another study Edwards (1967) selected eighty college students in an introductory psychology course from a pool of 250 students who had been previously tested on the IAM. She was able to select twenty male and twenty female high aggression Ss, each with an average IAM intensity score of 5 or 6, and twenty male and twenty female low aggression Ss, each with an average IAM intensity score of 1 or 2. Half of each of these four groups was retested on the IAM in the usual, nonretaliatory (NR) condition. The Ss were told that once they were finished correcting their partners, the task would be over and they would be dismissed. In this way they were assured the other Ss would have no opportunity to retaliate. The other half of these four groups was retested on the IAM in a retaliatory (R) condition. The Ss were told that after they had helped the other subjects to learn a task by correcting them, the other subjects would do the same in return.

The data of the male subjects in this study were very similar to those in Meyerson's research (see Table 4.14). Low aggressive males were more aggressive in the nonretaliatory condition than in the retaliatory condition. However, neither high aggressive males nor

TABLE 4.14
Mean IAM Aggression Scores[a] for High and Low Aggressive Subjects
in Retaliation and Nonretaliation Conditions in Edwards's Study (1967)

| | | Retaliation | | Nonretaliation | |
		HA	LA	HA	LA
	Mean	5.90	1.72	6.46	5.96
Male	σ	2.47	1.26	2.25	2.89
	N	10	10	10	10
	Mean	4.90	1.48	4.60	2.30
Female	σ	1.48	.60	1.73	1.32
	N	10	10	10	10

[a]"Mean aggression score" refers to mean of the button pushed for five trials averaged over all Ss in that condition.

female Ss, whether high or low in aggression, were affected by the retaliation manipulation. This result supports the idea that low aggressive males are low as a result of preretaliatory cues. When there is no possibility of retaliation, their aggression is equal to that of the high aggression males. Edwards's study indicates that those behaviors that avoid retaliation in a retaliatory condition are included in what we have called aggression anxiety. The same thing does not happen with high aggression males since they have not learned to avoid retaliation: they give aggression and take it in return and, in fact, seem to seek out situations in which the likelihood of retaliation is high (see results of Peterson's study, described below). The females, both high and low in aggression, also are not affected because (1) they probably do not have a history of being hit back and (2) they do have a history of having learned nonaggressive behaviors other than sheer avoidance of retaliation. This consistency of response in all girls is related, no doubt, to the previously discussed observation that prediction from home to school is better for girls than for boys. We may surmise that the third-grade boys with low peer-rated aggression have learned aggression anxiety as a retaliation avoidance behavior which is incompatible (or interferes) with aggressive responding under unprotected retaliatory conditions. These aggression avoidance behaviors do not have to be characterized by cringing in a protective corner. Dick Gregory, writing in his book, *Nigger* (1964), about his childhood in St. Louis, says he learned to be a stand-up comic and raconteur while under threat of retaliation. When cornered by stronger, more belligerent peers, he avoided punishment by doing something to make his potential attackers laugh. In such situations, when aggression avoidance behaviors are negatively reinforced, they become a more prominent behavior. They may then, as in Gregory's case, come under the control of environmental conditions other than the threat of retaliation, e.g., fame and fortune.

Peterson (1971), in an experiment with eight-year-old boys, attempted to define more explicitly the conditions under which the possibility of retaliation affects aggressive behavior by controlling the aggression level of both his subjects and their targets. Following on the results of Meyerson (1966) and Edwards (1967), he expected aggression to be reduced when the target of the aggression had a high potential for retaliation, especially if the Ss were low aggressive. He selected his Ss on the basis of their scores on the peer-rating index that had been administered to eleven third-grade classes. High aggressive Ss and targets were boys whose scores fell in the upper 25 percent of their class; low Ss and targets were boys whose scores fell in the lower 25 percent of their class. From each class, two high aggressive Ss, two low aggressive Ss, one high aggressive target, and one low aggressive target were randomly selected for the experiment. Since the target was supposed to represent an individual with a particular probable intensity of retaliation, there was a further stipulation that each S must himself view the target as high or low as defined by the class. Each S was tested with the Iowa Aggression Machine. On five trials he was required to "correct" the low aggressive target, and on five trials, the high aggressive target. Half of the Ss were placed in a nonretaliation condition in which their anonymity was assured and they were told the game would be over when they finished correcting their teammates. The other half of the Ss were placed in the retaliation condition in which they were told that, after they finished "correcting" their teammates, their teammates would have a chance to "correct" them. As predicted, there was a significant interaction between aggression level and retaliation condition (see Figures 4.1 and 4.2 for graphic presentation of results). However, not only did the low aggressive Ss respond less aggressively under the retaliation condition, but the high aggressive Ss responded more aggressively under this condition than when there was no possibility of retaliation. Actually, the low aggressive Ss responded more aggressively than the high aggressive Ss under the nonretaliation condition. Furthermore, high aggressive Ss responded more aggressively toward high aggression targets than toward low aggression targets; and low aggressive Ss responded more aggressively toward low aggression targets than toward high aggression targets. Thus the highest mean score was for high aggression Ss toward high aggression targets under the retaliation condition. The second highest mean score was for low aggressive Ss toward low aggressive targets under the nonretaliation condition. Thus low aggressive Ss diminish the intensity of their responses when they interact with high aggressive partners who are more likely to hit them back harder than low aggressive partners. However, high aggressive Ss respond more aggressively toward high aggressive than low aggressive partners, as if inviting counterattack. In other words, threat of punishment engenders aggression anxiety in low aggressive Ss, and the aggression anxiety diminishes when there is no possibility of punishment. But in the high aggressive Ss, the anticipated punishment does not serve to produce aggression anxiety but rather seems to serve as a positive secondary reinforcer for the aggressive response or, perhaps, as an indication that "a good offense is the best defense." The threat of punishment is no threat at all, and aggressive behavior is increased, thus qualifying threat of punishment as a discriminative stimulus (S^D) for aggression. One expects that under these conditions aggressing has

FIGURE 4.1

The Intensity of Aggression Scores[a] for the High and Low Peer-Rated Aggressors for the Threat of Retaliation and No Threat of Retaliation Conditions[b]

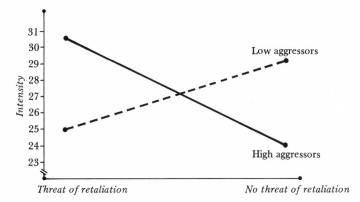

[a]"Intensity of aggression score" refers to the sum of the numbers of the buttons pushed on five trials, averaged over all Ss in that condition.

[b]Reprinted by permission of the American Psychological Association and the author from Rolf A. Peterson, "Aggression as a Function of Retaliation and Aggression Level of Target and Aggressor," *Developmental Psychology*, 5 (July 1971), pp. 161-166.

FIGURE 4.2

The Intensity of Aggression Scores[a] for the High and Low Peer-Rated Aggressors for the High and Low Peer-Rated Aggression Targets[b]

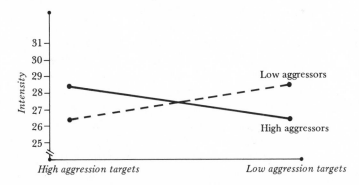

[a]"Intensity of aggression score" refers to the sum of the numbers of the buttons pushed on five trials, averaged over all Ss in that condition.

[b]Reprinted by permission of the American Psychological Association and the author from Rolf A. Peterson, "Aggression as a Function of Retaliation and Aggression Level of Target and Aggressor," *Developmental Psychology*, 5 (July 1971), pp. 161-166.

in the past led to reinforcement. The high aggressive S seems to seek out the possibility of punishment. This is not inconsistent with the point of view of Quay (1965) and others that aggressive psychopaths can be differentiated from nonpsychopaths by the extent to which they engage in pathological stimulation-seeking.

A series of studies by Feshbach and his associates (Feshbach and Jaffe, 1969; Feshbach, Stiles, and Bitter, 1967; Licht, 1966; Rubenstein, 1967) deals more directly with aggression anxiety, and the results support the notion that under permissive conditions high aggression anxiety Ss (i.e., low aggressive Ss) respond as low aggression anxiety Ss (i.e., high aggressive Ss). Feshbach and Jaffe found a significant interaction between aggression anxiety and an individual versus group dimension. Thus high aggression anxiety Ss in an individual, anonymous situation administered higher intensity shocks to their peers in a Buss-type aggression machine procedure than did low aggression anxiety Ss. (Ss had been selected as high or low in aggression anxiety on the basis of a paper and pencil test.) However, when participating in teams, the low aggression anxiety Ss administered shocks of higher intensity than the high aggression anxiety Ss. Furthermore, in a verbal conditioning experiment, Rubenstein found that when reference to aggression was highly indirect, high aggression anxiety Ss used more shocks than did low aggression anxiety Ss; but when aggression was directly labeled and encouraged, the high anxiety Ss decreased in aggressive behavior while the low anxiety Ss did not. Thus, it would seem that the high aggression anxiety S (or low aggressive S in our reference) is very responsive to retaliatory cues in the environment. When there is the possibility of censure or physical counteraggression, he does not respond aggressively; however, when these possibilities are removed, he responds as aggressively as the high aggressive S. The finding of increased inhibition of aggression with increased probability of retaliation is also consistent with the results of Buss (1961) and Edwards (1967) with college students, the results of Parton (1964) with third graders, and the results of Patterson et al. (1967) with nursery-school subjects. Thus it would appear that the relation between anticipation of punishment and aggressive behavior in low aggressive Ss develops early in life and is maintained at least through early adulthood.

Summary

Central to our theoretical understanding of the learning of aggression was the role of the reinforcement and punishment of this behavior by parents. In attempting to measure the relevant concepts, we soon learned that parents admit to very few rewards for aggressive behavior, and we consequently dealt only with punishment in the survey study. However, the effects of reward were examined in relating findings of the survey study to laboratory and observational investigations. Reasoning from laboratory studies with animals and nursery-school children, we anticipated that punishment for aggressive behavior would lead to inhibition of aggression in situations similar to the one in which punishment was originally administered. Findings of field studies contradicted these predictions derived from laboratory research in that increased aggression was routinely found to be associated with increased punishment for this behavior. It was believed at first that the contradiction was due to lack of control for intensity of punishment in field studies. After many attempts, we were able to construct a questionnaire that yielded scores with an expanded range of intensity of punishment and also sampled different types. However, the results with punishment intensity as it related to peer-rated aggression remained the same — the more intense the punishment by the parents at home, the higher the aggression as rated by the children's peers at school. This result held up for punishment by mothers and fathers but was especially marked for mothers. The greater relevance of mothers' punishment was consistent with other studies. A more detailed analysis of the data by type of punishment revealed that there was a consistent increase in children's mean aggression scores as the number of physical punishment items endorsed by their parents increased. Again, this was especially true for mothers. Other data to be presented in subsequent chapters deal with the greater saliency of mothers in the home as socializing agents. Following Azrin, it thus seems inappropriate to refer to these parent behaviors as punishment since they do not reduce the subsequent probability of the "punished" child behavior.

A related consideration was the correspondence between parents' ratings of their children's aggression at home and the children's peer-rated aggression scores. For the whole sample of girls and for those few boys (approximately 5 percent of the sample) who seemed to behave consistently at home, there was a positive relation between home and school aggression. The conditions under which the relation between home and school aggression is either positive or negative are explored in subsequent chapters.

The hypothesis that low aggressive boys learn aggression anxiety as a way of avoiding retaliatory behavior (punishment) from their peers or others was supported by reference to laboratory studies of aggression with an aggression machine. When there was no possibility of punishment for aggressive behavior, low aggressive boys responded just as aggressively as high aggressive boys. Only when there was the likelihood of punishment did their aggressive behavior become inhibited. High aggressive boys were shown to be unaffected by aggression anxiety, and, in fact, the anticipation of punishment seemed to facilitate rather than inhibit their aggressive behavior. This difference between the high and low aggressive subjects is a possible reason for discrepant findings between laboratory and field studies of aggressive behavior and punishment.

Evidence shows the following effects of rewards and punishments on aggressive behavior:

1. Reward for aggression increases subsequent aggressive behavior.
2. "Punishment" for aggression:
   a. decreases subsequent aggressive behavior in some subjects by the development of aggression anxiety, and facilitates aggression in other subjects by acting as a conditioned positive reinforcer;
   b. increases subsequent aggressive behavior by the increase in instigation; and
   c. increases subsequent aggressive behavior by the provision of a salient model of behavior.

Punishment as an instigation is discussed further in Chapter 5. In Chapter 6 there is additional treatment of punishment as a model for behavior.

INSTIGATION TO AGGRESSION

Chapter 5

One of the possible reasons given in the previous chapter for the positive relation between aggression and punishment for aggression was that punishment sometimes acts as an instigator rather than an inhibitor of aggressive behavior. Berkowitz (1962) made this point, and, as noted in the previous chapter, Peterson demonstrated that high aggressive *S*s actually seek out punishment. Ulrich et al. (1965) state, "Since physical punishment is by definition the delivery of aversive stimulation following a response, it may be expected that social aggression will occur as an elicited reaction to such punishment. Thus, our main objective of eliminating a response by punishment may have the completely unexpected effect of producing aggression by the punished organism" (p. 124).

Obviously, that which is called "physical punishment" is really some compound of noxious stimulation of the sort described by Ulrich plus a host of associated unpleasant responses. For example, the child who is attacked on the playground in some contact sport receives at least as much physical discomfort as he does when strapped by his father. However, his friend who tackles him is smiling while his father is frowning, speaking in an unpleasant way, perhaps threatening worse consequences, and implying rejection. Pavlovian conditioning of the unpleasantness of these words and gestures of the father have been studied in the laboratory (Diven, 1937). Most laboratory studies, however, involved pairs of animals in small enclosures where alternative behaviors, such as escape, were impossible. Thus, whether or not the aversiveness of the punishment is conditioned, the fact that the child has little opportunity to escape from his father's strap and words may be an important condition for punishment to act as an instigator.

At the outset of this research, we saw frustration as a likely instigator to aggression. As noted in Chapter 2, we recognized that punishment had some of the qualities of frustration, but we believed that its other properties would distinguish it from less complicated measures of instigation. In the search for likely instigators to aggression, we looked at situations in the home atmosphere that could be frustrating to children and thus incite them to aggressive behavior. We believed that the presence of such factors as rejection by parents, lack of nurturance, and restrictiveness, if persistent, could serve to heighten responsiveness, including aggressive responding. We were convinced that the major role of punishment was not as an instigator. Table II.1 in Appendix II (pp. 193–195) lists eight of the presumed instigators (numbers 4, 10, 13, 14, 15, 17, 18, 19) with definitions and examples of items used to measure them. These variables were analyzed in the early study with parents of sixty preselected children. Only parental rejection was significantly related to peer-rated aggression ($r = .40$ for mothers and .31 for fathers). Furthermore, mothers and fathers agreed significantly in their ratings on only four of these variables: residential mobility ($r = .91$), parental rejection ($r = .64$), parental disharmony ($r = .46$), and parental restrictiveness ($r = .38$). These four variables were retained intact in the final interview as was nonrecognition of the child's needs. The following measures were dropped: punishment for dependency, punishment for nurturance signals, and dependence avoidance.

Parental Rejection versus Child Rejectability

The finding of a high correlation between rejection by fathers and rejection by mothers alerted us to the notion that perhaps rejection of children was less a characteristic of the parents than it was of the children. The children might just be rejectable. This belief was supported by the relation of rejection by the parents to both rejection by peers ($r = .35$ for mothers and .20 for fathers) and ratings of school aggression ($r = .40$ for mothers and .31 for fathers).

To clarify these questions about rejection, we added a number of items to that scale. Since the scale consisted of the number of complaints indicated by a parent's answers to questions about his child — e.g., (a) "Does he read as well as could be expected for a child of his age?" and (b) "Are you satisfied with his manners?" — it could have been tapping either a realistic evaluation of the child (his rejectability, as in example a above) or a trait of the parent

94

(feelings of rejection toward the child independent of the child's actual performance, example *b* above). The former interpretation was supported by the high correlations, noted above, between mothers' and fathers' rejection and between mothers' and peers' rejection. Children who are rejected by one tend to be rejected by the others.

Thus we added items to the rejection scale in order to take into account the emotional reaction of each parent in response to his child's undesirable behavior — e.g., "Do you think he wastes too much time?" If the answer was "yes" or "sometimes," then the question was asked, "Does this annoy you when he wastes too much time?" If the parent answered "no" to the first question, he received a score of zero for this item; if he answered "yes" or "sometimes," he received a score of 1 or 2 depending on his answer to the second question. This revision of the rejection scale did not substantially change the obtained relation to school aggression, but we were confident that the scale reflected more of the parents' behavior as opposed to the children's behavior than the previous scale had. The correlation between mothers' rejection and fathers' rejection was significantly reduced from .64 to .42 by this refinement.

We also added to the rejection scale items of complaint about aggressive behavior that had been deliberately excluded from the earlier study to ensure a measure of rejection uncontaminated by the aggression criterion that we were predicting. We hoped that the inclusion of these items would give an indication of how general the complaining tendency was in the parents and would also add to our understanding of the concept of rejection. Table 5.1 indicates that the rejection scale is somewhat independent of parents' complaints about their children's aggressive behavior, which confirms the appropriateness of keeping aggressive behavior content out of the rejection scale. The parents' ratings of aggression are not just general complaints about their children's behavior, indicating rejection; they refer specifically to aggression or to non-aggression.

Derivation of a Composite Score of Instigation

The first step in the analysis of the data obtained in the countywide study was to relate each of the five instigation measures individually to the aggression criterion. Each of these scales was then intercorrelated with every other scale. The results appear in Table 5.2. There is a positive but not very large correlation between aggression in school and rejection by either parent (not significantly dif-

TABLE 5.1
Correlations between Parents' Reports of Home Aggression
and Complaints about Aggressive and Nonaggressive Behaviors

	Source			
Variables	Mothers vs. mothers	Fathers vs. fathers	Fathers (odd) vs. mothers (even)[a]	Mothers (odd) vs. fathers (even)[b]
1. Frequency of aggression 2. Recency of aggression	73	74	26	27
3. Recency of aggression 4. Complaints about aggression	55	55	30	32
5. Frequency of aggression 6. Complaints about aggression	51	53	28	30
7. Complaints about aggression 8. Complaints about nonaggression	45	46	23	21
9. Frequency of aggression 10. Complaints about nonaggression	38	36	25	19
11. Recency of aggression 12. Complaints about nonaggression	35	36	20	16

[a]Fathers' rating on odd-numbered variable correlated with mothers' rating on even-numbered variable.

[b]Mothers' rating on odd-numbered variable correlated with fathers' rating on even-numbered variable.

ferent from the correlations obtained in the preliminary study).[1] Three of the instigators (rejection, lack of nurturance, and parental disharmony) are positively intercorrelated, but the remaining two (restrictiveness and residential mobility) show no relation to the others. Therefore, a composite instigation score was calculated based on a mean of the three intercorrelated measures (converted to standard scores), and the other two were dropped from further analyses. In the following discussion the instigation score refers to this composite of the three intercorrelated scales.

As indicated in Table 5.3, the trend of results with instigation is in the same direction as with punishment (significant only for fathers of girls at .05 level of confidence). The more instigation at home, the more aggression there is in school. The similarity between punishment and instigation to school aggression supports the notion that punishment is just one more instigator. When mothers'

[1] This order of relation between rejection by parents and aggression in school is remarkably constant from one study to another, even cross-nationally. In Holland we obtained a correlation of .32 between rejection by mothers and peer-rated aggression in school (see Chapter 7). Lesser (1952) found a similar order of relation between his measures of rejection by mothers and peer-rated aggression.

TABLE 5.2
Intercorrelations among School Aggression and Presumed Instigators to Aggression

	1 Aggression		2 Rejection		3 Lack of nurturance		4 Parental disharmony		5 Restrictiveness	
	Mothers	Fathers	Mothers	Fathers	Mothers	Fathers	Mothers	Fathers	Mothers	Fathers
1. Aggression										
2. Rejection	.25	.24								
3. Lack of nurturance	.02	-.02	.18	.24						
4. Parental disharmony	.09	.06	.32	.22	.10	.25				
5. Restrictiveness	.09	.02	.04	.09	.04	.03	-.01	.02		
6. Residential mobility	.02		.04		.03		.10		.06	

TABLE 5.3
Mean Aggression Scores of Subjects According to Total
Instigation Level at Home

Informants	Instigation level		
	Low	Middle	High
	BOYS		
Mothers	13.12 (69)[a]	13.92 (108)	15.70 (68)
Fathers	13.09 (85)	12.65 (81)	16.95 (79)
	GIRLS		
Mothers	5.64 (72)	10.30 (70)	12.09 (64)
Fathers	5.61 (62)	8.55 (81)	13.64 (63)

[a]The number in parentheses represents the number of subjects in the cell.

TABLE 5.4
Mean Aggression Scores of Subjects According to Instigation Level
of Mothers and Fathers Combined

		Mothers		
		Low	Middle	High
		BOYS		
	Low	12.44 (36)[a]	13.20 (35)	14.50 (14)
	Middle	12.71 (24)	12.38 (37)	13.10 (20)
	High	16.89 (9)	16.22 (36)	17.74 (34)
Fathers		**GIRLS**		
	Low	5.06 (34)	5.13 (15)	7.61 (13)
	Middle	6.30 (30)	9.55 (29)	10.32 (22)
	High	5.62 (8)	14.11 (26)	15.45 (29)

[a]The number in the parentheses represents the number of subjects in the cell.

and fathers' instigation scores are considered conjointly, as in Table
5.4, the main effect of instigation by fathers appears more pronounced (significant for girls at .02 level of confidence and for boys
at .05), but mothers' instigation still shows no significant effect,
and there is no interaction between mothers' and fathers' instigation.

Differences between Fathers and Mothers
in Effect of Instigation

It seems that instigation is a more efficient predictor of children's
school aggression for fathers and that punishment is a better pre-

TABLE 5.5
Mean Aggression Scores Classified by Punishment and Instigation Levels

Instigation level	Punishment		
	Low	Middle	High
	BOYS		
Low	12.36 (25)[a]	13.35 (31)	13.45 (29)
Middle	8.38 (29)	14.12 (34)	16.22 (18)
High	17.79 (19)	15.93 (29)	17.39 (31)
Fathers	GIRLS		
Low	3.04 (26)	5.95 (21)	9.60 (15)
Middle	7.08 (25)	7.62 (29)	10.93 (27)
High	8.87 (23)	15.55 (18)	17.09 (22)
	BOYS		
Low	12.52 (23)	9.18 (28)	20.00 (18)
Middle	13.00 (33)	11.00 (34)	17.14 (41)
High	14.71 (21)	15.75 (20)	16.44 (27)
Mothers	GIRLS		
Low	3.19 (32)	6.78 (18)	8.27 (22)
Middle	11.30 (20)	7.80 (26)	12.17 (24)
High	5.81 (16)	10.85 (26)	18.14 (22)
	BOYS		
Low	10.87 (24)	9.18 (27)	18.22 (23)
Middle	10.85 (39)	15.45 (22)	15.04 (27)
High	14.63 (19)	15.52 (29)	20.26 (35)
Mothers and fathers	GIRLS		
Low	2.60 (23)	6.55 (20)	6.17 (18)
Middle	7.09 (21)	5.57 (28)	11.25 (24)
High	9.58 (29)	14.27 (13)	13.97 (25)

[a]The number in the parentheses represents the number of subjects in the cell.

dictor for mothers. Table 5.5 stratifies punishment by instigation separately for mothers and fathers. At the low instigation level for fathers, the boys' aggression scores are low (below the mean) at all levels of punishment; and at the high instigation level, the aggression scores are high (above the mean) regardless of punishment level. However, for mothers at the low punishment level, the boys' aggression scores are low; and at the high punishment level, the aggression scores are high, regardless of instigation level. Thus it seems that instigation and punishment are probably conceptually

99

different kinds of variables since they enter into different relations with school aggression. The distinction between punishment and instigation will be examined further in Chapter 6, where the difference between these two variables in covariation with identification is considered.

Frustration-Aggression Hypothesis

If the instigators measured here are indeed frustrators, these results can be taken as evidence in favor of the traditional paradigm of increased frustration leading to increased aggression.[2] However, just as punishment does not act as an instigator in every respect, perhaps our so-called instigators do not always act as frustrators but as models of aggressive behavior for children (see Chapters 6 and 8).

This finding of a significant positive relation between supposed frustrating conditions in the home and aggression on the part of the child has not been characteristic of other studies that have attempted to implement a test of the frustration aggression hypothesis by the use of parent questionnaires. Fairly typical are the results of Radke-Yarrow et al. (1968), who found nonsignificant correlations between measures of current frustration (global ratings from interviews with mothers of maternal restrictiveness, warmth, and response to dependency) and aggression both at home and in school. They question whether or not their own results and those of others indicate a lack of support for the traditional paradigm since low coder reliabilities in their own study and others may have covered up any "true" relation. More important, however, they believe the variables themselves, emphasizing parental demands and restrictions, actually might not have sampled frustration as intended. Children who comply with parental demands and limits (e.g., going to bed at a set time) are likely not to be frustrated and perhaps to have lower levels of tension than children for whom no limits are set. We may have obtained significant positive findings precisely because of these two factors. As noted in Chapter 3, we did not use ratings made independently by two or more judges of the parents' interview protocols. Each parent responded for himself, and his response, unfiltered by the judgment of others, entered into the data that we analyzed.

Furthermore, the variables we assumed to be frustrators (parental

---

[2] Further evidence, such as results with judgment of punishment which was not originally conceived as a scale to measure instigation, might also be cited. See Chapter 4, 79–80.

disharmony, rejection, and lack of nurturance) [3] might have captured more relevant antecedents of frustration since they did not involve the usual questions about parental demands. As a matter of fact, the scale that assessed the latter parental behaviors, parental restrictiveness, was dropped from the instigation composite score because of its lack of correlation with both the criterion and the other presumed frustrators. Our positive findings relating current frustration at home to aggression in school when other survey studies have found no relation between frustration level and child aggression might thus be a function of less complicated methodology and more pertinent content.

Another reason for the lack of results in the studies cited by Radke-Yarrow et al. (1968) is that for the most part they deal with the relation between frustration in infancy and later (preschool) behavior (e.g., Sears et al., 1953). It may be that the effects of frustration dissipate rapidly, as has been indicated with the effects of punishment (Skinner, 1938; Estes, 1944). Our data refer to current frustrations that would be more likely to have an effect on current aggressive behavior in school. Palmer (1960) compared fifty-one male murderers and their brothers nearest in age on the basis of their mothers' ratings of physical and psychological frustration in infancy, childhood, and adolescence. He found significantly more *continuing* frustration in the lives of the aggressive brothers. Of course, the likelihood of bias in the mothers' reports must be considered in interpreting those results. Our own findings, however, cannot be criticized on this basis since the criterion rating of aggression was independent of the parents' reports.

An Alternative View of Instigation

The findings relating instigation to aggression have thus far dealt with conditions imposed by the environment. In short, certain events, such as rejection, lack of nurturance, and parental disharmony, may frustrate certain needs. These frustrating events then, presumably, serve as instigators to aggression. Although the origin of these needs may be biological, the findings of our research concern the manner in which aggression is related to learning. Thus

[3] Sample items:
   Nurturance: Do you usually have time so that NAME can talk to you about things that interest him? (no, yes)
   Parental disharmony: Do you and your spouse ever disagree about choice of friends? (no, yes)
   Rejection: When NAME has money to buy something for himself, are you displeased with what he buys? (no, yes)

101

throughout our study the learning conditions for aggression have been stressed. However, other models might invoke different variables as instigators that should be considered, at least briefly, to see if they can add to an understanding of the learning conditions for aggression. It should be remembered, however, that the explication and elucidation of learning conditions are the chief purposes of this book.

In the main these alternative models are biological and have received current exposition within the framework of ethology (Lorenz, 1965, 1966; Tinbergen, 1951; Ardrey, 1966). Bridger (1962), although he does not subscribe to the ethologists' instinct theory, provides a succinct summary of their general position. In the ethological view, instinctual acts are the result of phylogenetically derived patterns of behavior that are built into the central nervous system and are related to the satisfaction of certain basic needs or drives such as reproduction and food-getting. These preformed or preprogramed neurobehavioral patterns are released by specific sign stimuli that in turn trigger an innate releasing mechanism. At this point, specific action (behavior) occurs. Each innate behavior pattern is associated with a reaction specific energy. Sometimes this energy is displaced so that behavioral patterns governed by one instinct are expressed under a different instinct activity.

Lorenz's view of behavior is strongly Darwinian. Adaptation, the keystone in Lorenz's theory, is the phylogenetic and ontogenetic process that molds the organism to fit its environment in a way that enhances its survival. Behavior, either innate or learned, has a phylogenetic basis. Innate behavior, acquired through the long process of evolution, provides an instantaneous adaptation to the immediate requirements of the environment. In this sense, innate behavior is similar to the Pavlovian unconditioned response.

Learning is also related to the phylogenetic process but it provides for adaptive modification of behavior through interaction between the organism and its environment rather than through the process of evolution. Information or what has been learned is, perhaps, stored in neural tissue. Change in function, i.e., new behavior, produces or is related to a corresponding change in structure. Thus Lorenz conjectures that either an adaptive modification of neural structure occurs or that, biochemically, information is coded in chain molecules in a manner similar to that in which phylogenetic information is retained. The following quotation from Lorenz (1965) explains his position on learning: "It is . . . an inescapable logical necessity to assume that learning, like any other organic function regularly achieving survival value, is performed by organic structures evolved in the course of phylogeny under the

102

selection pressure of just that survival value. All observational and experimental evidence goes to confirm this assumption. None contradicts it" (p. 18).

For Lorenz, aggressive behavior is based on phylogenetic adaptation, not in the sense of the modification of biological structure through function but rather in the sense of innate behavior developed during phylogenesis. Aggression is, therefore, an instantaneous adaptive response of the organism to an environmental requirement. Thus aggression closely resembles an unconditioned response and is manifested as a released mechanism when a stimulus or trigger in the environment acts upon certain phylogenetic information presumably stored in the genes. Lorenz seems to be describing the biological phenomena underlying the frustration-aggression relationship. Although possibly heuristic, the application of these assumptions to all levels of the phyletic scale may, we believe, be misleading. Lorenz in his earlier work, *On Aggression,* explains all of human aggression, such as war and religious or ideological conflict, as subject to the laws of phylogenetically developed instinctive behavior. At best, reasoning or cultural conditions serve only as stimuli for releasing the aggressive mechanism. Intraspecies killing, such as human warfare, is an anomaly of evolution as viewed by ethologists. Lorenz implies a lacuna in phylogenesis in which the development of inhibitions against killing among humans lags behind the remarkable technology of weapons development. Of particular importance in this regard are long-range weapons that shield the actor from the bloody consequences of his act, physically and emotionally. Recently, however, in *Evolution and Modification of Behavior,* Lorenz has allowed for the greater influence of learning and cultural effects on behavior. Yet in explaining how learning occurs, he adheres to a strict biological, albeit Lamarckian, model. According to Lorenz, information generated by the interaction of the organism with its environment is genetically stored and eventuates biologically in the modification of, presumably, the central nervous system structure.

Tinbergen (1951) examines the question of whether certain behaviors occur spontaneously, independent of external stimulation, or only as a reaction to external stimulation. Based on instinct theory, the argument for spontaneity holds that the mechanism for any kind of behavior is present in the organism and is released at the appropriate time. Appropriateness is defined in terms of survival value. The argument that all behavior is a reaction to environmental stimulation is grounded in the learning theory that manifested itself in the 1920's as reflexology. This Watsonian form of behaviorism was based on the conditioned reflex principle that

103

certain stimuli regularly produce reflex responses (Hilgard, 1948). Pavlov's discovery provided Watson with a working model. Tinbergen holds that, to a certain extent, both views are correct. Behavior is reaction when it is dependent on external stimulation; but it is spontaneous when it is dependent on internal motivational factors which are activated by an urge or a drive. An alternative explanation of what appears to be spontaneous behavior is offered by Hebb (1949). He relates learning to phylogenetic level and shows that certain organisms, such as insects, possess a very rapid learning rate for certain acts. Consequently, what has been interpreted as instinct is actually due to learning which requires only a few seconds for completion. This is a further example of the destruction of the concept of instinct as the highly uniform behaviors of many species are critically and experimently analyzed (cf. Lehrman, 1953).

Tinbergen discusses the fighting drive in animals and man and reasons that the drive has survival value. Fighting enhances reproduction, because it tends to aid in the distribution of sexual objects. Furthermore, fighting serves in warding off a predator or in the acquisition and maintenance of territory. It also has its disadvantages when individuals are excluded from reproduction because they are damaged or killed. According to Tinbergen, therefore, the compromise reached in nature is to have releasers that intimidate without causing damage. In animals and humans these releasers include bluff and threat, and in humans particularly they include the gladiatorial vestments of the Middle Ages and the uniforms and hand weapons of today. The balance of terror concept so evident in world affairs today seems to be consistent with Tinbergen's point of view. Tinbergen argues that man has an instinctive reluctance to kill, particularly within his own species. Moreover, this reluctance is strengthened by the very sight of death and destruction.

If man is instinctively inhibited against killing, why has there been such mass slaughter in the history of man's relationships? Tinbergen explains this seeming paradox by pointing to the relatively easy manner in which killing is accomplished by modern, long-range weapons of war that, in effect, obscure the disastrous results for the aggressor. This view of instinctive inhibition against killing may also be stated in learning terms: the sight of slaughter is the aversive consequence that serves to diminish the probability that the response, namely fighting or slaughter, will occur. Therefore, the necessity to invent yet another instinct, that of an inhibition against killing, is obviated. Furthermore, fighting to obtain a sexual partner, to ward off a predator, or to obtain or maintain

104

territory is behavior that just as readily may be interpreted as a generalized response to instigators to aggression.

Ardrey (1967) states that man is instinctively a killer who possesses an innate proclivity for destruction of his fellow man through the use of weapons. He believes that man has "an aggressive imperative" and that war and the weapons of war are necessary for his survival. Thus, Ardrey eschews the consideration that man is born tabula rasa and rather subscribes to the Hobbesian notion of man's innate brutishness. He bases his discussion of human aggression on generalizations derived from animal behavior. These generalizations are greatly lacking in validity according to Scott (1967), Montagu (1968), and Gorer (1968). Ardrey's thesis that man has an instinct for territoriality is sharply criticized by Scott as unscientific and unsophisticated. He criticizes Ardrey for his tendentiousness and readiness to generalize from, for example, a band of lemurs in Madagascar to a modern human nation. Gorer holds that man does not have a killer instinct. He argues that although violence, torture, and killing seem to be ubiquitous, such behavior may be attributed to learning and cultural tradition.

From the viewpoint of certain anthropologists, animals and human beings tend to live in packs. In the latter case the pack is society, generally, and some segment, particularly. Killing of members within the pack is always forbidden except under carefully defined rules. However, these restrictions do not exist outside of the pack, which at the human level has been variously defined throughout the ages as the nation state, religion, an ideological group, and so forth. Members of other packs may be viewed or defined as inferior and the learned proscriptions against killing do not apply to them. History furnishes too many examples of the dehumanization and denigration of human beings in order to rationalize and thus permit their slaughter. The first step is to redefine the pack, those within the pack, or both. Examples of such redefinition by the use of labels are infidel, redskin, Hun, non-Aryan, Jap-rat, yellow-peril, and gook. A concomitant of all wars and massacres is the attempt to portray the enemy as a lesser or nonhuman being. Since he is no longer within the same pack of humans he can become the target of aggression without violating cultural traditions or moral conditioning. Real or imagined frustrators then serve as instigators to an aggressive act which culminates in injury or death of the victim. This process was vividly demonstrated in the 1968 massacre of Vietnamese civilians by American troops in My Lai. Many Americans tend to view Asians as lesser human beings, if human at all, and American troops refer pejoratively to the Vietnamese as "gooks," "dinks," and "slopeheads." Such dehumanization is attested to by Fried (1969), an anthropologist at the East Asian Institute of Columbia University. In his frequent trips to Asia, Fried's seatmates during long Pacific flights were often United States officers and enlisted men returning to Viet Nam from leave. Fried states that on a number of occasions they "expressed the most horrifying opinions of the Asians among whom they were serving. To put it quite mildly, they did not regard Asians, whether friend or foe, as quite human." Fried felt that these attitudes may have been consciously inculcated, or at least strengthened, during military indoctrination. Thus, what ethologists term a "killer instinct" in man may be explained more parsimoniously by learning theory. Interestingly, a nationally known newspaper columnist, in discussing the Songmy massacre, attributes the incident to the "beast in man" that is let loose by the conditions of war (Wicker, 1969). The similarity of this position to that of the ethologists is clear.

Gorer argues that, rather than possessing a killer instinct, man has no inhibition against killing his fellow men who do not belong to the same pack. Such inhibitions are culturally given, or conditioned to prevail across packs or societies as well as within packs. In this context, Gorer conceives of the international youth movement, typified by its hairstyle, dress, and behavior, as a repudiation of pack differences. For example, the outer trappings of male and female sex roles lose their distinctiveness in the unisex mode of dress and appearance. The symbols of aggressive masculinity are obliterated in the attempt to merge the male and female packs. However, the style and appearance of the youth movement may, paradoxically, have increased pack differences such as seen in the generation gap.

Carrying the construct of instinct over into social psychology, Aronfreed (1969) postulates the existence of what he terms "aggressive dispositions" in human beings. These mechanisms are manifested through the agency of a releasing stimulus. The probability of the occurrence of aggressive behavior increases in the presence of situations that provide social facilitation. Aronfreed maintains, for example, that observation of aggression facilitates the expression of aggression in the observer. Furthermore, the aggression manifested by the observer need not imitate or correspond to the aggression he observes. The aggressive actions of the observer are determined mainly by the modes and targets that are present in the situation and that provide the opportunity for the expression of aggression. Accordingly, the mere presence of the observer when an aggressive act occurs is enough to facilitate the expression of aggression in the observer. Generalized arousal of an aggressive drive results in aggressive behavior that, it seems, is the result of the drive rather than of modeling or of discriminative control over the observer's behavior. However, evidence cited in Chapter 4 (p. 84) indicates that only specific behaviors are learned, not a whole class of behaviors labeled aggressive.

Actually, there is no firm evidence for the supposition that the central nervous system is innately set to react to specific signs or releasing mechanisms. None of the postulates of the ethologists has been demonstrated by the methods of experimental verification. This objection is particularly relevant to the problem of human aggression because the methods used in the modification of human aggression would vary greatly, depending on the theory on which the methods were based. If a choice must be made between instinct theory and learning theory to account for the data of aggression in humans, then in our view the criterion of parsimony should serve as the deciding factor. In short, the theory which encompasses and explains the data of human aggression with the fewest assumptions and from which testable hypotheses may be deduced is, pragmatically, the best theory. As Scott says (1963, 1968), genetics has an unquestionable effect on behavior, and the issue of whether nature or nurture is more important is really spurious. The interdependence of these conditions is accepted by most behavioral scientists as almost axiomatic. The questions of how constitutional factors affect behavior and how they interact with learning remain largely unanswered. It seems probable that the science of genetics will resolve these questions and thus eliminate the need for the somewhat metaphysical assumptions of instinct theory.

Summary

By "instigation" we mean the frustrating conditions in the home that are likely to instigate aggression or at least to heighten the drive level as postulated in the frustration-aggression hypothesis. Rejection, lack of nurturance, and parental disharmony are three of five such instigators that we ultimately investigated. Rejection in and of itself had the highest correlation to aggression; and parental disharmony and lack of nurturance correlated moderately with rejection, whereas the other two (restrictiveness and residential mobility) did not. Thus, these three were combined into a composite instigation score and related to school aggression. The results were much the same as for punishment: the more instigation at home as reported by either mothers or fathers, the higher the peer-rated aggression score. This was especially marked for fathers. This positive relation between aggression and instigation seems to bear out the frustration-aggression hypothesis. In addition, it is unlikely that punishment acts as an instigator since it relates differently to other variables than does instigation. Instigation by fathers is more important than punishment by fathers in its relation to peer-rated aggression, but for mothers, punishment is more important than instigation. Further differences that tend to emphasize the distinction between punishment and instigation are examined in Chapter 6. An alternative view of instigation is that offered by the ethologists who meld instinct and evolution in order to account for aggressive behavior throughout the phyletic scale. This point of view was considered, and the theoretical structure was found unnecessary for our understanding of the learning of aggression in children.

IDENTIFICATION AND AGGRESSION

Chapter 6

As stated in Chapter 2, we had to consider at least two aspects or dimensions of identification in relating this construct to aggressive behavior in children: (1) children's internalization of their parents' standards; and (2) the model of behavior presented to children by their parents. Appendix IV details our early attempts at operationalizing these constructs, including the derivation of a measure of role expectations, i.e., standards, for aggressive behavior in eight-year-old children. This measure was obtained from both parents and their children. A discrepancy score was obtained that, we hoped, would yield a measure of the extent to which children internalized their parents' standards about aggressive behavior in eight-year-old children. We also attempted a measure of aggressive role modeling by having parents rate themselves and their spouses on the likelihood of particular aggressive responses to specific frustrating situations.

Internalization Measure

In the early study an alternative measure of internalization was a simple two-item scale of confessing (see Appendix II, Table II.1, for definition and sample item). A child who was described by his parents as confessing to a transgression was said to blame (or to punish) himself (or to expose himself to parental blame or punishment) for the transgression. He thus acted as the parent in punishing the child (himself). We found a significant negative relation between confessing as reported by fathers and school aggression ($r = -.31$); the correlation was in the same direction but not significant for mothers ($r = -.20$). Thus this confessing measure was carried over intact from the preliminary study.

Additional measures of internalization of standards were built for the new study. A five-item scale (called "guilt identification"), the content of which was suggested by items from the Minnesota Multiphasic Personality Inventory (MMPI), attempted to tap the component of guilt (presumed to be self-punishment) more directly than did confessing, by asking such questions as "Would NAME tell a fib or lie to keep out of serious trouble?" and "When he disobeys, does he feel sorry about it afterwards?" We expected the use of this new guilt measure to enhance the obtained inverse correlation of the criterion with confessing.

Role Modeling Measures

Three measures were used to tap the aspect of identification referred to as role modeling. The previous self-rating of parents' aggression was replaced by a twelve-item scale, the Personal Opinion Inventory, that was developed by Walters and Zak (1959). The authors of this scale selected the items on the basis of their relation to overt aggression. The scale itself was reported to have a retest reliability of .86, and the authors felt it was a valid measure of aggression. This conclusion was based on a number of studies, including an experiment demonstrating the sensitivity of the test to situationally-produced aggression.

The data resulting from analysis of the Personal Opinion Inventory with social status controlled are presented in Table 6.1. Direct support for the role modeling concept of identification is provided by this analysis. Boys whose fathers obtain higher scores on this measure of aggression tend to be rated as more aggressive by their peers ($p < .05$). Moreover, this relation is more pronounced for boys with low social status fathers than for boys with high social status fathers ($p < .025$). Similarly, mothers' aggression as measured by the Personal Opinion Inventory is related to peer-ratings of girls' aggression ($p < .005$). From this analysis it seems probable that identification is occurring through same-sex modeling: high aggressive mothers have high aggressive daughters and high aggressive fathers have high aggressive sons.

Another measure of role modeling, role identification, was also included in the parent interview. The set of items attempted to gauge how much each parent participated in traditionally sex-typed

110

TABLE 6.1

Mean School Aggression Scores of Subjects Classified by Social Status
and Parents' Aggression (Walters-Zak Scale)

| | | Girls | | | Boys | | |
		Low	Middle	High	Low	Middle	High
		FATHERS' AGGRESSION					
Social status	Low	7.5	10.3	14	15	21	19
	Middle	7.8	7.3	13.8	7	13	15
	High	6.9	9.7	8.6	9	13.6	13.9
		MOTHERS' AGGRESSION					
Social status	Low	3.2	8.8	16.5	22.6	18.5	16.3
	Middle	6.4	6.8	13.7	15.4	9.5	15
	High	2.7	7.9	10.6	16.5	13.3	12.6

behaviors such as cooking, cleaning, mowing the lawn, and doing minor repairs around the house.

Related to role modeling, but also including an aspect of internalization, was a new method designed to assess the discrepancy between children's and parents' self-descriptions. Called "discrepancy in identification," it was a variation of the semantic differential technique (Osgood et al., 1957). The parents rated themselves on a series of eighteen biopolar adjectives having to do with perceived self-expressive behavior. Three of the eighteen items are as follows:

I walk

fast _____ _____ _____ _____ _____ slow
loud _____ _____ _____ _____ _____ soft
often _____ _____ _____ _____ _____ not often

To deal with one of the problems of response set, adjectives were chosen that, on their face, seemed to have no value loading on either end of the continuum. The same items were administered to the children in the classroom. Thus it was possible to get a measure of identification between children and parents in terms of similarity in self-described expressive behaviors. A measure of profile similarity, Cronbach's D (Cronbach and Gleser, 1953), between parents' and children's responses yielded a hard-to-fake measure of similarity of stylistic characteristics. The lack of a more valued end point not only reduced a favorability response tendency but also made this the least obvious and most theoretically pure measure of general similarity between parent and child.

Interrelations of Identification Measures

The intercorrelations of the five identification measures are presented in Tables 6.2 and 6.3 for boys and girls respectively. Also included in the tables of intercorrelations are the peer-rating measure of aggression and the classroom measure of masculine-feminine identification (i.e., preference for girlish or boyish games). These scales are identified in the tables as follows:

1. MAGG — Children's school aggression score.
2. LFWZ — Fathers' score on Walters and Zak scale of aggression (a measure of respondents' aggression).
3. LMWZ — Mothers' score on Walters and Zak scale of aggression.
4. LFCI — Children's tendency to confess as reported by fathers.
5. LMCI — Children's tendency to confess as reported by mothers.
6. LFPI — Discrepancy between children's self-perception and fathers' self-perception.
7. LMPI — Discrepancy between children's self-perception and mothers' self-perception.
8. LFGI — Extent of children's internalized guilt feelings as reported by fathers.
9. LMGI — Extent of children's internalized guilt feelings as reported by mothers.
10. MBGA — Tendency of children to prefer boyish games and activities.
11. MGGA — Tendency of children to prefer girlish games and activities.
12. LFRI — Tendency of fathers to perform masculine role activities.
13. LMRI — Tendency of mothers to perform feminine role activities.

Some of the relations of variables in these tables have been examined already; for instance, Table 6.1 shows the relation of parental aggression to child aggression (with social status controlled). Table 6.3 shows the significant positive relations of mothers' aggression to daughters' aggression, but a similar relation of fathers' to sons' aggression is *not* found in Table 6.2. This suggests that social status is particularly relevant for boys (see Chapter 7 for support of this idea). In any case, there is a same-sex parent to child similarity with respect to aggression level.

The fact that the mother-daughter relation appears without controlling for social status may reveal an important difference between the socialization of aggression in boys and in girls by fathers and by mothers. Social status does not seem to affect the mothers' influence as it does the fathers'. The mothers' identification measures are uniformly equal to or greater than the comparable measures for fathers in their relation to children's aggression, no matter whether the children are boys or girls. Perhaps this is because mothers are home with their third-grade children more than fathers are. This greater presence would make for more influence, including a modeling influence. The boys' data suggest that eight-year-old boys are making a transition from mothers in the direction of fathers. See Kohlberg's (1966) independent description of this phenomenon.

Fathers' or mothers' engagement in sex-typed activities at home seems to bear no relation to either boys' or girls' aggression in school. However, boys' preference for girlish type games, as revealed in self-report, is negatively related to their peer-rated aggression. Thus, based on the data in our study, the relation between aggression and socially typed masculine behavior is equivocal.

The predicted negative relations between confessing and aggression and between guilt and aggression for both mothers and fathers of girls are also evident in the matrices (see Table 6.3). Confessing enters into the predicted relation with boys' aggression only as reported by mothers of boys. No significant relation obtained between the guilt items and boys' aggression.

Types of Punishment and Identification

As noted in Chapter 4, the type of punishment administered by parents in response to their children's aggressive behavior, i.e., the extent of use of physical punishment, is positively related to aggression. Similarly, the negative relation between confessing and aggression increases as a function of the number of physical punishment items parents admit to using. Table 6.4 shows the progressive increase in these coefficients within the four physical punishment categories, as well as the increase in aggression score and decrease in confessing score. These results suggest that those children who have internalized the interdictions of the socializing agent are less aggressive than those who have not. The foregoing results are consistent with those of two earlier studies, one by Sears et al. (1957) and the other by Miller and Swanson (1958). Both studies report that psychological punishment (exposure to love followed by conditional withdrawal) is more effective in "development of conscience" than

113

TABLE 6.2
Correlation of Identification Measures with Aggression, N = 254 Boys

	1 MAGG	2 LFWZ	3 LMWZ	4 LFCI	5 LMCI	6 LFPI	7 LMPI	8 LFGI	9 LMGI	10 MBGA	11 MGGA	12 LFRI	13 LMRI
1. MAGG													
2. LFWZ	04												
3. LMWZ	-07	17											
4. LFCI	-03	-06	-13										
5. LMCI	-17	-02	-15	36									
6. LFPI	16	22	05	-00	-03								
7. LMPI	22	23	16	-11	-13	64							
8. LFGI	-01	-02	-02	47	26	00	-05						
9. LMGI	-09	-07	-10	30	53	-02	-07	30					
10. MBGA	08	-09	-07	-19	-04	-13	-12	-00	-01				
11. MGGA	-18	01	01	10	-02	-02	-08	-02	06	-40			
12. LFRI	-02	09	00	-06	04	-02	05	-07	-02	-10	06		
13. LMRI	-06	16	09	-06	-01	05	14	-00	-14	-02	-04	25	

A correlation of .12 is significant at the .05 level of confidence.
A correlation of .16 is significant at the .01 level of confidence.

114

TABLE 6.3
Correlation of Identification Measures with Aggression, *N* = 206 Girls

	1 *MAGG*	*2* *LFWZ*	*3* *LMWZ*	*4* *LFCI*	*5* *LMCI*	*6* *LFPI*	*7* *LMPI*	*8* *LFGI*	*9* *LMGI*	*10* *MBGA*	*11* *MGGA*	*12* *LFRI*	*13* *LMRI*
1. MAGG													
2. LFWZ	13												
3. LMWZ	32	34											
4. LFCI	-25	-12	-17										
5. LMCI	-29	-04	-26	35									
6. LFPI	13	25	18	-07	-10								
7. LMPI	25	23	21	-08	-09	54							
8. LFGI	-28	-07	-11	59	31	-04	02						
9. LMGI	-28	-10	-25	34	57	-06	-06	33					
10. MBGA	01	-08	-02	10	06	-05	-04	01	06				
11. MGGA	-03	04	-14	01	08	05	-03	08	06	-66			
12. LFRI	-03	03	-04	-06	06	-01	06	-04	-11	-11	10		
13. LMRI	-12	04	02	-16	02	05	02	-17	-09	-04	02	35	

A correlation of .14 is significant at the .05 level of confidence.
A correlation of .18 is significant at the .01 level of confidence.

TABLE 6.4

Relation of Extent of Physical Punishment to Mean Aggression and Confessing Scores and Their Correlation

Number of physical punishment items	N	$\bar{X}$ Aggression	$\bar{X}$ Confessing	r	t	P
			MOTHERS			
0	428	11.08	6.30	-.13	2.60	.01
1	180	13.71	5.82	-.15	2.05	.05
2	63	16.19	5.52	-.23	1.82	ns
3 and 4	28	18.39	5.46	-.50	2.93	.01
			FATHERS			
0	353	9.79	5.96	-.07	1.26	ns
1	138	14.96	5.19	-.16	1.88	ns
2	45	15.16	5.78	-.14	.93	ns
3 and 4	19	14.18	5.16	-.52	2.49	.05

is physical punishment. Our confessing score can be interpreted as an indication of "conscience."

Differential Effects for Boys and Girls

Evidence in our study of a differential punishment system for boys and girls is contained in Table 6.5. Approximately twice as many fathers employ the love withdrawal technique of discipline with girls as with boys, and mothers just slightly favor the boys with this technique. Examination of the proportion of parents using physical punishment or the withholding of tangible objects shows that this disciplinary technique is more often used with boys than with girls by at least one of the parents and in many cases by both.

A comparison was made of parents' judgments of how harsh a standard set of punishments would be for boys and for girls. Table 4.11 (p. 79) shows that girls whose mothers judge a standard series of punishments to be harsh for them tend to be rated less aggressive in school than girls whose parents judge such punishments not to be harsh; this is not so for boys. Thus not only is there differential punishment for boys and girls, but also the judged sensitivity of girls relates to school aggression whereas the same judgment about boys does not.

Theoretically, differential punishment involving love withdrawal for girls and physical punishment for boys (see Table 6.5) should lead to two other predictions in addition to that pertaining to the

TABLE 6.5
Percentage of Parents Endorsing Love Withdrawal
and Physical Punishment Items[a]

Item	Mothers		Fathers	
	Boys	Girls	Boys	Girls
1. Would you tell NAME you don't love him for grabbing things from another child?	3	2	6	11
2. Would you tell NAME you don't love him for getting very mad at you?	4	3	4	9
3. If you heard NAME say mean things to another child, would you wash out his mouth with soap?	11	6	8	7
4. If NAME were rude to you, would you wash out his mouth with soap?	7	4	5	5
5. Would you spank NAME until he cried if he were rude to you?	33	30	36	27
6. If NAME got very mad at you, would you slap him in the face?	12	12	12	6
7. If you heard NAME say mean things to another child, would you say, "Get on that chair and don't move until you apologize"?	37	35	39	33
8. If NAME were rude to you, would you say, "Get on that chair and don't move until you apologize"?	41	35	38	34
9. If NAME got very mad at you, would you send him to another room where he would be alone and without toys?	51	46	40	38

[a]Items 1 and 2 pertain to love withdrawal; items 3 through 9 pertain to physical punishment.

negative relations between confessing and aggression and between guilt and aggression: (1) boys should be more aggressive than girls, and (2) girls should be more identified in terms of the guilt and confessing measures than boys. The first prediction is borne out since the mean aggression score of boys is five points higher than that of girls. Some evidence for the second prediction is found in Table 6.6, which shows the means and standard deviations of confessing and guilt measures. Although the mean differences are slight, all are in the expected direction.

Sex-Role Identification

Two indices (one for boys and one for girls) were developed to assess sex-role preference of boys and girls (Lefkowitz, 1962). These measures, the Games and Activities Preference Lists (GAP), were composed of items defined empirically as high or low masculine or

117

TABLE 6.6
Means and Standard Deviations of Confessing and Guilt Measures

		Boys	Girls			Boys	Girls
LFCI	$\bar{x}$	5.67	5.81	LMCI	$\bar{x}$	6.02	6.21
	σ	1.67	1.65		σ	1.62	1.72
LFGI	$\bar{x}$	9.33	9.40	LMGI	$\bar{x}$	9.42	9.48
	σ	1.40	1.45		σ	1.40	1.37

high or low feminine (see Appendix I.B). Examples of the item pairs presented to each child follow:

Would you rather
1. Go shooting or go bowling?
2. Use lipstick and powder or use a razor and shaving cream?
3. Learn boxing or learn dancing?

Differentiated on the basis of scores on this measure, boys and girls were partitioned into high and low masculine and high and low feminine sex-role preference groups. This permitted analysis of differences between groups based on responses made by the children or their parents to other variables: usual disciplinary agent, social status, nurturance, aggression, IQ, and first figure drawn in response to the Draw-a-Person technique. The results show that boys who are strong in masculine sex-role preference may have more nurturant mothers than low sex-role preference boys. High sex-role preference boys are also more likely than low sex-role preference boys to have parents who both take responsibility for discipline, a home environment tending toward the upper social status categories, a disposition to drawing their own sex first in Draw-a-Person, and a significantly higher mean intelligence score. There were no significant relations for girls.

Scoring the GAP indices on a continuous rather than on a dichotomous basis (see Table 6.2) results in a negative relation for boys between aggression and preference for feminine games or, more specifically, between aggression and feminine sex-role identification. The lack of a significant relation between preference for masculine games, masculine sex-role identification, and aggression suggests that feminine and masculine sex roles are not always antipodal. That is, high masculine sex-role preference does not necessarily imply low feminine sex-role preference for the same individual and vice versa. However, the negative correlations between these measures for boys and girls as seen in Tables 6.2 and 6.3 suggest that sex-role preference does indeed tend toward polarization.

118

Discrepancy in Identification

Discrepancy in identification (the difference between the way the child looks at himself and each parent looks at himself) is the final identification variable to be considered here. As this discrepancy increases, the aggression score in school becomes higher (see Table 6.7). This effect holds when we consider mothers and/or fathers and boys and/or girls, and it is particularly pronounced for mothers of boys and fathers of girls. It seems that cross-sex identification is important (see p. 115 regarding presence of mother). However, an examination of Table 6.8 shows that if children have a close identification with at least one parent they will tend to be nonaggressive, regardless of their degree of identification with the other parent. This is true for both boys and girls as shown by a comparison of the High-High cell entry (those children who identify with neither parent) with all other entries in each half of the table. Children who are rated as very aggressive by their peers tend to view themselves differently from the way *both* parents view themselves. It is interesting that a simplistic measure such as this one would relate so directly to aggression in school. Furthermore, the same order of relation was obtained in the study done in Amsterdam, Holland (see Chapter 7). The correlation between aggression in school and discrepancy in identification was .27 in Amsterdam and .24 in Columbia County. Analysis of variance as described above, which at this writing has not yet been performed on the Dutch data, would undoubtedly show the same strong relation (see Chapter 4, p. 62). This is testimony to the stability of both the measure and the relation.

TABLE 6.7
Mean Aggression Scores According to Discrepancy in Identification

Model	Discrepancy in identification		
	Low	Middle	High
	BOYS		
Mothers	10.28 (77)[a]	14.16 (82)	17.50 (86)
Fathers	11.78 (73)	14.16 (94)	16.71 (78)
	GIRLS		
Mothers	7.00 (68)	7.81 (77)	13.42 (68)
Fathers	7.64 (74)	8.20 (61)	15.51 (64)

[a]The number in parentheses represents the number of subjects in the cell.

119

TABLE 6.8

Mean Aggression Scores of Subjects According to Discrepancy in Identification with Mothers and Fathers

		Discrepancy in identification with mothers		
		Low	Middle	High
		BOYS		
	Low	10.87 (46)[a]	12.96 (29)	14.33 (3)
	Middle	9.14 (22)	15.89 (45)	15.42 (26)
Discrepancy in	High	9.67 (3)	11.65 (17)	18.77 (54)
identification				
with fathers		GIRLS		
	Low	6.52 (42)	10.44 (18)	6.75 (4)
	Middle	8.25 (24)	6.53 (39)	11.35 (20)
	High	3.67 (3)	7.88 (18)	15.21 (38)

[a]The number in parentheses represents the number of subjects in the cell.

Fathers' aggression and mothers' aggression as measured by the Personal Opinion Inventory are related in a statistically significant manner to the measures of guilt, confessing, and discrepancy in identification. Table 6.2 shows that when fathers' aggression is high, boys' discrepancy in identification with their fathers and with their mothers also tends to be high. When mothers' aggression is high, the discrepancy in identification between boys and mothers is high, but no relation obtains under this condition between boys and fathers.[1] Table 6.2 also illustrates the significant inverse relations between mothers' aggression and both parents' reports of their children's confessing.

When the foregoing relations are examined for girls, as in Table 6.3, high fathers' aggression is significantly related to high discrepancy in identification between girls and fathers and between girls and mothers. Similarly, when mothers' aggression is high, discrepancy in identification between girls and fathers and girls and mothers tends also to be high. Table 6.3 also shows that high aggression for mothers is significantly related in inverse fashion to both parents' reports of their daughters' confessing behavior, but only mothers' reports of daughters' expression of guilt. In general all of these relations may be contained in a paradigm of high parent aggression associated with low child identification with parent.

[1] The reader is referred to comparison of correlation (r) procedures with analysis of variance in Chapter 4 (pp. 61–62), demonstrating that r underestimates the relation.

Relation of Punishment and Discrepancy
in Identification

When we stratify identification by punishment (Table 6.9), an interesting finding emerges that may help clarify the paradoxical results obtained in survey studies relating child-rearing practices of parents to aggression of children. At least for boys, when there is a close identification with their fathers, the relation between punishment and aggressive behavior is what one would predict from traditional notions about socialization: behavior that is punished tends not to appear in situations similar to the one in which the training occurs. According to findings with this measurement operation sons who identify with their fathers tend to be less aggressive the more they are punished for this behavior; and boys who do not identify closely with their fathers tend to be more aggressive the more they are punished. (The interaction between punishment and discrepancy in identification is significant at the .02 level for boys.) Although the relation appears to be curvilinear since boys with high discrepancy in identification have lower aggression scores than those with medium discrepancy, the scores are not significantly different from each other. It seems that for both non- and poorly-identified boys, punishment acts either as an instigator or as a model of behavior.

That instigation and punishment are not identical variables, however, is seen in Table 6.10. When discrepancy is held constant, there

TABLE 6.9
Mean Aggression Scores of Children Classified by Fathers' Punishment and Discrepancy of Identification

| | | Discrepancy of identification with fathers | | |
		Low	Middle	High
		BOYS		
	Low	13.10 (30)[a]	10.48 (25)	13.05 (18)
	Middle	11.07 (30)	13.86 (37)	19.30 (27)
	High	10.77 (18)	17.48 (31)	16.72 (29)
Fathers' punishment		GIRLS		
	Low	4.87 (30)	7.03 (30)	7.35 (14)
	Middle	9.46 (24)	6.85 (27)	12.58 (17)
	High	11.60 (10)	10.96 (26)	14.79 (28)

[a]The number in parentheses represents the number of subjects in the cell.

121

TABLE 6.10

Mean Aggression Scores of Children Classified by Fathers' Instigation and Discrepancy in Identification

		Discrepancy in identification with fathers		
		Low	Middle	High
		BOYS		
	Low	10.41 (29)[a]	16.22 (32)	12.17 (24)
	Middle	8.10 (23)	10.12 (33)	20.28 (25)
	High	16.65 (26)	16.57 (28)	17.68 (25)
Fathers' instigation		GIRLS		
	Low	4.00 (23)	4.42 (26)	10.85 (13)
	Middle	7.23 (22)	9.39 (36)	8.52 (23)
	High	12.53 (19)	10.86 (21)	17.13 (23)

[a]The number in parentheses represents the number of subjects in the cell.

is no systematic effect of instigation on aggression scores of boys; for girls there is still a main effect for instigation, significant at the .05 level. Instigation and punishment do not relate to aggression in the same way when identification is held constant. This reinforces our belief that they are two conceptually different variables.

Summary

In this chapter we explored two facets of identification in their relation to aggression: identification through modeling and identification through the internalization of parental standards. In addition, a corollary of modeling — sex-role identification — was investigated through the study of children's preference for sex-typed games and activities. Concerning internalization of standards, it was found that confessing behaviors as reported by mothers and fathers of girls are negatively related to the peer-rating measure of aggression. For boys, the relation is manifested only in mothers' interviews. Similarly, significant correlations in the predicted direction were found between mothers' and fathers' reporting of children's expression of guilt and the criterion measure of aggression. This relation, however, was found to hold only for girls. Concerning the role modeling measures of identification, direct support for the modeling concept derives from an analysis of the results of the Walters and Zak Personal Opinion Inventory. When social class is taken into account, fathers and mothers who rate themselves as high in aggressive attitude have sons who are rated as more aggressive by their peers. This trend is more pronounced in low than in high social status categories. Another finding, probably associated with both internalization and role modeling, is the increase in school aggression as the discrepancy widens between childrens' and parents' ratings of their own expressive behavior. The effect is particularly pronounced for mothers of boys and fathers of girls, suggesting the influence of cross-sex identification. However, as long as children can identify closely with one of their parents, they tend to be nonaggressive. Only children with discrepancy in identification with both parents tend to be rated as highly aggressive by their peers. The relation between children's aggression and preference for games and activities is statistically significant only for boys and only for the feminine scale. Specifically, boys who prefer feminine type games and activities, and who thus may have made a feminine sex-role identification, are rated by their peers as low in aggression.

The data on punishment for aggression presented in this chapter are pertinent to that aspect of identification occurring through internalization of standards. Children who have internalized the interdictions of the socializing agent are less aggressive than those who have not, and the magnitude of this negative relation appears to increase with an increase in parental use of physical punishment. Also, either fathers or mothers may serve as role models, but the relation is particularly strong for mothers of girls, suggesting that salience of the mother is an important variable in identification. Boys who identify strongly with their fathers tend to be less aggressive the more they are punished for aggression. However, boys who identify less tend to be more aggressive the more they are punished for aggression. Thus for boys who are not identified with their fathers, punishment appears to act as an instigator to aggressive behavior. However, other evidence presented in this chapter, as well as in Chapter 5, indicates that punishment and instigation differ in a number of ways.

SOCIOCULTURAL VARIABLES
AND AGGRESSIVE BEHAVIOR

Chapter 7

For many years it has been widely accepted that the effect of socio-cultural variables on behavior is pervasive. This is especially so for social class membership in its many ramifications (Warner et al., 1960). Statements in the literature have been largely unanimous that children from lower-class backgrounds are more aggressive than middle- and upper-class children (Davis, 1943; Goldstein, 1955; Mc-Kee and Leader, 1955; Stulz and Smith, 1959). Furthermore, aggression is said to be encouraged in the socialization of children in lower-class environments (Davis, 1941, 1943, 1948; Davis and Havighurst, 1946) since in some lower-class environments, aggressive behavior is necessary for the preservation of life (Duvall, 1946). An associated finding is that punishment for aggressive behavior is more severe among middle-class parents than among others (Davis, 1943).

Social class variables were included in this study because social status probably defines some important aspects of the learning environment. Attitudes about children, specifically expectations about how eight-year-old children behave, no doubt influence which behaviors of their children parents reward and which they punish. These attitudes and expectations have been shown to vary with such sociocultural variables as ethnic group (Barabee and von Mering, 1953), social class (Aberle and Naegele, 1952), rurality (Sorokin, Zimmerman, and Galpin, 1933), social mobility (McGuire and Clark, 1952), and social isolation (Merton and Kitt, 1950).

Fathers' Occupational Status

Social status in our study was measured by fathers' occupations according to the Bureau of Census classification (United States Bureau of Census, 1960), a ten-point scale that was collapsed to 3 classes: upper, middle, and lower. The cutting points were determined by the computer in order to get the closest approximation of thirds. Of the Bureau of Census classes, 0 and 1 were in the upper class, 2, 3, and 4 in the middle class, and 5 through 9 in the lower or working class.

We used just one indicator of social class because research of others (Kahl and Davis, 1955; Lawson and Boek, 1960) had shown this single index to be as efficient as any combination of occupation, education, place of residence, and so forth. In fact, this single index is probably better because exactly opposite relations are obtained when predicting to school aggression scores from education (the number of years of education completed by the parents) and occupation.

The data in Table 7.1 bear on the relation between aggressive behavior and social class. For both boys and girls there is a tendency for children of upper-class fathers to be more aggressive than children of lower- and middle-class fathers. This is significant at the .05 level of confidence only for boys. However, considering both fathers' occupations and fathers' punishment, that is, stratifying fathers' punishment by their social class (see Table 7.2), the results become much sharper, especially for boys: there is a main effect for punishment (significant at .05 level of confidence), a main effect for social class (significant at .025), and an interaction between social class and punishment (significant at the .025 level). For boys of low social status, it does not seem to make much difference what fathers' punishment is, but boys of upper status who are punished severely for aggression seem to be very aggressive — the more they are punished, the more aggressive they tend to be. In Chapter 6 it was pointed out that fa-

TABLE 7.1
Children's Mean Aggression Scores by Social Status as Defined
by Fathers' Occupations

Social status	Boys	Girls	Boys and girls
Low	13.2	8.6	11.3
Middle	12.7	9.2	10.9
High	18.7	10.7	14.9

TABLE 7.2
Children's Mean Aggression Scores According to Intensity of the Fathers'
Punishment and Social Status as Defined by Fathers' Occupations

| | Punishment intensity | | | |
Social status	Low	Middle	High	Total
		BOYS		
Low	13.3	12.5	13.9	13.2
Middle	11.2	15.6	12.0	12.9
High	11.3	16.5	28.5	18.8
Total	11.9	14.9	18.1	
		GIRLS		
Low	6.4	8.9	10.1	8.5
Middle	4.9	9.9	13.6	9.4
High	7.3	11.2	16.9	11.8
Total	6.2	10.0	13.6	

thers' self-rated aggression is also more strongly related to school aggression when their occupations are controlled, although there is no significant interaction. For girls, there is a main effect only for punishment; fathers' occupations do not seem to have such a strong influence, although there is a tendency toward the same effect. However, high-status girls who are severely punished are also the most aggressive of all girls. When we do the same analysis for mothers, that is, stratify mothers' punishment by fathers' occupations, we get a main effect only for mothers' punishment, significant for boys at the .005 level and for girls at the .01 level. There is no interaction with social class.

The effect of mothers' punishment seems to be overriding; social class does not contribute anything significant. This may explain Allinsmith's finding (1954) that the effect of discipline is independent of social class since she used only mothers as informants. However, even though her measure of aggression — projective story completions — was different from ours, her data and ours are quite consistent.

Occupational Status and Punishment
for Aggression

Since the effect of punishment is so clearly related to the social class of socializing agents, as measured by fathers' occupational status, we examined the possibility of different patterns of punishment from one status to another. These results are in Table 7.3. There is a significant relation ($p < .005$) between fathers' occupations and their punishment for girls, with lower-class girls being punished more severely for aggression. The trend is the same for mothers of girls, but not significant. For boys, there is no significant relation between fathers' occupations and severity of punishment by either mothers or fathers. Again, our results contradict those of many writers, especially sociologists who have said that aggression is encouraged by lower-class parents and discouraged by middle- and upper-class parents.

TABLE 7.3
Mean Punishment for Aggression Scores
According to Fathers' Social Status

Status	Mothers	Fathers
	BOYS	
Low	17.5	17.4
Middle	15.5	14.9
High	17.3	16.1
	GIRLS	
Low	17.2	17.9
Middle	15.3	15.0
High	15.4	13.9

Since two of the punishment items concerned punishment for aggression against peers and two concerned punishment for aggression against parents, we examined the responses to these two sets for differences between them. Social class does not affect punishment for aggression against parents: all parents regardless of social class punish severely for this aggression. However, social class does affect punishment for aggression against other children (see Table 7.4). Upper-

TABLE 7.4
Mean Punishment for Aggression against Other
Children Scores by Fathers' Social Status

Status	Mothers	Fathers
	BOYS	
Low	3.7	3.7
Middle	2.0	2.9
High	4.5	2.8
	GIRLS	
Low	4.8	4.8
Middle	2.7	3.1
High	2.6	2.2

class girls are punished less severely by both mothers and fathers for this behavior than are lower-class girls ($p < .005$ for fathers). Middle-class boys are punished less severely by their mothers than lower- and upper-class boys ($p < .005$). Thus it seems that, in our population, lower-class parents are much less permissive about aggression than middle- and upper-class parents. The only other investigators who have found similar results are Maccoby and Gibbs (1954). They worked with nursery school children and attributed the difference to age (others before them had worked with pre-adolescents). If they are correct, then even up to nine years we find this less permissive behavior among lower-class parents.

It has been said that lower-class parents tend to use physical punishment whereas middle-class parents use psychological punishment (Allinsmith, 1954; Bronfenbrenner, 1958; Kohn, 1959a, 1963; Miller and Swanson, 1960), and this is significant for establishment of identification in children. (The relation between psychological punishment and identification was examined in Chapter 6, p. 116.) We tried to check the sociocultural aspect of this relation by comparing the proportion of parents in each class who said they would respond to specific behaviors with a physical or psychological punishment. We utilized four questions for this analysis, two concerning aggressive acts against other children and two concerning aggressive acts against parents. One act of each set evoked a psychological punishment and one a physical punishment. In all cases the physical and psychological punishments had a similar intensity value — high punishment — as rated in the previous study (see Chapter 4, p. 70). The results are shown in Table 7.5, and it is apparent that the relative frequency of the use of psychological or physical punishment by parents is not a distinguishing feature of class among these subjects. The only apparent trend is that upper-class mothers use more physical punishment for their children's aggression against other children and lower-class fathers use more psychological punishment for their daughters' aggression against both parents and other children. Differences in these results from those of Allinsmith (1954) may be due to measurement operations. She used ratings of audio-recorded interviews, whereas our measure is a simple count of "yes" responses to four questions having to do with the likelihood of a parent using a specific punishment for specific behavior. Other possible reasons for discrepancies include geographical and urban-rural differences in the samples. However, all results reported here tend to suggest that some traditional notions about the differential distribution of socialization practices and child behaviors among various social classes may be in need of revision. Bronfenbrenner (1958) points out that the gap between social classes has been narrowing over the years, with middle-

TABLE 7.5
Percentage of Parents by Class Who Say They Would Use
a Given Punishment for a Given Aggressive Act

Object of aggression	Type of punishment	Upper-class		Middle-class		Lower-class	
		Boys	Girls	Boys	Girls	Boys	Girls
				MOTHERS			
Child	Psychological	2	5	2	5	4	5
Child	Physical	16	5	3	8	11	10
Adult	Psychological	2	5	3	2	5	5
Adult	Physical	6	0	2	7	6	7
				FATHERS			
Child	Psychological	4	7	3	7	8	15
Child	Physical	6	2	12	10	6	9
Adult	Psychological	4	5	2	3	4	15
Adult	Physical	0	5	7	3	5	6

class parents becoming more permissive and lower-class parents becoming more conforming and restrictive. Thus the traditional differences between the two classes tend to disappear. Littman, Moore, and Pierce-Jones (1957), studying child-rearing practices of middle- and lower-class parents in Eugene, Oregon, and comparing their findings with those of other studies in different communities (primarily Boston and Chicago), contended that no demonstrable, consistent differences permitted any particular socialization practice to be described as characteristic of any class. Our data, collected in 1960, contribute additional evidence of the similarity in patterns of punishment at that time among different social class levels. Although no type of punishment is exclusively characteristic of any social class, we do not say that social class membership is an unimportant influence on aggressive behavior of children, since there is an interaction between social class and intensity of punishment.

It may indeed seem that we have substantiated some important class differences in our sample. For example, lower-class girls are punished more severely by their parents than are upper-class girls for aggression against other children, and at the same time lower-class girls are rated as less aggressive by their peers than are upper-class girls. In addition, middle-class boys are punished least for aggression against other children and are rated as least aggressive by their peers. However, these findings do not tell us anything about the relation between punishment for aggression and aggressive behavior in individual boys and girls. The best information on the basis of our data is that a positive relation prevails between punishment for aggression and the appearance of that behavior in school and that this relation is heightened by social class membership, with upper-class children who are punished severely by their parents being rated by their peers as most aggressive.

Effect of Social Status Composition of Classrooms

In addition to the correlation between aggressive behavior of individual children and the social class membership of their parents, we also investigated the ecological correlation between the social class composition of a total classroom and the amount of aggressive behavior displayed there.

It is possible that the atmosphere of certain classrooms is conducive to the expression of aggressive behavior. This was investigated with our data by Toigo (1962). He encountered definite ecological findings, with classroom aggression increasing as the proportion of upper-status children in the class declined. The ecological effect was different for children of contrasting status backgrounds: aggression in upper-status children declined with decreasing upper-status concentration in the classroom, and aggression in lower-status children increased with decreasing upper-status concentration. Rural occupational background of fathers emerged as a pertinent ecological variable since aggression at all occupational status levels increased as the proportion of children in the classroom with fathers in farm-centered occupations increased.

Attitudes

Attitudes can affect parents' socialization practices, as pointed out above. One set of attitudes that was thought to be important has been subsumed under the concept of "anomie" (Durkheim, 1951), which refers to a generalized attitude of alienation from people and a lack of social cohesion. Srole (1956) developed a scale which purportedly measures this attribute, and we adopted it in our early study. We expected a socializing agent who is high in anomie, i.e., with a jaded outlook toward life, social institutions, and people, to tend to encourage expression of aggression in the child because his own behavior, which might serve as a model for the child, stems from a "dog-eat-dog" attitude. A very strong relation was indeed found between social class and anomie, with lower-class parents scoring higher on this variable ($r = -.58$ for fathers and $-.51$ for mothers). Anomie was also significantly related to a number of other variables within the interview, particularly class-related items such as social participation ($r = -.56$ for mothers and $-.37$ for fathers)

130

and church attendance ($r = -.26$ for mothers and $-.31$ for fathers). However, it was not related to any of the independently obtained measures (school aggression, popularity, etc.). This strongly suggested that the measure of anomie was method-bound in that relations to it obtained only with responses supplied by the same subject. Since the items are all relatively obvious and slanted in the same direction, both acquiescent response set and social desirability are uncontrolled. Because of this and because the measure of anomie did not contribute anything new to the social class measure, we decided to drop the variable.

F Scale

In place of anomie we used Christie's Reversed F Scale (Christie et al., 1958), which we adapted for a face-to-face interview. In addition to giving us a measure of attitude, this scale yields its own measure of acquiescence set and can thus be used to check on the presence of such a set in the other scales in the interview (see Chapter 3, p. 56, for application of this check). We made one change in the Christie scale: because of public relations considerations we believed it best to eliminate the question which read, "People ought to pay more attention to new ideas, even though they seem to go against the American way of life. Do you agree?" Thus our F Scale score refers to a composite of nine items.

Although the F Scale score, like its predecessor, anomie, is unrelated to the independently obtained peer-rating aggression measure, it is related to a number of other interview measures. Keeping in mind the response bias which might affect the results when both predictor and criterion are obtained from the same respondent, it is still interesting to note which correlations with approximately 100 variables are significantly higher than zero. Table 7.6 contains all

TABLE 7.6
Correlation of F Scale Scores with Other Variables
in Mothers' and Fathers' Interviews[a]

	LFWZ	LMWZ	LFRO	LMRO	LFPU	LMPU
LFFS	.31	.16	.28	.18	.31	.16
LMFS	.13	.25	.14	.12	.12	.33

	LFBK	LMBK	LFEA	LMEA	LFED	LMED
LFFS	-.23	-.20	-.20	-.20	.37	.31
LMFS	-.11	-.15	-.13	-.13	.21	.28

[a]See Appendix V.A for explanation of codes.

correlations between mothers' and fathers' F Scale scores and another variable in mothers' and fathers' interviews in which at least three of the tetrad of correlations is significantly better than zero. Both mothers and fathers with high authoritarian attitudes as reflected in F Scale scores tend to rate themselves as more aggressive, are more punitive of aggression in their children, are less influenced by child care books such as Spock, are of lower educational level, and have lower educational aspirations for their children than parents with low F Scale scores. Fathers who are high on authoritarianism also tend to assume more traditionally sex-typed behaviors around the house (e.g., do minor repairs, mow the lawn, etc.). The positive relation between F Scale score and acquiescence was cited in Chapter 3, p. 57.

Mobility Orientation

We hypothesized that the mobility orientation of parents affects aggression level of children in school. Mobility was assessed by a series of questions (Farber and Jenne', 1963) dealing with the respondent's willingness to disrupt his usual routine in order to improve his station in life; for example, both mothers and fathers were asked, "How willing would you be to give up friends . . . move around the country a lot in order to get ahead?" Response alternatives were "not at all willing," "a little willing," "somewhat willing," and "very willing." Mobility was thus considered as a value in competition with other parental values. The original six-item scale was part of a written interview schedule. In our study, the scale was modified for face-to-face administration. In addition, one item was omitted which proved objectionable to some parents in the pretest: "How willing would you be to keep quiet about political views in order to get ahead?"

Table 7.7 examines the aggression scores for boys and girls grouped according to the joint occurrence of three levels of fathers' and mothers' mobility orientation. The marginals for boys show a regular increase in aggression score with increased mobility orientation of fathers, although not of mothers. Unfortunately, the results of the test of significance are unavailable and irretrievable due to computer error. Thus the mean scores per cell are presented as descriptive of the data in this sample.

Education

Table 7.8 considers the mean aggression score as a resultant of both education and occupational status of fathers. Fathers' education and occupation relate to school aggression in opposite directions (more

TABLE 7.7
Mothers' Mobility Orientation x Fathers' Mobility Orientation
and Their Relationship to Children's Mean Aggression Scores

		Fathers' mobility orientation			
		Low	*Middle*	*High*	*Total*
		BOYS			
	Low	10.54 (24)[a]	14.20 (30)	15.62 (21)	13.43 (75)
	Middle	14.35 (23)	13.68 (40)	17.52 (29)	15.05 (92)
	High	11.06 (17)	16.46 (28)	14.39 (41)	14.41 (86)
Mothers'	*Total*	12.05 (64)	14.63 (98)	15.67 (91)	
mobility		GIRLS			
orientation	*Low*	11.00 (23)	9.33 (27)	7.35 (17)	9.40 (67)
	Middle	8.29 (21)	7.23 (31)	9.07 (29)	8.16 (81)
	High	14.38 (13)	7.46 (28)	11.20 (35)	10.37 (76)
	Total	10.77 (57)	7.97 (86)	9.63 (81)	

[a]The number in parentheses represents the number of subjects in the cell.

distinct for boys than girls, though operative for both). The higher
the occupational status, the higher is the mean aggression; the higher
the education, the lower is the mean aggression. The traditional procedure of combining education and occupational status into a single
index of social class is based on the positive correlation between these
two indices, as is the case in this research ($r = .48$). However, our
finding that, when making predictions from education and occupational status to aggression, opposite results are obtained calls this
practice into question. Since the .48 correlation between education
and occupational status can account for less than 25 percent of the
variance, each of these variables could easily relate to a third variable in opposite ways. Some hypotheses about the circumstances under which education and occupation would relate differently can be
developed by examining those cells containing *S*s in which the two
variables diverge. For example, the highest mean aggression score is
in the cell which corresponds to children whose fathers did not graduate from high school yet have high occupational status. They are
men, no doubt, who, by dint of extreme striving (i.e., aggression),
have achieved a high social status.

Ethnicity

Our measure of ethnicity refers to the ethnic background of either
parent in terms of the number of generations his ancestors have been
in the United States. A nonethnic in our terms is someone whose

TABLE 7.8
Fathers' Occupations x Fathers' Education as Related to
Children's Mean Aggression Scores

			Fathers' education			
		High (some college)	High medium (high school)	Low medium (10–11 years)	Low (0–9 years)	Total
				BOYS		
	High	12.28 (25)[a]	20.15 (13)	30.83 (6)	15.17 (6)	16.90 (50)
	Middle	11.70 (27)	18.00 (27)	13.71 (14)	14.67 (12)	14.63 (80)
	Low	16.57 (7)	11.12 (60)	10.94 (35)	16.89 (56)	13.37 (158)
	Total	12.53 (59)	14.15 (100)	13.82 (55)	16.39 (74)	
Fathers' occupations				GIRLS		
	High	7.24 (29)	11.22 (9)	6.50 (2)	18.92 (12)	10.60 (52)
	Middle	9.43 (28)	5.46 (28)	11.86 (14)	10.50 (10)	8.60 (80)
	Low	3.29 (7)	5.74 (34)	9.35 (40)	10.38 (56)	8.56 (137)
	Total	7.77 (64)	6.32 (71)	9.88 (56)	11.71 (78)	

[a]The number in parentheses represents the number of subjects in the cell.

forebears came to the United States many generations before; an ethnic is someone whose parents or grandparents were not born in the United States. In the earlier study we found that fathers' ethnicity is more important than mothers' in predicting to children's aggressive behavior in school. Whereas mothers' ethnicity is not significantly related to any other variables, fathers' ethnicity is significantly related to school aggression (.26), rejection by peers (.41), and home aggression of child (−.29), among other things (Eron et al., 1963).

The relations between fathers' ethnicity and children's behavior are especially significant for fathers and sons. For example, fathers' ethnicity relates +.53 ($p < .001$) to their sons' school aggression and −.53 to their sons' home aggression.

One possible interpretation is that ethnic fathers do not tolerate aggression in the home, and thus the tendency on the part of the sons to aggress is displaced to the school context. Another possibility is that ethnic fathers may provide more aggressive role models by their punitive behavior at home. It seems that fathers' ethnicity thus has a more important influence on their children's behavior and the reaction of others to the children than does mothers' ethnicity, at least for boys. Correlation between fathers' ethnicity and daughters' aggression fails to reach significance at the .05 level. However, the relation between fathers' ethnicity and aggression is further clarified when we look at the ethnicity of both fathers and mothers for any

TABLE 7.9
Relationship of Ethnicity to School Aggression

| | | Fathers' ethnicity | |
		High	Low
Mothers ethnicity	High	15.5	6.0
	Low	69.0	16.0

particular child. (There is zero correlation between mothers' and fathers' ethnicity; some children have mothers who are high ethnic and fathers who are low ethnic and vice versa.) If, as in Table 7.9, we compare the median aggression scores of four groups of children according to whether their mothers and fathers are high or low ethnic, the relation between fathers' ethnicity and their children's school aggression is clarified. Only when there is a high-ethnic father and a low-ethnic mother is the aggression score very much elevated. When both the mother and father are ethnics or both are nonethnics, the aggression score is near the median for the entire group. On the other hand, when the mother is high ethnic and the father low ethnic, the median school aggression score is noticeably low. This suggests that there may indeed be a conflict of cultural values behind the obtained ethnicity-aggression relation. The high-ethnic woman married to either a low- or a high-ethnic man perhaps brings Old World values into her relationship with him, deferring to him as the decision-maker, authoritarian, etc. Their roles are well-defined. However, the low-ethnic woman married to a high-ethnic man perhaps has a different conception of the marital relationship that conflicts with the expectations of her husband. Value conflicts ensue, role definitions are not agreed upon, and their children are deviant, at least in their level of aggression.

Cross-National Differences and Similarities

The interesting relation noted in the previous section between ethnicity of parents and school aggression of children leads naturally to the question of whether the socialization experiences of children in other countries lead to similar kinds of classroom behavior. Variations in disciplinary practices in different countries in Western civilizations as well as in other more dissimilar cultures have been related to the inhibition and expression of aggression (Cooney, 1967; Lester, 1967; Stoodley, 1959; Whiting and Child, 1953). In 1968 it became possible to determine whether the relations we found between learning conditions and aggression in Columbia County, New York, could be generalized to a community in another country, Amsterdam, Holland. A small scale replication was conducted by a team of Dutch psychologists [1] working in close collaboration with one of the authors. Although it was possible to translate the peer-rating procedure into Dutch quite literally, it was necessary to adapt the parent interview to a greater extent by eliminating some of the questions and variables that were felt to be inappropriate for or offensive to Dutch parents. The Dutch interviews thus contained 237 items. However, only twenty-two variables in the interview were analyzed, primarily because of restrictions imposed by the available computer [2] and because it would have been difficult to interpret some of the results with so few subjects. The selection of variables to be analyzed was ultimately based on the results with the Columbia County data.

The classroom procedures were administered to five classrooms of eight-year-old children located in four schools from divergent socio-economic areas in Amsterdam (two lower-class and two upper-class). There were complete classroom data for ninety-seven children. An attempt was made to interview all mothers and fathers of these children. However, there was less success in obtaining cooperation from fathers in Amsterdam than in Columbia County, New York. Only fifty-four fathers agreed to be interviewed. Scorable interviews were obtained from seventy-two mothers, and these data were analyzed in relation to the peer-rating scores of the corresponding children (forty-one girls and thirty-one boys).

All the variables were intercorrelated, and a rough comparison between the Dutch and American data was attempted first by computing a Spearman rank-order correlation ($\rho = .56$, $p < .01$) between the Dutch and American correlation coefficients (between peer-rated aggression and other variables). These results appear in Table 7.10. There is a similar order of relation in both samples between school aggression and the predictor variables.

A factor analysis of the Dutch interview and peer-rating data combined yielded five factors. This analysis included twenty-eight variables of which twenty-two were from the mothers' interview, five were peer-rating scores, and one was sex of child. This factor analysis is not directly comparable to the ones done on the Columbia County data and reported in Appendix I.A and Appendix II.A since the latter were done separately for the peer-rating procedures and the interviews. Furthermore, the Columbia County analyses were done on

[1] Drs. B. Remmo Hamel, nej. Drs. Suus van Hekken, Rene Kaskens, and Adrianna Stroo.

[2] The data were analyzed on an EL-X8 at the Mathematische Centrum, Amsterdam. Thanks are due to Drs. Gerrit van der Veer for his expert counsel and assistance in programming the data for this machine.

TABLE 7.10
Correlations between Peer-Rated Aggression and Other Variables for Columbia County and Amsterdam Samples[a]

Variable[b]	Code	Columbia County	Amsterdam
1. Mother's age	LMAG	.014	.014
2. Social class	LMRO	.039	.189
5. Rejection	LMRJ	.251	.318
7. Educational aspirations	LMEA	-.055	.051
8. Acquiescence	LMFP	.128	-.080
9. Frequency of home aggression	LMFR	.158	.078
10. Respondent's aggression	LMWZ	.089	.033
11. F Scale	LMFS	-.013	-.149
12. Discrepancy in identification	LMPI	.240	.266
13. Judged harshness of punishment	LMJP	.052	-.023
15. Lack of nurturance	LMNU	-.021	-.206
17. Shame at home	LMSH	.027	.042
18. Confessing	LMCI	-.229	-.008
19. Punishment	LMPU	.192	.064
20. Toilet-training	LMEN	.014	.063
21. Respondent's education	LMED	.049	.118
22. Church attendance	LMRG	-.156	-.303
24. Activity level	MACT	.065	-.382
25. Aggression anxiety	MANX	-.303	-.141
26. Success in aggression	MSAG	.835	.650
27. Popularity	MPOP	-.253	-.190
		$N = 451$	$N = 72$
		$.05; r = .09$	$.05; r = .232$
		$.01; r = .12$	$.01; r = .302$
		(two-tailed)	(two-tailed)

[a]From Stroo, 1970
[b]Interview variables taken from mothers' interviews only. Five variables were not included in this table because of different scoring procedures used in the American and Dutch samples.

preliminary versions of these procedures and included additional variables. The five factors extracted from the Dutch interviews, with their loadings, appear in Table 7.11 (lower limit for factor loadings was taken as .40).

Factor I in the Dutch interview with mothers is quite similar to the second factor in the American interviews with both mothers and fathers (see Appendix II.A, pp. 209–212). In the United States we labeled this factor as social mobility potential. In Holland it has been called a millieu factor. None of the other factors extracted from the Dutch interview were identical with the American factors, although there was considerable overlap. This is not surprising in terms of the differences noted above in the procedures used. That there was as much overlap as indicated in the two factor structures

TABLE 7.11

Ordered Factor Loadings — Dutch Mothers ($N = 72$)

No.	Code	Loading	Meaning
			FACTOR I
21	LMED	−770	High education level of mother
2	LMRO	−747	High social class
7	LMEA	−609	Mother has high educational aspirations for child
19	LMPU	−578	Low punishment for child's aggression by mother
10	LMWZ	−569	Mother low in aggression
12	LMPI	−534	Strong identification, child-mother
8	LMFP	−465	Mother has low score on F Scale acquiescence (no response-set)
22	LMRG	+446	Mother attends church often
			FACTOR II
27	MPOP	+853	Child is popular
25	MANX	+795	Child is anxious about aggression
24	MACT	+744	Child is not active in school
14	LMPD	+568	High parental disharmony
1	LMAG	+398	Mother is relatively old
			FACTOR III
26	MSAG	+836	Child is successful in aggression
23	MAGG	+727	Child is aggressive
28[a]	sex	−575	Boy
4	LMRE	−478	Mother is not restrictive
22	LMRG	−449	Mother does not attend church very often
5	LMRJ	+409	Child is rejected by mother
11	LMFS	−397	Mother has a low score on F Scale (nonauthoritarian)
			FACTOR IV
9	LMFR	+784	Child has a high frequency of aggression at home
18	LMCI	−648	Child tends not to confess transgressions
5	LMRJ	+543	Child is rejected by mother
13	LMJP	−500	Judged intensity of punishment by mother is low
6	LMGI	−486	Child does not feel guilty
6	LMRA	+475	Child recently aggressive at home
			FACTOR V
20	LMEN	+595	Late toilet-trained child
16	LMRA	+554	Child recently aggressive at home
6	LMGI	+490	Child feels guilty
1	LMAG	−456	Mother relatively young
3	LMRI	−446	Sex-appropriate roles in the family

[a]Because of restricted N, separate analyses were not done by sex of child. All subjects were pooled and sex was treated as another variable.

is an affirmation of the stability of these measures and relations across national samples.

It would be redundant to detail all the specific similarities in relation that obtained between aggression and parent variables in the two samples. As in the American study, the product-moment correlations masked more striking relations which became apparent when the predictor variables were categorized into three levels, low, medium, and high. Especially striking was the increased school aggression with increased rejection by the mother and with increased discrepancy in identification between mother and child (whether son or daughter). These results parallel the American findings exactly.

Although punishment for aggression reported by the mothers in Amsterdam did not relate to school aggression in the same increasing monotonic fashion as it did in Columbia County, the results with the judgment of punishment scale indicated that those Dutch mothers of boys who rated the listed punishments as not harsh for their children had sons who were more aggressive than those mothers who rated the punishments as indeed harsh for their children. Thus this indirect measure of punishment did relate for boys in the same way as in the United States. The judgment of punishment scale may render a more accurate reflection of the conditions of punishment in the home. (See p. 79 for an explanation of how the judgment of punishment scale serves as a subtle measure of punitiveness on the part of parents.) This leads us to question how accurate the Dutch mothers were in reporting on their own punishment behaviors. The intensity of punishment responses by parents in Columbia County are higher than in Amsterdam. The high punishers in Amsterdam have intensity of punishment scores equivalent to the moderate punishers in Columbia County and the moderate Dutch punishers are no more punitive than the low punishers in the United States (Stroo, 1970). However, it is possible, in view of the results with the judgment of punishment scale, that the Dutch mothers were not reporting punishment accurately or else did not interpret the response alternatives in the same way as the American parents.

The intercorrelations of the identification measures in the two samples are strikingly similar as noted in Table 7.12. The way these five measures cluster together in the same way in both samples reinforces the plausibility of the interpretations we made in Chapter 6 about identification and aggression.

Despite the similarity between the Dutch and American results, there were some interesting differences in terms of the interrelations of the peer-rating composite scores (see Table 7.13). Although the scores for popularity, activity level, and aggression anxiety formed a tight cluster in both samples, as did aggression and

TABLE 7.12

Intercorrelations among Identification Measures in Dutch Sample[a]

	LCI	LGI	LWZ	LRI	LPI
Confessing (LCI)	1.00				
Guilt (LGI)	.46 (.58)	1.00			
Parent's aggression (LWZ)	.01 (–.17)	–.21 (–.20)	1.00		
Role identification (LRI)	–.09 (–.12)	.01 (.01)	–.07 (.05)	1.00	
Profile identification (LPI)	–.04 (–.07)	–.08 (–.12)	.23 (.19)	.07 (.07)	1.00

[a]Comparable American correlations are in parentheses.

TABLE 7.13

Interrelation of Composite Scores in Dutch Sample[a]

	MAGG	MSAG	MANX	MPOP	MACT
MAGG	1.00				
MSAG	.65 (.84)	1.00			
MANX	–.14 (–.33)	.00 (–.24)	1.00		
MPOP	–.19 (–.28)	.27 (–.06)	.74 (.61)	1.00	
MACT	–.38 (.04)	–.08 (.13)	.71 (.64)	.72 (.55)	1.00

[a]Comparable American correlations are in parentheses.

success in aggression, differences between the two samples in the interrelations among the members of the clusters merit mention. In the American sample there was a negative relation between success in aggression and aggression anxiety, but no relation between success in aggression and popularity. In Holland, however, there was *no* relation between success in aggression and aggression anxiety and a positive relation between success in aggression and popularity. Furthermore, in Holland there was a negative relation between aggression and activity level, and in America there was no relation at all.

Our original interpretation of the American findings was quite modest. It was felt that whatever relations were found with either success in aggression or popularity were accounted for primarily by their high correlations with aggression and aggression anxiety respectively. However, the Dutch results, which differed from the American results, indicate that there is more here than method variance.

The lack of relation between aggression and aggression anxiety in the Dutch sample corroborates the interpretation made on the basis of the American findings that these two variables are largely independent of each other and do not constitute opposite ends of the same continuum.

Gender

As stated in Chapter 2, it has been a pervasive finding in research studies, to say nothing of ordinary, every-day observations, that boys are more aggressive than girls. Indeed, one of the first items of information about validity we obtained on both the peer-rating and aggression machine measures was that boys obtained higher scores in aggression than girls. Thus, in reporting our findings, results for boys and girls have usually been stated separately, as they have been for mothers and fathers, since mothers are almost routinely perceived, at least by children, as more loving and nurturant, less strict, and less apt to use physical punishment than fathers (Emmerich, 1955a,b; Kagan and Lemkin, 1960). Indeed Becker (1964) states, "It is becoming more and more apparent that separate evaluations of developmental issues for sex groups (parent and child) may be needed to encompass fully the individual differences" (p. 171).

Another aspect of gender that is important in determining the intensity of aggressive expression is the sex of the target of aggression. Although aggression is frequently reinforced within the young male peer culture (Hess and Handel, 1956), aggression against girls is regularly punished by parents and other socializing agents. Buss (1966b) found that college males are significantly less aggressive (in terms of intensity of shock administered) toward female targets than toward males. In fact, he found that gender difference in the target is even more important than gender difference in the aggressor, since females are more aggressive toward males than males are toward females. Thus the taboo against aggressing toward females exerts a more potent influence on the intensity of the aggression response than does the inclination of males generally to be more aggressive than females. This taboo is learned early in life and persists at least until college age, but an experiment by Hedges (1969) demonstrates that it is unlearned or disinhibited easily. Of his Ss, all of whom were males, half had a female target and half had a male target in the traditional aggression machine situation in which the S corrects the "errors" of a confederate by administration of noxious stimuli (in this case, loud sound). During the instruction phase, which was presented on videotape, half of the Ss saw a male model delivering high intensity noxious tones to a male target and half to a female target. A third manipulation had to do with the possibility of retaliation. Control groups who were tested with no video target and no retaliation manipulation did respond to either male or female targets. Hedges found that generally Ss obtained significantly higher scores when responding to a male target than to a female target in both the control and the experimental groups. However, those Ss who observed a female target being administered high intensity sounds did themselves administer significantly higher intensity sounds to female targets than those who observed a male target. Furthermore, those Ss who had an actual male target but observed a female target being corrected pushed buttons of significantly higher intensity than Ss who observed a male target. In fact, the group with the actual male and observed female target had the highest scores of all. It seems, then, that if it is permissible in a specific situation to be aggressive toward a female target, it is indeed permissible to be aggressive toward a male. Observation of a male model responding aggressively toward a female seems to be a sufficient condition for disinhibiting a long-standing prohibition against being aggressive toward females.

With his random selection of Ss, Hedges did not replicate Edwards's (1967) findings of disinhibition of the aggression response when there is assurance of no retaliation. However, in a post hoc analysis, he selected Ss who were high and low aggressive according to Edwards' criteria, based on initial responses on the aggression machine, and corroborated her findings exactly: low aggressive Ss who are assured that there is no possibility of retaliation respond as aggressively as high aggressive Ss.

Summary

An investigation of sociocultural variables was included in our study of learning and aggression because it has been demonstrated that learning conditions are influenced by such factors as social class membership, education of parents, attitudes, mobility, ethnicity, cross-national differences, and gender. We used fathers' occupations as a single index of social class and found that upper-class children tend to be rated more aggressive by their peers than lower-class children. With social class controlled, the relation between fathers' punishment and aggression becomes more marked, upper-class children who are punished severely for aggression are the most aggressive. There is a positive relation between mobility orientation of fathers and aggression scores of their sons. However, education of fathers is inversely related to aggression scores, with children of better educated parents being less aggressive. We examined reasons for the difference between occupation and education in direction of relation to aggression, and we questioned the appropriateness of combining both into a single index of social class. Another surprising finding is that lower-class parents are less permissive of their children's aggression toward peers than are upper- and middle-class parents. However, children's aggression toward parents themselves is severely punished by parents of all classes. There is no difference in application of physical versus psychological punishments among classes. Ethnicity (number of generations that the parents' families have been in the United States) proved to be an important variable. Children of high-ethnic parents tend to be less aggressive at home and more aggressive in school than children of low-ethnic parents. Especially aggressive are children whose fathers are high ethnics and whose mothers are low ethnics.

A small-scale replication of the survey study was done in Amsterdam, Holland, with surprisingly similar results in the relation of school aggression as rated by peers to information furnished by parents about reinforcers, instigators, and identification variables. This attests to the stability and generality of our original findings.

Although some of the findings reported in this chapter support traditional notions about the effect of social status on aggressive behavior, most of them do not, and it seems that a reevaluation of many of these ideas is essential. The relation between aggression and sociocultural variables is consistently and dependably greater for boys than for girls. We anticipated this on the basis of some of the analyses in Chapter 6 dealing with role modeling. Chapter 8 will deal further with these factors. An additional factor briefly considered in this chapter was the gender of the target of aggression. The early learned inhibition against aggressing toward females is easily unlearned as demonstrated in experiments in which models performed aggressive behaviors toward females.

THE LEARNING CONDITIONS
OF AGGRESSION

Chapter 8

An understanding of how children learn to be aggressive may be achieved from an assimilation and integration of the antecedent conditions that, in the foregoing chapters, have been shown to relate to aggression. These antecedents were rationally derived from current theories of the development of aggression. However, which are the antecedents and which are the consequents cannot really be determined on the basis of relational study. There is no question that the environment that supports and changes a child's behavior is at least partly shaped by that child. As we organize our findings, we shall examine this reciprocal influence.

The results detailed in Chapters 4 through 7 indicate that each set of variables presumed to measure instigation, reinforcement, identification, and sociocultural status is indeed related to aggression. However, these sets of variables do not operate independently of each other. We can now evaluate and perhaps reformulate the four classes of variables in order to simplify the results and to make them more meaningful as well as to help resolve the contradictions that emerge when comparing findings from other studies. Radke-Yarrow et al. note in a recent volume (1968) that previous researchers in parent-child interaction tended to deal with one variable at a time. Thus studies are not comparable since concomitantly varying factors are not controlled. In our attempt to see the relations among the variables we have been trying to get some idea of what specifically happens to the child in concrete ways, to delineate the specifics of the learning conditions for aggression.

Instigation

The least equivocal, although not the most powerful, of our find....
was the relation between instigation as reported by parents and
school aggression. This was an operationalization of the frustration-
aggression paradigm and it worked exactly as hypothesized. We
selected three variables that we believed would add to children's
frustration at home and thus serve to heighten their aggressive responding — rejection and lack of nurturance by each parent and
disharmony between them. We selected these variables in the arm-
chair; other factors that could also be presumed to be frustrators
might have related even better to the criterion. The finding,
however, was uncomplicated: the higher the total instigation score,
the higher the aggression, regardless of whether it comes from mothers, fathers, or both. There is no interaction between mothers' and
fathers' instigation or between instigation and any of the other variables we measured in predicting to school aggression.

As outlined by Berkowitz (1962), we can assume that the frustration caused by the rejecting, nonnurturant, disharmonious behavior
of parents produces anger, an emotional drive state that increases
the probability of aggressive behavior. This response of anger to
frustration is innate, according to Berkowitz, and supplies the energy
behind the aggressive behavior. The effect of learning is to modify
the innate relation between anger and aggression. However, in these
data the relation of instigation to aggression is direct and uncomplicated by identification, sociocultural factors, or punishment. The
total effect of instigation adds to the total effect of punishment and
helps improve prediction to school aggression.

However, in comparing mothers and fathers, we found that instigation by fathers is a better predictor to aggression than punishment
and for mothers the opposite is true. This finding is consonant with
the theorizing of Sears and others on a developmental theory of identification (Levin and Sears, 1956; Mussen and Distler, 1959; Payne
and Mussen, 1956; P. Sears, 1953). A child's identification with his
father, according to this view, depends on a positive, affectionate interaction between them. It can be assumed that children who do not
identify with their fathers tend not to internalize their fathers' interdictions. Our own data show that when identification between
fathers and sons is maximal, punishment for aggression acts as an inhibitor of this behavior. In other words, children who identify closely
with their fathers learn the rules well and their behavior is more
likely to generalize from one situation to the other. However, children who do not have this affectionate, accepting relationship with

145

their fathers will probably not be socialized as readily, will respond to their fathers as if they were instigators, and will tend to be aggressive, especially in situations where their fathers are not likely to administer punishment (i.e., the classroom). This close identification with their fathers characterizes only a minority of the boys in the sample. Thus fathers' instigative behavior toward their children is an important factor in the occurrence of aggression in school for both boys and girls in this sample.

What is there about instigation that would tend to increase aggressive responding? The instigation score, it will be remembered, taps parental rejection, lack of nurturance, and parental disharmony. A high rejection score, reflecting many complaints of the parent about the child, suggests (1) that the child is not receiving rewards from the parent for prosocial (nonaggressive) behaviors, (2) that most of the child's present responding is below the parent's threshold for emitting rewards, and (3) that the parent has a view of proper child care as *correcting* the child rather than "catching the child being good" (Madsen, Becker, Thomas, and Rules, 1968). As a result, the child's prosocial (nonaggressive) behaviors have not developed as a means of controlling ("reaching") his parent; rather, only antisocial (aggressive) behaviors reach the parent. Adding to the effects of rejection, a high lack-of-nurturance score, reflecting the parent's lack of sensitivity (responsiveness) to the child, suggests that the parent does not detect signals from the child unless they are very loud, disturbing, disruptive, aversive, and so forth — namely, aggressive. It suggests that the child may well receive rewards and/or attention from the parent only after such behaviors; thus the conditions are here for the systematic strengthening of aggressive behaviors by often negative-appearing parental responses. Furthermore, a high parental disharmony score, reflecting the parent's distraction with the marital discord, suggests even more insensitivity to the child's small prosocial behaviors. (In addition, of course, the child is threatened by loss of parental support.) The parent with such a high instigation score not only is raising a child who is more controlled by avoiding and escaping negative consequences than by seeking positive ones, but also may well be himself a person whose behaviors are largely under aversive control.

Reinforcement

A reinforcement interpretation of the development of aggression is consistent with our data on the child's current level of aggressive and related behaviors in the home and in the school and on the consequences to the child following his emission of these behaviors. The current level of aggressive behavior at home is relevant to the level of aggression at school. This relation is substantial and dependable for girls in general. For boys, it depends upon the agreement between their two parents regarding the amount of home aggression. Those few boys who are consistent in their aggression at home (reflected by perfect agreement between ratings of fathers and mothers) are also more consistent in their aggression at home and at school. The majority of the boys, however, are much less consistent in their aggression at home and at school.

Punishment as a contingent response to aggression at home has been theoretically troublesome in past survey studies. Generally, these studies have yielded results that indicate that increased contingent punishment is associated with increased aggression rather than with suppression of the aggressive behavior. However, in our survey study we found what has usually been seen only in the direct observation laboratory — decreased aggressive behavior with increased, contingent punishment. But this was found in our analysis of punishment only when we controlled for identification. The highly identified child in a survey study behaves as a child in the laboratory. The importance of identification as a control variable confirms Sears' point of view that, as we indicated earlier, influenced us in selecting variables and building measures. Below we explore *why* high identification makes it likely that a survey subject will respond as a laboratory subject, i.e., will inhibit punished behavior and increase rewarded behavior. The large proportion of children in our survey sample did not have high identification scores, and they yielded results that are typical of survey children: the more punishment for aggression, the more aggression. Thus a survey study that does not control for amount of identification may indeed conclude that punishment is "ineffectual over a long term as a technique for eliminating the kind of behavior toward which it is directed" (Sears et al., 1957, p. 484).

Also important is the school situation in which the child emits aggressive and related behaviors and in which consequences of these behaviors occur. Behavior theory would suggest that the school situation is actually more relevant to school aggression than is the generalization of effects from the home situation. This is so even though we may make useful predictions from home to school aggression for girls in general and for those boys who show enough within-individual consistency of home aggression. The level of school aggression has been shown to be relevant to a variety of other school aggression measures, and the results of these studies thus make it possible to assert that this criterion measure is indeed a measure of the response class of school aggression.

When we examined behaviors that are related to school aggression, such as boys' interests in playing feminine games, we found, as might be expected, that such interests are associated with lower school aggression. This can be taken as an example of interference with the aggression response class by a nonaggression response class, i.e., the boys engage in activities that do not call for overt aggressive behavior. Other possible examples of this class of incompatible nonaggression behaviors are aggression anxiety, popularity, school achievement, and confessing.

It is now possible to examine the contingent consequences of school aggression. Aggression anxiety, which is negatively related to school aggression, may well be a behavioral result of punishment for aggression. It has been shown in the laboratory that Ss who exhibit a lower level of aggression on a pretest exhibit an increase in aggression in a subsequent permissive situation in which retaliation (punishment) for aggression is not likely. The reinforcement of aggression at school was studied with the success in aggression measure. Although this measure is very method-bound to aggression, the relation of success in aggression to aggression is consistent with a reinforcement interpretation of aggression. That the lowered aggression level of females is a function of lack of reinforcement for aggressive behavior is seen in the results of Hokanson and Edelman (1966) who found that female Ss did not demonstrate the quickened reduction of physiological arousal after the opportunity to counteraggress against a confederate. Such quickened reduction of heart rate and blood pressure to basal levels was routinely seen in male Ss, however.

In summary, aggression of consistent children (girls and some boys) is general in home and school. For highly identified boys, punishment of aggression in the home suppresses aggression in school. In general, the level of aggression at school is a function of the aggression tendencies and nonaggression tendencies. The aggression tendencies are increased by contingent reinforcements received in the school situation. The nonaggression tendencies can be increased by punishment of aggression and reinforcement of nonaggression, at least for boys who are highly identified with their fathers. Girls and some boys are quite consistent in their level of aggression in various places. Boys tend to be most discriminating in their aggression, especially those with low peer-rated aggression scores. Under proper conditions, high aggressive boys are also responsive to local situational controls. Some of the controlling stimuli are threat or anticipation of retaliation. For the low aggressive boy these act as a deterrent; for the high, these act as an incentive. Girls do not seem to be responsive to cues of retaliation.

Identification

Internalization

Both the psychoanalytic and reinforcement theories of behavior would predict that identification serves either to inhibit aggressive behavior or to encourage nonaggressive behavior. Although a number of measures of identification were employed in our study, only three entered into meaningful relations with other variables as predicted from the then current theories of identification. Actually, two of these measures focused on children's internalization of parental standards and pertained to the readiness of children to express guilt or to confess when they violate parental interdictions. The third measure was believed to be an assessment of both internalization and role modeling. Concerning the measure of guilt, a simple inverse relation was predicted between parents' reports of this behavior and the peer-rating measure of aggression in the school situation. Tentative support for this prediction emerged from the data, but only for girls. Again, for the confessing measure of identification, psychoanalytic and reinforcement theories would predict that when children of their own accord confess to acts the parents have trained them to believe are wrong, such behavior would be associated with low aggression in the school context. Indeed we found this prediction to be borne out in both parents' reports for girls but only in mothers' reports for boys. Thus, although there was some tendency for the predicted relation between aggression and internalization to hold for boys, this relation was much more evident for girls. Girls seem more prone to internalize parental standards and in this sense are more readily socialized. This observation is consonant with our finding that girls are significantly less aggressive than boys. To restate this idea, boys may be more aggressive than girls because their ability to identify with parents is not as great. This difference will be discussed in the next section.

The relations examined so far are fairly straightforward: the tendency on the part of children to internalize parental standards is associated with lower peer-ratings of aggression, and this tendency occurs most prominently for girls. A related phenomenon is manifested in the association of parents' expression of aggression and children's internalization of standards: internalization on the part of children seems to be enhanced when parents evince low aggression. Thus both mothers and fathers tend to report less confessing behavior for their children when mothers are high in aggression. Under the same condition, mothers are also inclined to report fewer expres-

149

sions of guilt on the part of their daughters. Since the relation obtains only for mothers, salience of the mother appears paramount in fostering or suppressing internalization.

The third measure of identification focused on discrepancy in self-descriptions between parent and child. We hypothesized that the more discrepant the child's view of himself from the parent's view of himself, the more the child would exhibit aggression in the classroom. Marked support was adduced for this hypothesis: the greater the discrepancy between self-ratings of parents and children, the greater the peer-ratings of classroom aggression. This measure of identification is also significantly related to parents' own aggression: fathers and mothers tending toward high aggression have children who are inclined not to be identified with them in the sense discussed and who tend to be more aggressive in school. Simply stated, we can conclude from these data that children tend not to identify, in terms of internalization of standards, with highly aggressive parents.

In summary, the child who has failed to internalize parental proscriptions tends to be rated as aggressive by his peers in the classroom context, a finding particularly prevalent for boys. Boys were found to be more aggressive than girls and may be so for this very reason. That children seem unable to identify with highly aggressive parents may be the counterpart of the relation showing children with low identification to be more aggressive in the classroom. From these data it seems that children who are highly identified with their parents internalize their proscriptions and obey and that children who are not identified with their parents tend to copy their parents' aggressive behavior, i.e., they "do as they do, not as they say." This becomes more apparent in the next section.

Role Modeling

As indicated above, when children's identification with socializing agents was taken into account, the results with the punishment scale were of two types. For a small group of male subjects who were closely identified with their fathers, i.e., rated themselves in the same way their fathers rated themselves, aggressive behavior was inhibited when it was punished by the fathers. However, for the male subjects who were only moderately or very little identified with their fathers (and who comprised the majority of the subjects), heightened punishment was associated with increased aggression in school.[1] For mothers

---

[1] It was stated above that the highly identified survey child behaves as the usual laboratory subject. He tries very hard to please his parents, to figure out what they want him to do, and then behaves accordingly. This is the way the usual *S* also responds. He is met at the laboratory door by a sympathetic,

and girls the latter was usually the case. A likely interpretation of this result is that the punitive parent furnishes an aggressive role model for the child to copy and thus has a disinhibiting effect on the occurrence of aggressive behavior. This is especially true since it was shown that primarily the parents who are likely to use physical punishment contribute to this finding.

Supporting this notion of role modeling is the significant relation between the aggressive behavior of the parent and the child's aggressive behavior in school, when social status as measured by the father's occupation is controlled. This is a within-sex relation, holding only for fathers compared with sons and mothers compared with daughters. It thus seems to be a more meaningful measure of parent and child role modeling than the discrepancy between self-ratings. The latter measure may be more properly understood, perhaps, as a measure of internalization, and, indeed, in its interaction with punishment it does seem to operate in that way. The discrepancy between self-ratings is not a direct measure of imitation of evaluations and proscriptions; rather, it is a direct measure of imitation of self-described, expressive motor behaviors. However, we may hope that a parent-child pair that shares such self-descriptions would also share moral standards, a hope justified by studies such as that of Gewirtz and Stingle (1968). In any case, discrepancy in self-ratings does function as a measure of imitation of moral judgments.

As indicated in previous chapters, Bandura and his associates (1961) were among the first to demonstrate the disinhibiting effect of an aggressive model on the occurrence of aggressive behavior. Bandura contends (1962b) that the observation of responses of a class labeled aggressive may lead the child to display these or other responses of the same general category if the behaviors already exist in the child's repertoire. Children exposed to filmed aggressive models subsequently displayed not only specifically imitative, novel responses (i.e., for the child) but also a relatively large number of aggressive responses that had not been performed by the model (Bandura et al., 1961). However, Meyerson (1966), in a study noted in the discussion of reinforcement, found that when he controlled for similarity between film and post-film settings and also for the subjects' characteristic aggression level, he did not obtain such generality. Exposure to a model and to a confederate in an aggressive interaction different from the post-film setting did not lead to increased aggressive responding. Only when the model performed the specific aggressive actions that

---

warm figure who promises him rewards such as candy and interesting playthings and activities if he will play games with the E. To get these rewards he "internalizes the standards" of E immediately.

were called for in the post-film setting did observation of the model's behavior lead to increased aggression on the part of the subjects. Specific behaviors are learned. The permissiveness that is inherent in the observation situation in which the models perform the behaviors without being punished extends only to those specific behaviors.

A study by Williams (1966) on the semantic mediation of motor aggression indirectly supports the contention that specific behaviors are learned and/or are evoked and that mere exposure to aggression does not arouse a broad class of behaviors labeled aggression. He induced an attitude of hostility in one group of third-grade subjects by having them associate one nonsense syllable with a series of hostile words and another nonsense syllable with nonhostile, inactive words. A second group received a similar number of hostile and passive word pairings but learned the correct pairing by the color in which the words were typed. Thus both groups were exposed to hostile stimuli, but hostility was the crucial concept for the first group only. A third group received pairings of active, nonhostile words with one nonsense syllable and passive words with the other. The subjects then used the Iowa Aggression Machine (see Chapter 3) to correct another (nonexistent) subject's mistakes. On half the trials mistakes were preceded by one nonsense syllable and on the remaining trials by the other nonsense syllable. The subjects in the first group pressed significantly higher numbered buttons (made responses which were more aggressive) when the preceding nonsense syllable was the one associated with the hostile words. Children in the other two groups did not respond differentially to the two nonsense syllables. It was necessary to learn a specific hostile attitude that mediated the aggressive response. Exposure to a similar number of hostile stimuli or learning a high activity concept did not affect aggressive responding.

Thus, although Bandura and also Aronfreed (1969) stress the importance of the model's behavior in eliciting a general class of behaviors labeled as aggression, not merely the imitation of his specific behaviors, these laboratory studies emphasize the importance of learning specific habits. Unfortunately, the survey data do not help in clarifying this disagreement. The attitudes assessed by the Personal Opinion Inventory do not duplicate the ten aggressive items included in the peer-rating index of aggression. The significant relation between the two measures, when social status is controlled, may or may not be a function of specific behaviors. At one time in the history of the project (see Appendix II), we attempted to construct a measure of parent aggression that would parallel the items in the peer-rating procedure but this was unsuccessful and was dropped when the Walters and Zak (1959) procedure became available.

What do we know now about identification and aggression? The child who is to become identified with a parent (in the sense discussed here) develops an imitative repertoire of behaviors, including evaluative reactions to his own behaviors. To progressively match his behaviors to his parent's, the parent's behaviors have to be distinctively present and the child's behaviors that copy them have to be reinforced. In the ordinary course of events this requires that the parent be a source of reinforcement so that not only can he strengthen imitative behaviors of the child, but also the presence of parent-like behaviors in the child will acquire positive properties. Although in principle it is not important that the child imitate only those parent behaviors for which the parent is reinforced (Williams, 1970), it is likely that only those reinforced behaviors will be supported when the child emits them. A parent may serve as a strong or influencing model even when infrequently present. Thus a father who possesses a clear image of his own identity, e.g., occupational, will by his consistent behavior provide a model that pervades the child's life space.

Sociocultural Status

Several sociocultural variables were demonstrated to have both a direct and an indirect bearing on expression of aggression in the classroom. A consideration of the simple relation between social class and aggression illustrates that children of upper-class fathers are more aggressive than children of lower-class fathers. In addition to this fundamental relation, however, social class serves to sharpen what would otherwise appear to be weak or obscure relations between other variables and aggression. For example, when the intensity of fathers' punishment is stratified according to their social status — considering both variables jointly — upper-class fathers who punish severely for aggression have highly aggressive children as rated by their peers. Further analysis of these data indicates that the intensity of punishment has little effect on the manifestation of aggression of boys in the lower social status category. In the upper class, however, severe punishment of boys and girls by their fathers is associated with marked aggression in the classroom.

In addition to this differential in the manifestation of aggression among the social status categories, a differential in the intensity of parental punishment for aggression was also discovered. Although a generalization may be made from sociological studies that aggression is condoned and encouraged by lower-class parents, our data seem to indicate that just the opposite is true. Lower- as compared to upper-class fathers punish their sons more severely for the expression of aggression. Similarly, girls whose parents are in a lower social status category are punished more severely by both parents for aggression than girls in high social status categories. For our population in general, therefore, lower-class parents prove to be much less permissive about aggression than middle- and upper-class parents. If punishment and classroom aggression are directly related, as is strongly suggested by the results of our study, then these data pertaining to punishment, aggression, and social class membership present an apparent contradiction.[2] Specifically, although lower-class children are the objects of more intensive punishment, the upper-class children are most aggressive. Resolution of this paradox may lie in the observation that severe punishment has a different kind of effect when administered by upper-class as compared with lower-class parents. Classroom aggression scores of lower-class children show considerably less variability as a function of intensity of parental punishment than those of upper-class children. In the latter case, as already mentioned, high intensity punishment is related to especially high ratings of aggression by peers. Furthermore, when social class is controlled, the parents' own aggressive behavior is directly related to school aggression. This is especially true for lower-class boys.

Another aspect of social class and its influence on aggressive behavior is the context effect of the social class membership of children in the classroom. In this sense, social class may be viewed as an ecological variable: classroom aggression increases as the proportion of upper-status children in the class decreases. Moreover, this ecological effect on aggression differs for different social classes. For upper-status children, aggression tends to diminish with diminishing upper-status concentration in the classroom. For low-status children, however, aggression increases as the concentration of upper-status children in the classroom decreases. It seems that for upper-status children, other children of the same class serve as a goad to aggression, whereas for lower-status children, the classroom predominance of upper-status children serves as a deterrent to the expression of aggression. Perhaps when children of contrasting social classes are merged in the same classroom, the unknown or alien quality of the other social class's behavior governs the expression of aggression. Also relating to aggression is the rural occupational background of the child's father: the more the classroom is saturated with children whose fathers have farm-centered occupations, the greater is the aggression among the other social class categories.

Fathers' mobility orientation is another sociocultural variable that is directly related to their sons' aggression. The more fathers report willingness to make personal sacrifices in order to enhance their eco-

[2] It should be pointed out that these are findings based on two measures obtained from large groups of subjects and do not indicate anything about the relation between punishment and aggression in individual boys and girls. The reader is referred to the controversy over the interpretation of ecological correlations (Duncan and Davis, 1953; Lazarsfeld and Menzel, 1961; Robinson, 1950).

nomic opportunities, the more aggressive their sons are viewed in the classroom by peers. One might speculate that the role modeling variant of identification is in evidence when boys copy their fathers' aggressive behavior that might be entailed in the process of economic striving and the boys are in turn aggressive in the classroom.

When the education and occupations of fathers are considered jointly, the relation of these variables to classroom aggression is in opposite directions. As already noted, fathers with higher occupations (that is, higher social class) have more aggressive children; but the higher the fathers' education, the less their sons are inclined to express aggression in the classroom. The result of the combination of high-status occupation but low education may very well be the kind of striving behavior so often termed aggressive in the world of work. That is, these fathers have achieved an occupational end or income considerably beyond that to be expected on the basis of their educational achievement. Hypothetically, their aggressive behavior has served to compensate for the insufficiency in their formal education. These data again can be parsimoniously embraced by the concept of role modeling in which fathers serve as aggressive models available for imitation. This is the same interpretation as for the relation between high mobility orientation and peer-rated aggression.

Ethnicity is the final sociocultural variable to be considered. A rather marked relation obtained between fathers' ethnic background and their sons' school aggression. This finding may be interpreted by either of two hypotheses, one involving role modeling and the other displacement. In the former, ethnic fathers, because of their punitive behavior in the home, provide aggressive role models for their children, particularly their sons. Such behavior is imitated by boys (Bandura and Walters, 1963) and manifested in the high peer-ratings of aggression they receive in school. In the displacement hypothesis, ethnic fathers are intolerant of aggression in the home, and behavior that is not permitted expression in the home is manifested in the school situation. In either case, it seems that ethnic fathers have brought to this country the authoritarian child-rearing methods so aptly described by Schaffner (1948) and by Adorno, Frenkel-Brunswick, Levinson, and Sanford (1950). Explicit in the latter study is the finding that children of foreign-born parents reported a harsh and threatening type of home discipline, experienced as arbitrary and authoritarian. Contributing to the ethnicity-aggression relation is the combination of a high-ethnic father and low-ethnic mother. Under this condition the peer-rating measure of aggression is very much elevated. Perhaps the juxtaposition of the Old World values of the father and the egalitarian values of the American mother exacerbates the ordinary marital conflicts and is reflected in the deviant (i.e., aggressive) behavior of their children in the classroom.

Differences in Socialization between Boys and Girls

The reader has probably noticed in this welter of findings that boys and girls respond differently to what goes on inside and outside the home. An examination of the pattern of differences reveals consistencies that provide an opportunity to generate hypotheses that should be tested at least in a replication. Differences between boys and girls in patterns of predictor scores are of interest. Moreover, boys score consistently and dependably higher than girls on the school aggression measure that consists of items tapping verbal and indirect expression of aggression as well as direct, physical acting-out.

Two interview predictor scores that relate to girls' school aggression scores but not to boys' are the composite home aggression score and the composite instigation score. In addition, the punishment for home aggression score relates to school aggression more for girls than for boys. These three scores that are distinctively relevant to girls' aggression at school are derived from mothers' and fathers' interview responses about events which take place at home. However, the parent interview scores which are distinctly relevant to boys' school aggression are not responses to questions about events at home. Three scores that are relevant for boys and not for girls are fathers' occupational status, fathers' mobility orientation, and fathers' ethnicity. Two other scores that are more relevant for boys than for girls are fathers' educational attainment and various combinations of fathers' occupational status and educational attainment. These five scores are concerned with the position of the boys' families in society and may represent various aspects of the models that fathers make available for their sons to copy.

The difference in pattern may be broadly stated: boys' school aggression is affected by those aspects of their fathers that interest sociologists; girls' school aggression is affected by those aspects of their mothers' and fathers' home-making characteristics that interest child psychologists.

The cause of the failure of boys' home aggression to be relevant to their school aggression, except for those 17 out of 284 cases for whom the two parents agree completely, may be that we have built a measuring device that is appropriate for parents of girls but not for parents of boys. One may try to guess why the measure does not relate to boys as it does to girls. Could it be that the items evoke two conflicting desirability tendencies for those parents describing their boys' aggression? On the one hand, aggression is an undesirable behavior in general; on the other hand, aggression is a desirable masculine

156

behavior. The rating of boys' home aggression may be confused by their parents' ambivalence. Those parents describing their daughters' aggression have no such conflict since aggression is undesirable for people in general and for girls in particular.

Another interpretation may be based on the fact that only 17 of 284 boys aggress consistently in their fathers' presence, in their mothers' presence, and in their peers' presence. The remaining 267 boys are such specialists in aggression that ratings from one parent do not relate to the ratings of either the other parent or the peers. Thus the boys respond aggressively in discriminating ways.

This lack of consistency may well be relevant to the second major difference between the scores of boys and girls — the higher aggression scores of boys. To understand this and the greater inconsistency of boys' aggression we shall explore here some relevant boy-girl differences. Which behaviors of boys are part of or facilitate aggression? Boys tend to develop large muscle skills, such as pushing, shoving, throwing, lifting, running, etc., the better to aggress physically. With more reinforceable aggressive skills, boys' aggressive repertories increase and differentiate. This differentiation of aggression may be another term for a reduction in the consistency of aggression on different occasions, in different places, with different people, and under different conditions. Which behaviors of girls are part of or facilitate nonaggression? Girls tend to develop small muscle skills, such as reading, writing, speaking, etc., the better to nonaggress. With more reinforceable, nonaggressive skills, the girls' nonaggressive repertories increase. It is interesting that, as mentioned in Chapter 6, boys who prefer feminine games and activities (small muscle skills) have low aggression scores.

The differential learning conditions influencing boys and girls seem to be long-standing in their effect. Differences in responses attributable to early social learning are seen in college-age men and women. Edwards (1967) found that her female Ss were not affected by the possibility that their teammates might retaliate against them for making aggressive responses (see Chapter 4, pp. 86–87). Girls do not seem to be sensitive to cues of possible retaliation in the same way that their male counterparts are. Similarly, Hokanson and Edelman (1966) found that male college-student Ss who were permitted to counteraggress to an interpersonal provocation showed a relatively rapid return of autonomic processes, such as systolic blood pressure, to pre-frustration level accompanying the expression of aggression. This did not occur with their female Ss who presumably had not learned that counteraggression is an appropriate response that can either make one "feel better" or be effective in terminating noxious social stimulation.

157

Males and females have different cue values as targets of aggression. This also results from differential learning conditions. Boys are frequently rewarded, especially by their peers but also by their parents, for aggressing toward other males. However, they are punished for aggressing toward females. The effects of this differential training are also long-lasting since inhibitions against aggressing toward females are found in both young children and college-age subjects. However, this inhibition can easily be unlearned, as demonstrated by experiments in which Ss observe a female target being punished by a male model (see p. 142).

The foregoing hypotheses search for possible sources of the difference in amount of aggression in boys and girls and the difference in patterns of relations between aggression and other variables. We should point out that a definitive study has not yet been done.

Summary and Theoretical Conclusions

The results support our initial theoretical position that four major classes of parent-child relation characteristics are important in the development of aggressive behavior in children: instigation, reinforcement, identification, and sociocultural status.[3] We have even more confidence in our findings now that they have been largely replicated in a study in another country, Holland. However, while the major outlines of these classifications remain, the details of the theory become more explicit. We may now specify details in each of the four constructs and begin to describe the joint action of any two of them in producing more or less aggression. We may also speculate about the combined action of three or more of these constructs.

The data generated by this research may be encompassed within any of a number of theoretical models. Because of their simplicity and because they seem most appropriate for describing how behavior develops in a natural environment, we shall cast our conclusions and also the recommendations for child-rearing in the following chapter in behavior analytic terms (Ferster and Perrott, 1968; Skinner, 1968). It is not an accident that our results fit a Skinnerian model, even though our original notions and measures derived from a Hull-Spence orientation. Terms derived from both systems will be used, which is testimony to the relevance of the two systems to the same set of events. Since our methodology was essentially behaviorally based, it permitted the test of this relevance.

In the production of aggressive behavior, instigation (one aspect

[3] Although the data themselves are largely correlational and do not imply causality, they are consistent with theoretical positions that do assert such cause and effect relations.

of a parent-child relationship) is of paramount importance. Our view of the construct instigation is, of course, limited to the measures of it that we tried. At the same time, however, our experience with these measures and familiarity with their content suggest that a child's aggression in school increases as he receives a low level of positive response (e.g., nurturance) from his parents. A low level of positive parental response to a child not only increases his rate of aggression at school but also reduces the possibility that his parents use punishment effectively as an inhibitor of aggressive behavior. Instigation can first be viewed as a low density of reinforcement. The child who is rejected (whose parents complain about his behaviors and accomplishments), who receives little nurturance from his parents, and who is witness to their disharmony (thus diminishing his confidence in the stability of his home) is receiving little reinforcement to begin with. Only with an ordinarily adequate density of reinforcement can a contingent punishment have the desired effect. Thus reinforcement of behaviors is directly affected by instigation since if the child has little to lose by continuing in the behaviors his parents profess to discourage, he will tend not to change them. This assumes that the child whose interaction with his parents is such that he is instigated to aggression is already in an unpleasant situation and the punishment can hardly be effective in inhibiting his aggressive behavior.

The second aspect of instigation is that the child is forced to control his parents through aversive, antisocial, and perhaps aggressive means. The parents deliver few reinforcements to their child since (1) they tend to concentrate on the child's deficiencies that "need correcting," and (2) they are not supportive of those aspects of the child's behavior that could be built into desirable, prosocial, nonaggressive behaviors. The attention from the parents is sparse, negative, and contingent upon the child's negative behaviors.

Instigation is thus a chronic state of affairs that reduces the income from the parents, reduces or reverses the effectiveness of punishers, builds aggressive behaviors and weakens nonaggressive behaviors in the child, and reduces the likelihood of the development of identification with the instigating parent.

Reinforcement is even more complex than instigation. It includes a number of variables: contingent punishment for aggression, amount of child's aggression in the home, success in aggression at school, avoidance of retaliation (aggression anxiety), and the child's entire repertory of behaviors, both aggressive and nonaggressive. Reinforcement thus deals with temporally contingent positive and negative responses to the child's aggression and lack of aggression in different settings. As previously stated, instigation and reinforcement are related. The parent who generally provides reinforcement is in a better position than one who does not provide reinforcement to weaken a behavior by contingently reducing the child's reinforcements. The parent who provides little general reinforcement may be chagrined to find that the punishment he delivers after a nondesired behavior by his child is ineffective in reducing that behavior. A closer look reveals that the child may well be copying the parent's punishing behavior. This is so because a parent who does not regularly present positive reinforcement to the child (especially for completing prosocial, nonaggressive behaviors) has little opportunity to withhold these responses as a form of punishment. Instead he is left with only noxious stimuli to present as punishment; his repertory of reinforcing behaviors is limited. Thus the model the child copies will be, by definition, an aggressive one. The failure of the parents to be viewed by the child as a dispenser of a wide variety of reinforcers affects not only punishment specifically but also what has been called identification; and punishment is effective in reducing aggressive behavior only for the highly identified child. Those few children who have developed similarity to a parent on stylistic, noninstrumental, or expressive behaviors get the message when punished. The remainder seem to copy the punishment itself. In fact, those children who have not developed such similarity to either parent (approximately one-fifth of the total sample) exhibit very high aggression. However, when we consider another facet of identification, internalization of parental proscriptions, we find that highly identified children so defined manifest lowered aggression.

As noted above, highly relevant to the concept of reinforcement is the behavioral repertoire of the child that delimits at any given time which behaviors are available for subsequent reinforcement. If a behavior is not emitted, it cannot, of course, be reinforced, especially if a parent does not approach the child at the child's level, i.e., build in whatever positive behavior the child emits. Constitutional and experiential factors largely determine the range of behaviors available to a particular child and probably account in great part for the difference in aggression level between boys and girls. Girls tend to be consistent in the amount of aggression they emit under a variety of conditions. But boys, in addition to emitting more aggression generally, tend to be more responsive to the specific conditions, displaying aggression here but not there and avoiding aggression now but not then. Those boys who avoid aggression will often avoid it less if the threat of retaliation is reduced. Girls in general are not sensitive to cues of retaliation: since they have learned a wider repertory of behaviors with which to respond to instigation, they are not as likely to counteraggress.

Various sociocultural factors operate both to ameliorate and intensify the relation between aggression on the one hand and instigation, reinforcement, and identification on the other hand. These social variables are not as susceptible to manipulation and control as the other three. However, it is our expectation that the behaviors and the environmental conditions that ultimately define sociocultural status can be understood and therefore manipulated and controlled similarly and to the same extent as the other three classes of variables shown to influence aggressive behavior in eight-year-old children. In the concluding chapter we consider the implications of these findings for the control (up or down) of aggressive behavior in children.

IMPLICATIONS FOR CHILD-REARING

Chapter 9

From the material in the preceding eight chapters a number of implications for child-rearing practices regarding aggression emerge. If, indeed, one desired to produce a child with either high or low aggressive qualities, then the foregoing findings could well serve as a mold — albeit incomplete. That is, our data strongly suggest that by manipulating the environment in which a child develops, the outcome with respect to aggressiveness would be reasonably assured. Perhaps the parallel most appropriate at this juncture is with Emile, Rousseau's fictional child (1762), who was raised in a manner conforming to a predetermined outcome. Rousseau of course subscribed to the notion that a child is born tabula rasa and is thus completely malleable. Well aware of genetic and constitutional influences on a child's development, we eschew such an assumption. At the same time, however, our data do not lend support to the contention of Camus (1955) that because one has no choice of family and little of environment, life is essentially absurd. Because the individual has no control over the conditions that shape his life, Camus believes life is devoid of meaning. The findings of our study suggest that one's approach to life, largely shaped by experience, may very well be a modifiable condition. Specifically, parental response to a child's aggressiveness or lack of aggressiveness may appear to be an immutable condition so that behavior begets response which begets behavior in an infinite progression without change. However, if parents can be provided with skills enabling them to interrupt this concatenation of parents' and children's behavior, then the change in parents' behavior should be reflected by a change in children's behavior. In this sense, the meaninglessness that Camus attributes to existence is obviated by the purposeful acts of behavior modification toward a specified end or goal. Rousseau's eighteenth-century prescriptions for rearing Emile are still quite applicable to child development generally, and particularly so if they are updated by the current philosophy of the behavior modification protagonists who believe that the relevant variables for change of behavior are socioeducational in nature. The results of our research may be best utilized within this framework.

Our study delineates a number of conditions that singly and/or in combination have been shown to be consistently associated with children's expression of aggression in the school context. Consequently, by abstracting these elements and introducing them systematically into children's environments, the regulation of aggression may hypothetically be accomplished. It is by now almost trite to say that aggressive behavior is overdetermined in the sense that it is instigated, supported, and maintained by many features of the environment, a number of which we have explicated in previous chapters. These environmental influences are of differential importance for different children. Two children with highly similar patterns of aggression may well be influenced by quite different features of the environment. Conversely, children with similar forces impinging upon them may manifest different aggressive behaviors.

Tools for Managing a Child's Aggression

The person who is responsible for a child's development may well be concerned with such a behavior as aggression. We have considered philosophical issues as well as the general societal context. However constraining these outside influences are, the family still has some room to maneuver, some choices to make. We shall write as if the parent's choices are limitless and assume that he has decided how aggressive his child should be, a decision that carries with it some consequences for that child both inside and outside of the family and for society itself. These consequences will be discussed later.

Is it proper to give to ordinary people the tools of behavior change? Will they not be misused? Bandura (1962a) answers those who say that parents who fail to help their children behave in desirable ways without realizing it really want their children to behave in less desirable ways. He analyzes how parents may punish their children in such a way as to inadvertently increase or maintain some undesired behavior. His analysis leads to the conclusion that parents need information about behavior management in doing their job to guide their children's development. For too long parents have been blamed for the results of errors of child-rearing, but we professionals have not given them the technical skills needed to fulfill their responsibilities (Schopler, 1969). The skills of behavioral technology are needed if one is to promote the "mental health" of another. This approach toward education for mental health is examined elsewhere (Walder et al., 1970).

We shall therefore present four hypothetical examples of behavior change, two in which the problem is to decrease aggressive behavior in a child of each sex and two in which the problem is to increase or to instate (increase from zero) aggressive behavior in a child of each sex. We hope that these examples will illustrate the approach. This chapter contains the broad outlines, and Appendix VI contains the technical terms and the specifics of "how to do it."

To analyze behaviors one must note carefully the ABC's of those behaviors. A stands for the immediate *a*ntecedent conditions under which the behavior occurs; B for the *b*ehavior itself, either aggressive or nonaggressive; and C for the *c*onsequences which immediately follow the behavior. The behavior can be modified by systematically changing the antecedent conditions and/or the consequences of that behavior.

Aggression that is instigated by pain or by frustration is directly responsive to the antecedent. A natural place to find aggression is under these unpleasant antecedent conditions. Poke a child and he may well poke back. He will often take other aggressive actions if he is insulted or disappointed. If aggression is very likely after a pain stimulus, aggression might be interpreted as being under respondent control. The possibly erroneous interpretation that elicitation of aggression by pain is a natural reflex (Ulrich et al., 1965) may then result in the recommendation that to decrease "respondent" aggression one should decrease the child's pain.

The distinction between operant and respondent behavior is increasingly difficult to maintain (Miller, 1969). Although frustration-aggression or pain-aggression looks like respondent or reflex behavior, the function of the immediately antecedent stimulus to aggression (a conditioned or an unconditioned negative stimulus) may be to set an occasion for reinforcement of a behavior. The aggressive behavior following the provoking stimulus may, on a sufficient number of occasions, reduce or terminate the provocation and thus be strengthened or maintained by negative reinforcement. An aversive enough stimulus, removed a varying percentage of the time by aggression (a variable ratio schedule), may result in a very strong and dependable stimulus-response relation and erroneously be considered to be a respondent. No matter what the theoretical source, there is no question that for a large number of people there is a close and dependable relation between an aversive stimulus and an immediately following aggressive response.

In addition to the immediate response to a painful provocation, especially when other escape responses are not possible, there is the chronic instigation revealed by our study. This chronic instigation describes a parent-child relationship in which (1) the child has reduced opportunity to receive positive consequences and increased opportunity to receive negative consequences from his parents; (2) the child's more disruptive, antisocial behaviors are strengthened, and the more prosocial, nonaggressive behaviors are weakened; (3) the child's imitation of the parents' proscriptions is reduced; and, finally, (4) neither the parents nor the child can influence each other in the exchange of positive attention, goods, and services. In this context, the pattern of reinforcement seems ideally designed to increase the aggression and counteraggression between the parents and the child.

Aggression may also become controlled by its consequences. The painful antecedent may well instigate respondent-like aggression, but the consequence will either strengthen the aggression or weaken it. With proper programing even the painful antecedent can become the occasion for a nonaggressive behavior. For example, sometimes the child must endure pain but must not aggress; instead he must "grin and bear it." If the antecedent pain can become the occasion on which grinning and bearing it leads to reward and aggression does not lead to reward, the pain will no longer elicit aggression. In this way operant nonaggression (grinning and bearing it) may become more likely. This new operant control is established by programing the consequences of aggression and of nonaggression to the discriminative stimulus of pain. These consequences in the home or in the school are of great importance for behaviors such as aggression.

A parent or teacher who wishes to reduce the frequency of an aggressive behavior may consider various ways of doing it: (1) The amount of instigation to aggression may be reduced. Bickering between the parents, criticizing the child, and not nurturing the child are instigations that can be reduced.[1] (2) Aggressive models may be made less available to the child. Some parents and teachers tell children to be gentle while they themselves are aggressive. Parents may reduce the violence observed by the child, whether on TV, in the disciplinary practices of the parents, in the parents' social and occupational behaviors in general, or in the actions of people in low and

[1] Notice that these are the chronic instigating conditions we found to be antecedent to aggression.

high places in government. (3) Nonaggressive models may be made more available to the child. Parents may attempt to present nonviolent behaviors on TV, in their disciplinary practices, in their general social and occupational behaviors, and in their government. (4) Finally, the consequences of aggression and of nonaggression can be programed so that decreasing amounts of aggression and increasing amounts of nonaggression will occur.

To be an effective disciplinarian, the parent must systematically present to his child a wide variety of consequences of aggression. The parent who presents only negative, noxious consequences offers an aggressive role model (as noted above), cannot punish by withholding positive consequences, and cannot easily strengthen nonaggressive behaviors. Although such an extreme parent is probably very rare (if he exists at all), a parent who is an approximation of this hypothetical specialist in negative discipline will be unable to control behaviors efficiently and will instill behaviors in the child that serve merely to avoid punishment. Such avoidance behaviors will be in evidence just as long as the parent is present and is strong enough to punish; only with luck will they be strengthened and routinely maintained by nonparental reinforcing agents. Any time the parent is not present or if, even when present, he no longer punishes, the suppressed behaviors will emerge.

The parent who presents both positive and negative consequences of aggression offers both an aggressive and a nonaggressive role model, can punish both by presenting noxious consequences and by withdrawing positive ones, and can more easily strengthen nonaggressive behaviors. Such a parent is in a position to control behaviors efficiently and to develop behaviors in the child that serve to gain positive consequences as well as to avoid negative ones. It is obvious that behaviors responsive to both positive and negative controls are more likely to be desirable behaviors than are those under only negative control.

Another general benefit for the parent who dispenses an adequate number of positive consequences is that his child will work to please him. This implies that the child will copy not only the parent's disciplining but also the parent's rules and instructions about how he should behave (referred to as internalization in Chapter 6). This will serve to control the child's behavior in situations where the parent is not present, e.g., in school.

In addition to providing a broad range or variety of consequences, the parent must arrange for the child to receive these consequences in a generally systematic way so that the child, by behaving either well or badly, can influence the kind and amount of positive and negative consequences dispensed by the parent (and in this sense control the parent). Also the parents must set requirements for the child that are appropriate to his development in order to ensure that he is most often successful in behaving well and learning through trial and success. Such a state of affairs keeps the chronic instigation to aggression down to a minimal level.

Let us now examine a hypothetical example of a parent who would like to reduce the frequency of aggressive behavior in an eight-year-old boy. The complaint is that he "teases" his younger sister. The mother notices that this occurs more often when she is present than when she is not. She also notices that she intervenes only after the screams of the girl are aversive enough to force her to do something. At that point she slaps her son and comforts her daughter. She also berates her son, saying such things as "You're not nice." She would like to reward him if possible, but he simply does not behave well enough to justify a reward.

Here is a parent who may very well dispense positive and negative consequences to one child, her daughter, but for some reason dispenses only negative consequences to her son. Our advice to her would be to look carefully at her son's current actions that can be supported by positive consequences. Such a parent may need help to state what she wants her son to do in place of teasing and to identify his current behaviors that can be built into the desired behaviors.

She also will need to examine the positive stimuli she now dispenses without making them contingent upon a behavior that she would like to strengthen and to search for ways of increasing the variety, number, and effectiveness of positive consequences for her son. Once she delivers a large quantity of small positive consequences to her son's desired behaviors, she will notice that the reinforced behaviors are more dependable. At that time she can raise the standards for him, but she should be careful not to raise them too much and too soon lest she hinder opportunities to reward him.

When she deals with him in a positive way, she can — as his behavior warrants — deal with him negatively. A transgression by him can now result in withholding the positive and, if desired, in presenting the negative. An angry mother who temporarily stops rewarding good behavior will suppress bad behaviors more quickly and easily than an angry mother who has never rewarded good behavior (e.g., with her pleasant attention) but has attended to the child only when she has been angry. By this time in our consultation, it is likely that mother and son will be doing well.

The younger, six-year-old sister not only is getting teased but also may well be supporting her brother's teasing behavior. It is inviting to regard her as aggressive in the brother-sister interaction in that she may encourage her brother to engage in teasing behaviors that

167

get him "punished" (quotes provided because the "punishment" from mother did not reduce the frequency of the "punished" behavior). If she is regarded as aggressive, we may wish to reduce that type of aggression and replace it with another kind; if she is not regarded as aggressive, we may wish to increase some kind of aggression. In either case, let us presume that the mother asks the girl to "protect herself" from her brother's teasing. Before the change program for her brother was started, the girl screamed in response to her brother's teasing and was comforted by her mother. To reduce the frequency of the boy's teasing, the girl may learn some kind of aggressive behavior, e.g., a social behavior called "snubbing," withholding ordinarily offered social attention. This may be viewed as a time-out or a DRO [2] nonreinforcement contingent upon some behavior, a technique that reduces immediately preceding behavior.

To build such a behavior in her daughter, the mother may simply speak to her, telling her that some positive consequence will be hers if she will ignore her brother's teasing *and* respond to her brother's nonteasing. The mother may also build cooperative behaviors for both children by making a positive consequence, e.g., parental attention, available to both when they interact in desirable ways (specified by her perhaps in consultation with the children). It has been our experience that "catch the child being good" is one of the best general forms of advice that can be given child-care workers, including parents.

Another hypothetical example concerns a father who would like to increase from zero (i.e., instate) an aggressive behavior in his son. The boy has become known as a sissy at school and is the butt of jokes from his third-grade classmates. He avoids relating to the boys at school and engages in such avoidance behaviors as being excessively polite and relating mostly with teachers, girls, and younger children.

The father has a conference with the teacher. On the basis of their exchange of information about the boy, they conclude that the boy initiates no physical contact with his male peers. At home he gets along well. However, his parents implore and nag him to spend more time with the boys, but to no avail.

---

[2] DRO, the *differential reinforcement of other* behaviors, involves changing the reinforcement contingencies from the behavior that has been supported to any *other* behavior. In this example the younger sister would pay attention to any of her brother's behaviors other than teasing. Thus some nonteasing behaviors would be strengthened and teasing behaviors would be weakened. This is an especially effective technique of behavior change in that it not only weakens the behavior (as do time-out and nonreinforcement) but it also strengthens other behaviors that might interfere with the weakened behavior.

The teacher notices that when the physical education instructor takes the boys into the play and exercise area he praises the physically proficient boys but ignores or berates those less proficient ones. The teacher confers with the physical education instructor and they arrange a series of graded activities that (1) involve a limited amount of physical contact and (2) assure that all students can succeed (and therefore be praised). As the boys succeed, the physical education instructor moves them up to an activity involving slightly more physical contact. To ensure growth in competitive, contact activities, the danger to any boy is kept controlled by careful restriction of the amount of contact allowed at any stage. Step by step, more behavior is praised, more behavior is expressed, and more behavior is required. The ultimate behavioral goals are pushing, shoving, wrestling, etc., with few limits. As the children proceed through the programs, playful enthusiasm is encouraged in closely supervised activities such as boxing, wrestling, football, and basketball. Any attempt on the child's part to retaliate to either playful or more serious aggression is privately and publicly praised. As these behaviors continue to emerge, natural reinforcers such as the positive attention of his age and sex peers supports and further develops these new behaviors.

Thus far in our examples we have illustrated techniques that may be utilized to shape the behavior of a boy who is deemed to be too aggressive, a boy who is considered not sufficiently aggressive, and a girl for whom some aggressive behavior is believed desirable. However, an example of a girl with too much aggression at home is not as easy to find. We have drawn largely from our clinical experience for the previous examples, and no such cases of excessively aggressive girls have come to our attention. The overaggressive girl is often in some special treatment environment, and we have therefore turned to a special education therapeutic center for the example. We report a clinical study by Bernstein, Perry, and Friman (1969) in which the goal was to learn about reducing a girl's aggression. A fourteen-year-old girl was described as extremely disruptive by both her teacher and the staff at the center that she attended. She was chosen for study because of her frequent aggressive behavior in and out of the classroom setting. The study took place in a small classroom holding approximately five students and a teacher. Unfortunately, the classroom was so small that there was room for only one observer at a time, and since the teacher did not have time to take objective data, no dependable index of interjudge agreement was available. However, the changes in the child were so large, so dramatic, and so consistent that it is not very likely that they were due to adventitious circumstances. Also, they are consistent with other reports (Hamblin, Buckholdt, Bushell, Ellis, and Ferritor, 1969).

Two types of observation were made: the girl's aggressive behavior and the teacher's response to the girl's aggressive behavior. The teacher was instructed at the outset (baseline) of the study to respond to the girl as he always had. In this period the girl was aggressive in 31 percent of the observation intervals. At the start of the experimental procedure the teacher was instructed to give positive social responses to the girl contingent upon any good behavior. In this period the girl was aggressive in 2 percent of the observation intervals. A DRO procedure in which the teacher responded only to any *not good* behavior by this girl was so effective (she was aggressive in 31 percent of the observation intervals) that it was terminated after one day. A return to the experimental procedure of the teacher responding to any good behavior was accompanied by an immediate return to a low level of aggression (aggressive in 1 percent of the observation intervals).

Although there are many other aspects of behavioral control to be considered, further discussion is beyond the scope of this volume. Suffice it to say that applications from the behavior theory underlying this study have been shown to be appropriate to the management of aggression (see Appendix VI for further examples and references).

Conclusion

Assuming that aggression can be regulated, certain ethical and moral considerations of such regulation deserve to be raised. For example, what are the ramifications for a human being's development if his behavior is shaped to minimize aggressiveness? In a chiefly capitalistic, competitive economy such as the United States, low aggressiveness may seriously handicap an individual in coping with the socioeconomic environment. Certainly our early American heros could not be described as passive individuals. We could construct an almost endless list of figures chosen from all areas of endeavor, such as the military, commerce, government, literature, art, and science, and across all of recorded history who, in our culture, are revered and adulated and held up as models for emulation to our children. Many of these figures would be rated as high in aggressiveness.[3] Thus the attempt to shape behavior toward the end of low aggressiveness may prove to be crippling not only economically but also psychologically.

[3] We are perhaps assuming a relation between aggression and assertiveness that is not entirely warranted by our own data but that is nonetheless reasonable (see, e.g., the quotation by Frankel below).

It seems that a nonaggressive American male would stand at variance and appear inferior to the image of the strong, masculine American, aggressively engaged in the conquest of the Western frontier in the last century or of space in this century.[4] Although frequent lip service is given to the Sermon on the Mount, it is rare to discover a child or an adult ready to "turn the other cheek" or to choose Christ as a role model.

But what are the consequences of shaping a child's behavior towards the goal of aggressiveness? Some of the positive results that presumably may ensue have been implied in the foregoing section and relate to successful coping in a competitive economy and to social adjustment. The negative consequences of training in aggressiveness are seen in the pattern of American violence and are aptly stated by Max Frankel:

> We are known for our violence, we Americans. The creative violence with which we haul down the good for what we fancy as better. The cruel violence with which we have treated red men, and black. The intoxicating violence of our music and art. The absurd violence of our comics and cartoons. The organized violence of our athletic and corporate games. The coarse violence of our speech, even our jokes.
>
> And now we have come violently to disagree about the nature of our violence in Vietnam or Dallas or Watts or Hiroshima. We seek the primitive within ourselves and bemoan the failure of affluence to civilize. Our young deplore the violence of the old and are tempted to use violence against them. The old deplore the ferocity of the young and are tempted to use violence to suppress them [1968, p. v].

That aggressiveness can be systematically inculcated into a person's behavioral repertoire has been conclusively demonstrated by the acts of military and paramilitary forces and of law enforcement agents. These acts, the manifestations of training in aggressiveness, are strongly encouraged by society and highly rewarded. Paradoxically, however, they may also serve as models for aggressiveness — just as the striving father serves as an aggressive model for his son — for individuals and groups in which society strongly condemns the expression of aggression. Murder, assault, arson, looting, and rioting are examples of aggressive behavior that may result from unsystematic inculcation of aggressiveness, but they are deemed opprobrious acts when performed in a nonsanctioned context.

The major problem of systematic training for aggressiveness in-

[4] We emphasize males in these examples because, as noted above, they more frequently exhibit behaviors commonly referred to as aggressive. However, under appropriate conditions girls might be observed to behave as aggressively as boys.

heres in its control. Examples abound of aggressive behavior that is learned, expressed, and rewarded in one context (e.g., military or police) generalizing to another context where it is condemmed, viewed as criminal behavior, and punished. Similarly, parents' manipulation of the socioeducational environment in the attempt to engender aggressiveness in their children may also get out of control. Although we may have discovered through our research several components of the formula for developing aggressive behavior, this formula is in no way precise. In American society today we are probably witnessing the deleterious effects of unplanned yet systematic education for aggressiveness. Factors such as parental instigation, parental punishment, and lack of identification between child and parent, in inadvertent coalescence with the aggressive role model and awesome frustrations provided by society, may be responsible for the violence and bloodshed produced by many of its members in such diverse contexts. Moreover, the inability of society to provide adequate opportunities for reinforcing some prosocial behaviors exacerbates the situation even further. If such social chaos is the result of the lack of systematic training in aggressiveness, dare we attempt by design to create aggressive behavior? Perhaps even more important, dare we not plan for its regulation and control and replacement? These are some ethical and moral questions with which behavior scientists and concerned citizens must struggle in the face of mounting aggressiveness on both the domestic and the international scenes.

CLASSROOM MEASURES

Appendix I

A. Development of a Peer-Rating Measure of Aggression

In order to build a peer-rating measure of aggression we started out with approximately one thousand short descriptions of behavior, presumed to tap aggression or anxiety about expressing aggression. These descriptions had been garnered from a review of the literature and interviews with experts (psychologists, guidance counselors, teachers, social workers, psychiatrists, and mothers) about how eight-year-old children express aggression. The instances included items of various types and objects of aggression and both provoked and unprovoked aggression. The vast majority of the items had high content validity. We then reworded items for clarity for third-grade school children according to the word counts of Rinsland (1945) and Thorndike and Lorge (1944), discarding inappropriate items. At that time we also eliminated the obvious duplicates. Two hundred and seventy-one items then remained, each of which was subsequently judged by six experts for its relevance to aggression or to anxiety about expressing aggression. At least five of the judges agreed that 177 of these items were relevant. Further judgments were then made as to type of aggression being expressed, i.e., whether physical, verbal, indirect, or acquisitive. All 155 items on which at least four judges agreed about type were classified. The other twenty-two items were considered unclassified aggression. After some less obvious duplicates were culled, 106 items remained which had been judged with minimal disagreement by experts to be relevant to the definition of aggression which had been adopted for the study, and which were deemed appropriate for third-grade children.

The 106 items were then submitted to empirical test. The purpose was to find items on which the children as judges could agree as to which of their classmates were described by each item. The items were divided by stratified random procedure into two pools, A and B, of fifty-three each so that either pool contained items of each category of type and object of aggression and provocation level. Each pool was then randomly divided in half and administered to all the members of a third-grade class. In all, four classes were used at this stage, two urban and two rural, each receiving twenty-six or twenty-seven items. The purpose of this preliminary tryout was to see if the children could cooperate with this type of procedure, to work out various technical problems in the administration, and to select items on the basis of interjudge agreement. For each of the 106 items the question asked was, "How well do the children, as judges, agree in their rating?" From each pool twenty-eight items were selected which had the highest variance and interjudge reliability. It was possible to eliminate all items with a split half r of less than .50, uncorrected for test length. No items with feeling words in them, e.g., "Who feels angry a lot?" or "Who is afraid of being hit?" achieved sufficient interjudge reliability to survive this screening.

Pilot testing was then carried out in thirty-four classes, sixteen classes receiving Form A and eighteen classes receiving Form B. The actual data for analysis were provided by the nine largest Form A classes and the nine largest Form B classes. For each form, six classes were used for intensive experimental analysis of the data and three classes were used for cross-validation of the findings with the first six. Interjudge reliability of the individual items was encouragingly high. In addition, three clusters of items were derived by a new method of cluster analysis, especially designed for this analysis of peer-rating data. (See monograph by Walder et al., 1961, for complete description of the method.) Cluster reliabilities remained high on cross-validation. The clusters had to do with (1) aggression against the teacher, (2) aggression against peers, and (3) acquisitive aggression. There were a number of other interesting findings. As anticipated, in every classroom boys scored higher than girls. There was no relation between peer-rating score and a nonverbal measure of intelligence (Davis and Eells, 1953), activity level as rated by the teachers, placement of the children's names on the list, or whether boys' or girls' names were on the right. The correlation between ratings by the teacher and ratings by peers was moderately high (.41 in Form A and

.63 in Form B) for all aggression items. For the cluster having to do with aggression against the teacher, however, the correlation was .84, indicating this must be a clearly salient form of behavior, obvious to both teachers and children. Furthermore, in every class the distribution of scores on this cluster took the form of a J-curve which is expected in most kinds of nonconforming behavior of which aggression against the teacher is certainly an example (Allport, 1934).

As for the distribution of the total aggression scores in either Form A or Form B among the subjects, there was remarkable consistency from one class to the next. Very few of the children received enough choices to be called highly aggressive; the vast majority of children were moderately aggressive. The more popular children were less aggressive, but even the most popular children were aggressive in some ways.

There was a moderate negative relation between popularity and aggression and between aggression and aggression anxiety. It will be remembered that the peer-rating of aggression anxiety had been planned as the low end of the peer-rating of aggression continuum. However, the magnitude of the negative correlation seems to contradict this assumption. (Actually, the evidence given below supported the hypothesis that aggression anxiety is more a part of popularity than of low aggression.)

Because these results, obtained from a pool of 974 children in forty third-grade classes, were so encouraging, we decided to take the best items of both forms and combine them into one aggression index. For this purpose we retained the fifteen items that comprised the three derived clusters and seven individual items of good interjudge reliability (at least .70), in order to tap different types of aggression, different objects, and different provocation levels. (See Table I.1 for items included in this version of the peer-rating measure.)

The content of the items that comprised this version of the peer-rating procedure made it obvious that our definition of aggression should be changed to "an act which injures another object." Each of the items described injurious acts and it was unnecessary to invoke intent as implied by the term "goal response" in the original definition.

In the following year, this one set of twenty-two items, called the "aggression index," was administered to a new sample of third graders (158 children in six classes). The same relations obtained, but the grouping of items, which in the earlier cluster analysis had yielded types of aggression, did not survive a factor analysis of the data (see Table I. 2), which revealed that only one factor accounted

TABLE I.I

The Aggression Index (not in order of administration)

Cluster 1

1. Who is a pest? (indirect)[a]
2. Who does not obey the teacher? (unclassified)[b]
3. Who takes the teacher's things without permission? (acquisitive)
4. Who is always getting into trouble? (unclassified)[b]
5. Who tattles to the teacher? (indirect)
6. Who is rude to the teacher? (verbal)

Cluster 2

7. Who starts a fight over nothing? (physical)[b]
8. Who says mean things? (verbal)[b]
9. Who makes it hard for children to get things done? (indirect)
10. Who pushes or shoves children? (physical)[b]
11. Who does things that bother others? (indirect)[b]

Cluster 3

12. Who forgets to return borrowed things? (acquisitive)
13. Who often says "Give me that"? (acquisitive)[b]
14. Who makes marks on the desk? (physical, against property)
15. Who takes other children's things without asking? (acquisitive)[b]

Individual aggression items

16. Who will always fight back if someone else hits them first? (physical)
17. Who gives dirty looks or sticks out their tongue at other children? (verbal)[b]
18. Who complains to the teacher when she tells them what to do? (verbal)
19. Who grabs things from other children? (acquisitive)
20. Who uses bad words when another child bothers them? (verbal)
21. Who gets very very mad at times? (unclassified)
22. Who makes up stories and lies to get other children into trouble? (indirect)[b]

Anxiety about aggression items

23. Who is always polite? (unclassified)
24. Who will never fight even when picked on? (physical)[b]
25. Who will never argue even when they are right? (verbal)
26. Who says, "Excuse me," even when they have not done anything bad? (unclassified)[b]

Rejection by peers

27. Who are the children that you wish were not in your class at all?

Popularity with peers

28. Who are the children that you would like to have for your best friends?[b]
29. Who do you know best of all?
30. Who would you like to sit next to in class?[b]
31. Who would you like to play with?

[a]Category within parentheses is the name we originally assigned when we asked the six experts to classify the items.

[b]These items were retained for use in final sociometric measure of aggression (ten aggression items, two aggression anxiety items, two popularity items). Also added to that measure were three items of success in aggression and three items for activity level.

TABLE I.2
Two Factor Analyses of Thirty-one Peer-Ratings by Third-Grade Children
(Aggression, Aggression Anxiety, Popularity, and Rejection)

First sample					Second sample			
N = 152					N = 78			
Original (test on six classes)					Replication (retest administration on three classes)			
Factors					Factors			
I	II	III	h^2		I	II	III	h^2
	(decimals omitted)			Item Number[a]		(decimals omitted)		
				AGGRESSION				
77	-19	-22	68	1	88	-18	21	85
90	-10	-14	84	2	88	29	-03	86
64	-01	-15	43	3	89	-06	23	85
88	-09	-05	79	4	95	00	01	90
69	-31	-10	58	5	86	-16	10	78
84	06	09	72	6	94	-05	14	91
82	10	20	72	7	87	01	-07	76
84	01	15	73	8	94	-04	-09	89
77	-23	-28	72	9	83	-17	-07	72
82	-07	07	68	10	88	-03	-24	83
90	-09	-15	84	11	94	-12	08	90
57	-17	-35	48	12	81	-19	05	69
75	-15	20	63	13	93	-03	-11	88
68	-12	-17	51	14	78	-04	00	61
83	-12	-03	70	15	96	00	02	92
67	24	32	61	16	73	26	-46	81
84	-09	05	72	17	92	-02	14	87
76	-04	-29	66	18	84	-12	03	72
82	-14	18	72	19	90	-10	-13	84
82	04	19	71	20	95	00	-04	90
65	13	33	55	21	79	09	-04	63
86	-05	09	75	22	93	-12	13	90
				AGGRESSION ANXIETY				
-54	71	-18	83	23	-54	67	17	77
-42	59	-28	60	24	-10	30	66	54
-29	49	-31	42	25	-27	57	49	64
-37	80	-08	78	26	-31	74	30	73
				REJECTION				
74	-42	-26	79	27	79	-38	-03	77
				POPULARITY				
-35	82	11	82	28	-35	84	-17	86
-32	81	13	78	29	-19	84	-16	77
-38	83	01	83	30	-29	84	06	79
-43	79	13	83	31	-38	84	04	85

[a]Item numbers listed here correspond to item numbers in Table I.1.

for a major portion of the variance. The same children tended to get nominated for all aggression items regardless of category and these same children tended to receive many nominations on rejection. A second factor differentiated aggression anxiety and popularity from aggression and rejection. A third factor's contribution seemed to be in the loadings of the first three aggression anxiety items and one item of justified or provoked aggression, "Who will always fight back if someone else hits them first?" An important finding here was that aggression anxiety did not constitute the low end of the aggression continuum since it loaded on a factor orthogonal to the first general factor. Similarly, rejection did not form the lower end of the popularity continuum.

However, we did have to face the explanation that we had not a measure of aggression but merely a measure of reputation for bad behavior. Perhaps the children as judges could not discriminate aggressive behavior and continually nominated those children who for some reason were considered "bad." (Perhaps they had been taught this by teachers who singled out certain children for attention.) This was an especially compelling argument since the measure of rejection (one item: "Who are the children that you wish were not in your class at all?"), used in previous studies, correlated .73 with the aggression score. We should note that the range of correlation between each aggression item and the aggression composite (which includes overlap) was .86 to .93. An alternative explanation (and one which we, of course, preferred) was that at age eight years children were not yet "specialists" in aggression. They were generally either aggressive or nonaggressive and had not yet discovered their preferred ways of being aggressive. Of course, we were also forced to consider that children as aggressors were indeed specialists but the children as judges of their peers' behavior were not sufficiently discriminating. However, patterns of data subsequently found (see pp. 41–45) strongly suggest that children are adequate discriminators of their peers' behavior.

In the year after the initial administration of the aggression index, we checked the generality of the measure. The previous factor analysis was replicated exactly, showing a remarkably stable factor structure for the aggression score. (See Table I.2 for the results of these two factor analyses.) This replication was done with a different sample of seventy-eight children and within a different item context.[1] Again the factor analysis revealed a first general factor of aggression and rejection and a second factor of aggression anxiety and

[1] Two weeks previously these children had responded to some of the same items embedded within a group of other items.

popularity. However, we still had confidence that we were indeed measuring aggression and not a child's general undesirable reputation. Support for this contention lies in the fact that expert judges had agreed that the items were aggressive ones, the item wording was appropriate to third-grade understanding, and the aggression-rejection relation was much less marked in the teachers' ratings of the children.

We had to make sure, however, that when the children nominated their peers for those items they were actually responding to aggressive behavior displayed by their peers and not just to their peers' general undesirability. Therefore a new study was carried out to determine the interrelations among peer-ratings of socially desirable and undesirable aggressive and nonaggressive behaviors. The social desirability ratings of all items, both of aggression and of nonaggression, were determined empirically by administering a large pool of items to twelve classrooms. The format used in this attempt to get social desirability ratings included such questions as:

> Could you like a child your age who is a pest?
> . . . who talks a lot?
> . . . who gets good marks?
> . . . who picks his nose?
> . . . who sings nice?

Response alternatives were "surely yes," "yes," "no," or "surely no." This set of alternatives had been chosen on the basis of a previous study of three classes who were given thirty-three social desirability items, each with a different response format: "yes / no"; "yes / don't care / no"; "surely yes / yes / no / surely no." A fourth class received a self-rating format for these same items. Scale values obtained with the first three classes were related to the percentage of yesses on the self-ratings obtained in the fourth class. They correlated as follows: two responses, .41; three responses, .48; and four responses, .60. Also each set of scale values correlated higher with the self-ratings than with each other. Edwards (1957) has pointed out the very high relation between precentage of people endorsing an item and that item's social desirability ($r = .87$). Therefore, because the relation to self-ratings was highest for the four alternative response formats, because the children demonstrated that they could handle this number of alternatives, and because it gave the largest variance, the four-choice response format was selected for this procedure. Social desirability scores were then assigned to the behaviors on the basis of percentage of children in twelve new classrooms rating them as disliked in other children. Table I.3 presents the eight items in each of four types, clearly differentiated in that study by desira-

TABLE I.3

Rotated Orthogonal Factor Matrix of Peer-Rating Items (*N* = 151)

Percentage undesirable[a]	Item number		I	II	III	h²
				Factors		
				(decimals omitted)		
		CLUSTER 1				
		Bad aggression				
91	1.	Who does not obey the teacher?	34	-10	12	73
95	2.	Who is always getting into trouble?	89	-19	00	83
95	3.	Who starts a fight over nothing?	91	-11	-10	85
97	4.	Who is rude to the teacher?	88	-12	16	81
96	5.	Who takes other children's things without asking?	84	-16	22	78
98	6.	Who gives dirty looks or sticks out their tongue at other children?	84	-18	19	77
99	7.	Who makes up stories and lies to get other children into trouble?	84	-16	21	78
99	8.	Who uses bad words when another child bothers them?	87	-15	10	79
		Good aggression				
52	9.	Who always fights back if someone has been asking for it?	73	-01	-23	59
57	10.	Who pushes when some child has been asking for it?	87	-12	-18	80
63	11.	Who grabs things from someone who grabs things from them?	89	-14	-03	81
		CLUSTER 2				
		Good aggression				
66	12.	Who gets very, very mad at a bully?	86	10	-07	75
62	13.	Who bothers someone who has been asking for it?	88	01	-09	78
63	14.	Who says mean things to someone who says mean things to them?	94	-06	09	90
57	15.	Who will always fight back if someone else hits them first?	85	07	-12	74
60	16.	Who pushes someone who pushes them first?	90	-06	03	81
		Bad nonaggression				
94	17.	Who is a hog?	71	-20	15	57
91	18.	Who tells other children what to do?	88	04	-14	80
93	19.	Who always wants things done their way?	91	-06	-07	84
86	20.	Who has a messy desk?	39	-30	42	42
90	21.	Who dresses sloppy?	59	-20	67	84
91	22.	Who picks their nose?	58	-28	37	55

TABLE I.3 cont.

Percentage undesirable[a]	Item number		Factors			
			I	II	III	h^2
				(decimals omitted)		
96	23.	Who is always dirty?	51	-19	69	77
97	24.	Who acts like a baby?	66	-24	24	55

CLUSTER 3

Good nonaggression

3	25.	Who keeps their promise?	-35	75	-08	69
2	26.	Who sings nicely?	-15	74	-08	58
0	27.	Who has a nice smile?	-22	86	-13	80
1	28.	Who is good at games?	-24	71	-19	60
7	29.	Who gets the best marks?	-26	82	14	76
3	30.	Who helps others?	-30	89	04	88
1	31.	Who is ready on time?	-36	82	03	80
0	32.	Who reads well?	-22	88	05	83

[a]Percentage of children rating items as undesirable, combining judgment of "no" and "surely no" when asked, "Could you like a child your age who...."

bility score and content. All eight bad-aggression items were taken from the aggression index (Table I.1). Once the items were chosen they could then be used in the peer-rating procedure to determine the relation between good and bad aggressions and nonaggressions. Scores on each of the thirty-two items (based on number of choices by peers) were correlated with scores on every other item for 151 children in six new classrooms. The mean intercorrelations among items of different social desirability appear in Table I.4.

The highest mean is that of the correlations between items of good aggression and items of bad aggression, indicating that aggression is salient when these subjects make their sociometric choices. However, the mean correlation between items of bad aggression and bad non-aggression is also high. This indicates that a general reputation for

TABLE I.4
Mean Intercorrelations among Types of Items
of Varying Social Desirability and Aggression

	Bad aggression	Good aggression	Bad nonaggression
Good aggression	.71		
Bad nonaggression	.62	.52	
Good nonaggression	-.35	-.24	-.33

bad behavior influences choices to some extent. Next highest in magnitude is the mean correlation between good aggression items and bad nonaggression items suggesting that all aggression has some communality with bad behavior. However, the range of correlations with bad and good aggression is much lower for those items in the bad-nonaggression category that do not connote bothering others (e.g., "Who picks their nose?") than for those that do (e.g., "Who tells other children what to do?"). The latter type of item (17, 18, 19, 24) describes interpersonal activity that implies aggression more readily than the others in the bad-nonaggression category (20, 21, 22, 23). Thus the high mean correlation between bad aggression and bad nonaggression is probably a result of poor selection of items for the bad-nonaggression classification. Further, the moderately low negative correlations between good nonaggression and the three other classes of items means that the subjects are not choosing the same objects indiscriminately for all items. In general, these results can be interpreted as showing that although sociometric choices on aggression items are influenced by the general reputation for bad behavior of the individual objects, differentiation by the judges can be and is made between aggressive and nonaggressive behaviors. Moreover, no general "sociometric choice" (tendency to choose the same object for all items) pervades the procedures. A factor analysis of all thirty-two items, the results of which appear in Table I.3, corroborates the above interpretation. Indeed, the four undesirable nonaggression items noted above (17, 18, 19, 24) are factorially similar to the aggression items and are more relevant to aggression than to nonaggression; they were undoubtedly categorized incorrectly to begin with. It should be remembered that we wrote these items ourselves and, unlike the aggression items, they were neither submitted to outside experts for checking on classification or tried out empirically with groups of children beforehand. Aside from these four items, the factorial compositions of aggression items at the two levels of social desirability are indeed similar, and they are somewhat different from nonaggression items, especially the desirable ones.

In this same study, stability (test-retest reliability) was also found over a two-week period with the item context changed. Half the subjects was administered the same four sets of items after two weeks; the other half was administered only the twenty-two items of the aggression index. In both cases retest reliability was high. Individual item reliabilities ranged from .70 to .92. As has been said elsewhere:

> These results show that while the children may not be able to tell one aggression item from another, they can certainly tell

an aggression item from a nonaggression item (and a socially desirable item from a nonsocially desirable item). Also they are dependable in telling one child from another in very general terms. The stability coefficients suggest that by the spring semester the third graders have a reputation for aggression which the peers can rate at different times and in shifting item context [Walder et al., 1961, p. 542].

On the basis of the above results, especially the consistently high loadings on the first factor, ten aggression items were retained in the final measure. Another consideration in the selection of these items was to ensure representation of each type and provocation level so that in future studies, especially with different age groups, patterns of aggression might become available. These items appear in Table 3.1. The majority of results reported in this volume refer to the composite of these ten items as the aggression score. Although the items included are heterogeneous in content, they comprise a tightly packed, homogeneous scale. Interitem correlations range from .69 to .87; the item-total correlations, from .86 to .93; and there is very little variability in mean and range of scores among classes. The same relations seem to have held up on all versions of the aggression scale to date (Form A and Form B, each with twenty-eight items, the intermediate aggression index with twenty-two items, and the final ten-item aggression score).

An examination of the content of the ten aggression items suggested a final refinement in the definition. All the items refer to interpersonal aggression. Furthermore, a content analysis of the four items that were originally classified as undesirable nonaggression but that related so markedly to these aggression items (see Table I.3) indicated that high scorers are also children who irritate others. Thus the definition should read: "aggression: an act which injures or irritates another person." The aggression score refers only to interpersonal, extrapunitive behavior; there is no consideration of intent or provocation.[2] In this respect it most clearly resembles the definition of Buss (1961).

Table I.5 contains a set of data (correlations between aggression score and any variable, which were significant for either total correlation or within-classroom correlation), which justifies pooling of aggression scores for all classrooms (see Chapter 3, pp. 36–37).

---

[2] Items referring to provoked aggression did indeed relate empirically to the aggression items that were retained although they were not included in the scale. However, the items which included intent were eliminated on an empirical basis: lack of sufficient interjudge reliability.

TABLE I.5

A Comparison of Correlations between Aggression and Other Variables Based on Total Sample and Within-Classroom Populations[a]

	Total sample	*Within-classroom*
MCIQ[b]	−.31	−.29
MBGA	.19	.23
MGGA	−.21	−.25
LFFR	.22	.19
LMFR	.16	.19
LFRJ	.24	.22
LMRJ	.25	.28
LFRA	.19	.16
LMRA	.16	.18
LMCI	−.23	−.20
LFPU	.20	.17
LMPU	.19	.19
LFPI	.14	.13
LMPI	.24	.23
MCPI	.15	.10
LFGI	−.14	−.13
LMGI	−.17	−.17
LMRG	−.16	−.15
LFDE	−.14	−.11
LFPM	.17	.12
LMPM	.16	.14
LFPH	.21	.20
LMPH	.21	.21

[a]Included are all significant correlations of aggression with three non-peer-rating classroom measures and ninety-seven interview variables based on total sample. ($N = 451$)

[b]See Appendix V for explanation of codes.

B. Instructions for Classroom Procedures

FIRST SESSION

Instructions for Peer-Ratings

Materials

Two sets of instructions and items (one each for E and for assistant).

A prize for each subject (Tootsie Rolls).

A Number 2 pencil for each child.

A response booklet for each child (order of colors: Blue, Yellow, Pink, Green, White).

Instructions

(Class should be watered immediately before testing.)

(Introduce self and assistant; send teacher out.)

(Reseat class, alternating rows of boys and girls.)

"I am going to give each of you a pencil and a booklet with a lot of pages in it." (E distributes pencils and RESPONSE BOOKLETS, taking care that all the children in the class get the same booklet appropriate for that class.) "Put all other pencils or erasers inside your desks.

"Look at the front page. It is a colored page. What color is it?" (Class response: blue.) "That's right, it's a blue page. Does everybody have a blue front page?" (Pause.) "Look at the bottom of this blue page. There's a number at the bottom. What number is it?" (Class response: one.) "Does everybody have a *number one* on the blue front page?" (Pause.)

"I'll read you the question that goes with the *number one blue page*: B1. Who are you? Who are you?

"On the front page there are two lists of names. Your name is in one of these two lists. The first list has girls' (boys') names; the second list has boys' (girls') names. I'll read all the names in the list for you. First the (girls', boys') list." (E reads the names in the order in which they appear in the list to the left. When E reads NO BOY and NO GIRL he says, "Remember, NO BOY (GIRL) is a name.") "Now the boys' (girls') list." (E reads the names in the order in which they appear in the list to the right.)

"Now look for your own name. Find your name and put your finger on your own name. Put your finger on your own name.

"Keep your finger on your own name and watch what I do at the blackboard." (E writes his own name on the board.) "Here is my name. Mr. Blank. I'm going to draw a line through my name like this. Now you draw a line through *your* own name. Remember, you have a first name and a last name, so make sure you draw a line through your whole name, your first name and your last name." (*Check carefully*: E and assistant go to every child and read the crossed-out name aloud.) "If you want to change your mark, make a wavy line through it like this." (E demonstrates.)

"Now fold back the front page like this." (E demonstrates.) "The next page is yellow. Does everybody have a yellow page?" (Pause.) "What is the number of the yellow page?" (Pause.) "That's right, it's number two. It's a yellow two. Soon I will read you the question that goes with yellow two. *Listen*, from now on, do not draw a line through your own name. Remember, it's against the rules of the game to mark your own name.

"Now I will read you the yellow question, the number two question: Y2. Who are the children who always sit around you? Who are the children who always sit around you?

"You are sitting in different places now. Look through the names in *both* lists and find the children who always sit around you. Draw a line through the names of the children who sit around you every day. Make sure you find the names in both lists. First look at the names in the first list and draw a line through the names of all the children in that list who sit around you. Then look at the second list and draw a line through the names of all the children in that list who always sit around you." (Pause.) "Remember, NO BOY and NO GIRL are names, so if no boy sits around you, cross out the name NO BOY, and if no girl sits around you, cross out the name NO GIRL."

(If child marks only one name in either of the lists, ask:) "Aren't there any other boys (girls) who always sit around you?"

"We'll play this game the same way from now on. I'll read you the question for each page. You find the names in both lists that you think are right for the question. First look at all the names in the first list and draw a line through all the names that fit. Then look at all the names in the second list and draw a line through all the names in that list that fit. Here are the rules of the game: First rule, make a line through at least one name in each list. Do not make a line through your own name. Second rule, look only at your own game. Never look at your neighbor's game. Third rule, if you want to change your mark, make a wavy line through it. Fourth rule, do not answer out loud. Everybody who follows the rules gets a prize. Mark names in each list, don't mark your own name, don't answer out loud, don't look at your neighbor's game.

"Remember, for every question make sure that you look at every name in the *two* lists and make sure that you draw a line through any name that fits the question. Remember to look at the person's first name and last name. Do not mark your own name.

"In question number two, the yellow question, not everybody made lines through the same names. This is because the answer depends on where you always sit. So, what was the right answer for you was not the right answer for somebody else. On the other questions I'll ask you, different children draw lines through different names because there are no answers that are the same for everybody. On each page you will have to decide *for yourself* what names to make a line through. Do not cross out your own name. When we get finished, the two of us, Mr. —— (assistant) and I, will take the papers and we won't show them to anybody else.

"Now turn the page so that the pink page is on top. What number is it? That's right, number three. I'll read the question that goes with the pink three and you be sure to draw a line through names in the *two* lists — all the names that fit the question."

[The items are in Table 3.1 in Chapter 3.]

Instructions for Games and Activities Preference (GAP)
(Classes 03–38 Only)

"Everybody turn to page 24. We are going to play a game called 'Would You Rather.' "

(Assistant prints example on board while E is reading:)

Would you rather

eat ice cream   1   drink soda

"We play this game by choosing the thing that we would rather do or be. The way to choose is to draw a circle around the thing you would rather do or be. In a few seconds I'll do one on the blackboard. But first, write your first and last name on the top of the page. If you are a boy, draw a circle around the word 'boy.' If you are a girl, draw a circle around the word 'girl.'

"On your page is a list of numbers down the middle. All of us point to the top number. Who doesn't see the number 1? Next to each number are two different things. One thing is on each side of the number. The game is for you to choose one of these things and draw a circle around it.

"In this game I'm the leader. Everybody must wait until I say 'ready.' When I say 'ready' draw a circle around the thing you would rather be or do. Then wait until I say 'ready' for the next number.

"The rules of the game are to choose the thing you would rather do and draw a circle around it. Don't answer out loud and don't look at your neighbor's game. Those are the rules. All children who follow the rules will win a prize at the end of the class. Watch me do the first one on the blackboard.

"When I say 'ready,' those children who would rather eat ice cream must draw a circle around the words 'eat ice cream.' " (Demonstrate.) "Those children who would rather drink soda must draw a circle around the words 'drink soda.' " (Erase circle from ice cream and demonstrate.) "Notice you must draw a circle around either 'eat ice cream' or 'drink soda.' But you cannot draw a circle around both. If you want to erase, draw a wavy line through the circle." (Demonstrate and then erase board.)

"All right now, let's begin the game with #1, the same one I did on the blackboard. But this time you do it on your paper. Ready for number 1: Would you rather eat ice cream or drink soda?" (Repeat.) "Draw a circle around the thing you would rather do." (Pause for marking.) "Has everybody drawn a circle around either 'eat ice cream' or 'drink soda?' Has anybody drawn a circle around both?" (If so, say game cannot be played that way and repeat instructions. E and assistant check to see that each child has one and only one thing circled.)

"All right, ready for #2." (Read each question twice and say: "Draw a circle around the thing you would rather do/be." Pause for marking and continue with each item saying, "Ready," and then the number and the question twice.)

(After item #11, say:) "Everybody turn the page to page 25. Does everybody have a number 25 at the bottom of the page in the corner? All right, now everybody write their first and last name at the top of the page." (Pause.) "Ready for #12." (Same instructions.)

[Below are the pairs of items used.]

Would you rather

Eat ice cream	1	Drink soda
Play doctors	2	Play soldiers
Go roller skating	3	Draw and paint
Play blind man's bluff	4	Play musical chairs
Go shooting	5	Go bowling
Play house	6	Play dressing up
Play baseball	7	Play volleyball
Go hunting	8	Go hiking
Play marbles	9	Play puzzles
Be a daddy	10	Be a mother
Play darts	11	Play jacks
Use lipstick and powder	12	Use a razor and shaving cream
Wear girls' clothes	13	Wear boys' clothes
Play inventors	14	Play actors
Play see-saw	15	Play king of the mountain
Be an artist	16	Be a teacher
Play Indian princess	17	Play Indian chief
Learn boxing	18	Learn dancing
Play school	19	Play house
Pick flowers	20	Go fishing
Play bows and arrows	21	Play dominoes
Play follow the leader	22	Play dodgeball

Instructions for Occupational Aspiration (OAS)
(Classes 03–38 Only)

"Turn to page 23 and write your first and last name on top. If you are a boy, draw a circle around 'boy.' If you are a girl, draw a circle around 'girl.' On this page is a list of things grown-ups become. *Don't make any mark until I say ready.* When you grow up, what would you like to be? What kind of work would you like to do? The way to tell me is to draw a *circle* around the thing you would like to do or be. But first I shall read each one on the list to make sure we don't miss any. Follow along with me by putting your finger on the one I'm reading. Remember this rule: you can draw a circle around only one thing and no more than one."

(Read through list giving number and occupation. At #21, say:) "If what you want to be is not on the list, write it in the blank space next to #21.

"Ready now: draw a circle [demonstrate] around the one thing you would like to be when you grow up. Find what you would like to be and draw a circle around it."

[Below are the items used.]

1. truck driver	11. office clerk
2. policeman	12. storekeeper
3. factory worker	13. engineer
4. cook	14. teacher
5. artist	15. salesman
6. nurse	16. doctor
7. beautician	17. dress maker
8. lawyer	18. waitress
9. housewife	19. farmer
10. mechanic	20. postmaster
	21. _____

SECOND SESSION

Instructions for Profile Identification (SPID)
(Classes 03–38 Only)

(Assistant prints example on board.)

I like cocoa

hot __ __ __ __ __	cold
light __ __ __ __ __	dark
sweet __ __ __ __ __	not sweet

"Write your first and last name at the top of the page. If you are a boy, put a checkmark on the line next to boy. If you are a girl, put a checkmark on the line next to girl.

"This is a game in which you tell me how you do certain things. You're supposed to tell me how you walk, how you talk, how you stand, how you eat, how you write, and about yourself. The idea of the game is to tell me by using checkmarks instead of words. Therefore, the name of this game is checkmark.

"Look at the first page where it says 'I like cocoa.' Does everybody see it? Let's all point to 'I like cocoa.' Underneath is the word 'hot' and five spaces away is the word 'cold.' (E points and counts.)

"Look at the words 'hot' and 'cold.' You know how they are different. If you put your checkmark [point] next to 'hot,' this is the way to tell me without using words that you drink your cocoa hot. If you put your checkmark next to 'cold,' it means you drink your cocoa cold. If you place your checkmark here [#2] it means you like to drink cocoa a little less hot. If you put your checkmark here [#3] it means you like to drink cocoa not hot and not cold but inbetween. And if you put your checkmark here [#4] it means you like to drink cocoa when it's cool. If you put it here [#5] this is the way to tell me that you like cold cocoa.

"Anybody who does not understand how we play checkmark, please raise their hand." (To any questions, say:) "Listen carefully and I'll tell you some more about how to play.

"Now look at the next line where it says 'light' on one side [point to board] and 'dark' on the other. Does everybody see these words on their papers? We play the game the same way here. The closer you put your checkmark to the word 'light' the more it means you like to drink cocoa like the word says. The closer you put your checkmark to the word 'dark' the more it means you like to drink cocoa like *that* word says.

"Again, on the last line it's exactly the same way. If you want to tell me you drink cocoa sweet put your checkmark toward 'sweet.' If you want to tell me that you like cocoa not sweet, then put your checkmark toward the words 'not sweet.'

"Listen, I'm going to tell you something about the cocoa game and the games on the next two pages. The closer you put your checkmark to one or the other words at the ends of each line the more it means you do things like that word says."

"Now listen closely to the rules. All children who obey the rules will win a prize at the end of the class. *The rules are: you can use only one checkmark on each line. You cannot look at your neighbor's game. You cannot answer out loud. You must follow along with me.*

"Ready, let's begin with the cocoa game. Put a checkmark in one of the five spaces on the top line [point] to tell me about how you like cocoa. Ready, now on the middle line, where it says "light-dark" put a checkmark, *but only one*, in one of the five spaces [point] to tell me some more about how you like cocoa. Ready, on the bottom line, where it says "sweet-not sweet" put a checkmark in one of the five spaces [point] to tell me some more about how you drink cocoa.

(E and assistant inspect each protocol for one checkmark per line. For any extreme case, E says:) "Show me where you would put your checkmark if you liked cocoa a little less hot (cold)?" (Child must enter checkmark.)

"All right. Turn the page. Does everybody have a '2' in the corner on the bottom of their page? Write your first and last name on top. Now we play the game the same way. You must tell me how you walk just by using checkmarks. Listen carefully: remember, the closer you put your checkmark next to a word the more it means you do things like that word says. Remember, the rules are: you can use only one checkmark on each line. You cannot look at your neighbor's game. You cannot answer out loud. You must follow along with me.

"Ready, 'I walk.' Put a checkmark in one of the five spaces on the 'fast-slow' line telling me how you walk." (Pause.) "Now put a checkmark in one of the five spaces on the 'loud-soft' line telling me how you walk." (Pause.) "And put a checkmark in one of the five spaces on the 'often-not often' line telling me how you walk." (Pause.)

"Ready, 'I talk.' Put a checkmark in one of the five spaces on the 'slow-fast' line telling me how you talk." (Pause.) "Now put a checkmark in one of the five spaces on the 'soft-loud' line telling me how you talk." (Pause.) "And put a checkmark in one of the five spaces on the 'not often-often' line telling me how you talk." (Pause.)

"Ready, 'I stand.' Put a checkmark in one of the five spaces on the 'straight-lean forward' line telling me how you stand." (Pause.) "And put a checkmark in one of the five spaces on the 'at ease-firm' line telling me how you stand." (Pause.)

"Ready, 'I eat.' Put a checkmark in one of the five spaces on the 'much-little' line telling me how you eat." (Pause.) "And put a checkmark in one of the five spaces on the 'fast-slow' line telling me how you eat." (Pause.)

(After "I eat":) "Turn the page to number 3. Does everybody have a '3' in the corner on the bottom? Put your first and last name on top. Remember, the closer you put your checkmark to a word, the more it means you do things like the word says.

"Ready, 'I write.' Put a checkmark in one of the five spaces on the 'slow-fast' line telling me how you write." (Pause.) "Now put a checkmark in one of the five spaces on the 'small-large' line telling me how you write." (Pause.) "And put a checkmark in one of the five spaces on the 'heavy–light' line telling me how you write." (Pause.)

"Ready, 'My body is.' Put a checkmark in one of the five spaces on the 'light–dark' line telling me how you are.' (Pause.) "Now put a checkmark in one of the five spaces on the 'tall–short' line telling me how you are." (Pause.) "Now put a checkmark in one of the five spaces on the 'thick–thin' line telling me how you are." (Pause.) "Now put a checkmark in one of the five spaces on the 'hard-soft' line telling me how you are." (Pause.) "And put a checkmark in one of the five spaces on the 'strong-weak' line telling me how you are." (Pause.)

[Below are the pairs of items.]

I like cocoa

hot	__ __ __ __ __	cold
light	__ __ __ __ __	dark
sweet	__ __ __ __ __	not sweet

I walk

fast	__ __ __ __ __	slow
loud	__ __ __ __ __	soft
often	__ __ __ __ __	not often

I talk

slow	__ __ __ __ __	fast
soft	__ __ __ __ __	loud
not often	__ __ __ __ __	often

I stand

straight	__ __ __ __ __	lean forward
at ease	__ __ __ __ __	firm

I eat

much	__ __ __ __ __	little
fast	__ __ __ __ __	slow

I write

slow	__ __ __ __ __	fast
small	__ __ __ __ __	large
heavy	__ __ __ __ __	light

My body is

light	__ __ __ __ __	dark
tall	__ __ __ __ __	short
thick	__ __ __ __ __	thin
hard	__ __ __ __ __	soft
strong	__ __ __ __ __	weak

Instructions for Draw-a-Person (DAP)
(All Classes)

"Everybody turn to page 4 [a blank page with a 4 at the bottom]. Does everybody have a number 4 at the bottom of this page? Now write your first and last name at the top of the page. Draw a picture of a person on this page. Do not ask any questions." *(No questions allowed!)* "Just take a couple of minutes to draw a picture of a person. I shall tell you shortly before you are to stop. Draw a picture of a person, a whole person. Be sure to make a whole person."

(If questions are asked about what kind of drawing, answer:) "Any kind of drawing you want so long as it is a whole person." (If questions are asked about erasing, permit it. Allow two minutes for the drawing, say after 1½ minutes:) "You will have to stop soon.

"If you drew a picture of a girl or woman, write *G* under the drawing [demonstrate]; if you drew a picture of a boy or man write *B* under the drawing [demonstrate].

"Who wrote a *B*? You children who wrote a *B* turn to the next page [a blank page with a 5 at the bottom] and draw a picture of a girl or woman. Who wrote a *G*? You children who wrote a *G* turn to the next page and draw a picture of a boy or man. On the page with number 5 at the bottom, all of you should draw another picture of a person, but this time a person of the other sex than you drew the first time. Again, just take a couple of minutes to draw it. Be sure your name is on this page too." (Allow two minutes as before.)

"If you drew a picture of a girl or woman, write *G* under the drawing [demonstrate]; if you drew a picture of a boy or man write *B* under the drawing [demonstrate]."

PARENT INTERVIEW MEASURES

Appendix II

A. Derivation of the Parent Interview

The first set of variables we constructed with definitions and sample items for each appears in Table II.1. The median number of items for each of the twenty-three scales was ten with a range from one to twenty.

Responses to these items by sixty mothers and fifty fathers were related to aggression index scores obtained from their children as described in Chapter 3 of the text. The first step was an item analysis of the 272-item questionnaire. This was done in two ways. First, each of the items was related to the school aggression measures and to sex of child in a 3×2 (level of aggression by sex) analysis of variance design done separately for mothers and fathers (Walder, 1961). The two most striking findings were: (1) the lack of relation between aggression in school as rated by peers and teachers and aggression at home as rated by parents, even when the very same behaviors were under consideration; and (2) the consistent, positive relation between intensity of punishment for a specific behavior and the presence of that behavior in school. This was especially true for fathers' punishment and much less so for mothers' punishment. Evaluation of the items by this analysis of variance design permitted us to see if there were any single items that had a powerful relation to the criterion in and of themselves. No such items were found.

Second, in an attempt to establish relatively homogeneous sets of items that would constitute stable measures of our variables, item-

192

TABLE II.1

Parent Interview Variables (First Interview Study)

1. *Anomie:* General attitude of alienation from people characterized by a jaded, cynical outlook about other people's motivation, the hostility of the environment, and the futility of coping.

   Example: These days a person doesn't really know whom he can count on. Would you: 0 – disagree; 1 – don't know; 2 – agree?

2. *Approval of aggression:* Evaluate standards for aggressive behavior stated in terms of approval or disapproval of specific items of aggressive behavior which appear in the school aggression measure.

   Example: Suppose NAME said mean things to another child. Would you: 0 – strongly disapprove; 1 – mildly disapprove; 2 – not care (and don't know); 3 – mildly approve; 4 – strongly approve?

3. *Confessing by child:* Extent to which a child behaves as if he were monitoring his own behavior in a way he thinks a socializing agent would. These items are closed-end versions of two questions used by Sears et al. (1957).

   Example: When NAME has done something naughty *and* you haven't seen him do it, does he come and tell you about it without your having to ask him? 4 – all the time; 3 – most of the time; 2 – some of the time; 1 – almost never; 0 – never.

4. *Dependence avoidance of child:* Inability or unwillingness of the child to accept help or rely on others.

   Example: Does NAME seem embarrassed when you take his part? 0 – no; 1 – sometimes (and don't know); 2 – yes.

5. *Ethnicity* (generational level): Number of generations in which parents' forebears have lived in the United States.

6, 7. *Father's and mother's aggression:* Tendency of the parent to display aggressive behavior in situations which often elicit aggressive responses. Each parent rates himself and is rated by the other parent on each of these situations.

   Example: Suppose you are driving a new car and get into an accident which is clearly the other driver's fault. Would you show your anger if: 1 – he says, "What's the matter, can't you drive"; 2 – he apologizes; 3 – he says, "I'm not going to say anything until I see a lawyer"; 4 – he laughs it off?

8. *Home aggression of child:* Frequency of acts whose goal response is injury to another object.

   Example: How often does NAME say mean things to another child? 0 – never; 1 – rarely; 2 – occasionally; 3 – pretty often; 4 – frequently; 5 – daily. These alternatives were specifically defined in terms of frequency in time and typed on cards which were handed to the respondent.

9. *Lack of social participation:* Degree of participation of respondent in formal and informal social relationships.

   Example: About how many times in the past year have you attended meetings or affairs of any local organizations, societies, or clubs? 0 – 13+; 1 – 7 to 12; 2 – 4 to 6; 3 – 1 to 3; 4 – none.

10. *Nonrecognition of child's needs:* An aspect of nonnurturant behavior. (For other aspects of nonnurturant behavior see "Punishment for nurturance signals" below.)

    Example: Do you usually have time so that NAME can talk to you about things that interest him? 0 – yes; 1 – no (and don't know).

193

TABLE II.1 cont.

11. *Parental aspirations for child:* Level of education parent hopes child will attain.
    Example: How much education do you expect NAME to get? 1 – high school,
               specialized training, or college; 2 – high school graduate or less.

12. *Parental aspirations for self*
    Example: When you left school what particular kind of occupation or life work
               was it your ambition to reach some day? Aspiration for: 1 – professional
               status; 2 – minor profession, small business, or farm owner; 3 – skilled
               worker trades; 4 – semi-skilled or unskilled occupations.

13. *Parental disharmony:* The extent of disharmony in the home as measured by disagree-
    ment about various specific matters of importance in a family; items dealing with
    arguments between husband and wife and presumptive evidence such as separation,
    divorce, amount of time spent together, etc.
    Example: Are you satisfied with how your SPOUSE handles money? 0 – yes;
               1 – sometimes (and don't know); 2 – no.

14. *Parental rejection:* The number of changes in the child's behavior (aggression ex-
    cluded) and characteristics desired by the socializing agent. The parent is considered to
    be accepting when he indicates that his needs are satisfied by the child: "I like you the
    way you are."
    Example: Do you think NAME wastes too much time? 2 – yes; 1 – sometimes (and
               don't know); 0 – no.

15. *Parental restrictiveness:* Extent to which the child defines behaviors which are proper
    for him to perform rather than the agent defining proper behaviors for the child.
    Restrictiveness refers to the amount of control exercised by the agent over the child.
    Example: Do you make NAME finish up everything he is served at mealtime?
               2 – yes; 1 – sometimes (and don't know); 0 – no.

16. *Punishment for aggression:* Rewards and punishments of various intensities admin-
    istered by socializing agents contingent upon the child's aggressive behavior.
    Example: What do you usually do when NAME is rude to you? (Verbatim response
               and probes recorded, subsequently rated by three judges on a scale from
               1 to 7.) 1 – rewarding aggression; 2 – don't do anything; 3–7 – mild to
               severe punishment for aggression.

17. *Punishment for dependency:* Rewards and punishments of various intensities admin-
    istered by socializing agent when child asks for help.
    Example: What do you usually do when NAME asks for help? (Each response was
               rated by three judges on a scale from 1 to 4.) 1 – giving help; to 4 –
               punishing the child.

18. *Punishment for nurturance signals:* Rewards and punishment of various intensities
    administered to child by socializing agent in situations which might tend to lead to
    nurturant behavior on part of agent.
    Example: What do you usually do when NAME is afraid? (Each response was rated
               by three judges on a scale from 1 to 4.) 1 – giving nurturance; to 4 –
               punishing the child.

19. *Residential mobility:* A measure of the number of times the child changed residence
    and thereby had to change schools and/or find new friends.
    Example: How often has moving meant that NAME had to find new friends?
               o – none; 1 – once; 2 – 2 to 3 times; 3 – 4+.

20. *Rural background:* Population size of geographical area in which respondent was born
    and grew up.

TABLE II.1 cont.

| Example: | Where did the family live when you were born — on a farm, or in a village, town, small city, medium-sized city, or big city? 1 – big city; (500,000+); 2 – medium-sized city (100,000–500,000); 3 – small city (10,000–100,000); 4 – town (1,000–10,000); 5 – village (under 1,000); 6 – farm. |

21,
22.   *Shame, at home and out of home:* Tendency to punish in public assessed by items involving different kinds of punishment and different publics.

| Example: | Suppose NAME was naughty and you felt he deserved a scolding. Would you do it when: (1) your SPOUSE and other children could hear it; (2) one of NAME's friends could hear; (3) one of your close friends or relatives could hear; (4) a neighbor or acquaintance could hear; (5) you were in public and someone else might hear? 0 – no; 1 – sometimes (and don't know); 2 – yes. |

The first item constitutes a separate measure, punishing the child in front of his family, which defines home shame.

23.   *Social isolation of child:* Frequency and types of contacts with peers outside of school.

| Example: | About how many children of NAME's age live in the neighborhood? Would you say about one or two, three to five, or more than five? 3 – none; 2 – 1 to 2; 1 – 3 to 5; 0 – 5+. |

total correlations were calculated. The sets of items were analyzed separately from mothers and fathers. With initially small sets of items, correction for overlap and other procedures were used. Items were retained which had the highest item-total correlation (no items with correlations below .30 were retained), reducing the 272-item questionnaire to 180 items. This approach to interview-building capitalizes on traditional test-construction methods which are rarely used in devising interviews for the usual survey study. One result of this analysis was, in some instances, to create two measures from a set of items originally intended to provide a score on one variable. For example, two measures of dependency conflict were suggested by the intercorrelational data, one tapping sanctions administered when children are dependent, the other consisting of parental statements about whether their children find it difficult to accept help.

Once homogeneous sets of items had been derived, a number of correlational analyses were done. First, scores on each variable from the mothers' interview were correlated with scores on similar variables in the fathers' interview. As shown in Table II.2, of twenty-three correlations, only eleven were significantly better than zero ($p < .05$).[1] Obviously mothers' and fathers' responses cannot be substituted for one another, at least in this child-rearing questionnaire.

[1] We are aware that there is an error when a region of rejection for a set of intercorrelations is established by a procedure appropriate to single correlations. However, we know of no established procedure that is available for establishing a region of rejection for a set of intercorrelations (Harris, 1967).

TABLE II.2

Correlations between Mothers and Fathers on Interview Variables

Variable	Boys N = 26 $r_{.05} = .39$ $r_{.01} = .50$	Girls N = 24 $r_{.05} = .40$ $r_{.01} = .52$	Both N = 50 $r_{.05} = .28$ $r_{.01} = .35$
Anomie	.593	.519	.562
Ethnicity	.409	.142	.209
Home aggression of child	.394	.148	.250
Residential mobility	.910	.887	.909
Confessing by child	.178	.347	.252
Parental disharmony	.341	.601	.465
Parental rejection	.698	.514	.636
Parental restrictiveness	.286	.496	.385
Approval of aggression	-.007	.202	.091
Mother's aggression	.083	.406	.150
Father's aggression	.239	.291	.348
Rural background	.167	.463	.319
Shame, out of home	.231	.083	.164
Shame, at home	.098	-.251	-.058
Social isolation of child	.302	.549	.418
Lack of social participation	.623	.620	.627
Punishment for dependency	-.076	.211	.045
Child's dependency avoidance	-.099	.062	-.051
Parental aspirations for child	.595	.434	.516
Parental aspirations for self	.128	.061	.067
Punishment for aggression	.424	.411	.415
Nonrecognition of child's needs	.159	.176	.205
Punishment for nurturance signals	.345	-.028	.128

Two intercorrelation matrices were calculated, one for mothers and one for fathers (see Table II.3). Each matrix consisted of twenty-five interview variables and five classroom measures. Table II.4 contains a list of the variables and the items that were retained to comprise the measure of each. These intercorrelational analyses were exploratory and were used as a basis for making decisions as to retention or elimination of variables for the final interview (see below).

The wide range of the correlations in the two 30 × 30 matrices indicated the presence of at least several factors. A large number of insignificant correlations indicated independence of many of the variables, and many patterns of correlations suggested the presence of several unifying dimensions.

A factor analysis based on these two intercorrelation matrices (Tables II.5 and II.6) emphasized the difference between information obtained from mothers and from fathers. It is interesting that although the factors extracted from the two sets of interviews show some similarity, in general the factor compositions and loadings are quite different. For instance, Factor I in this version of the interview with fathers seemed to reflect a general tendency for the individual to rate himself and others as aggressive and no good in a variety of situations (perhaps a general social desirability effect). Mothers, however, from the loadings on Factor I, seemed to be more discriminating in their responses; their sanctions were more specific. This was one indication we had that mothers might really be better informants. They are less prone to a generalized set toward either the subject or the interviewer. The second factor in both sets of interviews seemed to be somewhat similar in composition. Social class, anomie, and low aspirations for self and child are highly loaded on this factor in both series. This constellation may be characterized as social mobility potential. Factor III for fathers seemed to reflect a permissive home atmosphere. Approval of aggression was positively loaded, whereas shame at home and punishment for aggression were negatively loaded on this factor. The factor composition, however, was not the same for mothers although shame at home was also highly loaded on this factor for mothers. Similarly, the loadings on other factors in mothers' and fathers' interviews were markedly different, except for Factors IV, V, and VI on which mothers and fathers had one highly loaded component in common. Another illustration of how method-bound (considering each parent to be a different method) must be the data obtained in the usual one-parent study is seen in the drop in relation when comparing correlations based only on information from fathers to correlations where every father variable is correlated with every mother variable. In all cases the size of correlation shrinks: the correlation between fathers' ratings of rejection and fathers' ratings of frequency of aggression is .46, but the correlation between mothers' ratings of frequency of aggression and fathers' ratings of rejection is only .15 (Banta, 1960).

TABLE II.3
Intercorrelations among Interview and Classroom Measures (First Interview Study)

LEGEND

	Variable	Low score signifies	High score signifies
1.	Aggression	Low aggression	High aggression
2.	Polite	Not polite	Polite
3.	Won't fight	Will fight	Won't fight
4.	Popularity with peers	Unpopularity	Popularity
5.	Rejection by peers	Not rejected	Rejected
6.	Anomie	Low	High
7.	Ethnicity	Nonethnic	Ethnic
8.	Home aggression, child	Low	High
9.	Residential mobility	Low	High
10.	Confessing	Hide, deny	Confessing
11.	Parental disharmony	Low	High
12.	Rejection by parent	Not rejected	Rejected
13.	Restrictiveness	Not restricted	Restricted
14.	Approval of home aggression	Disapprove	Approve
15.	Respondent's aggression	Low aggression	High aggression
16.	Spouse's aggression	Low aggression	High aggression
17.	Rurality	Urban	Rural
18.	Rural background	Urban	Rural
19.	Shame, out of home	Low	High
20.	Shame, at home	Low	High
21.	Social isolation of child	Nonisolated	Isolated
22.	Parents' social participation	Nonisolated	Isolated
23.	Social class	High class	Low class
24.	Dependency conflict, A	Reward	Punish
25.	Dependency conflict, B	Low	High
26.	Aspiration for child	High education	Low education
27.	Aspiration for self	High ambition	Low ambition
28.	Sanctions for aggression	Reward	Punish
29.	Nurturance, B	Nurturance	Lack of nurturance
30.	Nurturance, A	Reward	Punish

Fathers' $N = 50$. Any correlation coefficient with an absolute value equal to or greater than .22 is significant (for the hypothesis that $p = 0$ at the 5 percent level.
Mothers' $N = 59$. Five percent, $r \geqslant .23$.

198

TABLE II.3 cont.

INTERCORRELATIONS
(fathers above diagonal; mothers below diagonal)
(decimals omitted)

	1	2	3	4	5	6	7	8	9	10	11	12	13	14	15	16	17	18	19	20	21	22	23	24	25	26	27	28	29	30
1. Aggression[a]		-60	-42	-51	83	14	26	13	15	-31	-08	31	12	-11	13	-15	-18	-14	08	06	09	09	02	21	08	15	07	31	-06	12
2. Polite[a]	-63		72	88	-68	-10	-22	-09	-15	15	04	-17	-26	15	-06	01	02	07	-11	-09	01	-13	03	-26	12	-04	-11	-21	14	-04
3. Won't fight[a]	-50	77		70	-52	01	-14	12	02	22	09	02	-26	-11	08	22	-11	17	-15	05	-16	04	04	-11	25	-03	-18	-07	10	06
4. Popularity with peers[a]	-56	89	72		-74	-15	-30	10	-21	22	09	-12	-28	12	-02	-05	-02	-01	-23	-12	-02	-04	-04	-31	09	-11	-06	-11	-08	-14
5. Rejection by peers[a]	83	-67	-54	-74		26	41	-08	29	-29	-07	20	18	-09	-02	-20	-05	-04	19	18	11	15	16	24	-02	13	10	19	05	11
6. Anomie	23	-13	-24	-18	24		22	-15	29	-07	24	-02	-10	-06	09	22	-16	-04	16	23	-16	37	58	30	-06	32	12	07	30	18
7. Ethnicity	00	00	-03	08	-03	-15		00	26	-07	-13	-08	-01	-19	-22	-17	-11	-04	23	-05	-21	28	16	02	01	-12	-19	03	-12	-21
8. Home aggression, child	05	04	14	11	-17	-09	11		-28	-32	14	49	06	00	00	14	-26	-28	-05	00	-17	-12	-10	03	08	18	-07	46	-07	01
9. Residential mobility	10	-10	-01	-15	17	20	21	-28		05	09	23	00	-19	36	-11	-29	-10	-07	-04	-09	-34	10	03	01	-05	15	00	14	20
10. Confessing	-21	-01	00	-03	-10	04	03	21	04		-27	-58	-07	00	-02	-18	14	-21	-08	-01	-10	14	01	-28	01	02	-22	-35	-09	-28
11. Parental disharmony	04	00	06	-01	-01	30	-14	11	12	10		42	-17	-14	04	37	-03	13	10	29	-01	02	-08	27	08	-05	-16	18	17	04
12. Rejection by parent	40	05	-23	-29	35	-10	17	00	04	-32	-27		-04	00	32	17	-37	-16	-11	-49	41	41	-06	36	16	-05	-13	44	-12	19
13. Restrictiveness	-02	-37	-08	-06	-12	-01	-14	25	21	12	10	20		-06	-14	-11	10	15	08	09	06	-08	-05	05	-10	01	20	28	-09	-16
14. Approval of home aggression	14	-12	-08	-10	10	-28	14	-05	-21	00	-02	-03	-24		-06	00	05	07	-09	28	-05	18	04	-05	-17	-09	03	-28	16	04
15. Respondent's aggression	15	-12	01	-07	10	02	-12	-08	03	14	-17	11	12	-18		29	-27	26	-03	-01	42	24	00	33	11	-02	03	24	-02	25
16. Spouse's aggression	13	-09	01	01	02	09	-05	-01	03	08	01	-12	12	-19	29		-10	-06	17	-05	07	-09	14	26	08	21	-12	03	28	17
17. Rurality	-11	-03	-09	-02	10	-05	-01	09	-01	12	08	04	-06	-15	-15	-22		-15	22	08	18	14	23	-01	09	01	16	-04	-02	17
18. Rural background	-01	-01	08	-07	-07	-15	08	04	-31	00	-05	08	16	-03	30	06	-02		48	-05	15	14	08	15	10	04	10	-16	07	-26
19. Shame, out of home	04	00	-19	-04	02	04	-18	00	-30	00	-01	05	03	21	23	38	-22	-25		-37	-01	08	-03	-02	05	11	17	18	-06	-14
20. Shame, at home	-07	06	01	-07	04	28	-06	18	00	-24	12	03	00	-09	-05	22	-08	-05	01		-06	34	25	08	-10	13	-19	32	06	-24
21. Social isolation of child	03	-01	08	-04	04	-02	00	18	-09	04	13	07	22	-16	05	02	20	15	06	08		08	18	30	14	33	-11	19	00	-10
22. Parents' social participation	28	-04	-13	16	-13	-13	06	00	00	10	-07	-02	02	-25	12	07	-12	17	20	16	-24		21	34	35	00	22	24	24	13
23. Social class	07	-17	-03	-18	12	56	06	18	00	-19	11	20	11	-41	-10	18	01	08	29	04	-03	21		47	36	08	12	15	26	20
24. Dependency conflict, A[b]	-04	-18	24	23	26	51	-03	02	35	20	28	-06	04	04	-26	-17	-13	06	-09		13	34	47		03	24	17	39	15	38
25. Dependency conflict, B[b]	-01	-20	-12	-13	-08	29	00	-14	14	-17	-12	-10	-20	12	10	-20	-09	27	06		-11	35	36	03		-01	04	38	03	06
26. Aspiration for child	03	-05	-07	-09	08	25	15		-06	-04	-07		04	-14	24	21	02	-26	22		05	00	08	24	-01		-20	-02	32	13
27. Aspiration for self	18	-12	08	08	-13	25	06		-01				42	-18	-37	-01	-11	23	-01		-15	22	12	17	02	-06		-35	14	17
28. Sanctions for aggression	-04	-07	24	23	25	41	-09	47	22				-12	00	-01	05	00	00	24		-20		13	39		-09	22		-14	10
29. Nurturance, B[b]	03	-22	-26	-29	24	02	-03		20				14	-03			-18							37				07		49
30. Nurturance, A[b]	12	-34	-34	-34		26	-15	-11	04					08															42	

Fathers' N = 50. Any correlation coefficient with an absolute value equal to or greater than .22 is significant (for the hypothesis that $p = 0$ at the 5 percent level.
Mothers' N = 59. Five percent significant, $r \geq .23$.
[a]These are classroom measures obtained from peer-ratings. All other measures obtained from parent interviews.
[b]A refers to sanction-type items; B refers to non-sanction-type items.

TABLE II.4
Items per Preliminary Interview Variables

Note: Symbols to the left of the items are as follows:

M = item used to derive score for men
W = item used to derive score for women
– = item not used for one of the sexes

Whenever response foils are omitted, they are the same as for the previous item.

ANOMIE

M W 27A. These days a person doesn't really know whom he can count on.
           0 – disagree; 1 – don't know; 2 – agree
– W   B.   No one really understands me.
M W   C.   Most people don't really care what happens to the next fellow.
M W   D.   Nowadays, a person has to live pretty much for today and let tomorrow take care of itself.
M W 29C. Most people in public office are not really interested in the problems of the average man.
M W 123. It's hardly fair to bring a child into the world with the way things look for the future.
M W 162A. Next to health, money is the most important thing in life.
M W   B.   In spite of what people say, the lot of the average man is getting worse, not better.
– W   C.   To make money, there are no right and wrong ways any more, only easy ways and hard ways.
M W   D.   You sometimes can't help wondering whether anything is worthwhile any more.

ETHNICITY

M W   8.   Now, about your parents. Were either of them born outside the United States? Where was your father born? Where was your mother born?
M W   9.   (If both parents born in U.S., ask:) Were any of your grandparents born outside the United States? Where was your father's father born, etc?
           1 – Old Yankee; 2 – 3rd generation foreign-born; 3 – 2nd generation foreign-born; 4 – 1st generation foreign-born, e.g., respondent foreign-born

HOME AGGRESSION, CHILD

M W 125. How often does NAME get very mad?
           0 – never; 1 – rarely; 2 – occasionally; 3 – pretty often; 4 – frequently; 5 – daily
M W 126. How often does NAME say mean things to another child?
M W 127. How often does NAME grab things from another child?
M W 128. How often does NAME make it hard for another child to do the things that child wants to do?
M W 129. How often does NAME do things that bother others?
M W 130. How often does NAME push or shove another child (not accidentally)?
M W 131. How often does NAME use bad words when another child bothers him; that is, words that you consider to be bad?

200

TABLE II.4 cont.

M W	133.	How often does NAME take another child's things without asking — things they don't both own or share?
M W	135.	How often does NAME complain to you when you tell him what to do?
M -	136.	How often does NAME take your things without permission; that is, when you don't want him to?
M W	137.	How often does NAME pester you?
M W	138.	How often does NAME disobey you?
- W	139.	How often does NAME make marks on the furniture or walls — accidentally or not?
M W	140.	How often is NAME rude to you?
M W	141.	How often does NAME give you a dirty look?

RESIDENTIAL MOBILITY

M W	12A.	How many different houses or apartments has NAME lived in since birth? 0 - 1; 2 - 2-3; 3 - 4+
M W	B.	How often has moving meant that NAME had to find new friends? 1 - none; 1 - once; 2 - 2-3 times; 3 - 4+
M W	C.	How many times has NAME had to change schools because of moving? 0 - none; 1 - once; 2 - twice; 3 - 3+

CONFESSING

| M W | 93B. | When NAME has done something naughty *and* you haven't seen him do it, does he come and tell you about it without your having to ask him?
4 - all the time; 3 - most of the time; 2 - some of the time; 1 - almost never; 0 - never |
| M W | 94A. | When you ask NAME about something naughty he has done; how often does he deny it?
0 - all the time; 1 - most of the time; 2 - some of the time; 3 - almost never; 4 - never |

PARENTAL DISHARMONY

M W	23.	Do you and your SPOUSE disagree about choice of friends? 0 - no; 1 - yes and don't know
M W	24.	Do you and your SPOUSE disagree about your social life (free time)?
M W	30A.	About how many Sundays or days off do you and your SPOUSE spend a good part of the day together; about half of them, almost all, some? 0 - almost all; 1 - one-half; 2 - some; 3 - none
- W	30B.	What sort of things do you like to do together? 1 - nothing; 2 - 1+
M W	31.	About how many evenings a week, in general, have you and your SPOUSE spent together at home and *without company*? 0 - 6-7; 1 - 3-5; 2 - 2 or less

			Yes	Sometimes and DK	No
- W	64.	Do you and your SPOUSE have serious disagreements about raising NAME?	2	1	0
M W	77A.	Can NAME hear when you and your SPOUSE argue?	2	1	0

201

TABLE II.4 cont.

				Yes	Sometimes and DK	No
-	W	B.	Does NAME get involved in disagreements between you and your SPOUSE?	2	1	0
-	W	160.	Are you satisfied with how much your husband helps around the house?	0	1	2
M	-		Do you feel that your wife is interested enough in your work?	0	1	2
M	W	161.	Are you satisfied with how your SPOUSE handles money?	0	1	2
M	W	164.	Do you or your SPOUSE ever leave the home during an argument?	2	1	0
M	W	165.	Is it easy for you to make up?	0	1	2
M	W	166.	Do arguments between you and your SPOUSE settle anything?	0	1	2

			REJECTION BY PARENT	Yes	Sometimes and DK	No
M	W	36.	Does NAME show enough responsibility in doing routine chores around the house?	0	1	2
M	W	38.	Are you bothered that NAME doesn't follow directions when he runs an errand?	2	1	0
M	W	39.	Are you satisfied with how NAME takes care of his things?	0	1	2
M	W	67.	When NAME has money to buy something for himself, are you displeased with what he buys?	2	1	0
M	W	68.	Do you think NAME wastes too much time?	2	1	0
M	W	69.	Do you get annoyed because NAME is not ready on time or isn't where he is supposed to be on time?	2	1	0
M	W	70.	Is NAME too forgetful?	2	1	0
M	W	71.	Are you satisfied with NAME's manners?	0	1	2
M	W	118.	Are you annoyed that NAME does not read as well as *you* think he should? 0 - yes; 1 - somewhat; 2 - no			
M	W	119.	Are you pleased with the quality of NAME's schoolwork?			

			RESTRICTIVENESS	Yes	Sometimes and DK	No
-	W	37.	Does NAME have chores around the house that you regularly require him to do?	2	1	0
-	W	57.	Do you have to quiet the kids down because they are making too much noise?	2	1	0
M	W	59.	Do you feel that it is all right for NAME to do anything else during mealtime; for example, getting up to play, reading, or watching TV?	0	1	2
M	W	61.	Do you make NAME finish up everything he is served at mealtime?	2	1	0
M	-	115.	Is it easy for you to say "no" to NAME and stick by it?	2	1	0

TABLE II.4 cont.

M	W	66A.	Does NAME receive a regular allowance?
		B.	Does NAME ever do things that make you withhold part or all of his allowance?
		C.	Can NAME usually spend his allowance however he wishes without asking you or your SPOUSE?

0 – regular allowance, never withholding, no questions asked; 1 – regular allowance, is withheld, *no* questions asked; 2 – regular allowance, never withheld, questions asked; 3 – regular allowance, is withheld, questions asked; 4 – no regular allowance

APPROVAL OF HOME AGGRESSION

M W 96. Suppose NAME gets very mad. Would you:
0 – strongly disapprove; 1 – mildly disapprove; 2 – not care and don't know; 3 – mildly approve; 4 – strongly approve

M W 97. Suppose NAME said mean things to another child?

M W 98. Suppose NAME grabbed things from another child?

M W 99. Suppose NAME makes it hard for another child to do the things that child wants to do?

M – 105. Suppose NAME forgets to return things he borrowed from another child?

M – 106. Suppose NAME takes another child's things without asking — things they don't both own or share?

M – 107. Suppose NAME makes up stories or lies to get another child into trouble?

M W 108. Suppose NAME complains to you when you tell him what to do?

M W 109. Suppose NAME takes your things without permission; that is, when you don't want him to?

M – 111. Suppose NAME disobeys you?

M W 112. Suppose NAME makes marks on the furniture or walls — accidentally or not?

M W 113. Suppose NAME is rude to you?

M W 114. Suppose NAME gives you a dirty look?

RESPONDENT'S AGGRESSION

M W 147. Suppose you were a boss and one of the workers did something wrong. Would you criticize him if he had done the same thing within the last week and you had talked to him about it?
0 – no; 1 – yes

149A. Suppose that you are driving a new car and get into an accident which is clearly the other driver's fault. Would you show your anger if:

M W   1. he says, "What's the matter, can't you drive?"

– W   2. he apologizes?

M W   3. he says, "I'm not going to say anything until I see a lawyer"?

M W   4. he laughs it off?

151A. (*For men:*) Suppose a man was angry at you and made as if to hit you. Would you get ready to defend yourself or try to calm things down if he:…
(*For women:*) Suppose a woman was angry at you and made as if to slap you. Would you get ready to defend yourself or try to calm things down if she:

M –   1. had a good reason to be angry at you;

M W   2. had little or no reason to be angry at you;

TABLE II.4 cont.

M	–		3. was just angry in general and was just picking on you?
			0 – nonaggressive responses; 1 – aggressive responses
M	–	154A.	Suppose someone is unnecessarily rude to you, would you be rude back?
			0 – nonaggressive responses; 1 – DK; 2 – aggressive responses
M	W	155A.	Suppose you're trying to get something important across to somebody and he doesn't seem to want to understand. Would you show your impatience?
M	–	156A.	Suppose you're in a store and in a hurry to pay for your purchase and get out. The person at the cash register is taking her time joking with the customer in front of you. Would you show your impatience?
M	W	157A.	Suppose when you're driving, someone passes you and cuts in real close. Would you show your anger?
M	–	158A.	Suppose you see an opportunity to sneak into a line. Would you?

SPOUSE'S AGGRESSION

		147B.	Suppose your SPOUSE were a boss and one of the workers did something wrong. Would your SPOUSE criticize the worker if:
M	–		1. the worker was new on the job?
M	W		2. the worker had recently done other things wrong?
			0 – no; 1 – DK; 2 – yes
		149B.	Suppose your SPOUSE is driving a new car and gets into an accident which is clearly the other driver's fault. Would your SPOUSE show anger if the other driver.
M	W		1. says, "What's the matter, can't you drive?"
M	W		2. apologizes?
M	W		3. says, "I'm not going to say anything until I see my lawyer"?
M	W		4. laughs it off?
		151B.	(For men:) Suppose a woman was angry at your wife and made as if to slap her. Would your wife get ready to defend herself or try to calm things down if she: ...
			(For women:) Suppose a man was angry at your husband and made as if to hit him. Would your husband get ready to defend himself or try to calm things down if he:
M	W		1. had good reason to be angry at SPOUSE?
M	W		2. had little or no reason to be angry at SPOUSE?
M	W		3. was just angry in general and was just picking on SPOUSE?
			0 – nonaggressive response; 1 – DK; 2 – aggressive response
–	W	154B.	Suppose someone is unnecessarily rude to your SPOUSE, would SPOUSE be rude back?
M	W	155B.	Suppose your SPOUSE were trying to get something important across to somebody and he doesn't seem to want to understand. Would your SPOUSE show impatience?
M	W	156B.	Suppose your SPOUSE were in a store and in a hurry to pay for the purchase and get out. The person at the cash register is taking her time joking with the customer in front of your SPOUSE. Would SPOUSE show impatience?
M	W	157B.	Suppose when your SPOUSE is driving, someone passes and cuts in real close. Would your SPOUSE show anger?

TABLE II.4 cont.

- W 158B. Suppose your SPOUSE saw an opportunity to sneak into a line. Would he?

RURALITY

M W 4C. Rurality of place of residence.
0 – Hudson (urban); 1 – other village; 2 – open country; 3 – farm in village; 4 – farm not in village

M W 5E.[a] How many months in the past year did you work full time on the farm?
1 – under 3; 2 – 3–5; 3 – 6+

M W F.[a] Is farming the major source of your income; that is, does more than half of your income come from farming?
1 – no; 2 – yes

RURAL BACKGROUND

M W 7A. Where did the family live when you were born; on a farm, or in a village, town, small city, medium-sized city, or big city?
1 – big city (500,000+); 2 – medium-sized city (100,000–500,000);
3 – small city (10,000–100,000); 4 – town (1,000–10,000);
5 – village (under 1,000); 6 – farm

M W B. Now, where did you grow up? Did you spend most of your childhood up to the age of 16 on a farm, in a village, in a town, in a small city, in a medium-sized city, or in a big city?

SHAME – AT HOME AND OUT OF HOME[b]

146. Suppose NAME was naughty and you felt he deserved a scolding. Would you do it when:
M W 1. your SPOUSE and other children could hear it?
M W 2. one of NAME's friends could hear?
M W 3. one of your close friends or relatives could hear?
M W 4. a neighbor or acquaintance could hear?
M W 5. you were in public and someone else might hear?[c]
0 – no; 1 – sometimes and don't know; 2 – yes[c]

M W 148. Suppose NAME was naughty and you felt you ought to take away some privilege. Would you do it when: . . .

M W 150. Suppose NAME was naughty and you felt he deserved a spanking. Would you do it when: . . .

M W 152. Suppose NAME was naughty and you felt he deserved a warning. Would you do it when: . . .

SOCIAL ISOLATION OF CHILD

M W 14. About how many children of NAME's age live in the neighborhood? Would you say about one or two, three to five, or more than five?
3 – none; 2 – 1–2; 1 – 3–5; 0 – 5+

[a]These questions asked of or about fathers only.
[b]The first item of each group constitutes a separate measure, punishing the child in front of his family, which defines home shame.
[c]Questions and response alternatives are the same for the four different kinds of punishment.

TABLE II.4 cont.

M	W	15.	About how many days a week does NAME play with children other than (sibs and/or the children who live in your home)? 0 – every day; 1 – 5–6 days; 2 – 3–5 days; 3 – 2 or less
M	W	16.	Are his friends mostly boys, mostly girls, or both? 0 – both; 1 – same sex only; 2 – other sex only; 3 – no friends
M	–	17.	Are NAME's friends the same children he goes to school with? 2 – yes; 1 – some of them; 0 – no
M	W	19.	Can you give me an idea of about how many good friends NAME has? Would you say one or two, three to five, or more than five? 3 – none; 2 – 1–2; 1 – 3–5; 0 – 5+

PARENTS' SOCIAL PARTICIPATION

M	W	20A.	How many families who are relatives of yours live in or around Columbia County? 0 – 6+; 1 – 2–5; 2 – 1; 3 – none
M	W	B.	How many of these families do you see fairly often; i.e., at least five or six times a year?
M	W	21.	About how many neighbors or friends around here do you see fairly often; i.e., at least five or six times a year?
M	W	25.	All together, about how many people are there whom you consider to be *close* friends; i.e., people you can confide in and sound off to?
M	W	28A.	Could you tell me the names of the *local* organizations, societies, and clubs you belong to? 0 – 6+; 1 – 4–5; 2 – 2–3; 3 – 1; 4 – none
M	W	B.	Which of these are you active in; i.e., attend at least some of their meetings or affairs?
M	W	C.	About how many times in the past year have you attended meetings or affairs of any *local* organizations, societies, or clubs? 0 – 13+; 1 – 7–12; 2 – 4–6; 3 – 1–3; 4 – none
M	W	29A.	Have you ever been a member of a committee in any of the *local* groups you have belonged to? 0 – yes; 1 – no
M	W	B.	Have you ever been an officer in any of the *local* groups you have belonged to?

SOCIAL CLASS[d]

5B.	Could you tell me what you are now doing for a living?
C.	Are you working for yourself or for others?
D.	(If self:) How many people do you have working for you? (If others:) Do you have any people working under you; that is, people for whom you make decisions on the job?
5G.	Do you own the farm, or are you a tenant or employee? 1 – owner (include partner); 2 – tenant; 3 – farm worker
171A.	Now about yourself — how far did you go in school? 1 – graduate or professional school degree; 2 – college graduate; 3 – 1–3 years college; 4 – high school graduate; 5 – 10–11 years; 6 – 7–9 years; 7 – under 7 years of schooling

[d]Social class index for each family based on father's occupation and education.

TABLE II.4 cont.

B.   (If R mentions vocation or technical type of school not usually requiring college degree – e.g., music, secretarial, trade, nursing, etc., proceed as follows. Ask:) What was the last regular kind of school (e.g., grammar, high school, or college) you attended? (And ask:) What year did you complete in it? Then get details on other schooling, type and number of years.

DEPENDENCY CONFLICT, A

M W 46A.   What do you *usually* do when NAME asks for help? (If necessary, ask:) What did you do the last time? Is this what you typically do?
        (Each response was coded by three judges on a scale from 1 to 4.)
        1 – giving help; to 4 – punishing the child

M W B.   What if it happens again *soon*; that is, NAME asks for help, what do you do you do then? (Probe:) Have you ever had to do anything else?

M W 49.[e]   What do you usually do when NAME asks for attention?

M W 81.[e]   What do you usually do when NAME wants sympathy?

DEPENDENCY CONFLICT, B

M W 41.   Does NAME try to hide the fact that he needs a lot more attention on some days than on most other days?
        0 – no; 1 – sometimes and don't know; 2 – yes

– W 42.   Does NAME sometimes resent your taking care of him when he is sick?
        0 – no; 1 – yes

– W 55C.   When NAME is afraid, does he often object to your trying to find out why?
        0 – no; 1 – sometimes; 2 – yes

M W 72B.   Does NAME try to hide his feelings when he is upset?
        0 – no; 1 – sometimes and don't know; 2 – yes

M W 74.   Does NAME seem embarrassed when you take his part?

– W 82.   Does NAME object to too much sympathy even when he has a problem?

SOCIAL MOBILITY ASPIRATIONS FOR CHILD AND SELF

Analysis of the following two items revealed such low intercorrelations that no meaningful score could be derived. However, two of the items were used in the correlation matrix on the supposition that they might be useful measures of aspirations.

M W 175A.   How much education do you expect NAME to get?
        1 – college, or high school plus specialized training; 2 – high school graduate or less

M – 176.   When you left school what particular kind of occupation or life work was it your ambition to reach some day?
        1 – professional status; 2 – minor profession, small business, or farm owner; 3 – skilled worker trades; 4 – semi-skilled or unskilled occupations

– W 176.   When you left school, what were your ambitions for the future?
        1 – high occupational status aspirations; 2 – medium; 3 – low

SANCTIONS FOR AGGRESSION

M W 50A.   What do you usually do when NAME says mean things to another child?

[e]The format of these questions is the same as for questions 46A and B.

TABLE II.4 cont.

			What did you do the last time? Is this what you typically do?
			(Each response was coded by three judges on a scale from 1 to 7.)
			1 – rewarding aggression; 2 – don't do anything; 3–7 – mildest to severe punishment for aggression
M W		B.	What if it happens again soon; that is, NAME says mean things to another child, what do you do then? Have you ever had to do anything else? What?
M W		51.[f]	What do you usually do when NAME does things that bother another child?
M W		52.[f]	What do you usually do when NAME pushes or shoves another child?
M W		53.[f]	What do you usually do when NAME grabs things from another child?
M W		56.[f]	What do you usually do when NAME makes up stories and lies to get another child into trouble?
M W		78.[f]	What do you usually do when NAME gets very mad?
M W		79.[f]	What do you usually do when NAME pesters you?
M W		84.[f]	What do you usually do when NAME takes your things without permission; that is, when you don't want him to?
M W		88.[f]	What do you usually do when NAME is rude to you?
M W		89.[f]	What do you usually do when NAME complains to you when you tell him what to do?

NURTURANCE, A

M W		45A.	What do you *usually* do when NAME has a nightmare or bad dream? What did you do the last time? Is this what you typically do?
			(Each response was coded by three judges on a scale from 1 to 4.) 1 – giving nurturance; to 4 – punishing the child
M W		B.	What if it happens again *soon*; that is, NAME has a nightmare or bad dream, what do you do then? Have you ever had to do anything else? What?
M W		54.[g]	What do you usually do when NAME is afraid?
M W		85.[g]	What do you usually do when NAME is unhappy?
M W		90.[g]	What do you usually do when NAME cries?

NURTURANCE, B

M W		18.	Do you know the names of the children NAME usually plays with?
			0 – yes; 1 – some of them; 2 – no
M W		33.	Do you usually have time so that NAME can talk to you about things that interest him?
			0 – yes; 1 – no and don't know
M W		35.	When NAME wants to, do you let him help you in doing things around the house?
			0 – yes; 1 – sometimes; 2 – no
M W		40.	Does NAME seem to need a lot more attention on some days than on most other days?
			0 – yes; 1 – no
M W		44.	What does NAME dream about?
			0 – mentions 1+; 1 – don't know
M W		55A.	Do you often find yourself trying to figure out what NAME is afraid of?
			0 – yes; 1 – sometimes; 2 – no

[f]The format for all these questions is the same as for questions 50A and B.
[g]The format for these questions is the same as for questions 45A and B.

TABLE II.4 cont.

M W	B.	What is NAME afraid of?	
		1 – don't know; 0 – mentions 1+	
M W	62.	*(For mothers:)* How many days a week, on the average, do you do something special to make the main meal more pleasant?	
		(For fathers:) How many days a week, on the average, is it possible for you to eat the main meal with NAME?	
		0 – 6-7; 1 – 3-5; 2 – 1-2; 3 – never and don't know	
M W	72A.	What upsets NAME?	
		1 – don't know; 0 – mentions 1+	
M W	73.	How do you try to show NAME that you are on his side?	
		0 – any attempt; 1 – cannot say and don't know	
M W	86.	What makes NAME unhappy?	
		1 – don't know; 0 – mentions 1+	
M W	91.	What makes NAME cry?	
		1 – don't know; 2 – mentions 1+	

TABLE II.5
The Ordered Factor Loadings — Mothers (N = 59)

Variable	Loading (decimals omitted)
FACTOR I	
Punishment for aggression	89
Home aggression of child	53
Parental restrictiveness	40
Nonrecognition of child's needs	–36
Confessing by child	–26
Parental disharmony	25
FACTOR II	
Anomie	73
Lack of social participation	69
Social class	67
Low aspirations for self	61
Low aspirations for child	55
Approval of aggression	–47
Parental disharmony	32
Residential mobility	29
FACTOR III	
Shame, out of home	–75
Shame, at home	–67
Mother's aggression	–44
Father's aggression	–39
Child's dependence avoidance	–25

TABLE II.5 cont.

Variable	Loading (decimals omitted)
FACTOR IV	
Ethnicity	−54
Residential mobility	−43
Parental rejection	−36
Social isolation of child	25
FACTOR V	
Punishment for nurturance signals	−75
Nonrecognition of child's needs	−65
Punishment for dependency	−52
Anomie	−40
FACTOR VI	
Low aspirations for child	51
Rurality	47
Social isolation of child	27
FACTOR VII	
Child's dependence avoidance	64
Approval of aggression	37
Father's aggression	−31
Confessing by child	−29
Parental restrictiveness	−26
FACTOR VIII	
Punishment for dependency	−48
Parental disharmony	38
Father's aggression	−31
Confessing by child	−29
Parental restrictiveness	−26
FACTOR IX	
Confessing by child	35
Home aggression of child	−32
Low aspirations for self	29
Parental restrictiveness	28
Parental disharmony	28
FACTOR X	
Rural background	71
Residential mobility	−46
Approval of aggression	34
Social isolation of child	−28
Parental restrictiveness	−25

210

TABLE II.6

The Ordered Factor Loadings — Fathers ($N = 50$)

Variable	Loading (decimals omitted)
FACTOR I	
Parental rejection	84
Punishment for aggression	64
Home aggression of child	62
Confessing by child	-51
Father's aggression	48
Punishment for dependency	46
Rurality	-37
Parental disharmony	34
Punishment for nurturance signals	28
Mother's aggression	26
FACTOR II	
Social class	76
Anomie	69
Low aspirations for self	36
Shame, out of home	36
Punishment for dependency	34
Nonrecognition of child's needs	33
Low aspirations for child	28
Punishment for nurturance signals	26
FACTOR III	
Shame, at home	-81
Approval of aggression	53
Residential mobility	-34
Punishment for nurturance signals	26
Punishment for aggression	-25
FACTOR IV	
Lack of social participation	-80
Residential mobility	-61
Parental restrictiveness	-39
Rurality	31
Ethnicity	-29
Anomie	-29
FACTOR V	
Nonrecognition of child's needs	65
Punishment for nurturance signals	55
Ethnicity	-45
Low aspirations for child	37
Shame, out of home	-33

TABLE II.6 cont.

Variable	Loading (decimals omitted)
FACTOR VI	
Social isolation of child	72
Parental restrictiveness	53
Rurality	44
Punishment for aggression	34
Ethnicity	-33
Residential mobility	-27
FACTOR VII	
Rural background	-48
Child's dependence avoidance	39
Low aspirations for self	-25
FACTOR VIII	
Parental disharmony	54
Mother's aggression	51
Low aspirations for self	-28
FACTOR IX	
Confessing by child	-52
Father's aggression	-35
Rurality	30
Home aggression of child	-30

TABLE II.7
Final Status of All Measures

A. Original variables retained throughout study	Final status
Classroom	
Aggression	22 items reduced to 10
Aggression anxiety	4 items reduced to 2
Popularity	4 items reduced to 2
Activity level (rated by teacher)	Now rated by peers (3 items)
IQ — Davis-Eells	Replaced by California Mental Maturity Test
Role expectations	Ranking of 8 behaviors replaced previous format which gave no spread
Interview	
Parental restrictiveness	No change
Parental disharmony	No change
Parental rejection	No change in original items which were included in an expanded set of items to differentiate it from rejectability and general complaint

212

TABLE II.7 cont.

A. *Original variables retained throughout study*	*Final status*
Nurturance	Broken into 2 scales on basis of item total r: (*a*) Nonrecognition of child's needs — no change (*b*) Punishment for nurturance signals — this one finally dropped because of high r with *a* above
Shame	16 items reduced to 2
Ethnicity	No change
Role expectations	Changed in same way as classroom measure
Religion	No change
Education of parents	No change
Occupation of parents	No change
Owner-renter status	No change
Residential mobility of parent	No change
Geographic mobility of child	No change
Achieved mobility	No change
Mobility perception	No change
Educational aspirations for child	No change
Family structure	Simplified
Household composition	Simplified
Social isolation of child	Simplified
Parental aspirations for self	Replaced by mobility orientation because of lack of relation to criterion or other variables
Father's and mother's aggression (Role modeling)	Replaced by Walters and Zak measure (called by us "respondent's aggression") because of lack of spread and relations with our original measure
Confessing by child	No change
Direct identification	No change
Occupation aspirations for child	No change
Punishment for aggression	Eventually evolved as precoded, objective, and in 2 scales — one subtle (judgment of punishment) and one direct
Home aggression of child	Replaced by frequency and recency of aggression which was less ambiguous than previous scale, giving greater spread, and making socially unacceptable responses easier to give

B. *Variables tried out at various times and dropped*	*Reason for dropping*
Classroom	
Rejection	Not differentiated from aggression
Sarason scales	No relation to our data
Intensity of punishment (children's rating)	Inadequately tested

213

TABLE II.7 cont.

B. Variables tried out at various times and dropped	Reason for dropping
Interview	
Anomie	Contaminated by social desirability — replaced with Christie's Reversed F Scale
Dependency conflict	No relation to criterion or other variables

C. Variables used in final study but not previously used	Reason for introduction
Classroom	
Success in aggression	Measure of reward for aggression by peers
Identification measures	
(a) Occupational aspirations	Previously only obtained from parents — now obtained from children also and D score calculated
(b) Expressive behavior profile	To compare with measure obtained from parents as in a above
(c) Games and activities preference ("Would you rather")	To get at sex-typed behavior of child
Interview	
Identification measures	
(a) Guilt	To measure guilt more directly than the confessing measure and to supplement it
(b) Expressive behavior profile	To correspond to classroom measure for direct comparison with self-ratings of child
Interview	
(c) Masculine-feminine role identification	To get at sex-typed behavior of parent — compared with GAP on child (above)
Value preference and behavior profile[a]	Attitude measures to supplement role expectations
Parental presence	As control variable
Child presence	As control variable
Christie's Reversed F Scale	As check on acquiesence set
Calibration	As control variable
Questionnaire practice	As control variable
Interviewer-ratings	As control variable
"Ladies Home Journal"	Direct questions to assess some popular notions about relation of aggression to socialization practices of parents

[a]These variables are not dealt with in this volume. They were included in the interview to obtain data for a doctoral dissertation of one of the participants (Toigo, 1962).

214

TABLE II.8

All Variables for Which Agreement between Mothers' and Fathers' Rating Is Significantly Greater Than Zero

Variable[a]	Code[b]	r[c]
Frequency of home aggression of child	FR	.31
Educational aspirations for child	EA	.43
Parents' aggression (Walters-Zak)	WZ	.26
Rejection of child	RJ	.42
Recency of aggression	RA	.28
Nurturance	NU	.16
Parental disharmony	PD	.30
Confessing of child	CI	.36
Restrictiveness	RE	.32
Social isolation of child	SI	.55
Punishment for aggression	PU	.34
Residential mobility	RM	.38
Ethnicity	GL	.30
Judgment of punishment	JP	.13
Discrepancy in identification	PI	.61
Role identification	RI	.31
Guilt identification	GI	.36
Length of marriage	LM	.74
Number of children	NC	.95
Family intactness	FI	.57
Child presence	CP	.20
Parental association with child	PW	.19
Age of respondent	AG	.70
Child-rearing books	BK	.30
Shaming of child	SH	.13
Religiosity	RG	.43
Mobility perception	MP	.16
Mobility orientation	MO	.24
F Scale	FS	.17
Acquiescence	FP	.18
Enuresis	EN	.62
Education	ED	.50
Comic books	CB	.38
Hours of television	TV	.37

[a]Of a total of ninety-seven variables.

[b]The first letter of the code, "L," which signifies that the variable is taken from the parent interview, and the second letter of the code, "M" or "F," which signifies mother or father, have been omitted from this table.

[c]$r_{.05} = .13$.

TABLE II.9

Correlation of Acquiescence Score with Scores on Other Variables in Mothers' and Fathers' Interviews

Variable	Code[a]	Fathers' acquiescence	Mother's acquiescence
Frequency of child's home aggression	FR	.02	.03
Geographic mobility	GM	-.08	.03
Educational aspirations for child	EA	-.25	-.05
Respondent's aggression (Walters-Zak)	WZ	.42	.26
Respondent's occupation	RO	.20	.03
Rejection	RJ	.03	.14
Recency of child's home aggression	RA	.00	.05
Nurturance	NU	-.04	-.05
Parental disharmony	PD	.00	.06
Confessing by child	CI	-.04	-.07
Restrictiveness	RE	.00	.01
Social isolation of child	SI	.03	-.02
Punishment for aggression	PU	.33	.27
Residential mobility	RM	-.07	-.04
Ethnicity	GL	-.05	.06
Judgment of punishment	JP	-.01	.02
Profile identification	PI	.19	.13
Role identification	RI	-.01	.05
Guilt identification	GI	.05	-.07
Length of marriage	LM	.11	.12
Number of children	NC	.07	.16
Family intactness	FI	-.03	-.16
Child presence	CP	-.01	-.06
Parental association with child	PW	-.08	-.06
Parental presence	PX	.17	.07
Age of respondent	AG	.19	.15
Child care books read by parents	BK	-.12	-.11
Estimate of popularity in school	CA	.05	-.06
Use of shame	SH	.09	.00
Religiosity	RG	-.14	-.14
Mobility perception	MP	-.07	.01
Mobility orientation	MO	-.04	.02
Interviewer-rating	IR	.01	-.03
F Scale	FS	.41	.31
Enuresis	EN	.01	.51
Education of parent	ED	.30	.17
Comic books	CB	.06	.02
TV hours	TV	.05	.01
Consistency of punishment	CN	-.10	-.02

[a]The first letter of the code, "L," which signifies that the variable is taken from the parent interview, and the second letter of the code, "M" or "F," which signifies mother or father, have been omitted from this table.

216

TABLE II.10

All Variables Which Correlated Significantly with Random Composite Score in Either Mothers' or Fathers' Interviews

Variable[a]	Code[b]	Correlation coefficient[c]	
		Random score from fathers' interviews	Random score from mothers' interviews
Educational aspiration (fathers)	FEA	.07	.17
Educational aspiration (mothers)	MEA	-.01	.13
Rejection (fathers)	FRJ	.29	.17
Rejection (mothers)	MRJ	.14	.32
Nurturance (mothers)	MNU	.05	.13
Parental disharmony (fathers)	FPD	.15	.09
Parental disharmony (mothers)	MPD	.05	.14
Profile identification (fathers)	FPI	-.01	-.13
Profile identification (mothers)	MPI	.05	-.14
Guilt identification (fathers)	FGI	-.10	-.15
Religiosity (fathers)	FRG	.04	.13
Religiosity (mothers)	MRG	-.07	.14
Mobility orientation (fathers)	FMO	.08	.15
Mobility orientation (mothers)	MMO	.05	.22
Acquiescence (fathers)	FFP	.02	-.18

[a]Of a total of 208 variables.
[b]The first letter of the code, "L," which signifies that the variable is taken from the parent interview, has been omitted from this table.
[c]$r_{.05} = .13$.

TABLE II.11

Classification of Items in the 1960 Rip Van Winkle Child-Rearing Questionnaire

Code no.	Code[a]	No. of items[b]	Question nos.[b]	Classification
01	AMO	1	130A–D	Achieved mobility
02	ANY	1	140	Anything else
03	BEP	16	48A and B	Behavior profile
04	CAL	2	55, 125	Calibration
05	CHI	5	25, 40, 45A and B, 66	Child presence
06	CID	2	49, 83	Confessing identification
07	COM	27[c]	19, 22, 29, 32, 35, 37, 41, 47, 52, 53 58, 60, 71, 72, 84, 87, 91, 94, 95, 98, 103, 115, 119, 120, 121, 123, 134	Complaint

217

TABLE II.11 cont.

Code no.	Code[a]	No. of items[b]	Question nos.[b]	Classification
08	DID	1	44	Direct identification
09	EAC	2	21A and B	Educational aspirations for child
10	EDU	1	126A	Education of parent
11	ENU	1	96	Enuresis
12	FAS	18	6, 7, 8, 9, 10, 11	Family structure
13	FRA	7	23, 26, 30, 36, 39, 51, 100	Frequency of aggression
14	FSC	10	56.1–10	F Scale
15	GEL	2	5A and B	Generational level
16	GEM	1	54	Geographic mobility of child
17	GID	7	20, 28, 76, 99, 104, 105, 109	Guilt identification
18	HOC	3	12, 13, 14	Household composition
19	IND	10	Facesheet, 1, 2	Independent items
20	INT	9	141.1–9	Interviewer-ratings
21	JUP	16	102A–P	Judgment of punishment
22	LHJ	7	38, 78, 97, 114A and B, 124A and B	"Ladies Home Journal"
23	MOO	6	40.1–6	Mobility orientation
24	MOP	1	135	Mobility perception
25	NUR	8	33, 62, 70, 75, 85, 110, 112, 116	Nurturance
26	ORS	3	138	Owner-renter status
27	PAD	10	31, 34, 63, 64, 77, 79, 101, 108, 118, 131	Parental disharmony
28	PAP	9	16, 57, 69, 73, 74, 86, 88, 122, 127	Parental presence
29	PID	19	65A and B	Profile identification
30	PUN	24	50.1–6; 61.1–6; 80.1–6; 90.1–6	Punishment
31	QPR	3	81A and B, 126B	Questionnaire practice
32	RAG	12	24.1–12	Respondent's aggression
33	REA	8	42, 67, 92, 107, 117, 132, 133, 136	Recency of aggression
34	RES	5	18, 46, 89, 106, 128	Restrictiveness
35	REL	2	139A and B	Religion
36	RID	5	17, 59, 93, 129A and B	Role identification
37	RMO	2	3, 4	Residential mobility
38	ROC	4	15A–D	Respondent's occupation
39	SHA	2	43, 113	Shame

TABLE II.11 cont.

Code no.	Code[a]	No. of items[b]	Question nos.[b]	Classification
40	SIC	5	68, 82A and B, 111, 137	Social isolation of child
41	VAP	9	27A–D	Value preference
Total		286 items		

[a]The first letter of the code, "L," which signifies that the variable is taken from the parent interview, has been omitted from this table.

[b]The "No. of items" column and the "Question nos." column do not necessarily have to agree; e.g., family structure has eighteen items, but only six question numbers associated with it.

[c]The following items constitute the rejection scale: 19, 35, 47, 58, 71, 72, 84, 98, 103, 119. Complaints about aggression: 22, 37, 52, 60, 94, 121, 123, 134. General complaints: 29, 32, 41, 53, 87, 91, 95, 115, 120.

B. 1960 Rip Van Winkle Child-Rearing Questionnaire

LENGTH

The questionnaire consists of 37 pages. Of these 37 pages, seven contain instructions or response examples only; the remaining 30 pages are IBM coded.

AMOUNT OF INFORMATION IN THE QUESTIONNAIRE

There are 286 items, or units of information, in the questionnaire. An "item" is here defined as the smallest unit of information assigned to a location in the IBM card. (E.g., GEOGRAPHIC AREA OF RESIDENCE is a two-column code, but it is *one* item. PID consists of 18 scales on which a concept is rated by the respondent — each rating scale is *one* item; there are 18 items in PID altogether.)

ORGANIZATION

Parts of the questionnaire are randomized, other parts are not. The six parts of the questionnaire that are not randomized are as follows, in order of appearance in the questionnaire:

1. Facesheet, race, age, mobility, generational level, family structure, household composition, and respondent's occupation.
2. Value preference.[a]
3. School behavior preference.[a]
4. Profile identification.
5. Judgment of punishment.
6. Owner-renter status, religion, interviewer-ratings.

The placement of the remaining 173 items (60% of the interview), between each of the six parts of the questionnaire given above, was determined by randomization.

[a][These variables are not dealt with in this volume. They were included in the interview to obtain data for a doctoral dissertation of one of the participants (Toigo, 1962).]

The value preference instrument, noted above, lists 18 values, all of which appear as alternatives in each questionnaire. In order to analyze for potential order and sequence effects, six "value orders" were utilized. The value order used in a given questionnaire is coded at the bottom of page 8.

QUESTIONNAIRE AS IBM CODE MANUAL

To facilitate locating a piece of information on an IBM card, each page of the questionnaire contains a reference to the Source Card into which that page has been punched. This reference is located next to the page number at the top of each page. E.g., page 2 is punched into Card 1; all IBM columns and IBM codes on page 2 refer to Card 1.

Every item in the questionnaire is allocated to a variable. These variables are denoted by a three-letter mnemonic code. This code appears in the left margin opposite each item or block of items. Table II.11 presents a summary of the codes, their respective variables, the number of items allocated to each variable, and the question numbers associated with each variable.

IBM CODING

The 340 IBM-card columns used in coding this questionnaire can be allocated as follows:

Card-deck identification	5 columns (1 col./card)
Respondent identification	25 columns (5 cols./card)
Control punches	4 columns
Precoded data punches	283 columns
Postcoded data punches	23 columns
Total	340 columns

The questionnaire is punched into five IBM cards. The number of columns per card is as follows:

Card 6-Y01	77 columns
Card 6-Y02	70 columns
Card 6-Y03	71 columns
Card 6-Y04	65 columns
Card 6-Y05	57 columns
Total	340 columns

Each card uses five columns to identify the person interviewed: two columns for the classroom from which the child was sampled; two columns for the identification of the child in the classroom; and one column to identify the sex of the parent or parent-surrogate.

In addition, a sixth column is used for identification of the study, the card deck, and the card number within the deck. A "Y" in the sixth column identifies the 1960 RVW child-rearing study. A "0" in the sixth column specifies that the card belongs to the Source Deck. Any punch, 1–5, in the sixth column of each card specifies Card 1 to Card 5 respectively. *Thus the sixth column of every Source Card is triple-punched.*

COLOR CODING[b]

The first page of the interview is green, the last page is red. In addition, pages 7, 13, 19, and 24 are printed on green paper. These pages provide space for the identification number of the respondent which must appear on every IBM card; it is at these points in the questionnaire that the new IBM cards must be started. The green pages aid the interviewer in transferring the identification numbers rapidly from page 1.

ERROR CHECKING

There are three phases in the questionnaire checking process. They are as follows:

1. *During the interview.* On p. 29 of the questionnaire, after question 140, there are instructions to check the questionnaire in the presence of the respondent. The *only* purpose of this check is to be sure that all questions which should have been asked, were asked. A more detailed check on the coding is done when the interviewer returns.

2. *Right after the interview.* When the interviewer has returned from the respondent's house, the questionnaire is edited by the interviewer. This consists of checking that every precoded column is marked, and that the identification numbers on the green pages are transferred from the facesheet. The interviewer initials EDITED BY INTERVIEWER on facesheet when this task is completed.

3. *Before key-punching.* Double checking is done when the postcoding is completed, and after enough questionnaires have accumulated to justify sending to key-puncher. This will repeat the checking on IBM codes plus the post-codes. When this task is completed, DOUBLE CHECKED is initialed.

Note: Steps 1 and 2 are done in black pencil. Only step 3 is to be done in red pencil — red pencil supersedes any other markings or corrections.

---

[b][The original questionnaire form included colored pages, which are not included in the reproduction of the form in this volume.]

1960 RIP VAN WINKLE CHILD-REARING QUESTIONNAIRE

Family name _____

Address _____

_____

Phone _____

1-	2-		3-	4-		5-	
class			child			1	male
						2	female

Child's name _____

boy   girl   6-Y01

GEOGRAPHIC AREA OF RESIDENCE   7,8- [|]

INTERVIEWER   9,10-   00 Eron   06 M. Eron
                                       01 Walder   07 Lawrence
                                       02 Banta   08 Hurley
                                       03 Lefkowitz   09 Collins
                                       04 Toigo
                                       05 LaLiberte   [|]   OTHER
                                                                    (name)

LOCATION OF INTERVIEW   11-   1 home address
                                     2 RVW Foundation House
                                     3 other _____

DATE _____ 12-   1 Jan 1-15   7 Apr 1-15
     day   month   year   2 Jan 16-31   8 Apr 16-30
                                     3 Feb 1-15   9 May 1-15
                                     4 Feb 16-29   0 May 16-31
                                     5 Mar 1-15   X Jun 1-15
                                     6 Mar 16-31   Y Jun 16-30

SCHEDULED STARTING   13-   1 before 10:00 AM   5 4:00 - before 6:00
TIME: _____   2 10:00 - before Noon   6 6:00 - before 8:00
                                     3 12:00 - before 2:00   7 8:00 - before 10:00
                                     4 2:00 - before 4:00   8 10:00 PM or after

STARTED ON TIME?   14-   1 yes
                                     2 no, half hour late
                                     3 no, one hour late
                                     4 no, more than one hour late

TIME CONSUMED IN INTERVIEW.   15-   0 not completed   5 1-1/2 hours
IF NOT COMPLETED, NOTE WHY.   1 1/2 hour   6 1-3/4 hours
                                     2 3/4 hour   7 2 hours
                                     3 1 hour   8 2-1/4 hours
                                     4 1-1/4 hours   9 2-1/2 hours +

EDITED BY INT'WER _____   DOUBLE CHECKED _____
                  (initial)   (initial)

222

TIME QUESTIONS STARTED_____ A.M.
P.M.

IND 1. RACE:

16- 1 White
     2 Negro
     3 Other _____
     4 DK

IND 2. Let's see, your age is...?
        WRITE IN AGE. (IF NECESSARY,
        ESTIMATE AGE AND WRITE IT IN.)

17,18- [|]

19- 1 age estimated by int'wer
     2 age given by R

RMO 3. Did your family live in Columbia
        County when you were born?

20- 1 yes
     2 no, but in U.S.
     3 outside U.S.
        What country?_____

RMO 4. How many years did you live in
        Columbia County before you were
        18 years old?

21- 0 none
     1 1-3 years
     2 4-6 years
     3 7-9 years
     4 10-12 years
     5 13-15 years
     6 16-18 years

GEL 5. Now about your parents:

                    CIRCLE SPECIFY
     A. Where was your
        father born?   U.S. Other_____

     B. Where was your   U.S. Other_____
        mother born?

22- / ___ / RT

     IF BOTH PARENTS BORN IN U.S., ASK:
     Were any of your grandparents born
     outside the United States?

23- 1 yes
     2 no
     3 DK
     4 DNA

223

FAS 6. When were you married?   24,25-

                                    year

FAS 7. Have there been any other marriages?   26- 6 no other marriages

       IF YES, Are any of your present   0 no children from
       children from a previous marriage?   previous marriages
                                    1 child
                                    2 children
                                    3 children
                                    4 children
                                    5 children +

FAS 8. Is NAME your own child or is he   27- 1 own child
       adopted?   2 adopted
                                    3 other _____

FAS 9. You are presently married and living   28- 1 yes
       with your SPOUSE?   2 married, not living with
                                       SPOUSE
       IF NO, PROBE FOR DETAILS   3 divorced
                                    4 widowed
                                    5 separated
                                    6 other

       IF NO, ASK: How many years have   29- 1 month
       you been the only parent at home   2 2-6 months
       with NAME? (NO SUBSTITUTE PARENT)   3 7 months - 1 year
                                    4 2-3 years
                                    5 4-5 years
                                    6 6-7 years
                                    7 all of NAME'S life
                                    8 DNA

FAS 10. How many children do you now have   30- 1   6
       in your family? (ALL CHILDREN)   2   7
                                    3   8
                                    4   9+
                                    5

FAS 11. I'd like to know about all the children
in your family...what their names are,
and their ages. Let's start with your
oldest. (INCLUDING "NAME")

OLDEST (NAME:_____)   31-   1 boy   3 boy twin
                                            2 girl   4 girl twin

How old is he? WRITE IN AGE   32,33- ☐☐

SECOND OLDEST (NAME:_____)   34-   1 boy   3 boy twin
                                            2 girl   4 girl twin
                                                        5 DNA

How old is he? WRITE IN AGE   35,36- ☐☐

THIRD OLDEST (NAME:_____)   37-   1 boy   3 boy twin
                                            2 girl   4 girl twin
                                                        5 DNA

How old is he? WRITE IN AGE   38,39- ☐☐

FOURTH OLDEST (NAME:_____)   40-   1 boy   3 boy twin
                                            2 girl   4 girl twin
                                                        5 DNA

How old is he? WRITE IN AGE   41,42- ☐☐

FIFTH OLDEST (NAME:_____)   43-   1 boy   3 boy twin
                                            2 girl   4 girl twin
                                                        5 DNA
How old is he? WRITE IN AGE   44,45- ☐☐

RECORD ON OTHER SIDE OF PAGE IF
MORE THAN FIVE CHILDREN

TRANSFER INFORMATION ABOUT "NAME"   46-   1 boy   3 boy twin
                                            2 girl   4 girl twin

                                      47,48- ☐☐

HOC 12. Which children are now living at home?   49- 1 oldest   6 sixth
                                                      2 second   7 seventh
              MULTIPLE CODES ALLOWED   oldest   8 eighth
                                                      3 third   9 ninth
                                                      4 fourth
                                                      5 fifth

HOC 13. Is there anyone besides your own children
and your SPOUSE living in your home now?

    IF YES, ASK: Who? RECORD AGE, SEX, RELATION

50- 0 no one
   1 person
   2 people
   3 people
   4 people
   5 people +

HOC 14. Has anyone else lived in your home during NAME'S
lifetime for a year or more?

    IF YES, ASK: Who? RECORD AGE, SEX, RELATION,
               AND TIME IN CHILD'S LIFE

51- 0 no
   1 yes

ROC 15 A. At present, are you working full-time or part-
time for a living, or are you presently not
working?

52- 1 not working TO B
   2 part-time TO B
   3 full-time TO C

   B. In the year, 1959, how many months were you
working on a full or part-time basis?
NEAREST NUMBER OF MONTHS

53- 0 none TO D
   1 1-3 months TO C
   2 4-6 months TO C
   3 7+ months TO C
   4 DNA

   C. What sort of work do you do? RECORD
(PROBE: What sort of day-by-day activity does
this involve?)

Do you do any other sort of work,
or have you done any other sort
of work in 1959?

____ No EXIT TO D

____ Yes: What kind of work is
this? RECORD

What sort of work do
you usually do?
RECORD AND EXIT TO D

54- / / RT

   D. What sort of work does your SPOUSE do for a
living? RECORD (PROBE: What sort of day-by-
day activity does this involve?)

55- / / RT

226

56-Ⓧ

PAP 16. How often does your work or other
duties force you to be away from home
in the evening before NAME is asleep?

57- 1 never
    2 once in a while
    3 almost daily
    4 daily

RID 17. Who prepares the family meals?

58- 1 father mostly
    2 both
    3 mother mostly
    4 neither
    5 other _____

RES 18. Do you have to quiet the kids down
because they are making too much noise?

59- 1 no
    2 yes

COM 19. Do you think NAME reads as well as could
be expected for a child of his age?
    IF NO, ASK: Are you annoyed that he
             does not read as well as
             you think he should?

60- 0 yes

    2 yes
    1 no

GID 20. When NAME tells a fib or lie, does he
seem to be worried about it?

61- 1 no
    2 yes
    3 DK or other

EAC 21 A. How much education do you expect NAME
to get? (If you had your wish, how
far would you like him to go?)

62- 1 graduate or profes-
      sional training
    2 college graduate
    3 1-3 years college
    4 high school graduate
    5 10-11 years
    6 7-9 years
    7 under 7 years

    B. What type of work do you hope NAME
will do? RECORD (If you had your wish,
what would you like him to do?)

63- ⬭   MML

COM 22. Do you think NAME hits other children
too often?

64- 1 no
    2 yes

FRA 23. How often does NAME do things that bother
others in the family? Does it happen...

    READ ALTERNATIVES ONE AT A TIME.
    CODE FIRST ONE ACCEPTED.

65- 5 at least once a day?
    4 at least once a week?
    3 at least once a month?
    2 less than once a month?
    1 never?

RAG INSTRUCTIONS TO RESPONDENT: I am going to read
a number of statements to you. For each one I
would like you to tell me if you agree or disagree.

    24.1 There are two kinds of people in this
world: the weak and the strong.

66- 1 disagree
    2 agree

227

RAG 24.2 Dealings with policemen and government officials are always unpleasant.

67- 1 disagree
2 agree

.3 Most people get killed in accidents because of their own reckless driving.

68- 1 disagree
2 agree

.4 Horses that don't pull should be beaten and kicked.

69- 1 disagree
2 agree

.5 At times we enjoy being hurt by those we love.

70- 1 disagree
2 agree

.6 Many a decent fellow becomes a crook or a criminal because he can't stand to be pushed around so much.

71- 1 disagree
2 agree

.7 I easily lose patience with people.

72- 1 disagree
2 agree

.8 I often do things which I regret afterwards.

73- 1 disagree
2 agree

.9 It makes me mad when I can't do things for myself the way I like to.

74- 1 disagree
2 agree

.10 Occasionally I was in trouble with the police or law.

75- 1 disagree
2 agree

.11 I almost never dare to express anger toward people for fear I may lose their love or approval.

76- 1 disagree
2 agree

.12 As a young kid I often mixed with the wrong crowd.

77- 1 disagree
2 agree

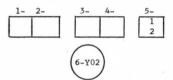

CHI 25. Would NAME rather play inside or outside? (GOOD WEATHER ASSUMED)

7- 1 outside mostly
2 both equally
3 inside mostly
4 DK

FRA 26. How often does NAME make up stories and lies to get another child into trouble with you? Does it happen...

READ ALTERNATIVES ONE AT A TIME.
CODE FIRST ONE ACCEPTED.

8- 5 at least once a day?
4 at least once a week?
3 at least once a month?
2 less than once a month?
1 never?

VALUE PREFERENCE - VAP - INSTRUCTIONS

TEAR OUT NEXT PAGE AND HAND TO RESPONDENT.

27 A. This is a list of things parents consider desirable in third-grade children. I'd like you to choose the 3 most desirable things in a third-grade <u>boy</u> - but first, let's read them to be sure we haven't missed any.

TURN PAGE AND READ WITH RESPONDENT^a

DO NOT READ THIS LIST	
01 Able to defend himself	10 Good student
02 Able to play by himself	11 Happy
03 Acts in a serious way	12 Honest
04 Affectionate	13 Liked by adults
05 Ambitious	14 Neat
06 Calm	15 Obeys his parents
07 Clean	16 Popular with children
08 Curious about things	17 Reliable
09 Good manners	18 Thoughtful of others

Now, would you choose the 3 most desirable things in a third-grade boy?

WRITE IN ABOVE CODE NUMBERS <u>CLEARLY</u> IN ORDER GIVEN BY RESPONDENT.

1-----> 9,10

2-----> 11,12

3-----> 13,14

B. Now, I'd like you to tell me which of the 3 you've picked is the <u>most desirable</u> in a third-grade boy.

WRITE IN NUMBER <u>CLEARLY</u> ----------------------------------> 15,16

C. Let's try the same thing for girls. Would you tell me the 3 most desirable things in a third-grade <u>girl</u>?

WRITE IN ABOVE CODE NUMBERS <u>CLEARLY</u> IN ORDER GIVEN BY RESPONDENT.

1-----> 17,18

2-----> 19,20

3-----> 21,22

D. Of the 3 you've mentioned, which one is the <u>most</u> desirable in a third-grade girl?

WRITE IN NUMBER <u>CLEARLY</u> ----------------------------------> 23,24

ENTER VALUE ORDER CODE FROM NEXT PAGE---------------------> 25,26

^a[The questionnaire included two sheets, each with the list in random order, not alphabetized as below.]

CID 28. Has NAME ever told you that he thought   27- 1 no
         God was punishing him?   2 yes
                                                             3 DK or other

COM 29. Does NAME play in the house too much?   28- 1 yes
                                                             2 no

FRA 30. How often does NAME bother you when you
         are talking on the telephone. Does it
         happen...   29- 5 at least once a day?
         (IF R SAYS, "NO TELEPHONE," SAY: I mean   4 at least once a week?
         on any telephone you might use.)   3 at least once a month?
                                                             2 less than once a month?
                    READ ALTERNATIVES ONE AT A TIME.   1 never?
                    CODE FIRST ONE ACCEPTED.

PAD 31. Do you and your SPOUSE ever have dis-   30- 1 no
         agreements about raising NAME?   2 yes

COM 32. Do you think NAME is pretty good about   31- 1 yes
         leaving you alone when you are talking   2 no
         with another grown-up?

NUR 33. What makes NAME cry? WRITE   32- 1 DK
                                                             2 MENTIONS 1+

PAD 34. Do you and your SPOUSE ever disagree   33- 1 no
         about what to do on your time off?   2 yes

COM 35. Do you get annoyed because NAME is not   34- 1 no
         ready on time or isn't where he's supposed   2 yes
         to be on time?

FRA 36. How often does NAME say mean things to one   35- 5 at least once a day?
         of his playmates? Does it happen...   4 at least once a week?
                                                             3 at least once a month?
                    READ ALTERNATIVES ONE AT A TIME.   2 less than once a month?
                    CODE FIRST ONE ACCEPTED.   1 never?

COM 37. Are you displeased with the way other   36- 1 yes
         children sometimes take advantage of   2 no
         NAME by trying to play too rough?

LHA 38. What are NAME'S three favorite TV or   37- ⟋‾‾‾‾⟋ LDE
         radio programs? RECORD   ⟋____⟋

FRA 39. How often does NAME give you a dirty
         look? Does it happen...   38- 5 at least once a day?
                                                             4 at least once a week?
                    READ ALTERNATIVES ONE AT A TIME.   3 at least once a month?
                    CODE FIRST ONE ACCEPTED.   2 less than once a month?
                                                             1 never?

230

CHI 40. What time does NAME leave home to go
to school?_____

Does he come home for lunch?
_____ always
_____ sometimes
_____ never

What time does NAME come home from
school in the afternoon?_____

```
┌─────────────────────────────────────┐
│            POSTCODE                  │
│                                      │
│  DEDUCT LUNCH AS INDICATED:          │
│    1 HOUR  - ALWAYS                  │
│    1/2 HOUR - SOMETIMES              │
│       0     - NEVER                  │
│                                      │
│  39- 1  10        6  7-1/2           │
│      2  9-1/2     7  7               │
│      3  9         8  6-1/2           │
│      4  8-1/2     9  6 or less       │
│      5  8         0  DK              │
└─────────────────────────────────────┘
```

TEAR OUT NEXT PAGE AND HAND TO RESPONDENT.[b]

MOO Getting ahead in your job or place in the
community sometimes means that you have to
do certain things you may not like. How
willing would you be to do each of the
following things in order to get ahead?

40.1 How willing would you be (for your   40- 1 not at all willing
husband) to learn new skills in order   2 a little willing
to get ahead?   3 somewhat willing
                                                    4 very willing
                                                    5 DK

.2 How willing would you be to leave your   41- 1 not at all willing
friends to get ahead?   2 a little willing
                                                    3 somewhat willing
                                                    4 very willing
                                                    5 DK

.3   42-Ⓨ

.4 How willing would you be to move around   43- 1 not at all willing
the country a lot to get ahead?   2 a little willing
                                                    3 somewhat willing
                                                    4 very willing
                                                    5 DK

.5 How willing would you be (for your   44- 1 not at all willing
husband) to take on more responsibility   2 a little willing
in order to get ahead?   3 somewhat willing
                                                    4 very willing
                                                    5 DK

   [b][The questionnaire included a sheet with the response foils (except
DK) as below.]

MOO   40.6   How willing would you be to give up   45-   1   not at all willing
             spare time in order to get ahead?   2   a little willing
                                                               3   somewhat willing
                                                               4   very willing
                                                               5   DK

                        TAKE BACK PAGE

COM   41.   Do you think NAME is pretty good about   46-   1   yes
            leaving you alone when you are talking on   2   no
            the telephone?

REA   42.   When is the last time NAME took your things
            when you didn't want him to? Was it...   47-   5   today or yesterday?
                                                               4   just a few days ago?
                        READ ALTERNATIVES ONE AT A TIME.   3   in the past week?
                        CODE FIRST ONE ACCEPTED.   2   in the past month?
                                                               1   more than a month ago?
                                                               0   never?

SHA   43.   Suppose NAME was naughty and you felt you   48-   1   no
            ought to take away some privilege (MAKE   2   yes
            HIM DO WITHOUT SOMETHING HE LIKES) - would
            you do it when one of your close friends
            or relatives was there?

DID   44.   Whom does NAME resemble more in behavior,   49-   1   father more
            you or your SPOUSE?   2   mother more
                                                               3   both
                                                               4   neither

CHI   45 A. In the summertime, does NAME play   50-   1   always
             outside or at other children's houses   2   sometimes
             until dark? (WHENEVER HE CAN)   3   never
                                                               4   DK

         B. In the winter, does NAME play outside   51-   1   always
             or at other children's houses after   2   sometimes
             dark? (WHENEVER HE CAN)   3   never
                                                               4   DK

RES   46.   Do you make NAME finish up everything he   52-   1   no
            is served at mealtimes?   2   yes

COM   47.   Does NAME show enough responsibility in   53-   0   yes
            doing routine chores around the house?
                      IF NO OR SOMETIMES, ASK: 2   yes
                      Do you let this annoy you when   1   no
                      he doesn't show enough responsibility?

232

SCHOOL BEHAVIOR PREFERENCE - BEP - INSTRUCTIONS

Now just a moment; I'll hand the notebook to you. TAKE OUT THIS PAGE
AND HAND NOTEBOOK TO RESPONDENT.[C]

On that page is a list of different things a third-grade child might do
in school.

Would you place a 1 in the blank beside the behavior which you think is
the worst behavior for a child in school - but first, I would like to read these
behaviors with you, so we don't miss any.

Giving dirty looks to other children.
Making up stories and lies to get other children into trouble.
Acting rudely to the teacher.
Starting a fight over nothing.
Not obeying the teacher.
Taking other children's things without asking.
Using bad words when bothered by another child.
Getting into trouble frequently.

Now place a 1 in the blank beside the behavior which you think is the
worst behavior...
Now place a 2 in the blank beside the next worst behavior.
IF R CATCHES ON: Now just continue until you finish the 8 behaviors on the list.

IF R NEEDS HELP, CONTINUE INSTRUCTIONS: Now place a 3...
                                        Now place a 4... etc.

There is another list of different things a third-grade child might do in
school on the next page. Again place a 1 in the blank beside the worst behavior -
but first let's read these behaviors so we don't miss any.

Bothering another child who's asking for trouble.
Pushing someone who pushed first.
Fighting back when hit by another child first.
Saying mean things back to another child who first said mean things.
Fighting back if another child has been asking for it.
Pushing or shoving another child who has been trying to make trouble.
Grabbing things back from someone who grabbed them first.
Getting very, very mad at a bully.

Now place a 1 in the blank beside the behavior which you think is the worst...
IF R CATCHES ON: Now, just continue until you finish the 8 behaviors on the list.

IF R NEEDS HELP, CONTINUE INSTRUCTIONS: Now place a 2...
                                        Now place a 3...

BE SURE ALL BLANKS ARE FILLED WHEN RESPONDENT HANDS NOTEBOOK BACK.

[C][The questionnaire included two sheets, one with the first list below
and one with the second list.]

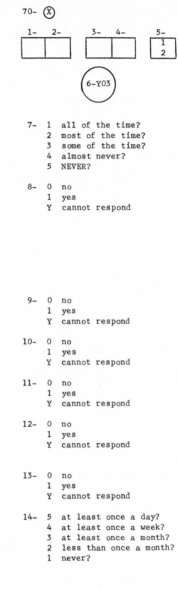

CID 49. When you ask NAME about something naughty he has done, how often does he deny it? Does he deny it...

    READ ALTERNATIVES ONE AT A TIME.
    CODE FIRST ONE ACCEPTED.

7- 1 all of the time?
    2 most of the time?
    3 some of the time?
    4 almost never?
    5 NEVER?

PUN 50.1 If you saw NAME grab things from another child, would you tell him that young men/ladies don't do this sort of thing?
IF R SAYS, "I NEVER SEE NAME GRAB THINGS FROM ANOTHER CHILD," ASK: What if it happens tomorrow?

    IF R CANNOT GO ALONG WITH THIS, CODE THESE SIX ITEMS Y AND EXIT TO 51.

8- 0 no
    1 yes
    Y cannot respond

  .2 If you saw NAME grab things from another child, would you say, "I would like to be proud of you."?

9- 0 no
    1 yes
    Y cannot respond

  .3 Would you make NAME apologize if he grabbed things from another child?

10- 0 no
    1 yes
    Y cannot respond

  .4 Would you tell NAME you don't love him for grabbing things from another child?

11- 0 no
    1 yes
    Y cannot respond

  .5 Would you point out how some close friend of his behaves better than NAME does, if he grabbed things from another child?

12- 0 no
    1 yes
    Y cannot respond

  .6 If you saw NAME grab things from another child, would you not let him play with his friends for two days?

13- 0 no
    1 yes
    Y cannot respond

FRA 51. How often does NAME forget to return things he borrowed from one of his playmates? Does it happen...

    READ ALTERNATIVES ONE AT A TIME.
    CODE FIRST ONE ACCEPTED.

14- 5 at least once a day?
    4 at least once a week?
    3 at least once a month?
    2 less than once a month?
    1 never?

COM 52. Does NAME ever use bad words when another   15- 0 no
         child bothers him?
                IF YES OR SOMETIMES, ASK: Are you annoyed   1 no
                when he uses bad words when another child   2 yes
                bothers him?

COM 53. When you have friends visiting, do they ever   16- 1 yes
         mention to you how well behaved NAME is?   2 no
                                                              3 no friends visiting

GEM 54. How often has moving to different houses or   17- 0   5
         apartments meant that NAME had to find new   1   6
         friends? CIRCLE # OF TIMES (0-9+)   2   7
                                                              3   8
                                                              4   9+

CAL 55. Do you think NAME is popular among the children 18- 1 no
         in the class?   2 DK
                                                              3 yes

FSC INSTRUCTIONS TO RESPONDENT: I am going to read a
     number of statements to you. For each one I would
     like you to tell me if you agree or disagree. If
     you don't know, tell me that you don't know.

     56.1   19- Ⓨ

     .2 Most people who don't get ahead just don't   20- 1 disagree strongly
         have enough willpower. Do you agree or   2 disagree slightly
         disagree?   3 neutral or DK
         IF AGREE, ASK: Do you agree strongly or do   4 agree slightly
         you agree slightly?   5 agree strongly
         IF DISAGREE, ASK: Do you disagree strongly
         or do you disagree slightly?

     .3 Sex criminals deserve more than prison; they   21- 1 disagree strongly
         should be whipped in public or worse. (Agree   2 disagree slightly
         or disagree?)   3 neutral or DK
         IF AGREE, ASK: Do you agree slightly or   4 agree slightly
         strongly?   5 agree strongly
         IF DISAGREE, ASK: Do you disagree slightly
         or strongly?

235

FSC 56.4 The findings of science may some day show that
         many of our most deeply held beliefs are wrong.
         (Agree or disagree?)
         IF AGREE,ASK: Do you agree strongly or slightly?
         IF DISAGREE,ASK: Do you disagree strongly or
         slightly?

22- 1 agree strongly
    2 agree slightly
    3 neutral or DK
    4 disagree slightly
    5 disagree strongly

     .5 The artist and the professor are probably more
        important to society than the businessman and
        the manufacturer. (Agree or disagree?)
        IF AGREE, ASK: Do you agree slightly or strongly?
        IF DISAGREE, ASK: Do you disagree slightly or
        strongly?

23- 1 agree strongly
    2 agree slightly
    3 neutral or DK
    4 disagree slightly
    5 disagree strongly

     .6 An urge to jump from high places is probably the
        result of unhappy personal experiences rather
        than something inborn. (Agree or disagree?)
        IF AGREE, ASK: Do you agree strongly or slightly?
        IF DISAGREE, ASK: Do you disagree strongly or
        slightly?

24- 1 agree strongly
    2 agree slightly
    3 neutral or DK
    4 disagree slightly
    5 disagree strongly

     .7 It is highly unlikely that astrology will ever be
        able to explain anything. (Agree or disagree?)
        IF AGREE, ASK: Do you agree slightly or strongly?
        IF DISAGREE, ASK: Do you disagree slightly or
        strongly?

25- 1 agree strongly
    2 agree slightly
    3 neutral or DK
    4 disagree slightly
    5 disagree strongly

     .8 Human nature being what it is, there must always
        be war and conflict. (Agree or disagree?)
        IF AGREE, ASK: Do you agree strongly or slightly?
        IF DISAGREE, ASK: Do you disagree strongly or
        slightly?

26- 1 disagree strongly
    2 disagree slightly
    3 neutral or DK
    4 agree slightly
    5 agree strongly

     .9 What young people need most of all is strict dis-
        cipline. (Agree or disagree?)
        IF AGREE, ASK: Do you agree slightly or strongly?
        IF DISAGREE, ASK: Do you disagree slightly or
        strongly?

27- 1 disagree strongly
    2 disagree slightly
    3 neutral or DK
    4 agree slightly
    5 agree strongly

     .10 Bosses should say just what is to be done and
         exactly how to do it if they expect us to do a
         good job. (Agree or disagree?)
         IF AGREE, ASK: Do you agree strongly or slightly?
         IF DISAGREE, ASK: Do you disagree strongly or
         slightly?

28- 1 disagree strongly
    2 disagree slightly
    3 neutral or DK
    4 agree slightly
    5 agree strongly

PAP 57. FATHERS ONLY: How often does your work or other
         commitments take you away from home and NAME on
         week-ends? (SATURDAY AND SUNDAY)

29- 1 every weekend
    2 one or two
       weekends a month
    3 rarely
    4 never
    5 female R

COM 58. Are you satisfied with how NAME takes care of
         his things?

30- 1 yes
    2 no

236

RID 59. Who does the minor repairs and odd jobs around the home, such as putting up shelves, mowing the lawn or fixing a light socket?

31- 1 mostly father
     2 both
     3 mostly mother
     4 neither
     5 other

COM 60. Do you think NAME should have a better-controlled temper?

32- 1 no
     2 yes

PUN 61.1 If you heard NAME say mean things to another child, would you tell him in a nice way how to act differently?
IF R SAYS, "I NEVER HEAR NAME SAY MEAN THINGS TO ANOTHER CHILD," ASK: What if it happens tomorrow?

IF R CANNOT GO ALONG WITH THIS, CODE THESE SIX ITEMS Y AND EXIT TO 62.

33- 0 no
     1 yes
     Y cannot respond

.2 If you heard NAME say mean things to another child, would you say, "Get on that chair and don't move until you apologize."?

34- 0 no
     1 yes
     Y cannot respond

.3 Would you not let NAME play with his friends for two days if you heard him say mean things to another child?

35- 0 no
     1 yes
     Y cannot respond

.4 If you heard NAME say mean things to another child, would you point out how some close friend of his behaves better than NAME does?

36- 0 no
     1 yes
     Y cannot respond

.5 If you heard NAME say mean things to another child, would you wash out his mouth with soap?

37- 0 no
     1 yes
     Y cannot respond

.6 If you heard NAME say mean things to another child, would you say, "I would like to be proud of you."?

38- 0 no
     1 yes
     Y cannot respond

NUR 62. What upsets NAME? WRITE

39- 1 DK
     2 MENTIONS 1+

PAD 63. Do you find that things important to you are considered unimportant by your SPOUSE?

40- 1 yes
     2 no

PAD 64. What sort of things do you and your SPOUSE like to do together?

41- 1 NOTHING
     2 ONE +

237

PROFILE IDENTIFICATION - PID - <u>INSTRUCTIONS</u>

TEAR OUT THIS PAGE AND HAND NOTEBOOK TO R.

We are interested in finding out how you do certain things such as walking, talking, and so forth. On the sheet of paper before you is a list of things described by sets of opposite words. Between each pair of words are five steps, or grades, ranging from one way of doing something to its opposite. I would like you to rate yourself for each type of activity, such as walking, talking, etc. by placing a check mark on one of the steps on each line. Notice that the closer you place your check mark to either of the opposite words, the more it means you act the way the word says.

Please turn the page and try the example. If I were to ask you how you like your coffee, how would you place your check marks?

IF R GIVES ONLY EXTREME RESPONSES ON EXAMPLE, SAY:

You showed that you liked your coffee very hot/cold.
How would you place your check mark if you wanted your
coffee just a <u>little</u> less hot/cold?

(<u>AFTER EXAMPLE IS COMPLETED</u>) Thank you, would you please turn the page back and complete that list.

SCAN PID FOR COMPLETION OF EACH ITEM AND THEN RETRIEVE INTERVIEW.

I walk

fast	___	___	___	___	___	slow
loud	___	___	___	___	___	soft
often	___	___	___	___	___	not often

I talk

slow	___	___	___	___	___	fast
soft	___	___	___	___	___	loud
not often	___	___	___	___	___	often

I stand

| straight | ___ | ___ | ___ | ___ | ___ | lean forward |
| at ease | ___ | ___ | ___ | ___ | ___ | firm |

I eat

| much | ___ | ___ | ___ | ___ | ___ | little |
| fast | ___ | ___ | ___ | ___ | ___ | slow |

I write

slow	___	___	___	___	___	fast
small	___	___	___	___	___	large
heavy	___	___	___	___	___	light

My body is

light	___	___	___	___	___	dark
tall	___	___	___	___	___	short
thick	___	___	___	___	___	thin
hard	___	___	___	___	___	soft
strong	___	___	___	___	___	weak

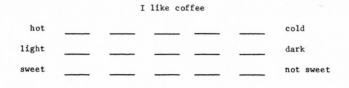

I like coffee

hot	____	____	____	____	____	cold
light	____	____	____	____	____	dark
sweet	____	____	____	____	____	not sweet

60- Ⓧ

65B. PROFILE IDENTIFICATION EXAMPLE

61- 1 passed
2 extreme, passed
3 extreme, failed
4 non-reader

CHI 66. Are there any clubs or groups, or
organizations that NAME takes part in
after school hours? (BROWNIES OR CUB-
SCOUTS, RELIGIOUS TRAINING, DANCING OR
MUSIC LESSONS?)

IF YES, ASK: About how many hours   62- 0 no   5
a week is NAME involved in these   1   6
activities away from home? (WITHOUT   2   7
PARENT'S PRESENCE THIS YEAR.)   3   8
                                        4   9+

REA 67. When is the last time NAME fought back
when a neighbor child hit him first?
Was it...   63- 5 today or yesterday?
                                          4 just a few days ago?
READ ALTERNATIVES ONE AT A TIME.   3 in the past week?
CODE FIRST ONE ACCEPTED.   2 in the past month?
                                          1 more than a month ago?
                                          0 never?
                                          6 DK

SIC 68. About how many children of NAME'S age
live close enough so that he can walk 64- 0   5
to their house by himself?   1   6
CIRCLE # OF CHILDREN (0-9+)   2   7
                                           3   8
                                           4   9+

PAP 69. When NAME wants to, do you let him   65- 1 no
help around the house?   2 yes
                                              3 doesn't want to

NUR 70. Do you often find yourself trying to   66- 1 no or not afraid
figure out what NAME is afraid of?   2 yes

COM 71. Are you bothered that NAME doesn't follow 67- 1 no
directions when he runs an errand?   2 yes

COM 72. Do you think NAME wastes too much time? 68- 0 no

IF YES OR SOMETIMES, ASK: Does this   2 yes
annoy you when he wastes too much   1 no
time?

PAP 73. How often do you, yourself, have break- 69- 1 never
fast with NAME?   2 once in a while
                                                  3 almost daily
                                                  4 daily

241

PAP 74. <u>FATHERS ONLY</u>: How often does your work   70- 1 every week
         take you out of town for more than a day   2 once or twice a month
         at a time?   3 rarely
              IF <u>NEVER</u>, ASK: Rarely or never?   4 never
                                                          5 female R

NUR 75. What makes NAME unhappy? WRITE   71- 1 DK
                                                          2 MENTIONS 1+

1-   2-   3-   4-   5-
[   ][   ]   [   ][   ]   [1]
                             [2]

(6-Y04)

GID 76. When NAME is punished, does he feel   7- 1 no
         that the punishment is justified?   2 yes
                                                          3 DK or other

PAD 77. Do arguments between you and your SPOUSE   8- 1 never argue
         settle anything?   2 yes
                                                          3 no

LHJ 78. Are you now a member of the PTA?
              IF <u>YES</u>, ASK: How often do you attend? 9- 0 DK
                                                          1 no
                                                          2 some of the meetings
                                                          3 all or most of the
                                                             meetings

PAD 79. Are you satisfied with how your SPOUSE   10- 1 yes
         handles money?   2 no

242

PUN 80.1 If NAME were rude to you, would you tell 11- 0 no
him, "I will give you something you like   1 yes
if you act differently."?   Y cannot respond
IF R SAYS, "NAME IS NEVER RUDE TO ME," ASK:
What if it happens tomorrow?

IF R CANNOT GO ALONG WITH THIS, CODE THESE
SIX ITEMS Y AND EXIT TO 81.

.2 If NAME were rude to you, would you wash out 12- 0 no
his mouth with soap?   1 yes
                                              Y cannot respond

.3 Would you remind NAME of what others will   13- 0 no
think of him if he were rude to you?   1 yes
                                              Y cannot respond

.4 If NAME were rude to you, would you say,   14- 0 no
"Get on that chair and don't move until you   1 yes
apologize."?   Y cannot respond

.5 Would you tell NAME that young men/ladies   15- 0 no
don't do this sort of thing - if he were rude 1 yes
to you?   Y cannot respond

.6 Would you spank NAME until he cries - if he 16- 0 no
were rude to you?   1 yes
                                              Y cannot respond

QPR 81A. Have you ever filled out a questionnaire   17- 1 no
before, or been interviewed for an hour or   2 yes, other_____
more - for a job, or anything else?   3 yes, previous RVWF
IF YES, What kind of interview?   interview

B. Have you talked to anybody who has been   18- 2 yes
interviewed in this study?   1 no

SIC 82A. Can you give me an idea of about how many   19- 0 5
good friends NAME has to play with?   1 6
CIRCLE # OF FRIENDS (0-9+)   2 7
                                                   3 8
                                                   4 9+

B. What are their names? (FIRST AND LAST NAME)   20- 1 knows none
WRITE   2 knows some
                                                 3 knows all

CID 83. When NAME has done something naughty and you 21- 1 NEVER?
haven't seen him do it, how often does he come   2 almost never?
and tell you about it without your having to   3 some of the time?
ask him...   4 most of the time?
          READ ALTERNATIVES ONE AT A TIME.   5 all of the time?
          CODE FIRST ONE ACCEPTED.

COM 84. When NAME has money to buy something for   22- 1 no
himself, are you displeased with what he buys?   2 yes

243

NUR   85. How do you try to show NAME that you   23-   1 CANNOT SAY
          are on his side?   2 ANY ATTEMPT

PAP   86. How often are you, yourself, home in the   24-   1 never
          afternoon when NAME comes home from school?   2 once in a while
                                                              3 almost daily
                                                              4 daily

COM   87. Do you ever get annoyed because NAME   25-   1 no
          makes it hard for another child to do   2 yes
          things?

PAP   88. How many days a week, on the average,   26-   0 4
          is it possible for you, yourself, to   1 5
          eat the main meal with NAME?   2 6
          CIRCLE # OF DAYS   3 7

RES   89. Is it easy for you to say "No" to   27-   1 no
          NAME and stick by it?   2 yes

PUN   90.1 If NAME got very mad at you, would you   28-   0 no
           get angry at him?   1 yes
           IF R SAYS, "NAME NEVER GETS VERY MAD   Y cannot respond
           AT ME," ASK: What if it happens tomorrow?

           IF R CANNOT GO ALONG WITH THIS, CODE
           THESE SIX ITEMS Y AND EXIT TO 91.

      .2 If NAME got very mad at you, would you   29-   0 no
         slap him in the face?   1 yes
                                                              Y cannot respond

      .3 Would you say, "That isn't a nice thing   30-   0 no
         to do" if NAME got very mad at you?   1 yes
                                                              Y cannot respond

      .4 Would you tell NAME you don't love him   31-   0 no
         for getting very mad at you?   1 yes
                                                              Y cannot respond

      .5 Would you tell NAME in a nice way how   32-   0 no
         to act differently if he got very mad   1 yes
         at you?   Y cannot respond

      .6 If NAME got very mad at you, would you   33-   0 no
         send him to another room where he would   1 yes
         be alone and without toys?   Y cannot respond

COM   91. Do some other children tease NAME un-   34-   1 no
          justly?   2 yes

244

REA 92. When is the last time NAME made marks on
the furniture or walls - accidentally or
not? Was it...

      READ ALTERNATIVES ONE AT A TIME.
      CODE FIRST ONE ACCEPTED.

35- 5 today or yesterday?
    4 just a few days ago?
    3 in the past week?
    2 in the past month?
    1 more than a month ago?
    0 never?

RID 93. Who does the daily housework, such as
cleaning, washing dishes, making beds?

36- 1 father mostly
    2 both
    3 mother mostly
    4 neither
    5 other _____

COM 94. Does NAME grab things from other
children?
      IF YES OR SOMETIMES, ASK: Does it
      annoy you when he grabs things from
      other children?

37- 0 no

    1 no
    2 yes

COM 95. Are you pleased with the way NAME
listens to you when you tell him what
to do?

38- 1 yes
    2 no

ENU 96. Has NAME ever wet the bed in the past
year?
      IF NO, ASK: How old was NAME when he
      stopped? (TO NEAREST YEAR)

39- 1 5
    2 6
    3 7
    4 8+ yes

LHJ 97. How often does NAME read comic books?

40- 1 never
    2 sometimes
    3 frequently

COM 98. Are you satisfied with NAME'S manners?

41- 1 yes
    2 no

GID 99. When he thought nobody was watching, has
NAME ever tried to get by with something
he wasn't supposed to do?

42- 1 yes
    2 no
    3 DK or other

FRA 100. How often does NAME disobey you? Does
it happen...

      READ ALTERNATIVES ONE AT A TIME.
      CODE FIRST ONE ACCEPTED.

43- 5 at least once a day?
    4 at least once a week?
    3 at least once a month?
    2 less than once a month?
    1 never?

PAD 101. Does NAME get involved in disagreements
between you and your SPOUSE?

44- 1 no disagreements
    2 no
    3 yes

245

JUDGMENT OF PUNISHMENT - JUP - INSTRUCTIONS

I am going to read to you some things parents do to their children. I want you to tell me how harsh, that is, how severe or how mean each would be as a punishment for NAME. Your job is to judge how harsh a punishment is, <u>even if</u> NAME is not punished that way.

REMOVE THIS PAGE AND HAND NOTEBOOK TO R.

On your page are lines. Each line has numbers from one to eight. For each thing I read you, I want you to circle one of the numbers. Circle a number toward eight for a very harsh punishment and circle a number toward one for a very mild punishment. The more harsh the punishment for NAME, the higher the number you should circle; the more mild the punishment is for NAME, the lower the number you should circle. The number you circle indicates your judgment of each punishment for NAME; is it very harsh, very mild, or somewhere inbetween?

READ LETTER AS PART OF ITEM. (HELP RESPONDENT ON A, B, C <u>ONLY</u>)

A. Giving NAME an angry look.

B. Sending NAME to his room without supper.

✓C. Encouraging NAME to try again.

IF R SAYS, E.G., "IT'S NOT A PUNISHMENT," SAY: Look at both ends of the line.

D. Saying to NAME, "You are a naughty boy/girl."

E. Saying, "That isn't a nice thing to do."

F. Taking away something that NAME likes.

G. Saying, "You're a lot of trouble to me."

H. Telling NAME, "I will give you something you like if you act differently."

I. Saying, "Get on that chair and don't move until you apologize."

J. Sending NAME to bed early.

K. Not permitting NAME to play with his friends.

L. Spanking NAME a couple of times on the bottom.

M. Telling NAME that what he did is stupid.

N. Shaking and slapping NAME.

✓ O. Telling NAME in a nice way how to act differently.

P. Saying, "You make me feel unhappy."

	Very mild punishment									
A	1	2	3	4	5	**6**	7	8	A
B	1	2	3	4	5	6	7	8	B
C	1	2	3	4	5	6	7	8	C
D	1	2	3	4	5	6	7	8	D
E	1	2	3	4	5	6	7	8	E
F	1	2	3	4	5	6	7	8	F
G	1	2	3	4	5	6	7	8	G
H	1	2	3	4	5	6	7	8	H
I	1	2	3	4	5	6	7	8	I
J	1	2	3	4	5	6	7	8	J
K	1	2	3	4	5	6	7	8	K
L	1	2	3	4	5	6	7	8	L
M	1	2	3	4	5	6	7	8	M
N	1	2	3	4	5	6	7	8	N
O	1	2	3	4	5	6	7	8	O
P	1	2	3	4	5	6	7	8	P

The "Very harsh punishment" label appears above columns 7–8.

247

61- Ⓧ

COM 103. Is NAME too forgetful?   62- 0 no

        IF YES OR SOMETIMES, ASK: Are you   2 yes
        annoyed when he is too forgetful?   1 no

GID 104. Will NAME tell you about something   63- 1 no
      naughty he has done before you dis-   2 yes
      cover it?   3 DK or other

GID 105. Would NAME tell a fib or lie to keep   64- 1 yes
      out of serious trouble?   2 no
                                                     3 DK or other

RES 106. Does NAME have chores around the house   65- 1 no
      that you regularly require him to do?   2 yes

1-	2-	3-	4-	5-
				1
				2

6-Y05

REA 107. When is the last time NAME pushed or   7- 5 today or yesterday?
      shoved a child in your home? Was it...   4 just a few days ago?
                                                     3 in the past week?
        READ ALTERNATIVES ONE AT A TIME.   2 in the past month?
        CODE FIRST ONE ACCEPTED.   1 more than a month ago?
                                                     0 never?

PAD 108. Is it easy for you and your SPOUSE to   8- 1 never argue
      make up after an argument?   2 yes
                                                     3 no

GID 109. When NAME disobeys, does he feel sorry   9- 1 no
      about it afterwards?   2 yes
                                                     3 DK or other

NUR 110. Does NAME seem to need a lot more atten-   10- 1 no
      tion on some days than on most other days?   2 yes

SIC 111. Are NAME'S friends boys, girls, or both   11- 1 both
      boys and girls?   2 same sex
                                                     3 other sex
                                                     4 no friends

NUR 112. Do you usually have time so that NAME   12- 1 no
      can talk to you about things that   2 yes
      interest him?

248

SHA 113. Suppose NAME was naughty and you felt   13- 1 no
          he deserved a spanking - would you do   2 yes
          it in front of the family?

LHJ 114A. Some of the parents we've talked to
          say they've read Dr. Spock's book.
          Have you had the opportunity to
          look at anything like this?
                  IF YES, ASK: What kinds of
                  things have you used it for?
                  RECORD:

POSTCODE
14- 0 (yes, but used inap-   propriately)
1 no
2 yes, but have not   used it
3 yes, used for child-   rearing information

      B. When NAME is sick or has other prob-   15- 1 no
          lems, have you found it helpful to use   2 yes
          any books about bringing up children?

COM 115. Does NAME complain to you when you tell 16- 0 no
          him what to do?
                  IF YES OR SOMETIMES, ASK: Does it   1 no
                  annoy you when he complains to you?   2 yes

NUR 116. What does NAME dream about? WRITE -   17- 1 DK, DNA
          MUST MENTION OBJECT OR EVENT IN DREAM   2 MENTIONS 1+

REA 117. When is the last time NAME complained to
          you when you told him what to do? Was it..18- 5 today or yesterday?
                                                       4 just a few days ago?
                  READ ALTERNATIVES ONE AT A TIME.   3 in the past week?
                  CODE FIRST ONE ACCEPTED.   2 in the past month?
                                                       1 more than a month ago?
                                                       0 never?

PAD 118. Do you and your SPOUSE ever disagree   19- 1 no
          about choice of friends?   2 yes

COM 119. Is the quality of NAME'S schoolwork   20- 0 yes
          as good as it should be?
                  IF NO OR SOMETIMES, ASK: Does it   2 yes
                  annoy you that his schoolwork is   1 no
                  not as good as it should be?

COM 120. Are you satisfied that NAME remembers   21- 1 yes
          to ask for something another child has   2 no
          before he takes it?

COM 121. Is NAME ever rude to you?   22- 0 no

                  IF YES OR SOMETIMES,ASK: Does it   1 no
                  annoy you when he is rude to you?   2 yes

249

PAP 122. How often do you, yourself, help NAME   23- 1 never
          with his homework?   2 once in a while
                                                         3 almost daily
                                                         4 daily

COM 123. Are you <u>satisfied</u> that NAME doesn't   24- 1 yes
          push or <u>shove</u> other children?   2 no

LHJ 124A. How many hours during the week-end   25- 0 5
           does NAME watch TV? CIRCLE # OF   1 6
           HOURS (0-9+) [SATURDAY AND SUNDAY]   2 7
                                                          3 8
                                                          4 9+
                                                          X no TV set

     B. How many hours during the rest of the   26- 0 5
        week does NAME watch TV? CIRCLE # OF   1 6
        HOURS (0-9+) [MONDAY THRU FRIDAY]   2 7
                                                          3 8
                                                          4 9+
                                                          X no TV set

CAL 125. Is NAME above or below average in   27- 1 below
          intelligence?   2 average
                                                          3 above

EDU 126A. How many years did you attend   28- 1 graduate or profes-
           school?   sional training
                                                          2 college graduate
                                                          3 1-3 years college
                                                          4 high school graduate
                                                          5 10-11 years
                                                          6 7-9 years
                                                          7 under 7 years

QPR B. How old were you when you finished
        your schooling? (NON-VOCATIONAL)   29,30- [|]
        WRITE IN AGE

PAP 127. Have there been any times in the past   31- 1 yes
          three years when you have been away   2 no
          from your family about a month or more:
          for vacations, family responsibilities,
          health, job reasons - or anything else?

RES 128. Do you feel that it is all right for   32- 1 no
          NAME to do anything else during meal-   2 yes
          time: for example, getting up to play,
          reading, or watching TV?

250

RID 129A. Who takes responsibility for NAME'S   33- 1 father mostly
discipline?   2 both
                                                    3 mother mostly
                                                    4 neither
                                                    5 other _____

B. Are there any other people at home   34- 1 yes _____
besides you and your SPOUSE who take
an important hand in bringing up NAME?

                                                    2 no _____

AMO 130A. When you were about 8 or 9 years old,
what kind of work was your father doing
for a living? RECORD

B. Is this what he regularly did for most
of your childhood? ___ yes EXIT TO 131
                            ___ no ASK C AND D

C. What other sorts of work did he do?
RECORD

D. What was his usual occupation during   35- ⟋⟋ RT
your childhood? RECORD

PAD 131. Do you or your SPOUSE ever leave the   36- 1 never argue
house during an argument?   2 no
                                                    3 yes

REA 132. When is the last time NAME pestered   37- 5 today or yesterday?
you? Was it...   4 just a few days ago?
                                 READ ALTERNATIVES ONE AT A TIME.   3 in the past week?
                                 CODE FIRST ONE ACCEPTED.   2 in the past month?
                                                   1 more than a month ago?
                                                   0 never?

REA 133. When is the last time you saw NAME get   38- 5 today or yesterday?
very mad? Was it...   4 just a few days ago?
                                 READ ALTERNATIVES ONE AT A TIME.   3 in the past week?
                                 CODE FIRST ONE ACCEPTED.   2 in the past month?
                                                   1 more than a month ago?
                                                   0 never?

COM 134. Do you think NAME controls his temper   39- 1 yes
well when he is outside playing and is   2 no
told to come in the house?

251

MOP 135. Which of these groups of people would you   40- 1 going up
          say you belong to: those who are going up   2 going down
          in the world, those who have gone down some-   3 not going up or down
          what, or those who are not really going up   4 DK
          or down?

REA 136. When is the last time NAME said mean things
          to a child in your home? Was it...   41- 5 today or yesterday?
                                                                4 just a few days ago?
                  READ ALTERNATIVES ONE AT A TIME.   3 in the past week?
                  CODE FIRST ONE ACCEPTED.   2 in the past month?
                                                                1 more than a month ago?
                                                                0 never?

SIC 137. About how many days a week does NAME   42- 0   4
          play with other children? CIRCLE # OF   1   5
          DAYS (0-7) [AFTER SCHOOL]   2   6
                                                              3   7
ORS 138. Do you own or rent your home?

              IF RENT, How much rent do you pay   43- 0 under $20
              per month?   1 20-29
                                                            2 30-44
                                                            3 45-59
                                                            4 60-79
                                                            5 80-99
                                                            6 100-124
                                                            7 125+
                                                            8 DK
                                                            9 DNA

              Are utilities included?   44- 1 yes
              (yes = AT LEAST HEAT)   2 no
                                                            3 DNA

              IF OWN, What is the approximate   45- 0 $7,999 or less
              value of your home?   1   8,000-11,999
                                                            2 12,000-14,999
                                                            3 15,000-19,999
                                                            4 20,000-24,999
                                                            5 25,000+
                                                            6 DK
                                                            7 DNA

REL 139A. How often do you attend church?   46- 0 never
                                                            1 a few times a year
                                                            2 about once a month
                                                            3 few times a month
                                                            4 once a week+

      B. Would you mind telling me your religion?   47- 1 Protestant
                                                            2 Catholic
                                                               Jewish
                                                               Greek Orthodox
                                                               Other _____

ANY 140.   Has there been anything which has happened in
your home lately which might have influenced
your answers to some of the things we've been
talking about - for example, arguments, sick-
ness or death in the family, or have you been
extremely busy lately? RECORD ON BACK OF
INTERVIEW.

48- 1 yes
    2 no

TELL RESPONDENT YOU MUST CHECK INTERVIEW.

DO INTERVIEWER RATINGS BEFORE CHECKING.

INT 141.1 Honesty of responses in this interview?

49- 1 faking good
    2 not faking good

.2 Was interview an easy job?

50- 1 not easy
    2 easy

.3 Interruptions in interview?

51- 1 yes
    2 no

.4 Were you bothered by the respondent's
semantic quibbling?

52- 1 yes
    2 somewhat
    3 no, did not occur

.5 Did respondent see this as a clinical interview at any time during the interview?

53- 1 yes
    2 no

.6 SOCIAL DISTANCE:
   (1) I would never like to see R again.
   (2) I have no strong feelings one way or
       the other.
   (3) I wouldn't mind seeing R occasionally.
   (4) I would like to get to know R better.
   (5) I would definitely like R for a friend.
   (6) Cannot say.

54- 1
    2
    3
    4
    5
    6

.7 Did other adults hear your interview?

55- 1 heard all of it
    2 heard parts of it
    3 heard none of it

.8 Did other children hear this interview?

56- 1 heard all of it
    2 heard parts of it
    3 heard none of it

.9 Did NAME hear this interview?

57- 1 heard all of it
    2 heard parts of it
    3 heard none of it

CHECK INTERVIEW; START ON PAGE 1.

TIME ENDED:_____

END OF INTERVIEW

253

C. Interviewer Manual to Accompany Questionnaire

No materials should be out of this office more than 48 hours!
Required for an interview[a] are:

1. Black (No. 2) wooden pencils
2. 1960 RVW Child-Rearing Questionnaire
3. Face sheet

Interviewer (E) receives a blank questionnaire (pp. 2–29) and a partially filled out face sheet (p. 1).

For assignments with preset appointments (Time and Place), the face sheet is filled out through SCHEDULED STARTING TIME (col. 13). For assignments with no preset appointment, the face sheet is filled out through INTERVIEWER (cols. 9, 10). In either case travel instructions will appear, if anywhere, on the back of p. 1.

When E turns in his completed questionnaire, the face sheet should be all filled out except for DOUBLE CHECKED and READY FOR PUNCHING initialing. Columns 1, 2, 3, 4, and 5 should be coded on all green pages (transferring from page 1 to pp. 7, 13, 19, and 24).

Erasures are not allowed. X-out the wrong mark and then recode.

ASSIGNMENT OF RESPONDENT TO INTERVIEWER

The assignment of a respondent (R) to an interviewer (E) is the responsibility of Mr. Toigo. He follows a procedure designed to allow chance factors to determine which R is assigned to which E.

Page 1 of the attached questionnaire is the face sheet. Receipt of face sheet by E constitutes an interview assignment. Interviewers will be notified by phone or by postcard, when they have an interview assigned to them. Interviewers are responsible for picking up the face sheet and questionnaire at the Foundation House. E should look on the back of face sheet for travel instructions. For a family with a telephone, everything down through SCHEDULED STARTING TIME will be already filled in: for a family without a telephone, everything down through INTERVIEWER will be filled in. In either case, E picks up face sheet, attaches it to questionnaire in notebook and is ready to attempt to meet with the respondent. Special instructions for the situation where an appointment is not made for E are discussed in RT's 12/29/59 memo on *Interview assignment and distribution procedures.* It is assumed here that the appointment has been made for E.

E should be at the designated place of the interview on time. He should remember that some parts of Columbia County are 20 miles from Hudson and that exigencies while traveling may develop. He should therefore allow enough time in order to arrive at the scheduled time. Arriving late may well lose part or all of the interview and perhaps create ill will for the project.

If interviewing must be stopped before the interview is completed, try to make another appointment or let R know that he will be contacted. It is vital that E realize that not only does a stopped interview become more expensive but also it is likely that the remainder of the interview will be either lost or subject to errors of unknown kind and size.

---

[a]Questionnaire = the assembled questions; interview = the administration of the questionnaire in a face-to-face situation.

THE FACE-TO-FACE INTERVIEW

E must see to it that, as much as he can do it courteously, the proper conditions of privacy are maintained. The ideal conditions are E interviewing R with no one else present. Deviations from the ideal are reported by E as part of INTERVIEWER RATINGS.

The interviewer is expected to appear neatly groomed. In general, we think the respondent should not be taken aback by the interviewer's appearance. E should not smoke or chew gum. He should not accept any liquid and/or solid refreshment before, during, or after the interview.

Before the interview starts, E has introduced himself, determined that he is talking to the person assigned to him, checked the accuracy of the address, learned what R calls NAME, and told R a minimum about the study. A good entrée is to ask R to say what he knows about the study. E then tells R as little as possible, promising to answer any questions after the interview is over. E's job is to get R's cooperation. He may use his judgment here.

E cannot give R any advice. E may not approve or disapprove in any way what R says. His job is to conduct the interview according to the rules and to code, postcode, or record R's responses to the questions. E should not guess R's responses; questions and probes must be used appropriately to obtain a codable response from R. When no clearly codable response to an item can be obtained from R, E writes in Y and circles it thus:

$$\textcircled{y}\,.$$

E's task is to administer the interview within the bounds specified by this manual. All deviations beyond these limits are to be communicated to the authors so that we may re-evaluate our procedures (and, of course, this manual). Thus the interview is conceived of as a standard test.

RATIONALE OF ERRORS

All interviewers are regarded as competent. In order to report this study to the scientific community it is vital to describe the means by which the data were collected. It is a contribution to report the extent of errors. In large part the interviewer can aid in this effort.

The methodology of interviewing is served by reporting of errors. Assignment of Rs to E on a random basis allows for the study of systematic interviewer differences. We can thus assess quantitative effects. With good reporting of errors of interview administration by each E we can put useful meat on these bones.

Sometimes E will "report" his errors by means of tape recording. When the interview is scheduled in the office, E may find the following sheets inserted at appropriate places in his interview:

1. This sheet allows E to ask R for permission to record a part of the interview. (Disregard sheets 2 and 3 if R does not give permission.)
2. This sheet tells E to start recording.
3. This sheet tells E to stop recording and to note footage on tape recorder.

Remember, we know that all people make errors. The study of errors is an important part of this research. Without it, no replication is possible.

The pace at which an interview goes can be manipulated by E. Two acceptable methods are as follows: (1) pop questions out, often interrupting as R begins to say something after the codable response; (2) let R speak beyond the codable response; E not reacting to R's verbal production tends to extinguish this type of response. E is to make no comments between items.

Note-taking behavior above and beyond the call of duty is a serious deviation from the rules. If E acts as if an item says RECORD when in fact it doesn't, this changes the nature and pace of the interview. E may record extra details on FAS questions and turn in such questionnaires especially earmarked.

E holds notebook and pages so R cannot see what's printed or written.

Format in the printing of the questionnaire provides the majority of the cues for E's behavior. General rules can be laid down not only for format but also for classes of item types. The final section of the manual gives specific rules for items not covered by the general format or item-type case.

An introduction to the rules of conduct for E will be made by discussing how examples of individual items are to be handled. The item is the unit of this questionnaire. E reads, says, or does whatever is appropriate to an item and then looks into R's face until R responds. The sequence of items as assembled into the questionnaire cannot be modified by E, with the exception of certain items that must be left out for different kinds of R (these columns are coded Y by the interviewer):

1. SPOUSE items. Any item which contains the word SPOUSE is not adminis-tered to Rs who do not now have a spouse living at home. (E learns this fact through Q 9 on p. 3.) An example of a SPOUSE item is: "108. Is it easy for you and your SPOUSE to make up after an argument?"
2. Restrictive items. Any items preceded by a restrictive category such as: "57. *FATHERS ONLY:* How often does your work or other commitments take you away from home and NAME on week-ends? (SATURDAY AND SUN-DAY)"
3. Non-readers. As soon as E learns R is a non-reader, E should not attempt Q 27, Q 48, Q 65, Q 102. E should not use p. 10a as a response sheet; rather E should offer R the alternatives with each question (Q 40.1–40.6).

We shall now describe in detail how some selected items are to be administered.

EXAMPLE 1

PAP 57.	*FATHERS ONLY:* How often does your work or other commitments take you away from home and NAME on week-ends? (SATURDAY and SUNDAY)	29– 1 every week-end 2 one or two week-ends a month 3 rarely 4 never 5 female R

The beginning of an item is identified by a three-letter code name and a number to the left (in this case "PAP 57."). E follows the directions in italicized caps ("*FATHERS ONLY*") and does not read the item to a female R; rather he circles the 5, the last of the five codes to the right. If R is male, E reads the lowercase words, "How often does your work or other commitments take you away from home and NAME [E substitutes the child's name in place of NAME] on week-ends?" If R requests it, E may reread the item or, if appropriate, the alternatives, "every week-end," "one or two week-ends a month," "rarely," and "never." In order for E to code 1, 2, 3, or 4, R must spontaneously say or select one of these alternatives. An item with this format is coded by E's circling one and only one of the five codes. Circling the code means drawing a circle around the number, not around the number *and* the words beside the number. Thus if R is a female, the coding is accomplished by:

⑤   female R.

E then proceeds with *no comment* to the next item.

EXAMPLE 2

CAL 55. Do you think NAME is popular among the   18– 1 no
children in the class?   2 DK
                                                         3 yes

Again the item starts at the code name and number ("CAL 55.") which are
not to be read. E substitutes the child's name whenever the word NAME appears
in caps. DK (= don't know), because it is in caps, cannot be offered to R as one
of the alternatives. It is apparent that the information to be key-punched is on
the right while the item to be administered is on the left.

Sometimes part of the item to be read is on the right. Example 3 illustrates this.

EXAMPLE 3

FRA 36. How often does NAME say mean things   35– 5 at least once a
to one of his playmates? Does it   day?
happen . . .   4 at least once a
                                                       week?
READ ALTERNATIVES ONE AT A   3 at least once a
TIME. CODE FIRST ONE ACCEPTED.   month?
                                                       2 less than once a
                                                       month?
                                                       1 never?

The full reading of this item for Johnnie's parent is as follows: "How often
does Johnnie say mean things to one of his playmates? Does it happen at least
once a day? (PAUSE.) . . . at least once a week? (PAUSE.) . . . at least once a
month? (PAUSE.) . . . less than once a month? (PAUSE.) . . . never?"

"(PAUSE.)" here indicates that E waits a moment for R to accept the alternative. If R does accept the last-read alternative, that alternative's number is circled
and E reads no further. If R does not accept an alternative, E reads the next alternative and pauses again. (E must be careful to give R a chance to reject the alternative; R's silence is not necessarily equal to "no.") If R spontaneously responds
in terms of an alternative that E has not yet read *in this item*, E reads without
pausing the rest of the alternatives down through the one picked.

Some items require E to code by writing numbers. The next example illustrates
this.

EXAMPLE 4

FAS 6.   When were you married?   24, 25–
                                                          year

E is required to write one legible digit for each rectangular box provided. Thus
he would write

if the year given to the question was 1948. If the year given to the question is
1908, E would write

Notice that E codes in this way into a rectangular box:

but not into a parallelogram:

FORMAT GLOSSARY

Item Directions

CAPS = don't read to respondent. E.g., Q 1 is not to be read to any R.

lower case = read as is printed. E.g., Q 2 is read, "Let's see, your age is . . . ?"

lower case italics = emphasis. E.g., Q 5A and B: *"father"* and *"mother."*

CAPS = titles and/or instructions to E not to be read to R., e.g., Q 5: *"CIRCLE SPECIFY."* (In this item, if R's parent(s) was born in the U.S., the *"CIRCLE"* instruction would be relevant; if not, E must *"SPECIFY"* on the line provided.

RECORD = item direction that E write R's response as verbatim as possible.

WRITE = item direction that E abstract R's response, often numerical information. E.g., Q 2:

WRITE IN AGE.   17, 18-

SPECIFY = item direction that E abstract R's response, often nonnumerical information. E.g., Q 5: *"SPECIFY"* means to write the name of a country.

(CAPS) = optional probe, may be paraphrased. Q 9: "(NO SUBSTITUTE PARENT)" may be paraphrased to clarify the meaning of "only parent" when E judges it to be needed.

(lower case) = optional probe, exact words. E.g., Q 21A. If E elects to use this probe, the probe must be as printed.

IF YES: lower case = mandatory probe, exact words. Instructions in caps, e.g., Q 13. Note also on p. 5, Q 15, the various paths through the item.

NAME = the child's name (preferably what R calls the child), *not* an appropriate pronoun.

"NAME" = NAME (as above) in all-cap sentence.

him, his, etc. — the feminine form is used when appropriate.

SPOUSE — translate to "husband" or "wife."

DNA = does not apply.

Coding (IBM codes are to right)

	Col. #	punches
1. On the spot coding, E circles either 1, 2 or 3 after R responds and before E can go to next item.	25-	1 yes 2 no 3 maybe
2. Same as #1 but if 3 is circled, record the required information on the line provided.	25-	1 yes 2 no 3 other _____
3. Same as #1 but more than one number may be circled.	49-	1 oldest 2 second oldest 3 third

258

4 fourth
5 fifth
6 sixth
7 seventh
8 eighth
9 ninth

4. Postcoding by E: E circles one code after interview is completed. The item provides space and/or instructions for E to record information to be coded by him later.

POSTCODE

DEDUCT LUNCH AS INDICATED:
1 HOUR - ALWAYS
½ HOUR - SOMETIMES
0   - NEVER

39- 1 10	6 7½
2 9½	7 7
3 9	8 6½
4 8½	9 6 or less
5 8	0 DK

5. On the spot coding by E: E writes in one digit as specified by item directions before E can go to next item.   25–

6. Same as #5, except E writes in one digit per box. In this case two digits are written.   24,25–

7. Postcoding by someone other than E: for example, E cannot write anything in any parallelogram. Item specifies in CAPS that E must record information to be coded by TB later.   25–

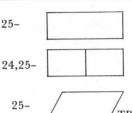

TB

8. For all items, when E cannot get R to accept one of the alternatives provided, E *writes* in Y and circles it. E.g., Y is used on Q 34 when not read to a SPOUSE-less R or on Q 90.1–90.6 if R cannot go along with the if-clause.   25–   1   2   3   (Y)

    If R says, e.g., on Q 66, "Two or three," E replies e.g., "I have to get one and only one answer. I wonder if you could tell me which you think is the best answer. Is it two or three?" (This rule does not apply when multiple codes are allowed.)

9. Whenever there is an interruption in the interview, E writes in

on left side of page:
Interruption is defined as any event which stops the flow of the interview. At end of interview, he uses this information to score Q 141.3: "Interruptions in interview?"

10. Respondent "codes" Q 48A and B, 65A, and 102 by writing numbers, making checkmarks, and circling numbers, respectively. E's responsibility is to see that R's marks are interpretable by the editor.

259

11. E stays away from circles such as the following: 56- ⊗ (p. 6)

   6-Y02 (p. 7).

12. If E makes error: no erasure allowed, X it out. Use pencil, not colored, no ink, no liquid lead, no ball point pen!

NOTES ON SPECIFIC ITEMS

Geographic Area of Residence Code (Cols. 7, 8 on p. 1)
(Done by RT before E gets face sheet.)

In coding geographic area, the location of the regular dwelling place of the respondent is to be determined. In some cases, this location can be determined in a preliminary way by means of the address from the school class list. However, the location of the dwelling will always be confirmed at the time telephone contact is made with the family.

Coding Rules

Residence in a city or village takes precedence over a residence in a town. That is, only when it has been determined that a respondent does not live within the boundaries of one of the listed cities or villages, will the township of residence be coded.

CODE	AREA	CODE	AREA
	Cities, villages		*Towns*
01	Hudson city	10	Ancram
02	Chatham village	11	Austerlitz
03	Philmont village	12	Canaan
04	Stottville (unincorporated village)	13	Chatham
		14	Claverack
05	Valatie village	15	Clermont
		16	Copake
		17	Gallatin
		18	Germantown
		19	Ghent
		20	Greenport
		21	Hillsdale
		22	Kinderhook
		23	Livingston
		24	New Lebanon
		25	Stockport
		26	Stuyvesant
		27	Taghkanic

Question 6

When were you married?   24,25-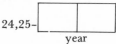

If R gives a date, E writes it in; if R says how long ago he was married, E may help R with the arithmetic.

260

Question 8

Is NAME your own child or is he adopted?

1 own child
2 adopted
3 other_____

If not (1) own child or (2) adopted, circle the 3-code, probe for relationship, and write it on the line provided.

Question 11

E writes in name of each child as given by R. Twins (etc.) are arbitrarily assigned successive positions and coded 3 or 4. All unoccupied positions are coded 5 (=DNA) and the age is coded as:

Y	Y

For example, an only-child family would receive 5-codes (DNA) in the sex columns and YY in the age columns for all positions except *OLDEST*. Age is calculated in the everyday way, that is the age achieved at the most recent birthday. Thus a child who is 12 years 6 months old is coded

1	2

;

a child 9 years 11 months old is coded:

0	9

;

a child 7 months old is coded:

0	0

.

A child 100 or more years old is coded:

9	9

.

Questions 15C and D; also questions 21B; 130A, C and D

In responding to Q 15C and D on occupation, some Rs will answer in terms of a job title (such as foreman, sales engineer, etc.), and some will answer in terms of specific occupational activities. The goal of probing here is to ensure that the job designation depicts in an accurate way these actual activities.

The following excerpt is taken from the 1960 Census Bureau Enumerator's Reference Manual, Paragraphs 165–168. It will serve as a guide to the use of the present occupation question:

165. *How to obtain a satisfactory occupation entry.* The best short description of a person's occupation is usually the title of his job; so, wherever possible, enter the title of the person's occupation. For example, "Auto mechanic," is satisfactory, you do not have to enter a description of his duties.

In some cases, the respondent will not give you enough information in answering the question, "What kind of work was he doing?" You should ask additional questions until you are satisfied that you have obtained the specific occupation of the person. For example, the respondent may say, "Teaching." You should then ask, "What subject did he teach?" For example the respondent says, "My daughter is a nurse." You should then ask, "What kind of a nurse is she, a registered nurse, practical nurse, nursemaid, or some other kind?"

Sometimes, the respondent will give you a lengthy explanation of the person's job duties. You should condense such statements in a few words which give the most important points about the kind of work the person is doing. For example, the respondent may say, "My husband runs a machine that takes dough and cuts it up before the dough is put into the oven." Your entry in the schedule should be "Dough cutting machine operator."

Another type of problem you may find is an answer for which you cannot think up a simple title. For example, the respondent may say, "He nails heels on shoes." It is satisfactory for you to enter on the schedule the words "Nails heels on shoes."

166. *Unusual occupations.* You may run across occupations which sound strange or funny to you. Accept such reports if the respondent is sure that the title is correct. For example, "sand hog" is the title for certain workers engaged in the construction of under-water tunnels, and "printer's devil" is sometimes used for an apprentice printer.

167. *Caution on occupations of young persons.* Professional, technical, and skilled occupations usually require lengthy periods of training or education which a young person normally cannot have. It may be found, upon further inquiry, that the young person is really only a trainee, apprentice, or helper (for example, accounting trainee, electrician trainee, apprentice electrician, electrician's helper).

168. *Occupations for which special care is necessary.* The following are occupations for which you must take special *care* to get satisfactory entries:

Not satisfactory	*Satisfactory*
A. Agent	Freight agent, insurance agent, sales agent, advertising agent, purchasing agent, etc.
B. Clerk	Stock clerk, shipping clerk, bookkeeper, statistical clerk, file clerk, etc. (A person who sells goods in a store, is a salesman, *not* a clerk.)
C. Engineer	Civil engineer, locomotive engineer, mechanical engineer, stationary engineer, aeronautical engineer, etc.
D. Fireman	Locomotive fireman, city fireman (city fire dept.), fire fighter, stationary fireman, fire boss, etc.
E. Mechanic	Auto mechanic, dental mechanic, radio mechanic, airplane mechanic, office machine mechanic, etc. (Do not confuse a mechanic with a machinist. . . .)
F. Nurse	Registered nurse, nursemaid, practical nurse, nurse's aide, student professional nurse, etc.
G. Teacher	Mathematics professor, music teacher, chemistry instructor, geography teacher, biology professor, etc. (If the teacher, instructor, or professor teaches more than one subject, enter the subject which he teaches the greatest number of hours; for an elementary school teacher who teaches many subjects, entries such as "primary teacher," "grade teacher," and "elementary teacher" are satisfactory.)

Question 20

When NAME tells a fib or lie, does he seem to be worried about it?

1 no
2 yes
3 DK or other

If R says, NAME doesn't lie, E codes 3.

Question 21A

If R says, "Nurse's training," code 3: 1–3 years college. If it is not clear how far in high school or college R means, probe. E.g., "How much college?"

Question 24.1

There are two kinds of people in this world: the weak and the strong.	1 disagree
	2 agree

1 is coded if R says either "disagree," "false," or "no."
2 is coded if R says either "agree," "true," or "yes."

Question 24.7

I easily lose patience with people.	1 disagree
	2 agree

An item such as 24.7 may elicit from R, "Who? You or me?" E may respond *only* by pointing to R.

Question 27

There are two identical pages following page 8. One is to be torn out of the notebook when E arrives at the instruction TEAR OUT NEXT PAGE AND HAND TO RESPONDENT on page 8; the other is retained in the notebook. The page retained in the notebook provides the order in which the "values" are read *to* R when E arrives at the instruction TURN PAGE AND READ WITH RE-SPONDENT on page 8. The designation in the lower right corner of the retained page provides the value order (VO) code to be entered into the 25,26 boxes on page 8. The two-digit VO-number is entered, not VO itself. There are six different value orders: 01, 02, 03, 04, 05, and 06.

If R gives three as most desirable and then gives a fourth for the single most desirable, E repeats, "Of the three you've picked, which one is the *most desirable* in a third-grade boy?" or, "Of the three you've mentioned, which one is the most desirable in a third-grade girl?" E accepts R's response after using this probe.

If R says, "Same as for a boy," E just copies. If R objects that NAME is girl, E smiles and repeats instructions for a *boy*.

Questions 33, 62, 75, 85, 116

What does R know about NAME?
No probes allowed! May reread.

Question 40

Round up. E.g., if 8.75 hours, code as if it were 9 hours.

Question 40.1, 40.5

Read parentheses "(for your husband)" as part of the items only for respondents who have husbands living with them.

Question 44

Whom does NAME resemble more in behavior, you
or your SPOUSE?

1 father more
2 mother more
3 both
4 neither

If R asks, E may interpret "father" and "mother" to mean *current* father or
mother surrogate. An *absent* biological parent is in the "neither" category.

Question 45 A,B

If R says, "yes," E asks, "always or sometimes?"

Question 54

How often has moving to different houses or apart-
ments meant that NAME had to find new friends?
CIRCLE # OF TIMES (0–9+)

0	5
1	6
2	7
3	8
4	9+

It is O.K. for E to help R to interpret the item so that a move made while
NAME was too small to have friends or to have to find friends may not be
counted. Also a small move need not be counted unless R indicates that NAME
had to find new friends.

Question 64

If R says, e.g., "I can't say," code 1: "NOTHING."

Question 65

If, for the example, R says, e.g., "I don't like coffee," E says, "For this example, just suppose you did like coffee. Pretend you like coffee and place your
checkmarks, one to a line."

Question 65A

One and only one response per line is required.

Question 65B

1 passed = at least one non-extreme checkmark on page 17b.
2 extreme, passed = all three checkmarks extreme on page 17b and then R
   moves one or two places.
3 extreme, failed = all three checkmarks extreme on page 17 and then R moves
   zero, three or four places.
4 non-reader = Q 65 has not been administered because interviewer had judged
   respondent to be a nonreader.

Question 66

Item is reworded as follows: Are there any clubs or groups, or organizations
that NAME takes part in after school hours — such as Brownies, Cub Scouts,
religious training, dancing or music lessons, and so forth?

264

"THIS YEAR" = the present school year (Sept. 1959 to the present).

Question 73

How often do you, yourself, have breakfast with NAME?

1 never
2 once in a while
3 almost daily
4 daily

If R says, e.g., "Sometimes," E asks, "Once in a while or almost daily?"

Question 78A

If R says, "Yes, but I don't attend," code 1: no.

Question 79

Are you satisfied with how your SPOUSE handles money?

1 yes
2 no

If R says SPOUSE doesn't handle money, E repeats item and reads alternatives to R. If R cannot choose "yes" or "no," code by writing in Y and circling:

Ⓨ

Question 81A

Have you ever filled out a questionnaire before, or been interviewed for an hour or more — for a job, or anything else? *IF YES*, What kind of interview?

1 no
2 yes, other _____
3 yes, previous RVWF interview

Questionnaire = any paper-and-pencil procedure.
RVWF = Rip Van Winkle Foundation (research interview).

Question 82A

If 0 is coded, code 82B Y and go to 83.

Question 82B

How many of these children do you know by name? What are their names? (FIRST *AND* LAST NAME) WRITE

1 knows none
2 knows some
3 knows all

If R asks someone for help, mark him down one category. Do not write names; just tally when names are given.

Question 96

Code the achieved age. ". . . when he stopped" is to be interpreted by the respondent with no help from the interviewer.

Question 102

If R says at any time before D something like, "It's not a punishment," E can, after reading what is provided in the interview, help R place his circle at or near 1.

It is proper to help R correct vertical errors. One and only one response per line is required.

When no number is circled on a line, E postcodes Y.

Question 122

How often do you, yourself, help NAME with his homework?

1 never
2 once in a while
3 almost daily
4 daily

If R says, e.g., "As often as needed," E asks, "How often has that been in the past month?" and reads the response alternatives starting at top.

Question 123

Are you satisfied that NAME doesn't push or shove other children?

1 yes
2 no

R may interpret item in any way. The key to the item is that R says "yes" or "no" to this item as R interprets it *with no help from E.*

Question 126A

Probe: (How far did you go in school?)

Question 126B

Schooling (NON-VOCATIONAL) means learning from books primarily.

Question 129A

If R says, "Nobody," code 4: neither.

Question 130A

Father = the "father" R was then living with.

Question 139A

If R says, "Once a year," code 1: a few times a year.

Question 139B

When needed, write in and circle 3, 4, or 5.

Question 141.1

Changed to:

> TELL RESPONDENT YOU MUST CHECK INTERVIEW.
> DO INTERVIEWER-RATINGS AFTER CHECKING.

Honesty of responses in this interview?

1 faking good
2 not faking good

1 faking good = making child or respondent better than he is.
2 not faking good = seemingly candid.

Question 141.3

| Interruptions in interview? | 1 yes |
| | 2 no |

Look for (INT) notations. If any, code 1: yes; if none, code 2: no.

Question 141.4

Were you bothered by the respondent's semantic   1 yes
quibbling?   2 somewhat
                                                    3 no, did not occur

Semantic quibbling = an attempt by R to rephrase, redefine, items.

Question 141.5

Did respondent see this as a clinical interview at any   1 yes
time during the interview?   2 no

Clinical interview = statements by R that indicate a belief that E came to diagnose or counsel about NAME's adjustment (mental health, emotional problems, etc.) or a belief that the study is concerned with problem kids and NAME is involved because we believe he is a problem.

Question 141.6

2 is the neutral category.
1 is the category for any amount of negative feelings.
3, 4, 5 — ordered amounts of positive feelings.

Question 141.9

If interview is tape-recorded, code 4.

ADDENDA TO INTERVIEW MANUAL

Procedure for Interviewer:

0. Before going to R, inventory pages.
1. E introduces self: "I am (Mr., Mrs., Miss) —— , the interviewer who was assigned."
2. E determines that he is talking to the person assigned to him (establishes that this person is R).
3. E must see to it that, as much as he can do it courteously, the proper conditions of privacy are maintained. The ideal conditions are E interviewing R with no one else present. Deviations from the ideal are reported by E in Q 141.7–141.9.
4. E checks accuracy of the address on the face sheet.
5. Tells R what child we're talking about and learns what R calls him. (This is what E substitutes for NAME.)
6. E tells a minimum about the study. A good entrée is to ask R to say what

he knows about the study. E then tells R as little as possible, promising to answer any questions after the interview is over. E can say that we are studying all the third graders in Columbia County and that R will see what we are studying by the kind of questions we ask.

7. E records time on the top of page 2 and starts interviewing. No smoking or gum-chewing by E is allowed at any time during the interview.

8. After E completes Q 140, he tells R that E must check through the questionnaire to see that nothing has been missed.

9. E checks through questionnaire, starting with page 1. He does this by seeing that all appropriate questions have been asked. E then completes Q 141.1 – 141.9.

10. E fills in TIME ENDED at bottom of page 29.

11. E leaves R as soon as possible. Keep talk and sociality to a bare minimum. No coffee, etc.

12. E edits questionnaire: being sure that all precoded columns are marked, postcoding (pp. 4, 10, and 25), and transferring the identification numbers from the face sheet to the other green pages (pp. 7, 13, 19, and 24). He then initials EDITED BY INT'WER on the face sheet.

REINFORCEMENT MEASURES

Appendix III

A. Development of a Home Aggression Composite Score (HAGG)

Tables III.1 and III.2 present the joint relation of mothers' and fathers' ratings of frequency of home aggression to school aggression for boys and girls.[1] It seems that the marginal scores (either parent's ratings) relate well only in the girls' table; there the cell entries form an additive pattern. As predicted from the agreement tables above, the home aggression score is not relevant to school aggression for a sample of boys that includes parents who disagree in their judgments of frequency of home aggression. The relations of mothers' and fathers' judgments of frequency of home aggression to school aggression for the girls, at least, encouraged us to form a new score, the sum of the two-parent frequency of home aggression (FR) ratings for each child.[2]

For the girls but not for the boys there is a consistent positive monotonic relation between frequency of home aggression as rated by composite parents and school aggression as rated by peers. Table III.3 shows the greater additivity of this frequency of home aggression measure for girls than for boys.

[1] A total of 545 subjects (281 boys and 264 girls) were used in this analysis. This included all children who were present on the one day the peer-ratings were done and both of whose parents were interviewed and yielded scorable records.

[2] Whenever scores were added together to form a composite, we routinely used standard scores.

TABLE III.1

Boys' Mean School Aggression Scores as a Function of Mothers'
and Fathers' Reports of Frequency of Home Aggression

| | | Mothers | | | |
		Low	Middle	High	Total
	Low	12.83 (41)[a]	12.45 (20)	15.33 (24)	13.45 (85)
Fathers	Middle	11.46 (33)	12.07 (28)	14.55 (31)	12.72 (92)
	High	14.84 (32)	18.56 (32)	15.43 (40)	16.21 (104)
	Total	13.04 (106)	14.76 (80)	15.12 (95)	14.23 (281)

[a]The number in parentheses represents the number of subjects in the cell.

TABLE III.2

Girls' Mean School Aggression Scores as a Function of Mothers'
and Fathers' Reports of Frequency of Home Aggression

| | | Mothers | | | |
		Low	Middle	High	Total
	Low	4.50 (48)[a]	5.64 (28)	11.00 (10)	5.63 (86)
Fathers	Middle	5.32 (28)	8.19 (31)	10.51 (35)	8.20 (94)
	High	10.43 (14)	8.96 (25)	16.98 (45)	13.50 (84)
	Total	5.68 (90)	7.57 (84)	13.80 (90)	9.05 (264)

[a]The number in parentheses represents the number of subjects in the cell.

TABLE III.3

Mean School Aggression Scores at Three Levels of the Composite
of Mothers' Plus Fathers' Ratings of Frequency of Home Aggression

		Boys	Girls	Both
LFFR	Low	12.41 (87)[a]	5.25 (103)	8.53 (190)
plus	Middle	13.88 (95)	9.25 (72)	11.89 (167)
LMFR	High	16.16 (99)	13.28 (89)	14.80 (188)
	Total	14.23 (281)	9.05 (264)	11.72 (545)

[a]The number in parentheses represents the number of subjects in the cell.

Another set of analyses on the 451 complete data cases (206 girls
and 245 boys) demonstrates essentially the same relations. Tables
III.4, III.5, III.6, and III.7 present 3×3 analyses of variance for par-
ent-ratings of recency (RA) and frequency of home aggression (FR)
for girls and for boys as these ratings relate to school aggression. Both
scores, recency and frequency of home aggression, relate for girls but
not for boys. This difference in relation supports the suggestion that
this measure is differentially useful, which was noted above from
examining Tables 4.2 and 4.3 in the text. In addition, for the girls

270

TABLE III.4
Recency of Aggression of Girls

		LMRA		
		Low	Middle	High
	Low	4.63	5.61	7.77
LFRA	Middle	6.64	9.29	14.84
	High	4.38	12.31	15.05

Summary

LMRA	$P < .005$
LFRA	$P < .025$
M × F	NS

TABLE III.5
Recency of Aggression of Boys

		LMRA		
		Low	Middle	High
	Low	11	12.52	17.81
LFRA	Middle	14.04	14.23	13.14
	High	16.80	13.71	16.04

Summary

LMRA	NS
LFRA	NS
M × F	NS

TABLE III.6
Frequency of Aggression of Girls

		LMFR		
		Low	Middle	High
	Low	5.4	5.0	6.2
LFFR	Middle	6.1	7.8	9.8
	High	9.0	7.5	18.3

Summary

LMFR	$P < .025$
LFFR	$P < .01$
M × F	NS

the relation to school aggression for recency of home aggression is not as uniform as it is for frequency of home aggression. Recency of home aggression seems relevant enough to attempt building a home aggression composite (RA + FR = HAGG) for each parent.

The 3×3 analyses of variance relating mothers' and fathers'

HAGG scores to the school aggression scores for girls and for boys are presented in Tables III.8 and III.9. The HAGG functions about as predicted from its components: a quite linear and dependable pattern for the girls, and nothing for the boys. Since for the girls the fathers' frequency of home aggression is a better prediction than

TABLE III.7

Frequency of Aggression of Boys

			LMFR	
		Low	*Middle*	*High*
	Low	11.1	15	14.2
LFFR	*Middle*	13.1	12.5	11.6
	High	15	19.6	15.5

Summary

LMFR	NS
LFFR	NS
M × F	NS

TABLE III.8

Recency and Frequency of Home Aggression, Girls

			LMRA plus LMFR	
		Low	*Middle*	*High*
LFRA	*Low*	5.56	3.84	6.4
plus	*Middle*	5.24	9.27	14.79
LFFR	*High*	3.64	7.86	19.21

Summary

LMRA + LMFR	$P < .025$
LFRA + LFFR	$P < .005$
M × F	$P < .05$

TABLE III.9

Recency and Frequency of Home Aggression, Boys

			LMRA plus LMFR	
		Low	*Middle*	*High*
LFRA	*Low*	10	12	18
plus	*Middle*	15	12.6	11.3
LFFR	*High*	17.8	13.9	18.2

Summary

LMRA + LMFR	NS
LFRA + LFFR	NS
M × F	NS

272

their recency of home aggression and the mothers' recency of home aggression is (better) than their frequency of home aggression, adding both parents' frequency and recency of home aggression into a single parental HAGG yields a useful composite. This single HAGG composite is useful in exploring the relation of home aggression to school aggression for boys and for girls. The reader is referred back to Table 4.4 in the text to see that this relation holds for girls only.

B. Development of Judgment of Punishment Scale (JUP)

During the pilot testing of the interview thirty respondents, mothers and fathers of third graders, were given forty punishment items to judge for harshness as it might be experienced by their third-grade children. The task was essentially a nine-point Thurstone scaling along intensity of punishment.

With the thought that the respondent reveals in an indirect way his tendency to use harsh or mild punishments by his average placement of items along this intensity continuum, the items were examined for their Q. Punishments with relatively large Q value (sixteen in all) were assembled into the JUP scale (item 102 in questionnaire, Appendix II.B). Original instructions for the scaling task and all forty items which were scaled follow.

Initial instructions

I am going to read to you some things parents do to their children. I want you to tell me how harsh, that is, how severe or how mean each would be as a punishment for NAME. Your job is to judge how harsh a punishment is, *even if* NAME is not punished in that way. (Take out this page and the next one and hand notebook to respondent.)

On your page are three lines. Each line has numbers from zero to eight. For each thing I read you, I want you to circle one of the numbers. Circle a number toward eight for a very harsh punishment and circle a number toward zero for a very mild punishment. The more harsh the punishment for NAME, the higher the number you should circle; the more mild the punishment is for NAME, the lower the number you should circle. The number you circle indicates your judgment of each punishment for NAME; is it very harsh, very mild, or somewhere in between?

(Read letter as part of item.)

        A. Giving NAME an angry look.
        B. Saying to NAME, "You are a naughty boy (girl)."
        C. Sending NAME to his (her) room without supper.

(If necessary, show R how to indicate *his* judgment; once R has done these correctly, read:) Now that we've tried these, I want you to turn the page and do some more.

Now let's make more judgments about how severe or how mild punishments are for NAME. Circle a number toward eight for a very harsh punishment and circle a number toward zero for a very mild punishment.

Scolding NAME in a crowded store.

Shaking NAME.

Saying, "That isn't a nice thing to do."

Spanking NAME a couple of times on the bottom.

Spanking NAME until (s)he cries.

Saying, "You make me feel unhappy."

Telling NAME, "If you want to get along with others, you'll have to behave differently."

Saying, "Get on that chair and don't move for half an hour."

Saying, "You're a lot of trouble to me."

Making fun of NAME.

Slapping NAME in the face.

Pointing out how some close friend of his (hers) behaves better than NAME does.

Not permitting NAME to play with his (her) friends.

Hitting NAME with a stick or strap.

Telling NAME that what (s)he did is stupid.

Telling NAME that young men (ladies) don't do this sort of thing.

Saying, "Get on that chair and don't move until you apologize."

Hitting NAME in front of people who are not in your family.

Saying, "I would like to be proud of you."

Telling NAME (s)he is acting like a baby.

Warning NAME that (s)he will have to be punished.

Telling NAME in a nice way how to act differently.

Telling NAME, "I will give you something you like if you act differently."

Shouting at NAME.

Shaking and slapping NAME.

Washing out NAME's mouth with soap.

Making NAME apologize.

Telling NAME, "You make me punish you when you act that way."

Sending NAME to bed early.

Getting angry at NAME.

Not letting NAME play with his (her) friends for two days.

Saying, "If you acted right, you'd be a big help to me."

Telling NAME (s)he won't be able to do something (s)he likes to do.

Encouraging NAME to try again.

Sending NAME to another room where (s)he will be alone and without toys.

Saying, "You shouldn't do this if you don't want others to do it to you."

Telling NAME you don't love him (her) for something (s)he has done.

Saying, "God doesn't like boys (girls) to act that way."

Taking away something that NAME likes.

ATTEMPTED MEASURES OF IDENTIFICATION

Appendix IV

We had little success in getting a measure of role expectations from either the children or the parents. In the first year of the study when 974 subjects were tested, a number of formats were tried with the aggression item stems, e.g., "Should (boys, girls) do . . . ," "Is it all right for (boys, girls) to . . . ," "Is it ever all right for (boys, girls) to . . . ," etc. Response alternatives were "yes" and "no" in half the classes, and "yes," "sometimes," "no" in the other half. None of these formats, however, yielded a sufficiently wide distribution of scores. These eight-year-olds would not admit to any extent that any of the aggressive behaviors mentioned were approved. The self-incriminatory response seemed to be too patent. A further attempt was made to establish a measure of role expectations that would yield some variance in scores by attaching two kinds of specifications to the aggression stems: provocation level (e.g., "pushing someone who pushes them first") and the kind of child who was the actor or object (e.g., "a boy who gets good marks," "a girl you like," etc.). The mean scores for the different classifications of actor and provocation level were compared and found to be similar, except that the girl-to-boy aggression was much more approved than girl-to-girl, boy-to-boy, or boy-to-girl. Apparently the effect of social desirability was still overriding. Thus the attempt to measure role expectations in this manner was abandoned.

An attempt was also made in the earlier interview to evaluate role modeling with a measure of the parents' own aggression as rated by each parent for both himself and spouse. However, this measure was unrelated to the independent aggression criterion, although it was related to other interview variables. In this measure a number of hypothetical frustrating situations were described to the respondent, and he was asked to choose from a series of alternatives how directly he would express his aggression in response to this situation (see Table II.4 Appendix II, questions 147–158). Here too the socially desirable response was perhaps too obvious and there was no relation to the criterion measure. Since it is central to the concept of role modeling that aggression of parents be related to aggression of children, this particular measure of the concept was dropped and another one substituted (Walters and Zak, 1959). Another reason for dropping the measure was the poor reliability (e.g., r between mothers' and fathers' ratings of mothers' aggression not significantly greater than zero).

SUMMARY STATISTICS

Appendix V

Explanations of Components of Each of 202 Scores

Note: M as first letter = child measure.
L as first letter = interview measure.
M as second letter = mother.
F as second letter = father.
B as second letter = composite of mother and father.

No.	Mnemonic	Translation
1.	MAGG	Peer-rating aggression, average of the percentage of judges choosing a child on ten aggression items.
2.	MANX	Peer-rating aggression-anxiety, average of the percentage of judges choosing a child on two aggression-anxiety items (child demonstrates fear and/or reluctance to perform aggressive acts).
3.	MPOP	Peer-rating popularity, average of the percentage of judges choosing a child on two popularity items.
4.	MSAG	Peer-rating success in aggression, average of the percentage of judges choosing a child on three success in aggression items.
5.	MACT	Peer-rating activity, average of the percentage of judges choosing a child on two activity items.
6.	MBGA	Unweighted composite of nine items selected from Games and Activity Preference for boyish games.
7.	MGGA	Unweighted composite of seven items selected from Games and Activity Preference for girlish games.
8.	LFFR	Unweighted sum of seven frequency of aggression items (father-interview).
9.	LMFR	Unweighted sum of seven frequency of aggression items (mother-interview).
10.	LFGM	A single geographic mobility of child item (father-interview).

No.	Mnemonic	Translation
11.	LMGM	A single geographic mobility of child item (mother-interview).
12.	LFEA	A single educational apsiration item (father-interview).
13.	LMEA	A single educational aspiration item (mother-interview).
14.	LFWZ	Unweighted composite of twelve Walters-Zak items (selected to assess aggression of father).
15.	LMWZ	Unweighted composite of twelve Walters-Zak items (selected to assess aggression of mother).
16.	LFRO	Respondent's occupation — the sum of mother's and father's ratings about father (0 = high; 18 = low occupational status).
17.	LMRO	Respondent's occupation — the sum of mother's and father's ratings about mother (0 = high; 18 = low occupational status).
18.	LFRJ	Unweighted composite of ten rejection items (father-interview) taken from 1958 Interview.
19.	LMRJ	Unweighted composite of ten rejection items (mother-interview) taken from 1958 Interview.
20.	LFRA	Unweighted composite of eight recency of aggression items (father-interview).
21.	LMRA	Recency of aggression. (Same.)
22.	LFNU	Unweighted composite of nine nurturance items.
23.	LMNU	Nurturance. (Same.)
24.	LFPD	Unweighted composite of ten parental disharmony items.
25.	LMPD	Parental disharmony. (Same.)
26.	LFCI	Unweighted composite of two confessing identification items.
27.	LMCI	Unweighted composite of two confessing identification items.
28.	LFRE	Unweighted composite of five restrictiveness items.
29.	LMRE	Restrictiveness. (Same.)
30.	LFSI	Unweighted composite of four social isolation items.
31.	LMSI	Social isolation. (Same.)
32.	LFPC	Unweighted composite of twelve punishment for aggression against another child items.
33.	LMPC	Punishment for aggression against another child. (Same.)
34.	LFPA	Unweighted composite of twelve punishment for aggression against respondent items.
35.	LMPA	Punishment for aggression against respondent. (Same.)
36.	LFPU	Unweighted composite of twenty-four punishment for both kinds of aggression items.
37.	LMPU	Punishment for both kinds of aggression. (Same.)
38.	LFRM	Unweighted composite of two residential mobility items.
39.	LMRM	Residential mobility. (Same.)
40.	LFDA	Date of interview (face sheet on father-interview).
41.	LMDA	Date of interview (face sheet on mother-interview).
42.	LFGL	Ethnicity generation level of father. Number of generations father's family has been resident in U.S.

No.	Mnemonic	Translation
43.	LMGL	Generation level of mother.
44.	LFJP	Unweighted composite of sixteen judgment of punishment items (how harsh the father judges these punishments to be for his child).
45.	LMJP	Judgment of punishment. (Same.)
46.	LFPI	Composite of eighteen profile identification items — child vs. father (Cronbach's D score).
47.	LMPI	Profile identification — child vs. mother (Cronbach's D score).
48.	LBPI	Profile identification — mother vs. father (Cronbach's D score).
49.	MCPI	Profile identification — child vs. mode of children of his own sex (Cronbach's D score).
50.	LFRI	A single role identification item (father).
51.	LMRI	A single role identification item (mother).
52.	LBRI	A single role identification item (composite of mother and father).
53.	LFBO	Birth order (father-interview).
54.	LMBO	Birth order (mother-interview).
55.	LBBO	Birth order (composite of father and mother).
56.	LFSP	A single substitute parent item.
57.	LMSP	Substitute parent. (Same.)
58.	LFGI	Unweighted composite of seven guilt identification items.
59.	LMGI	Guilt identification. (Same.)
60.	LFQP	Unweighted composite of three questionnaire practice items.
61.	LMQP	Questionnaire practice. (Same.)
62.	LFLM	Length of marriage (no. of years father reports being married).
63.	LMLM	Length of marriage (no. of years mother reports being married).
64.	LFNC	Number of children father reports having.
65.	LMNC	Number of children mother reports having.
66.	LFOP	No. of years father has been only parent.
67.	LMOP	No. of years mother has been only parent.
68.	LFFI	A composite of three family intactness items.
69.	LMFI	Family intactness. (Same.)
70.	LFBG	1 = boy; 2 = girl; 3 = boy twin; 4 = girl twin.
71.	LMBG	1 = boy; 2 = girl; 3 = boy twin; 4 = girl twin.
72.	LFCP	Unweighted composite of five child presence items (how much of the day child spends at home).
73.	LMCP	Child presence. (Same.)
74.	LFPW	Unweighted composite of four father associating with child items.
75.	LMPW	Unweighted composite of four mother associating with child items.
76.	LFPX	Unweighted composite of five parental presence items (how much of the day father spends at home).
77.	LMPX	Unweighted composite of three parental presence items.
78.	LFPP	LFPW + LFPX

279

No.	Mnemonic	Translation
79.	LMPP	LMPW + LMPX
80.	LFAG	Age of father.
81.	LMAG	Age of mother.
82.	LFAM	Achieved mobility (occupational status of father's father).
83.	LMAM	Achieved mobility (occupational status of mother's father).
84.	LFAN	Anything else?
85.	LMAN	Anything else?
86.	LFBK	Unweighted composite of two books (Spock, child-rearing) items.
87.	LMBK	Books (Spock, child-rearing). (Same.)
88.	LBBP[a]	Eight items behavior preference (low social desirability, unprovoked) father vs. mother. Cronbach's D score.
89.	LBCQ[a]	Eight items behavior preference (high social desirability, provoked) father vs. mother. Cronbach's D score.
90.	LFBP[a]	Four items behavior preference (low social desirability, unprovoked) child vs. father. Cronbach's D score.
91.	LMBP[a]	Four items behavior preference (low social desirability, unprovoked) child vs. mother. Cronbach's D score.
92.	LFCQ[a]	Four items behavior preference (high social desirability, provoked) child vs. father. Cronbach's D score.
93.	LMCQ[a]	Four items behavior preference (high social desirability, provoked) child vs. mother. Cronbach's D score.
94.	LFCA	"Calibration" — father's estimate of child's popularity in school (one item).
95.	LMCA	"Calibration" — mother's estimate of child's popularity in school (one item).
96.	LBCA	"Calibration" (LFCA–LMCA).
97.	LFOA	Father's occupational aspirations for child (one item).
98.	LMOA	Mother's occupational aspirations for child (one item).
99.	LFTI	Started on Time? (Lateness rated by father's interview.)
100.	LMTI	Started on Time? (Lateness rated by mother's interview.)
101.	LFTC	Time consumed in father's interview.
102.	LMTC	Time consumed in mother's interview.
103.	LFST	Scheduled starting time (time of day).
104.	LMST	Scheduled starting time (time of day).
105.	LFSH	Unweighted composite of two shame items (punishment of child in presence of others, rated by father's interview).
106.	LMSH	Shame. (Same.)
107.	LFRL	A single religion item.
108.	LMRL	Religion. (Same.)
109.	LFRG	A single religiosity item (how often father attends church).

[a]These variables are not dealt with in this volume. They were included in the interview to obtain data for a doctoral dissertation of one of the participants (Toigo, 1962).

No.	Mnemonic	Translation
110.	LMRG	Religiosity. (Same.)
111.	LFPT	A single PTA membership item.
112.	LMPT	PTA membership. (Same.)
113.	LFPR	Respondent's "race," rated by father's interview.
114.	LMPR	Respondent's "race," rated by mother's interview.
115.	LFOR	Owner-renter status (amount spent on housing).
116.	LMOR	Owner-renter status (amount spent on housing).
117.	LFRS	Restrictiveness from OA.
118.	LMRS	Restrictiveness from OA.
119.	LFMP	Mobility perception of father, single item.
120.	LMMP	Mobility perception of mother, single item.
121.	LFMO	Unweighted composite of five mobility orientation items.
122.	LMMO	Mobility orientation. (Same.)
123.	LFLO	Location of interview rated by interviewer.
124.	LMLO	Location of interview. (Same.)
125.	LFSC	Unweighted composite of three standard conditions items.
126.	LMSC	Standard conditions. (Same.)
127.	LFIR	Unweighted composite of six interviewer-ratings items.
128.	LMIR	Unweighted composite of six interviewer-ratings items.
129.	LFIN	Numerical name of interviewer.
130.	LMIN	Numerical name of interviewer.
131.	LFGE	Numerical name of geographic area of residence.
132.	LMGE	Geographic area of residence.
133.	LBGE	Geographic area of residence.
134.	LFFS	Unweighted composite of nine F Scale items.
135.	LMFS	F Scale. (Same.)
136.	LFFP	Nine F Scale items scored for acquiescence.
137.	LMFP	F Scale scored for acquiescence. (Same.)
138.	LFEN	Age when stopped wetting bed (enuresis).
139.	LMEN	Age when stopped wetting bed (enuresis).
140.	LDEN	LFEN–LMEN.
141.	LFED	Education of parent (1 = high; 7 = low).
142.	LMED	Education of parent. (Same.)
143.	LDED	LFED–LMED.
144.	LSED	LFED+LMED.
145.	LFCB	Frequency of child's reading of comic books.
146.	LMCB	Frequency of child's reading of comic books.
147.	LFDI	A single direct identification item.
148.	LMDI	A single direct identification item.
149.	LBDI	A composite of LFDI and LMDI.
150.	LFTV	Unweighted composite of two amount of television items.
151.	LMTV	Amount of television. (Same.)
152.	LF05	Frequency of TV category 05 (father) — cartoons (Huckleberry Hound, Popeye, Rough and Ready, etc.)
153.	LF06	Frequency of TV category 06 (father) — westerns (Wagon Train, Black Saddle, Bonanza, Rifleman, etc.)
154.	LF07	Frequency of TV category 07 (father) — other adventure (Vikings, Jungle, Riverboat, Rin Tin Tin, etc.)
155.	LF08	Frequency of TV category 08 (father) — super science (Superman, etc.)

No.	Mnemonic	Translation
156.	LF09	Frequency of TV category 09 (father) — scientific, educational (Mr. Wizard, Man and the Challenge, Meet the Press, etc.)
157.	LF10	Frequency of TV category 10 (father) — children, other (Captain Kangaroo, Glendora, Shirley Temple, Disneyland, etc.)
158.	LF11	Frequency of TV category 11 (father) — children, comedy (Three Stooges, Our Gang, etc.)
159.	LF12	Frequency of TV category 12 (father) — adult variety (Como, Shore, Sullivan, Bob Hope, etc.)
160.	LF13	Frequency of TV category 13 (father) — adult mystery (Sunset Strip, Perry Mason, Bourbon Street, etc.)
161.	LF14	Frequency of TV category 14 (father) — adult drama (U.S. Steel, Playhouse 90, movies, G.E., daytime soap operas, etc.)
162.	LF15	Frequency of TV category 15 (father) — family situational (Lassie, Fury, Father Knows Best, Beaver, Nelsons, etc.)
163.	LF16	Frequency of TV category 16 (father) — quiz shows
164.	LF17	Frequency of TV category 17 (father) — music appreciation (radio, ballet, opera, Bernstein TV concerts)
165.	LF18	Frequency of TV category 18 (father) — teen-age (American Bandstand, Teen-age Barn, etc.)
166.	LF19	Frequency of TV category 19 (father) — adult comedy (Lucy, Honeymooners, Fibber McGee, etc.)
167.	LF20	Frequency of TV category 20 (father) — sports
168.	LM05	Frequency of TV category 05 (mother) — cartoons
169.	LM06	Frequency of TV category 06 (mother) — westerns
170.	LM07	Frequency of TV category 07 (mother) — other adventure
171.	LM08	Frequency of TV category 08 (mother) — super science
172.	LM09	Frequency of TV category 09 (mother) — scientific, educational
173.	LM10	Frequency of TV category 10 (mother) — children, other
174.	LM11	Frequency of TV category 11 (mother) — children, comedy
175.	LM12	Frequency of TV category 12 (mother) — adult variety
176.	LM13	Frequency of TV category 13 (mother) — adult mystery
177.	LM14	Frequency of TV category 14 (mother) — adult drama
178.	LM15	Frequency of TV category 15 (mother) — family situational
179.	LM16	Frequency of TV category 16 (mother) — quiz shows
180.	LM17	Frequency of TV category 17 (mother) — music appreciation
181.	LM18	Frequency of TV category 18 (mother) — teen-age
182.	LM19	Frequency of TV category 19 (mother) — adult comedy
183.	LM20	Frequency of TV category 20 (mother) — sports

No	Mnemonic	Translation
184.	LFDE	Parent's deviation (eighteen random items).[b]
185.	LMDE	Parent's deviation (eighteen random items).[b]
186.	LMDE	Child's deviation (twenty-two random items).[b]
187.	LFRD	Unweighted composite of thirteen random scale items.
188.	LMRD	Random scale. (Same.)
189.	LFRN	Unweighted composite of thirteen RD's items randomly scored.
190.	LMRN	RD's items randomly scored. (Same.)
191.	LFPL	Unweighted composite of eight low punishment items.
192.	LMPL	Low punishment items. (Same.)
193.	LFPM	Unweighted composite of eight medium punishment items.
194.	LMPM	Medium punishment items. (Same.)
195.	LFPH	Unweighted composite of eight high punishment items.
196.	LMPH	High punishment items. (Same.)
197.	LFCN	Consistency − (LFPL-4) + (LFPM-4) + (LFPH-4).
198.	LMCN	Consistency − (LMPL-4) + (LMPM-4) + (LMPH-4).
199.	MDP1	Sex of the first picture drawn.
200.	MDP2	Sex of the second picture drawn.
201.	MDAP	Sameness (0) or oppositeness (2) of the sex of the first picture drawn with the sex of the artist.
202.	MCIQ	Child's IQ score on California Mental Maturity Scale.

Means and Standard Deviations for 451 Complete Data Cases

Code	Variable	Mean	σ
MAGG	Aggression	11.925	12.996
MANX	Anxiety	16.814	11.994
MPOP	Popularity	22.958	15.127
MSAG	Success in aggression	14.157	12.613
MACT	Activity level	15.177	9.002
MCIQ	IQ	104.373	14.189
MBGA	Boyish games and activity preference	14.572	3.583
MGGA	Girlish games and activity preference	8.998	2.642
LFFR	Frequency aggression	20.144	5.199
LMFR		21.104	5.196
LMGM	Geographic mobility of child	.712	1.255
LFEA	Educational aspiration for child	5.421	.949
LMEA		5.350	.995
LFWZ	Respondent's aggression	15.463	2.173
LMWZ		15.417	1.854
LFRO	Respondent's occupation	7.869	4.424
LMRO		9.525	2.585

[b]Each of these items was scored in terms of the percentage of respondents of the same sex as the respondent who picked that item. Thus a high score on this scale means that the respondent is not deviant (low deviation); a low score means that the respondent is deviant.

Code	Variable	Mean	σ
LFRJ	Rejection	12.827	2.207
LMRJ		13.428	2.247
LFRA	Recency of aggression	17.685	7.737
LMRA		20.698	7.582
LFNU	Nurturance	11.907	2.900
LMNU		13.184	2.675
LFPD	Parental disharmony	9.705	2.864
LMPD		9.222	2.538
LFCI	Confessing identification	5.729	1.628
LMCI		6.106	1.667
LFRE	Restrictiveness	8.452	1.042
LMRE		8.534	1.081
LFSI	Social isolation	11.457	6.340
LMSI		13.355	6.135
LFPU	All punishment items	16.390	8.705
LMPU		16.650	7.428
LFRM	Residential mobility	4.519	4.266
LMRM		5.075	4.293
LFGL	Generation level (ethnicity)	2.854	1.177
LMGL		2.931	1.153
LFJP	Judgment of punishment	51.231	15.443
LMJP		50.322	14.553
LFPI	Profile identification	6.608	1.832
LMPI		6.616	1.883
LBPI[a]	Profile identification	5.778	1.661
MCPI[b]	Profile identification	6.333	1.564
LFRI	Role identification	2.038	.608
LMRI		2.324	.574
LFGI	Guilt identification	9.366	1.423
LMGI		9.450	1.384
LFLM	Length of marriage	14.373	5.413
LMLM		14.188	4.762
LFNC	Number of children	3.483	1.629
LMNC		3.512	1.616
LFFI	Family intactness	1.867	.389
LMFI		1.876	.368
LFCP	Child presence	12.816	5.767
LMCP		13.226	5.499
LFPW	Parental association with child	11.439	3.573
LMPW		14.075	3.640
LFPX	Parental presence	15.634	2.255
LMPX		10.789	1.291
LFAG	Age of respondent	39.062	7.156
LMAG		35.632	5.934
LFBK	Books (Spock, child-rearing)	1.925	1.571
LMBK		2.741	1.956
LBCA	Calibration	.572	.705
LFSH	Shame	3.098	.799
LMSH		3.222	.711

[a]Discrepancy between child and composite of mothers and fathers.
[b]Discrepancy between child and modal profile for all children.

Code	Variable	Mean	σ
LFRG	Religiosity	2.226	1.570
LMRG		2.534	1.558
LFOR	Owner-renter status	3.907	2.118
LFMP	Mobility perception	2.528	.516
LMMP		2.421	.512
LFMO	Mobility orientation	15.188	2.919
LMMO		15.024	3.115
LFIR	Interviewer-ratings	24.115	4.445
LMIR		22.749	4.591
LFFS	F Scale	27.585	5.389
LMFS		28.541	5.087
LFFP	F Scale acquiescence	26.663	6.099
LMFP		32.787	6.985
LFEN	Enuresis	3.268	2.211
LMEN		3.220	2.337
LFED	Education of parent	4.386	1.460
LMED		4.120	1.282
LFCB	Comic books	2.064	.644
LMCB		1.949	.595
LFTV	Television	12.033	4.110
LMTV		12.029	3.896
LFDE	Parent's deviation-from-norm scoring	439.410	51.689
LMDE		445.865	44.232
LFRN	Randomly selected items randomly scored	58.880	6.721
LMRN		59.898	6.903
LFPL	Punishment low	5.051	1.389
LMPL		5.381	1.354
LFPM	Punishment medium	3.761	2.042
LMPM		3.929	2.057
LFPH	Punishment high	.920	1.388
LMPH		.951	1.321
LFCN	Consistency of punishment	6.322	1.733
LMCN		6.366	1.850

THE ENVIRONMENTAL MANAGEMENT
OF AGGRESSION

Appendix VI

We present here an introduction to the environmental management of aggression. The parent who wishes to use these techniques should be prepared to do some outside reading. For a start he might well study Holland and Skinner's *The Analysis of Behavior* (1961). This programed text will help the reader more appropriately to apply the techniques described here. Aggression has been treated in the current volume as a behavior that may be under respondent control and also under operant control.[1] In general we have described a series of investigations that were largely concerned with determining the resultants of training procedures in a community; we describe in Chapter 9 and in this appendix prescriptions to be followed by the parent who wants to be more effective in the management of aggression. Recommendations are based in part on the results of our study and in part on present knowledge about the laws of behavior. Behaviors other than aggression may also perhaps be managed by using the same principles presented here.

A few technical items first:

1. A *behavior* is some simple action or some complex series of actions of a person that can be observed to occur on some occasion. It is of interest to see how often this behavior reappears on certain types of occasions.

---

[1] The discussion of respondent or Pavlovian control of behavior should be tempered by Miller's (1969) paper which suggests that operant principles are sufficient to account for both respondent and operant behaviors.

2. A behavior that dependably occurs after the same stimulus, no matter what else happens before, during, or after that behavior, is said to be under *respondent* control. The eliciting stimulus, the behavior, and the dependability of the stimulus-behavior relation are referred to as a reflex. Pain seems to be an eliciting stimulus for aggressive behavior, and this combination of pain and then aggression is called a pain-aggression reflex (Azrin, Hake, and Hutchinson, 1965). Stimuli other than pain can be made to elicit aggression behavior. These stimuli, once neutral with respect to pain and aggression, become by respondent (Pavlovian) conditioning adequate substitutes for pain.

3. A behavior, whether or not it is under respondent control (part of a reflex), can come under *operant* control. A behavior may become more or less frequent under certain conditions depending on what happens just after the behavior (within about one second); this is referred to as operant control of behavior. An immediate consequence that maintains or increases the frequency of a behavior is by definition a *reinforcement*. If such a reinforcing consequence is not permitted to occur, the behavior becomes less frequent. The condition under which a behavior is reinforced (i.e., immediately followed by reinforcement) is called a discriminative stimulus (S^D, pronounced "ess dee"). The presence of an S^D increases the probability that the behavior will occur.[2]

4. Several *consequences* to behaviors are presented in Table VI.1. A reinforcement may involve the onset of a stimulus; such a stimulus is a positive reinforcer and its presentation is a positive reinforcement. Or a reinforcement may involve the termination or withdrawal of a stimulus; such a stimulus is a negative reinforcer and its withdrawal is a negative reinforcement. Notice that both types of reinforcement (positive and negative) maintain or increase the frequency of the behavior they immediately follow.

5. *Punishment*, defined as a consequence that reduces the frequency of the immediately preceding behavior, also comes in two general types: (1) withdrawing a stimulus (such a stimulus therefore being called a positive reinforcer) and (2) presenting a stimulus (such a stimulus therefore being called a negative reinforcer). This is also illustrated in Table VI.1. Another consequence of some import involves the presentation or withdrawal of *neither* a positive nor a negative reinforcer. This no-consequence (called extinction) serves to weaken or to reduce the frequency of the behavior. Thus

[2] Notice that a very dependable S^D behavior relation may well appear as if the S^D is an eliciting stimulus for the behavior, which might then be called "reflexive." The so-called reflex may well be no more than a very dependable, species-wide S^D-behavior relation.

TABLE VI.1
Four Types of Consequences of Operant Behaviors

	Behavior results in the occurrence of the stimulus	Behavior results in the withdrawal of the stimulus
Negative reinforcer ("painful" stimulus)	Punishment (decreases the frequency of behavior)	Negative reinforcement (increases or maintains the frequency of behavior)
Positive reinforcer ("pleasurable" stimulus)	Positive reinforcement (increases or maintains the frequency of behavior)	Punishment by time out from positive reinforcement (decreases the frequency of behavior)

extinction may be viewed as a punishment. The condition under which a behavior is punished or not reinforced is called an S^Δ (pronounced "ess delta"). The presence of an S^Δ decreases the probability that the behavior will occur.

To control behaviors one must note the ABC's of those behaviors: the *A*ntecedents (possible S^D's and S^Δ's), the *B*ehavior itself, and the *C*onsequences (reinforcement, punishment, or neither). To determine what controls a behavior, one must see how often the behavior occurs given certain antecedent conditions and certain immediately following consequences. To do this one must first define the behavior so it can be counted with some objectivity. After watching and counting the behavior as well as its context (its antecedents and consequences), one may guess what might be maintaining the behavior.

For example, a child hits his brother more often when the mother is present than when she is absent. (Guess: Is the mother's presence an S^D for hitting the brother?) Immediately after the child hits his brother with the mother present, the mother hollers at and hits the child. (Guess: This is reinforcement?!). But notice that the mother, after punishing the child, then puts on a "party" for the two brothers "so they can learn to be friendlier to each other." One may guess that the mother's "punishing" behaviors function as a conditioned *positive* reinforcer (i.e., maintain or reinforce the hitting) because of the subsequent milk and cookies and solicitude from the mother. To this point we have attempted a *functional analysis* of the child's hitting his brother. We have looked for the ABC's of this behavior.

Now we must proceed to an *experimental analysis* of that behavior. An experimental analysis involves systematically changing the antecedent and/or consequence of a behavior and watching to see if the frequency of the behavior changes. This is done to test the conjectures in the functional analysis. Notice that we assume that any behavior is maintained by its current relation to the environment. The relevant environmental factors in this case seem to be the mother's presence and her behaviors before and especially after the hitting.

We already know that the mother's presence is a relevant antecedent since the frequency of the behavior increases when she is present; thus this manipulation occurs naturally and has already been noticed. The consequence may be manipulated (perhaps by telling the mother what to do) to see if the mother's hollering at and hitting the child is a conditioned positive reinforcer. The simplest manipulation is to drop out the hollering and hitting *and* the subsequent "party" and to make sure that the mother does not respond to the hitting behavior at all.

Assuming that this manipulation of the consequences of hitting which occurs when the mother is present would put the behavior of concern on extinction, one needs to know the typical course of behaviors which are put on extinction. A not unusual effect is that at the outset the now nonreinforced behavior temporarily increases in frequency and intensity. The mother will be very tempted to intervene. If we are correct in our analysis so far, this would tend to develop even more frequent and more vigorous hitting (aggressive behavior) in the boy.[3]

The likelihood of such a response (i.e., intervening) by the mother suggests that we do not take the simple way out, i.e., eliminate the mother's hollering and hitting and the subsequent "party." We are more likely to conduct a test concerning the consequence if the mother eliminates only the party. This may well remove many of the positive aspects of the "punishment," and thus reduce the boy's hitting his brother in the mother's presence. (However, if the mother ordinarily does not talk to the boy except "when he needs correcting," then her hollering at and hitting him may still function as a reinforcement for his aggressive behavior. In this case, the mother may need to speak to her son even when he doesn't need correcting.)

An even surer way of changing the behavior of the boy and being able to test the reinforcing value of the party is to shift the temporal location of the party from systematically after the behavior of concern to systematically after either (1) *any* other behavior of the boy

[3] In fact Reynolds (1968) prescribes such a use of extinction and then reinforcement of the resulting larger and more vigorous responses to *shape* larger behaviors. Unfortunately, parents without such technical knowledge inadvertently shape bigger aggression, much to their own chagrin.

or (2) *some specific* other behavior of the boy that occurs with sufficient frequency so the number of parties is at least maintained. Presenting the party after any behavior other than hitting is an example of a powerful therapeutic technique which also yields information about a presumed reinforcer. This technique is called *D*ifferential *R*einforcement of *O*ther Behaviors (DRO). DRO often has two features: when the undesired behavior occurs, the mother announces (1) that a time out for reinforcement (the party) has started; and (2) that the reinforcement will be forthcoming only after no hitting has occurred for a specified time interval. If that time interval has passed with no hitting, then the party is awarded to the boys. The party thus follows a period of not hitting (i.e., a period of behaviors *other* than hitting), which may last, say, ten minutes. Thus the technique would be called "DRO–10 minutes." With this manipulation we would expect not hitting to increase and hitting to decrease if the party is in fact a reinforcer.

A final comment is in order. The cookie and milk party as a reinforcer has its problems. The boys could become satiated after one or two parties in a period of one or two hours. We may want to give smaller parties so they can be given more frequently (e.g., part of a cookie and a sip of milk and a little positive attention from the mother). Perhaps a point (or token) economy could be set up so that after a certain number of points (or tokens) had been earned, they could be used by the boys to buy a party. See Ferster and Perrott (1968, Chapter 2) for further discussion of the nature of the reinforcer.

If one can find some specific other behavior of the boy that already occurs with sufficient frequency and is incompatible with hitting, the reinforcer (parties, points, or tokens) can be presented after that behavior and, of course, no longer after the hitting. The same 10-minute time out, as suggested above, can be started by the hitting so that hitting is reduced.

Commonly available S^Δ's for not hitting in general (or for some not hitting behavior in specific) and S^D's for hitting are verbal instructions from the mother that set the rules with promises and threats about following or breaking the rules. A major type of S^D and S^Δ for hitting and not hitting is the model of behavior provided by the mother. Such S^D's and S^Δ's are developed as the child's tendency to imitate is built. With the development of that general abstract imitative repertoire which has been called identification, the child may be controlled by instructions; with less identification the child may be controlled by the modeled behavior (see Chapter 6 for the latter distinction).

The point of view of the behavior analyst is that he can change any behavior if he can control the antecedents and consequences. This suggests that behaviors, whether well-established or new and fragile, can be changed with proper programing. As stated at the outset, this Appendix only introduces some of the terms and techniques of applied behavior analysis (often called behavior modification). For more information, refer to the following sources: Bijou and Baer, 1961, 1965; Catania, 1968; Ferster and Perrott, 1968; Holland and Skinner, 1969; McIntire, 1970; Patterson and Gullion, 1968; Reese, 1966; Reynolds, 1968; Skinner, 1953, 1961, 1968; Ulrich, Stachnik, and Mabry, 1966; Valett, 1968; Walder et al., 1970; and issues of the *Journal of Applied Behavior Analysis* and the *Journal of the Experimental Analysis of Behavior*.

REFERENCES

Aberle, D. F., and Naegele, K. D. Middle class father's occupational role and attitudes toward children. *American Journal of Orthopsychiatry*, 1952, 22, 366–378.

Adorno, T. W., Frenkel-Brunswick, E., Levinson, D. J., and Sanford, N. R. *The authoritarian personality.* New York: Harper, 1950.

Allinsmith, B. B. Parental discipline and children's aggression in two school classes. Unpublished doctoral dissertation, University of Michigan, 1954.

Allinsmith, B. B. Expressive styles: II. Directness with which anger is expressed. In D. R. Miller and G. E. Swanson (Eds.), *Inner conflict and defense.* New York: Holt, 1960, 315–336.

Allport, F. H. The J-curve hypothesis of conforming behavior. *Journal of Social Psychology*, 1934, 5, 141–183.

Anastasi, A. *Differential psychology.* Third ed. New York: Macmillan, 1958.

Anderson, R. L., and Bancroft, T. A. *Statistical theory in research.* New York: McGraw-Hill, 1952.

Appel, J. B. Punishment and shock intensity. *Science*, 1963, 141, 528–529.

Ardrey, R. *The territorial imperative.* New York: Atheneum, 1966.

Aronfreed, J. The problem of imitation. In L. P. Lipsitt and H. W. Reese, *Advances in child development and behavior*, Vol. 4. 1969, 210–319.

Aronfreed, J., and Leff, R. The effects of intensity of punishment and complexity of discrimination upon learning of internalized suppression. Unpublished manuscript, University of Pennsylvania, 1963.

Azrin, N. H. Some effects of noise on human behavior. *Journal of Experimental Analysis of Behavior*, 1958, 1, 183–200.

Azrin, N. H. Punishment and recovery during fixed-ratio performance. *Journal of Experimental Analysis of Behavior*, 1959, 2, 301–305.

Azrin, N. H. Sequential effects of punishment. *Science*, 1960, 131, 605–606.

Azrin, N. H., Hake, D. F., and Hutchinson, R. R. Elicitation of aggression by a physical blow. *Journal of Experimental Analysis of Behavior*, 1965, 8, 55–57.

Azrin, N. H., and Holz, W. C. Punishment. In W. K. Honig (Ed.), *Operant behavior: Areas of research and application.* New York: Appleton-Century-Crofts, 1966, 380–447.

Azrin, N. H., Holz, W. C., and Hake, D. F. Fixed ratio punishment. *Journal of Experimental Analysis of Behavior,* 1963, 6, 141–148.

Azrin, N. H., Hutchinson, R. R., and McLaughlin, R. The opportunity for aggression as an operant reinforcer during aversive stimulation. *Journal of Experimental Analysis of Behavior,* 1965, 8, 171–180.

Bandura, A. Psychotherapy as a learning process. *Psychological Bulletin,* 1961, 58, 143–159.

Bandura, A. Punishment revisited. *Journal of Consulting Psychology,* 1962a, 26, 298–301.

Bandura, A. Social learning through imitation. In *Nebraska Symposium on Motivation.* Lincoln, Neb.: University of Nebraska Press, 1962b.

Bandura, A. Social learning theory of identificatory processes. In D. A. Goslin (Ed.), *Handbook of socialization theory and research.* Chicago: Rand-McNally, 1968, Ch. 3.

Bandura, A., and Huston, A. C. Identification as a process of incidental learning. *Journal of Abnormal and Social Psychology,* 1961, 63, 311–318.

Bandura, A., Ross, D., and Ross, S. A. Transmission of aggression through imitation of aggressive models. *Journal of Abnormal and Social Psychology,* 1961, 63, 575–582.

Bandura, A., Ross, D., and Ross, S. A. Imitation of film mediated aggressive models. *Journal of Abnormal Psychology,* 1963a, 66, 3–11.

Bandura, A., Ross, D., and Ross, S. A. Vicarious reinforcement and imitative learning. *Journal of Abnormal and Social Psychology,* 1963b, 67, 601–607.

Bandura, A., and Walters, R. H. *Adolescent aggression.* New York: Ronald Press, 1959.

Bandura, A., and Walters, R. H. *Social learning and personality development.* New York: Holt, 1963.

Banta, T. J. Convergent and discriminant validation of a child rearing survey questionnaire. Paper delivered at meetings of EPA, New York, 1960.

Banta, T. J., and Walder, L. O. Discriminant validity of a peer rating measure of aggression. *Psychological Reports,* 1961, 9, 573–582.

Barabee, P., and von Mering, O. Ethnic variations in mental stress in families with psychotic children. *Social Problems,* 1953, 1, 48–53.

Barsky, M. L. The relationship of some aggressive characteristics to reading achievement in fifth and sixth grade males and females. *Dissertation Abstract,* 1966, 27 (5-A), 1257–1258.

Becker, W. C. Consequences of parental discipline. In M. L. Hoffman and L. W. Hoffman, *Review of Child Development,* Vol. 1. New York: Russell Sage Foundation, 1964, 169–208.

Becker, W. C., Peterson, D. R., Luria, Z., Shoemaker, D. J., and Hellmer, L. A. Relations of factors derived from parent-interview ratings to behavior problems of five year olds. *Child Development,* 1962, 33, 509–535.

Berkowitz, L. *Aggression: A social psychological analysis.* New York: McGraw-Hill, 1962.

Berkowitz, L. Some aspects of observed aggression. *Journal of Personality and Social Psychology,* 1965, 2, 359–369.

Bernstein, N., Perry, S., and Friman, I. Reduction of aggressive behaviors through contingent use of social reinforcement. Unpublished paper, The American University, 1969.

Bijou, S. W., and Baer, D. M. *Child Development: I. A systematic and empirical theory.* New York: Appleton-Century-Crofts, 1961.

294

Bijou, S. W., and Baer, D. M. *Child Development: II. Universal stage of infancy.* New York: Appleton-Century-Crofts, 1965.

Block, J., and Martin, B. Predicting the behavior of children under frustration. *Journal of Abnormal and Social Psychology,* 1955, 51, 281–285.

Breithower, D. M., and Reynolds, G. S. A facilitative effect of punishment on unpunished behavior. *Journal of Experimental Analysis of Behavior,* 1962, 5, 191–199.

Bridger, W. H. Ethological concepts and human development. *Recent Advances in Biological Psychiatry,* 1962, 4, 95–107.

Bronfenbrenner, U. Socialization and social class through time and space. In E. E. Maccoby, T. M. Newcomb, and E. L. Hartley (Eds.), *Readings in social psychology.* New York: Holt, 1958, 400–424.

Bronfenbrenner, U. Freudian theories of identification and their derivatives. *Child Development,* 1960, 31, 15–40.

Bronson, F. H., and Desjardins, C. Aggression in adult mice: Modification by neonatal injections of gonadal hormones. *Science,* 1968, 161, 705–706.

Brown, R. M. Historical patterns of violence in America. In H. D. Graham and T. R. Gurr (Eds.), *Violence in America: Historical and comparative perspectives,* Vol. 1. Washington, D.C.: U.S. Government Printing Office, 1969.

Bugelski, R., and Miller, N. E. A spatial gradient in the strength of avoidance responses. *Journal of Experimental Psychology,* 1938, 23, 494–505.

Buss, A. H. *The psychology of aggression.* New York: Wiley, 1961.

Buss, A. H. The effect of harm on subsequent aggression. *Journal of Experimental Research in Personality,* 1966, 1, 249–255.

Buss, A. H. Instrumentality of aggression, feedback and frustration as determinants of physical aggression. *Journal of Personality and Social Psychology,* 1966, 3, 153–162.

Buss, A. H. Personal communication, 1967.

Buss, A. H., and Durkee, A. An inventory for assessing different kinds of hostility. *Journal of Consulting Psychology,* 1957, 21, 343–348.

Camus, A. *The myth of Sisyphus and other essays.* New York: Knopf, 1955.

Catania, A. C. (Ed.) *Contemporary research in operant behavior.* Glenview, Ill.: Scott, Foresman, 1968.

Chasdi, E. H., and Lawrence, M. S. Some antecedents of aggression and effects of frustration in doll play. In D. McClelland (Ed.), *Studies in motivation.* New York: Appleton-Century-Crofts, 1955.

Child, I. L. Socialization. In G. Lindzey (Ed.), *Handbook of social psychology,* Vol. 2. Reading, Mass.: Addison-Wesley, 1954, 655–692.

Christie, R., Havel, J., and Seidenberg, B. Is the F Scale irreversible? *Journal of Abnormal and Social Psychology,* 1958, 56, 143–159.

Cooney, N. C. Control of aggression in child rearing in Puerto Rico: A study of professed practices used with boys and girls in two socioeconomic urban groups. *Dissertation Abstract,* 1967, 28 (2-A), 777.

Cronbach, L. J., and Gleser, G. C. Assessing similarity between profiles. *Psychological Bulletin,* 1953, 50, 456–473.

Daut, R. L. TAT aggression anxiety as a function of prior aggression and the stimulus properties and sequence of the cards. Senior honors thesis, University of Iowa, 1969.

Davis, A. American status systems and the socialization of the child. *American Sociological Review,* 1941, 6, 345–354.

Davis, A. Child training and social class. In R. G. Barker et al. (Eds.), *Child behavior and development.* New York: McGraw-Hill, 1943, 607–619.

Davis, A. *Social class influence upon learning.* Cambridge: Harvard University Press, 1948.

Davis, A., and Eells, K. *Davis-Eells test of general intelligence and problem solving ability.* Yonkers-on-Hudson, N.Y.: World Book Company, 1953.

Davis, A., and Havighurst, R. J. Social class and color differences in child rearing. *American Sociological Review,* 1946, 11, 698–710.

Davitz, J. R. The effects of previous training on post-frustration behavior. *Journal of Abnormal and Social Psychology,* 1952, 47, 309–315.

Dawe, H. C. An analysis of 200 quarrels of preschool children. *Child Development,* 1934, 5, 139–157.

Dinsmoor, J. A. A discrimination based on punishment. *Quarterly Journal of Experimental Psychology,* 1952, 4, 27–45.

Diven, K. Certain determinants in the conditioning of anxiety reactions. *Journal of Psychology,* 1937, 3, 291–308.

Dollard, J., Doob, L. W., Miller, N. E., Mowrer, O. H., and Sears, R. R. *Frustration and aggression.* New Haven: Yale University Press, 1939.

Doob, L. W., and Sears, R. R. Factors determining substitute behavior and the overt expression of aggression. *Journal of Abnormal and Social Psychology,* 1939, 34, 293–313.

Duncan, O. B., and Davis, B. An alternative to ecological correlation. *American Sociological Review,* 1953, 18, 665–666.

Durkheim, E. *Suicide.* Glencoe, Ill.: Free Press, 1951.

Duvall, E. N. Conceptions of parenthood. *American Journal of Sociology,* 1946, 52, 195–203.

Edwards, A. L. The *social desirability variable in personality assessment and research.* New York: Dryden Press, 1957.

Edwards, A. L. *Experimental design in psychological research.* New York: Holt, 1960.

Edwards, N. Aggressive expression under threat of retaliation. Unpublished doctoral dissertation, University of Iowa, 1967.

Emmerich, W. Parental identification in young children. *Genetic Psychology Monographs,* 1959a, 60, 257–308.

Emmerich, W. Young children's discriminations of parent and child roles. *Child Development,* 1959b, 30, 404–420.

Epstein, R. Aggression toward out-groups as a function of authoritarianism and imitation of aggressive models. *Journal of Personality and Social Psychology,* 1966, 3, 574–579.

Eron, L. D. Social and cultural factors in mental illness. *Proceedings of the Rip Van Winkle Clinic,* 1956, 7, 2, 16–38.

Eron, L. D. Progress Report, Project M1726, U.S.P.H.S. *Psychosocial Development of Aggressive Behavior,* May 15, 1960.

Eron, L. D. Relationship of TV viewing habits and aggressive behavior in children. *Journal of Abnormal and Social Psychology,* 1963, 67, 193–196.

Eron, L. D., Banta, T. J., Walder, L. O., and Laulicht, J. H. Comparison of data obtained from mothers and fathers on child rearing practices and their relation to child aggression. *Child Development,* 1961, 32, 457–472.

Eron, L. D., Laulicht, J. H., Walder, L. O., Farber, I. E., and Spiegel, J. P. Application of role and learning theories to the study of the development of aggression in children. *Psychological Reports,* 1961, 9, 291–334 (monograph supplement 2-V9, 1961).

Eron, L. D., and Walder, L. O. Test burning: II. *American Psychologist,* 1961, 16, 237–244.

Eron, L. D., Walder, L. O., Toigo, R., and Lefkowitz, M. M. Social class, parental punishment for aggression and child aggression. *Child Development,* 1963, 34, 849–867.

Estes, W. K. An experimental study of punishment. *Psychological Monographs,* 1944, 57, 3 (whole no. 263).

Farber, B., and Jenne', W. L. Family organization and crisis. *Monograph of Society for Research in Child Development,* 1963, 28, 78.

Ferster, C. B., and Perrott, M. C. *Behavior principles.* New York: Appleton-Century-Crofts, 1968.

Feshbach, S., and Jaffe, Y. The effects of group versus individual decisions on aggressive behavior. Unpublished study, University of California at Los Angeles, 1969.

Feshbach, S., Stiles, W., and Bitter, E. The reinforcing effect of witnessing aggression. *Journal of Experimental Personality,* 1967, 2, 133–139.

Frankel, M. Introduction. In D. Walker, *Rights in Conflict.* New York: Bantam Books, 1968.

Freud, A. *The ego and the mechanisms of defense.* London: Hogarth Press, 1937.

Freud, S. *A general introduction to psychoanalysis.* Garden City, N.Y.: Garden City Publishing Company, 1920.

Freud, S. *Beyond the pleasure principle.* London: International Psychoanalytic Press, 1922.

Freud, S. *The ego and the id.* London: Hogarth Press, 1923.

Freud, S. Instincts and their vicissitudes (1915). In J. Strachey (Ed.), *The complete psychological works of Sigmund Freud,* Vol. 14. London: Hogarth Press, 1957.

Fried, M. H. Letters. *The New York Times,* November 30, 1969, 4, 13.

Gewirtz, J. L., and Stingle, K. G. Learning of generalized imitation as the basis for identification. *Psychological Review,* 1968, 75, 374–397.

Glueck, S., and Glueck, E. *Unravelling juvenile delinquency.* Cambridge: Harvard University Press, 1950.

Goldstein, A. Aggression and hostility in the elementary school in low socioeconomic areas. *Understanding the Child,* 1955, 24, 20.

Goodenough, F. L. *Anger in young children.* Minneapolis: University of Minnesota Press, 1931.

Goodenough, F., and Tyler, L. *Developmental psychology.* New York: Appleton-Century-Crofts, 1959.

Gorer, G. Man has no killer "instinct." In M. F. Ashley Montagu (Ed.), *Man and aggression.* New York: Oxford University Press, 1968, 27–36.

Gregory, D. *Nigger.* New York: Pocket Books, 1964.

Hamblin, R. L., and Buckholdt, D. Structured exchanges and childhood learning. Progress Report, Office of Education, Contract no. OEC 3-7-062875-3056, 1968.

Hamblin, R. L., Buckholdt, D., Bushell, D., Ellis, D., and Ferritor, D. Changing the game from "Get the Teacher" to "Learn." *Transaction,* January 1969, 20–31.

Harris, R. N. Multiple significance tests of correlational coefficients in correlation matrices. Unpublished doctoral dissertation, University of Maryland, 1967.

Hebb, D. O. *Organization of behavior.* New York: Wiley, 1949.

Hedges, L. E. Aggression as a function of gender and noxious stimulation. Unpublished M.A. thesis, University of Iowa, 1967.

Hedges, L. E. Aggressive responses as a function of target cues and the possibility of retaliation. Unpublished doctoral dissertation, University of Iowa, 1969.

297

Hess, R., and Handel, J. Patterns of aggression in parents and their children. *Journal of Genetic Psychology,* 1956, 89, 199–212.

Hicks, D. J. Imitation and retention of film mediated aggressive peer and adult models. *Journal of Personality and Social Psychology,* 1965, 2, 97–100.

Hilgard, E. R. *Theories of learning.* New York: Appelton-Century-Crofts, 1948.

Hokanson, J. Effects of frustration and anxiety on overt aggression. *Journal of Abnormal and Social Psychology,* 1961, 62, 346–351.

Hokanson, J. E., and Edelman, R. Effect of three social responses on vascular processes. *Journal of Personality and Social Psychology,* 1966, 3, 442–447.

Holland, J. G., and Skinner, B. F. *The analysis of behavior.* New York, McGraw-Hill, 1969.

Hops, H., and Walters, R. H. Studies of reinforcement of aggression. *Child Development,* 1963, 34, 553–562.

Hovland, C. I., and Sears, R. Minor studies in aggression: VI. Correlation of lynchings with economic indices. *Journal of Psychology,* 1940, 9, 301–310.

Jersild, A. T., and Markey, F. V. Conflicts between preschool children. *Child Development Monographs,* 1935, 40, 21.

Kagan, J., and Lemkin, J. The child's differential perception of parental attributes. *Journal of Abnormal and Social Psychology,* 1960, 61, 440–447.

Kahl, J. A., and Davis, J. A. A comparison of indexes of socioeconomic status. *American Sociological Review,* 1955, 20, 317–326.

Kahn, M. W. The effect of severe defeat at various age levels on the aggressive behavior of mice. *Journal of Genetic Psychology,* 1951, 79, 117–131.

Kahn, M. W. Infantile experience and mature aggressive behavior of mice: Some material influences. *Journal of Genetic Psychology,* 1954, 84, 65–75.

Kahn, M. W., and Kirk, W. E. The concepts of aggression: A review and reformulation. *The Psychological Record,* 1968, 18, 559–573.

Katz, M. M., and Lyerly, S. B. Methods for measuring adjustment and social behavior in the community. *Psychological Reports,* 1963, 13, 503–535.

Kinsey, A. C., Pomeroy, W. B., and Martin, C. E. *Sexual behavior in the human male.* Philadelphia: Saunders, 1948.

Klein, M. *Our adult world.* New York: Basic Books, 1963.

Kohlberg, L. A cognitive-developmental analysis of children's sex-role concepts and attitudes. In E. E. Maccoby (Ed.), *The development of sex differences.* Stanford: Stanford University Press, 1966, 82–173.

Kohn, M. L. Social class and the exercise of parental authority. *American Sociological Review,* 1959a, 64, 352–366.

Kohn, M. L. Social class and parental values. *American Journal of Sociology,* 1959b, 64, 337.

Kohn, M. L. Social class and parent-child relationships: An interpretation. *American Journal of Sociology,* 1963, 68, 471–480.

Kuhn, D. Z., Madsen, C. H., Jr., and Becker, W. C. Effects of exposure to an aggressive model and "frustration" on children's aggressive behavior. *Child Development,* 1967, 38, 739–745.

Lawson, E. D., and Boek, W. E. Correlations of indexes of family's socioeconomic status. *Social Forces,* 1960, 39, 149–152.

Lazarsfeld, P. F., and Menzel, H. On the relation between individual and collective properties. In A. Etzioni (Ed.), *Complex organization.* New York: Holt, 1961.

Lefkowitz, M. M. Some relationships between sex role preference of children and other parent child variables. *Psychological Reports,* 1962, 10, 43–53.

Lefkowitz, M. M. Aggression and size of human figure drawings. *Psychology in the Schools,* 1964, 3, 312–314.

Lefkowitz, M. M., Blake, R. R., and Mouton, J. S. Status factors in pedestrian violation of traffic signals. *Journal of Abnormal and Social Psychology*, 1955, 51, 704–706.

Lefkowitz, M. M., and Cannon, J. C. Physique and obstreperous behavior. *Journal of Clinical Psychology*, 1966, 22, 172–174.

Lefkowitz, M. M., Walder, L. O., and Eron, L. D. Punishment, identification and aggression. *Merrill Palmer Quarterly of Behavior and Development*, 1963, 9, 159–174.

Lehrman, D. S. A critique of Konrad Lorenz's theory of instinctive behavior. *Quarterly Review of Biology*, 1953, 28, 337–363.

Leibovitz, G. Comparison of self report and behavioral techniques of assessing aggression. *Journal of Consulting and Clinical Psychology*, 1968, 32, 21–25.

Leon, G. R. The observation of mother-son interactions before and after reinforcement of child's aggressive behavior. Unpublished doctoral dissertation, University of Maryland, 1967.

Lesser, G. Maternal attitudes and practices and the aggressive behavior of children. Unpublished doctoral dissertation, Yale University, 1952.

Lesser, G. The relationship between various forms of aggression and popularity among lower class children. *Journal of Educational Psychology*, 1959, 50, 20–25.

Lester, D. The relation between discipline experiences and the expression of aggression. *American Anthropologist*, 1967, 69, 734–737.

Levin, H., and Sears, R. R. Identification with parents as a determinant of doll play aggression. *Child Development*, 1956, 27, 135–153.

Licht, L. Direct and displaced physical aggression as a function of level of self-esteem and method of anger arousal. Unpublished doctoral dissertation, University of California, 1966.

Littman, R. A., Moore, R. C. A., and Pierce-Jones, J. Social class differences in child rearing: A third community for comparison with Chicago and Newton. *American Sociological Review*, 1957, 22, 694–704.

Loevinger, J., and Sweet, B. *Family problems scale* (Research Edition II). Privately distributed, 1956.

Loomis, S. D. EEG abnormalities as a correlate of behavior in adolescent male delinquents. *American Journal of Psychiatry*, 1965, 121, 1003–1006.

Lorenz, K. *Evolution and modification of behavior*. Chicago: The University of Chicago Press, 1965.

Lorenz, K. *On aggression*. New York: Harcourt, 1966.

Lovaas, O. I. Effect of exposure to symbolic aggression on aggressive behavior. *Child Development*, 1961, 32, 37–44.

Lovaas, O. I., Baer, D. M., and Bijou, S. W. Experimental procedure for analyzing the interaction of social stimuli and children's behavior. Paper read at S.R.C.D. Convention, Berkeley, 1963.

Maccoby, E. E., and Gibbs, P. K. Methods of child rearing in two social classes. In W. E. Martin and C. B. Stendler (Eds.), *Readings in child development*. New York: Harcourt, 1954, 380–396.

McCusick, V. A. *Human genetics*. Englewood Cliffs, N.J.: Prentice-Hall, 1964.

McGuire, C. Social status, peer status and social mobility. Unpublished memorandum, Committee on Human Development, University of Chicago, 1949.

McGuire, C., and Clark, R. A. Age mate acceptance and indices of peer status. *Child Development*, 1952, 23, 141–155.

McIntire, R. W. *For love of children: Behavioral psychology for parents*. Del Mar, Calif.: CRM Books, 1970.

McKee, J. P. The relationship between maternal behavior and the aggressive behavior of young children. Unpublished doctoral dissertation, University of Iowa, 1949.

McKee, J. P., and Leader, F. B. The relationship of socio-economic status and aggression to the competitive behavior of preschool children. *Child Development*, 1955, 26, 135.

Madsen, C. H., Jr., Becker, W. C., and Thomas, D. R. Rules, praise and ignoring: Elements of elementary classroom control. *Journal of Applied Behavior Analysis*, 1968, 1, 139–150.

Marcus, J. L. Examiner effects on two measures of aggression in children. Unpublished M.A. thesis, University of Iowa, 1966.

Masserman, J. H. *Principles of dynamic psychiatry*. Philadelphia: Saunders, 1946.

Meehl, P. E., and Rosen, A. Antecedent probability and the efficiency of psychometric signs, patterns or cutting scores. *Psychological Bulletin*, 1955, 52, 194–216.

Menninger, K. *Man against himself*. New York: Harcourt, 1938.

Merrill, B. Relation of mother-child interaction to children's social behavior. Unpublished doctoral dissertation, State University of Iowa, 1946.

Merton, R. A., and Kitt, A. S. Contribution to the theory of reference group behavior. In R. K. Merton and P. K. Lazarsfeld (Eds.), *Continuities in social research*. Glencoe, Ill.: Free Press, 1950, 40–105.

Meyerson, L. J. The effects of filmed aggression on the aggressive responses of high and low aggressive subjects. Unpublished doctoral dissertation, University of Iowa, 1966.

Miller, D. R., and Swanson, G. E. *The changing American parent: A study in the Detroit area*. New York: Wiley, 1958.

Miller, D. R., and Swanson, G. E. *Inner conflict and defense*. New York: Holt, 1960.

Miller, N. E. The frustration-aggression hypothesis. *Psychological Review*. 1941, 48, 337–342.

Miller, N. E. Theory and experiment relating psychoanalytic displacement to stimulus-response generalization. *Journal of Abnormal and Social Psychology*, 1948, 43, 155–178.

Miller, N. E. Learning of visceral and glandular responses. *Science*, 1969, 31, 434–445.

Montagu, M. F. A. The new litany of "innate depravity," or original sin revisited. In M. F. Ashley Montagu (Ed.), *Man and aggression*. New York: Oxford University Press, 1968, 3–17.

Morrison, E. Academic underachievement among preadolescent boys considered as a manifestation of passive aggression. *Dissertation Abstract*, 1967, 28(4-A), 1304–1305.

Mowrer, O. H. A stimulus-response analysis of anxiety and its role as a reinforcing agent. *Psychological Review*, 1939, 46, 553–565.

Mussen, P., and Distler, L. Masculinity, identification and father-son relationships. *Journal of Abnormal and Social Psychology*, 1959, 59, 350–356.

Nissen, H. W., and Elder, D. H. The influence of amount of incentive on delayed response performances of chimpanzees. *Journal of Genetic Psychology*, 1935, 47, 49–72.

Osgood, C. E., Suci, G. J., and Tannenbaum, P. H. *The measurement of meaning*. Urbana, Ill.: University of Illinois Press, 1957.

Otis, N. B., and McCandless, B. Responses to repeated frustrations of young children differentiated according to need area. *Journal of Abnormal and Social Psychology*, 1955, 50, 349–353.

Palmer, S. Frustration, aggression and murder. *Journal of Abnormal and Social Psychology*, 1960, 60, 430–432.

Parke, R. D., and Walters, R. A. Some factors influencing the efficacy of punishment training for response inhibition. *Monograph of Society for Research in Child Development*, 1967, 32, 1 (whole no. 109).

Parton, D. A. The study of aggression in boys with an operant device. *Journal of Experimental Child Psychology*, 1964, 1, 79–88.

Pastore, N. Role of arbitrariness in the frustration-aggression hypothesis. *Journal of Abnormal and Social Psychology*, 1952, 47, 728–731.

Patterson, G. R., and Gullion, M. E. *Living with children: New methods for parents and teachers*. Champaign, Ill.: Research Press, 1968.

Patterson, G. R., Littman, R. A., and Bricker, W. Assertive behavior in children: A step toward a theory of aggression. *Monograph of Society for Research in Child Development*, 1967, 32, 5 (serial no. 113).

Payne, D. E., and Mussen, P. H. Parent-child relations and father identification among adolescent boys. *Journal of Abnormal and Social Psychology*, 1956, 52, 358–362.

Peterson, R. Aggression as a function of retaliation and aggression level of target and aggressor. *Developmental Psychology*, 1971, 5, 161–166.

Pittluck, P. The relation between aggressive fantasy and overt behavior. Unpublished doctoral dissertation, Yale University, 1950.

Potter, E. H. Parents as role models for aggression. Unpublished honors thesis, Williams College, 1968.

Premack, D. Toward empirical behavior laws: I. Positive reinforcement. *Psychological Review*, 1959, 66, 219–233.

Quay, H. C. Psychopathic personality as pathological stimulation seeking. *American Journal of Psychiatry*, 1965, 122, 180–183.

Radke-Yarrow, M. Problems of methods in parent-child research. *Child Development*, 1963, 34, 215–226.

Radke-Yarrow, M., Campbell, J. D., and Burton, R. V. *Child rearing: An inquiry into research and methods*. San Francisco: Jossey-Bass, 1968.

Reese, E. P. *The analysis of human operant behavior*. Dubuque, Iowa: William C. Brown, 1966.

Reynolds, G. S. *A primer of operant conditioning*. Glenview, Ill.: Scott, Foresman, 1968.

Rinsland, H. D. *A basic vocabulary of elementary school children*. New York: Macmillan, 1945.

Robinson, W. S. Ecological correlations and the behavior of individuals. *American Sociological Review*, 1950, 15, 351–357.

Rosenbaum, M. E., and Tucker, I. F. The competence of the model and the learning of imitation and non-imitation. *Journal of Experimental Psychology*, 1962, 63, 183–190.

Rosenberg, B. G., and Sutton-Smith, B. The measurement of masculinity and feminity in children. *Child Development*, 1959, 30, 373–380.

Rousseau, J. J. *Émile ou de l'éducation*. Le Haye: Néaulme, 1762.

Rubenstein, B. The conditioning of aggressive verbs and aggressive behavior. Unpublished doctoral dissertation, University of California, 1967.

Schaeffer, E. S., and Bell, R. Q. Development of a parental attitude research instrument. *Child Development*, 1958, 29, 339–361.

Schaffner, B. *Fatherland, a study of authoritarianism in the German family*. New York: Columbia University Press, 1948.

Schopler, E., Parents of psychotic children as scapegoats. Presented at a symposium entitled, "Parents of impaired children as developmental agents." American Psychological Association, Washington, D. C., September, 1969.

Scott, J. P. *Animal behavior*. Garden City, N. Y.: Doubleday, 1963.

Scott, J. P. That old-time aggression. *The Nation*, 1967, 204, 53–54.

Scott, J. P. Tracing the expression of heredity in behavior. *Science,* 1968, 655–656.

Scott, J. P., and Marston, M. V. Non-adaptive behavior resulting from a series of defeats in fighting mice. *Journal of Abnormal and Social Psychology,* 1953, 48, 417–428.

Sears, P. Child rearing factors related to playing of sex-typed roles. *American Psychologist,* 1953, 8, 431.

Sears, R. R. Relation of early socialization experiences to aggression in middle childhood. *Journal of Abnormal and Social Psychology,* 1961, 63, 461–492.

Sears, R. R., Hovland, C. I., and Miller, N. E. Minor studies of aggression: I. Measurement of aggressive behavior. *Journal of Psychology,* 1940, 9, 275–295.

Sears, R. R., Maccoby, E. E., and Levin, H. *Patterns of child rearing.* Boston: Row Peterson, 1957.

Sears, R. R., Pintler, M. H., and Sears, P. S. Effect of father separation on preschool children's doll play aggression. *Child Development,* 1946, 17, 219–243.

Sears, R. R., Rau, L., and Alpert, R. *Identification and child rearing.* Stanford: Stanford University Press, 1965.

Sears, R. R., Whiting, J. W. M., Nowlis, V., and Sears, P. S. Some child rearing antecedents of aggression and dependency in young children. *Genetic Psychology Monographs,* 1953, 47, 135–234.

Semler, I. J., and Eron, L. D. Replication report: Relationship of aggression in third grade children to certain pupil characteristics. *Psychology in the Schools,* 1967, 4, 356–358.

Semler, I. J., Eron, L. D., Meyerson, L. J., and Williams, J. F. Relationship of aggression in third grade children to certain pupil characteristics. *Psychology in the Schools,* 1967, 4, 85–88.

Seward, J. P. Aggressive behavior in the rat: III. The role of frustration. *Journal of Comparative Psychology,* 1945, 38, 225–238.

Seward, J. P. Aggressive behavior in the rat: IV. Submission as determined by conditioning, extinction and disuse. *Journal of Comparative Psychology,* 1946, 39, 51–76.

Skinner, B. F. *The behavior of organisms.* New York: Appleton-Century-Crofts, 1938.

Skinner, B. F. *Science and human behavior.* New York: Macmillan, 1953.

Skinner, B. F. *Cumulative record.* Enlarged ed. New York: Appleton-Century-Crofts, 1961.

Skinner, B. F. *The technology of teaching.* New York: Appleton-Century-Crofts, 1968.

Sorokin, P. A., Zimmerman, C. C., and Galpin, C. J. *A systematic source book on rural sociology.* Minneapolis: University of Minnesota Press, 1933.

Spielberger, C. The role of awareness in verbal conditioning. In C. W. Erikson (Ed.), *Behavior and awareness.* Durham, N.C.: Duke University Press, 1962, 73–101.

Spock, B. *Baby and child care.* New York: Pocket Books, 1957.

Srole, L. Social integration and certain corollaries: An exploratory study. *American Sociological Review,* 1956, 21, 709–716.

Stolz, L. M. *Influences on parent behavior.* Stanford: Stanford University Press, 1967.

Stolz, R. E., and Smith, M. D. Some effects of socio-economic, age and sex factors on children's responses to the Rosenzweig Picture-Frustration Study. *Journal of Clinical Psychology,* 1959, 15, 200.

Stoodley, B. H. A cross-cultural study of structure and conflict in social norms. *American Journal of Sociology,* 1959, 56, 39–48.

Stroo, A. A. Hetverband tussen agressief gedrag bij kinderen van ± 8 jaar en opvoedingsvariabelen van moeders. Doctoraalscriptie, Vrije Universiteit, Amsterdam, 1970.

Sullivan, E. T., Clark, W. W., and Tiegs, E. W. *California short form test of mental maturity.* Los Angeles: California Test Bureau, 1957.

Telfer, M. A., Baker, D., Clark, G. R., and Richardson, C. E. Incidence of gross chromosomal errors among tall criminal American males. *Science,* 1968, 159, 1249–1250.

Thorndike, E. L., and Lorge, I. *The teacher's wordbook of 30,000 words.* New York: Bureau of Publications, Teacher's College, Columbia University, 1944.

Thurstone, L. L. Fechner's Law and the method of equal appearing intervals. *Journal of Experimental Psychology,* 1929, 12, 214–244.

Tinbergen, N. *The study of instinct.* London: Oxford University Press, 1951.

Toigo, R. Parental social status as a contextual and individual determinant of aggressive behavior among third-grade children in the classroom situation. Unpublished doctoral dissertation, Columbia University, 1962.

Toigo, R. Social status and schoolroom aggression in third-grade children. *Genetic Psychology Monographs,* 1965, 71, 221–263.

Toigo, R., Walder, L. O., Eron, L. D., and Lefkowitz, M. M. Examiner effect in the use of a near sociometric procedure in the third grade classroom. *Psychological Reports,* 1962, 11, 785–790.

Ulrich, R. E., Hutchinson, R. R., and Azrin, N. H. Pain elicited aggression. *Psychological Record,* 1965, 15, 111–126.

Ulrich, R. E., Stachnik, T., and Mabry, J. (Eds.) *Control of human behavior.* Glenview, Ill.: Scott, Foresman, 1966.

United States Bureau of the Census. *Classified index of occupations and industries.* U.S. Government Printing Office, 1960.

Urdang, L. (Ed.) *Random House dictionary of the English language.* College ed. New York: Random House, 1968.

Valett, R. *Modifying children's behavior.* Palo Alto: Fearon, 1968.

Walder, L. O. An attempt at an empirical test of a theory. In L. D. Eron (Ed.), Application of role and learning theories to the study of the development of aggression in children. *Psychological Reports.* 1961, 9, 291–334 (monograph supplement, 2-V9, 161).

Walder, L. O., Abelson, R., Eron, L. D., Banta, T. J., and Laulicht, J. H. Development of a peer-rating measure of aggression. *Psychological Reports,* 1961, 9, 497–556 (monograph supplement 4–49).

Walder, L. O., Cohen, S. I., Breiter, D. E., Warman, F. C., Orme-Johnson, D., and Pavey, S. Parents as agents of behavior change. In S. E. Golann and C. Eisdorfer (Eds.), *Handbook of community psychology.* New York: Appleton-Century-Crofts, in press.

Walder, L. O., Eron, L. D., and Laulicht, J. H. Manual of procedures in study of aggression. *Proceedings of the Rip Van Winkle Clinic,* 1957, 8, 1–30.

Walker, D. *Rights in conflict.* New York: Bantam Books, 1968.

Walters, R. H. Implications of laboratory studies of aggression for the control and regulation of violence. *Annals of the American Academy of Political and Social Science,* 1966, 364, 60–72.

Walters, R. H., and Brown, M. Studies of reinforcement of aggression: III. Transfer of responses to an interpersonal situation. *Child Development,* 1963, 34, 563–571.

Walters, R. H., and Parke, R. D. The influence of punishment and related disciplinary techniques on the social behavior of children: Theory and empirical findings. In B. A. Maher (Ed.), *Progress in experimental personality research,* Vol. 4. New York: Academic Press, 1967, 179–228.

303

Walters, R. H., and Zak, M. S. Validation studies of an aggression scale. *Journal of Psychology,* 1959, 47, 209–218.

Warner, W. L., Meeker, M., and Eells, K. *Social class in America.* New York: Harcourt, 1960.

Whiting, J. W. M., and Child, I. L. *Child training and personality.* New Haven: Yale University Press, 1953.

Wicker, T. In the nation: Only one kind of war. *The New York Times,* December 2, 1969.

Williams, D. L. The development of consequences of models' responses as discriminative stimuli for generalized imitation. Unpublished doctoral dissertation, University of Maryland, 1970.

Williams, J. F. Semantic mediation of motor aggression. Unpublished doctoral dissertation, University of Iowa, 1966.

Williams, J. F., Meyerson, L. J., Eron, L. D., and Semler, I. J. Peer-rated aggression and aggressive responses elicited in an experimental situation. *Child Development,* 1967, 38, 181–190.

Zak, M. S., and Walters, R. H. First steps in the construction of a scale for the measurement of aggression. *Journal of Psychology,* 1959, 47, 199–208.

INDEX OF AUTHORS

INDEX OF SUBJECTS

reward for nonaggression, 22, 23, 67, 146, 160, 166–167

Rip Van Winkle Child-Rearing Questionnaire, 10, 36, 222–253; classification of items in, 200–209 (table); derivation of, 49 ff., 192 ff.; factor analysis of, 196–197; interviewer manual for, 219–221, 254–268; and social desirability, 197, 276

role expectations, 275

role identification, 110, 135

sampling of subjects: Amsterdam, Holland, 35, 57, 136 ff.; Berkshire Farm, Canaan, N.Y., 78; Cedar Rapids, Iowa, 35, 40; Hudson, N.Y., 2–3, 4

sex differences, 28, 45, 86–87, 114, 118, 148, 149, 156, 160 (see also gender)

shaping, 22, 163, 171, 289

sociocultural factors, 9, 27–28, 124 ff., 153 ff., 161; cross-national differences, 135 ff.; social status of classroom, 130

sociometric, 31 (see also peer-rating measure of aggression)

success in aggression, 32–33, 34, 47, 80, 140–141; peer-rating items, 33 (table) (see also rewards)

survey research, 5, 9, 24

tardiness, 40

target of aggression, 28, 141 ff., 158

teacher-ratings, 174–175

television, 39–40

territoriality, 34

toilet training, 24

variables measured: glossary and abbreviations 277–283; means and standard deviations, 283–285

Viet Nam, 12, 105

violence, 12 ff.

war, 13 ff., 103 ff.

311